VOLUME TEN

ADVANCES IN TRANSPORT POLICY AND PLANNING

Cycling

VOLUME TEN

ADVANCES IN TRANSPORT POLICY AND PLANNING

Cycling

Edited by

EVA HEINEN

Department of Spatial Planning, TU Dortmund University, Dortmund, Germany; Faculty of Architecture and Design, Research Centre on Zero Emission Neighbourhoods (ZEN) in Smart Cities, Norwegian University of Science and Technology (NTNU), Trondheim, Norway; Institute for Transport Studies, University of Leeds, Leeds, United Kingdom

THOMAS GÖTSCHI

School of Planning, Public Policy and Management, University of Oregon, Eugene, OR, United States

ELSEVIER

ACADEMIC PRESS

An imprint of Elsevier

Academic Press is an imprint of Elsevier
50 Hampshire Street, 5th Floor, Cambridge, MA 02139, United States
525 B Street, Suite 1650, San Diego, CA 92101, United States
The Boulevard, Langford Lane, Kidlington, Oxford OX5 1GB, United Kingdom
125 London Wall, London, EC2Y 5AS, United Kingdom

First edition 2022

ISBN: 978-0-323-90156-7
ISSN: 2543-0009

For information on all Academic Press publications
visit our website at https://www.elsevier.com/books-and-journals

Publisher: Zoe Kruze
Acquisitions Editor: Mariana L. Kuhl
Developmental Editor: Naiza Ermin Mendoza
Production Project Manager: Sudharshini Renganathan
Cover Designer: Matthew Limbert

Typeset by STRAIVE, India

Contents

Contributors

Frauke Behrendt
TU Eindhoven, Eindhoven, The Netherlands

Klaus Bogenberger
Department of Mobility Systems Engineering, Technische Universität München, München, Germany

Jessica E. Bourne
Centre for Exercise, Nutrition and Health Sciences, School of Policy Studies, University of Bristol, Bristol, United Kingdom

Christian Brand
University of Oxford; UK Energy Research Centre, Oxford, United Kingdom

Ralph Buehler
Urban Affairs and Planning, Virginia Tech, Arlington, VA, USA

Winnie Daamen
Faculty of Civil Engineering and Geosciences, Department of Transport & Planning, Delft University of Technology, Delft, The Netherlands

Henk-Jan Dekker
TU Eindhoven, Eindhoven, The Netherlands

Angela Francke
Cycling and Sustainable Mobility, Universität Kassel, Kassel, Germany

Alexandra Gavriilidou
Transport & Planning Department, Delft University of Technology, Delft, The Netherlands

Regine Gerike
"Friedrich List" Faculty of Transport and Traffic Sciences, Technische Universität Dresden, Dresden, Germany

Rahul Goel
Transportation Research and Injury Prevention Centre, Indian Institute of Technology Delhi, New Delhi, India

Thomas Götschi
School of Planning, Public Policy and Management, University of Oregon, Eugene, OR, United States

Eva Heinen
Department of Spatial Planning, TU Dortmund University, Dortmund, Germany; Faculty of Architecture and Design, Research Centre on Zero Emission Neighbourhoods (ZEN) in Smart Cities, Norwegian University of Science and Technology (NTNU), Trondheim, Norway; Institute for Transport Studies, University of Leeds, Leeds, United Kingdom

Serge Hoogendoorn
Transport & Planning Department, Delft University of Technology, Delft, The Netherlands

Heather Kaths
School of Architecture and Civil Engineering, University of Wuppertal, Wuppertal, Germany

Paul Kelly
Physical Activity for Health Research Centre, Institute for Sport, Physical Education and Health Sciences, University of Edinburgh, Edinburgh, United Kingdom

Caroline Koszowski
"Friedrich List" Faculty of Transport and Traffic Sciences, Technische Universität Dresden, Dresden, Germany

Robin Lovelace
Institute for Transport Studies, University of Leeds, Leeds, United Kingdom

Nanette Mutrie
Physical Activity for Health Research Centre, Institute for Sport, Physical Education and Health Sciences, University of Edinburgh, Edinburgh, United Kingdom

John Parkin
University of the West of England, Bristol, United Kingdom

Marc Schlossberg
City and Regional Planning, University of Oregon, Eugene, OR, United States

Florian Schneider
Freiburg, Germany

Manuel Stoffers
Faculty of Arts and Social Sciences, Maastricht University, Maastricht, The Netherlands

Danique Ton
NS Stations, Utrecht, The Netherlands

Eugeni Vidal Tortosa
Institute for Transport Studies, University of Leeds, Leeds, United Kingdom

Simone Weikl
Department of Mobility Systems Engineering, Technische Universität München, München, Germany

Yufei Yuan
Transport & Planning Department, Delft University of Technology, Delft, The Netherlands

CHAPTER ONE

Cycling: Past, current and future

Eva Heinen[a,b,c,*] and Thomas Götschi[d]
[a]Department of Spatial Planning, TU Dortmund University, Dortmund, Germany
[b]Faculty of Architecture and Design, Research Centre on Zero Emission Neighbourhoods (ZEN) in Smart Cities, Norwegian University of Science and Technology (NTNU), Trondheim, Norway
[c]Institute for Transport Studies, University of Leeds, Leeds, United Kingdom
[d]School of Planning, Public Policy and Management, University of Oregon, Eugene, OR, United States
[*]Corresponding author: e-mail address: e.heinen@leeds.ac.uk

Abstract

Bicycle use brings various benefits to individuals and society. In the past decade, we have seen a sharp increase in attention toward cycling, both in terms of research into various aspects of cycling, as well as policies and programs to increase cycling or to make cycling safer or more enjoyable. We discuss recent trends and initiatives of cycling, and introduce the content of this volume. In this volume, we aimed to acknowledge the breadth of this research field and present some key aspects of contemporary cycling policy, practice, and research. These contributions—which focus on different elements of supply, demand and impacts—together provide an excellent overview of key contemporary research topics, as well as practice-ready design and planning tools.

Keywords: Bicycle, Cycling, Trends, Demand, Supply, Impacts

Cycling brings many advantages to the individual user as well as to society. For the individual, it provides a relatively cheap form of transport, which can be quicker than other modes within cities, which also provides health benefits. For society, the bicycle offers an opportunity to improve public health, reduce air pollution, carbon and noise emissions, and offers a form of transport that requires relatively little space. Consequently, over the past decades, we have seen a growing interest in cycling from policy makers, resulting in investments in cycling infrastructure, promotional campaigns, public bike sharing schemes, and subsidies for the purchase of e-bikes, to just name a few, all aimed at increasing cycling levels.

Due to Covid, urban mobility is one area that has seen dramatic changes in recent years. Within weeks, travel patterns have changed in magnitudes usually only attributable to decades-long policies and planning. While the long-term nature of these changes is still out for judgment, there seems to be universal consensus that cycling will come out of this pandemic as a winner. As a socially/physically distant form of travel and exercise, cycling has

Advances in Transport Policy and Planning, Volume 10
ISSN 2543-0009
https://doi.org/10.1016/bs.atpp.2022.04.001

seen an unprecedented boost in popularity. Some people rode a bike for the first time since their childhood. Bicycle stores worldwide reported record sales, and quickly supply could not keep up with demand. Some of this boom was certainly enabled by the fact that lock down measures and home office massively reduced motorized traffic volumes, a key deterrent of urban cycling. And many communities seized the opportunity of freed urban road space, and installed cycling facilities at a pace even the keenest advocates did not dare to dream of. So we may conclude that among the few positive outcomes of the COVID pandemic, there is an indisputable optimism about cycling.

Recently, there is also increased awareness of climate change as the top concern of our generation, and growing societal and political willingness to make (some) required changes. However, only more recently have governments and cities acknowledged the role of their urban and transport policies in reducing greenhouse gas emissions, and the reality that clean technology, i.e., electric vehicles, alone will not suffice. As a result there is increasing awareness of less-polluting forms of transport, such as cycling.

Having said that, the bicycle as an object itself, is also subject to change. One could argue that after decades with little change, bicycles have seen large changes in the past 20 years. Perhaps the largest change, has been that cycling technology itself is going through its "electric revolution," with the quickly emerging electric-assist bicycles redefining range, speed, target audiences and suited terrains of cycling. Also, partly thanks to advances in digital technology, bike sharing schemes have been introduced in various cities, and continue to operate. All these changes have made the bicycle more accessible, suitable for a wider group of individuals, and in case of bike sharing, removed concerns of theft and storage.

From a research perspective, these times present exciting opportunities to foster our understanding of cycling behavior, and policies that cater to increasing its use as part of the solution toward sustainable urban mobility and healthier lifestyles. Cycling research has increased almost 10-fold between 2000 and now (Fig. 1). Most papers come from the United States, and other western countries, such the United Kingdom, Canada and Australia. The contributions to cycling research come predominantly from the fields of social sciences (incl. planning), engineering, and medicine (incl. Public health), but also from a wide range of less obvious disciplines, such as psychology, computer sciences and mathematics, among others.

In this volume, we aimed to acknowledge the breadth of this research field and present some key aspects of contemporary cycling policy, practice,

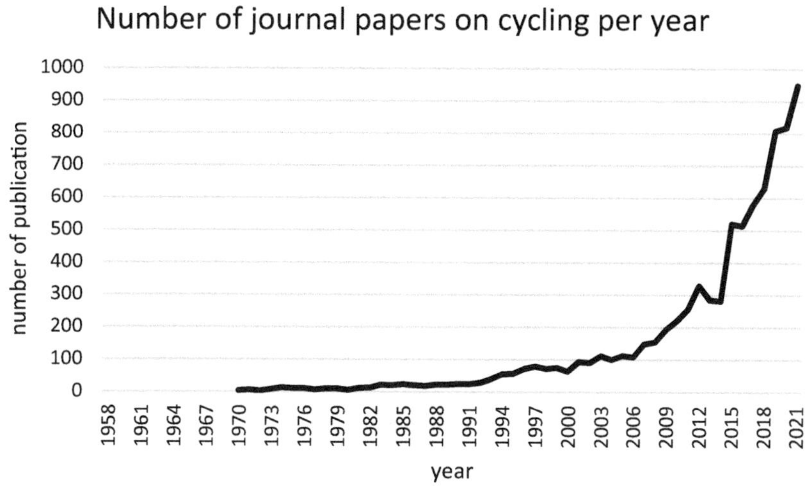

Fig. 1 Number of scientific articles by year (based on search in Scopus on "title, abstract, key words" on "bicycle" or "bicycling," and including "mobility," "travel" or "transport." Search was limited to journal publications in English.)

and research. We roughly align our presentation of research articles along a basic conceptual framework of cycling promotion along the domains of supply, demand, and impacts (Fig. 2). This framework postulates an iterative cycle where policies modify supply, e.g., of cycling infrastructure, which leads to changes (i.e., increases) in demand, resulting in impacts (e.g., health benefits or emission reductions). There are numerous feedback loops which close the cycle. An increase in demand triggers policy responses to increase supply. Personal impacts influence individuals' behavior (e.g., a negative experience, like a crash, will deter a person from further cycling), while societal impacts influence policy making (e.g., successful reduction of carbon emissions may induce further investments in cycling infrastructure). The iterative nature of this framework, in which policies lead to incremental improvements ultimately resulting in beneficial impacts, is not unlike how research contributes to our increasing understanding of cycling, and how to promote it.

Cycling research has come a long way and one dedicated volume can only provide a glimpse at the current state-of-the-art. As such the contribution in this volume on cycling provide compelling insights into a broad spectrum of provisions for cycling by policy makers, planners, and engineers, into cyclists' and non-cyclists' travel behavior, and into some of the resulting impacts for individuals and society.

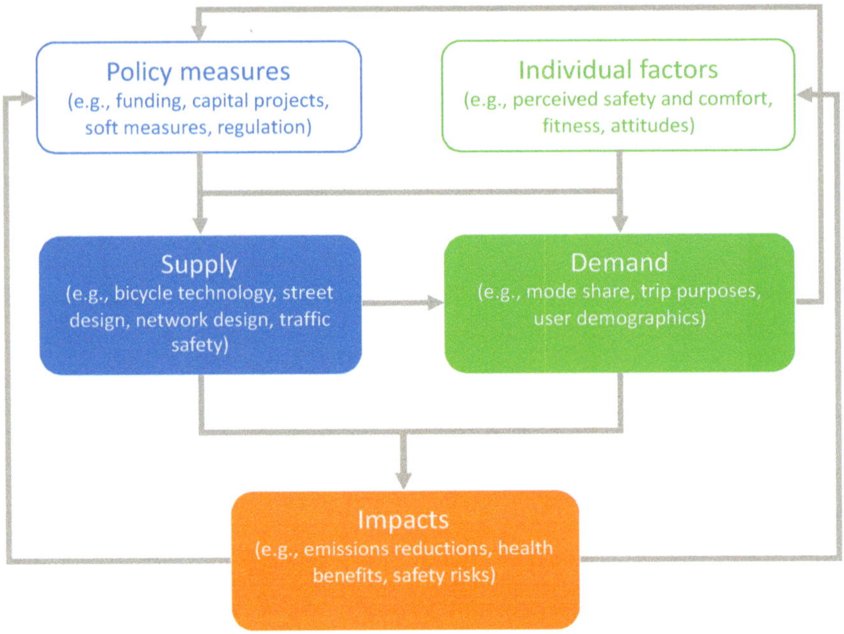

Fig. 2 Conceptual framework illustrating the relationships of cycling-related supply, demand and impacts. A number of feedback loops illustrate the cyclic, iterative nature of cycling promotion.

We acknowledge that an even wider range of topics could have been covered including, for example, but not limited to the most recent understanding of beneficial effects of cycling not only on physical but also mental health, the rapidly expanding portfolio of emerging data collection methodologies and sources (e.g., big data and smartphone-based location tracking), the role of cycling in lower income countries, or the challenges around translating scientific evidence into suitable formats for absorption into established planning practice.

The first part of the volume is dedicated to supply-side aspects. The first contributions focus on vehicle technology, infrastructure, systems/networks supporting cycling, as well as the development and trends of two-wheelers, street design, and urban planning more broadly. *Stoffers (2022)* starts this volume by providing a historical introduction to the bicycle and cycling. He provides a definition of the bicycle over time, and argues how technical properties of the bicycle are related to the interactions between technology and culture. *Bourne et al. (2022)* continues with a contribution on e-bikes, a relatively new addition to the bicycle "family" emerging since the mid-2000s. This chapter provides a broad overview of different strands of research on e-bikes, ranging from usage and sales, demographic of electric bicycle users, and the impact of electric bikes on transport, the environment, health, and safety.

The next three chapters step away from the vehicle, and instead focus on the design of infrastructure, such as street segments and cycling networks, and tools for planners. *Schlossberg (2022)* focuses on street-level designs that support cycling for a wide range of users. These include high quality design options that make cycling more comfortable and safer. He postulates that when it comes to cycling friendly street design there is little need for experimenting, as for most circumstances a design solution has been successfully implemented somewhere already. *Gerike et al. (2022)* look at design and planning at a higher level: cycle network planning. They first present main requirements for cycle networks, which are safety, cohesion, directness, comfort, attractiveness and adaptability. Then they discuss three approaches to network planning: networks based on desired lines and routes, networks linked to data driven approaches linked to user patterns, and optimization approaches to make decisions on investments. Finally, *Parkin (2022)* discusses guidance and tools for decision making and planning. This contribution focusses on a wide range of methods and tools, some cycling specific, others usable for cycling, ranging from methods to assess policy (e.g., the BYPAD audit tool), the technical process of modeling behavior needed for network planning (e.g., the Propensity to Cycling Tool), and appraisal and evaluation tools (e.g., WHO's Health Economic Assessment Tool for walking and cycling).

The second part of this volume is dedicated to demand-side aspects, with a focus on the use of bicycles and their users including patterns and trends in cycling, determinants of cycling, and modeling of cycling. *Buehler and Goel (2022)* start with providing a global overview of trends based on a data set of travel surveys from 16 countries. They compare differences in cycling levels, distances, durations and speeds between countries, as well differences in socio-economic characteristics. This comparison focusses both on "regular bicycles" as well as e-bikes. *Hoogendoorn et al. (2022)* follows with a discussion of how to model cyclists' behavior. Not only mode choice is discussed, but also very quick decisions when riding the bicycle, as well as activity choices and the locations where these activities are performed. As such, this chapter provides a good overview of how various behavior aspects of relevance to cycling can be modeled, and which correlates are associated with specific elements of cycling behavior. *Kaths (2022)* focusses on safety aspects of interactions between cyclists and other road users in various places. She discusses gap acceptance and problematic interactions, and focusses on interactions between cyclists and pedestrians, cyclists and passing motorists, and cyclists at bus stops.

The third part, which is dedicated to impacts of cycling, includes contributions on the inequalities associated with cycling, the contribution of cycling to reduce carbon and other emissions, and the impacts of COVID on cycling. *Vidal Tortosa et al. (2022)* describe inequalities in cycling and consequent socioeconomic disadvantage. Starting from the premise that socioeconomically disadvantaged have much to gain from cycling uptake, as they are most likely to suffer transport disadvantage and be less physically active, they look at inequalities in cycling levels and inequalities in the provisions in cycling facilities. *Brand et al. (2022)* focus on the topic of emission reductions. They report on the ability to reduce greenhouse gases and local air pollution emissions due to a modal shift to cycling and e-cycling, by means of life-cycle-analysis, which factors in production, use and end-of-life related emissions. Finally, *Francke (2022)* focusses on recent and ongoing changes in mobility related to cycling due to Covid. She provides an overview of changes in general mobility, and in cycling in particular, as well as actions taken by urban planners to cater to, encourage and address current and ongoing shifts toward more cycling.

These contributions jointly provide an excellent overview of key contemporary research topics, as well as practice-ready design and planning tools. We are confident that they provide the reader with both inspirations to advance further research as well as concrete take-homes to support practical activities to increase cycling, make cycling safer and healthier and more accessible to all individuals.

CHAPTER TWO

The bicycle: Technology and culture

Manuel Stoffers*
Faculty of Arts and Social Sciences, Maastricht University, Maastricht, The Netherlands
*Corresponding author: e-mail address: m.stoffers@maastrichtuniversity.nl

Contents

Abstract

Bicycle technology, except for its latest manifestations in "smart" bike sharing systems and in e-bikes, hardly attracts attention in analyses of contemporary bicycle use. If at all considered, the bicycle's characteristics are seen from a car driver's perspective, qualifying it as slow, physically demanding, vulnerable ("unsafe") and exposed. Based on existing historical research, the present contribution broadens the scope by addressing a wide ranch of technical qualities of bicycles and the effects these qualities have on the practice and appreciation of cycling. The single-track design, the self-moving principle and the increased speed and range of travel without increased energy consumption, are discussed as core characteristics leading on to a number of related characteristics, such as the bicycle's space efficiency and agility, its minimalist and lightweight construction, and its "openness." The contribution argues that the extent to which these qualities are appreciated or considered important for making modal choices depends on the various cultures of cycling, which can differ substantially from one temporal context to another, from one social group to another, and from one country to another.

Keywords: Cycling, Technology, Culture, History

Advances in Transport Policy and Planning, Volume 10
ISSN 2543-0009
https://doi.org/10.1016/bs.atpp.2022.04.002

1. Introduction

Apart from the e-bike and "smart" bicycle sharing systems, bicycle technology does not usually attract much attention in analyses of contemporary bicycle use. One of the reasons for this is that the basic design of the bicycle has stayed more or less the same since the so-called "safety bicycle" became the new standard at the end of the 19th century. The bicycle as we all know it, is a given and seems to need no further specification. It appears to constitute a common feature in all contexts, one that therefore can be left out of explanations for the differences in bicycle use between cities or countries. If at all addressed, the bicycle's characteristics are often defined from a car driver's perspective, qualifying it as slow, physically demanding, vulnerable ("unsafe") and exposed. Indeed, for a long time traffic engineers and planners have assumed that the demise of bicycle use in the 20th century was simply caused by it being technically superseded by the car; after the invention of the car, they argued, the bicycle only as a "niche product" still had some uses (e.g., still Filarski, 2004).

There are good reasons to question this limited view of bicycle technology in discussions of bicycle use. Of course it is true that, from the perspective of pure speed, the bicycle *was* superseded by the car. In fact, already the steam locomotive was faster than the bicycle and some 19th-century engineers saw the bicycle's dependence on human power as a foolish backsliding into the pre-steam engine era—despite its increasingly widespread use and its evident usefulness (Krausse, 1986, p. 64; Radkau, 1995). However, as historians and sociologists of transport technology have pointed out (and as will be seen further below), the bicycle's qualities shouldn't be reduced to the factor speed, nor should the bicycle just be seen as a (technologically inferior) precursor of the car as a form of individual transport (Burri, 1998; Cox and Van de Walle, 2007; Stoffers et al., 2010). The emphasis on technological progress and innovation often reduces the technological artifact to one of its characteristics (e.g., speed), whereas other characteristics may be equally or more important to their users and therefore may account for its continued use (Edgerton, 2006).

While it is therefore important to look more closely and at the same time more comprehensively at the technical characteristics of the bicycle, the most prominent analysts of the role of technology in society consistently warn against technological determinism: the view that technology as such is the sole or essential determinant in human practices. Bijker (1995) and other analysts of the social construction of technology, have emphasized that technology is always part of a complex social reality, in which different (groups of) actors have different views and interests and some groups are more powerful than others in defining the meaning of certain technologies and in pushing and promoting their use. What a technological artifact is, is from the constructivist perspective not determined by its technical qualities, but by its perception by powerful social actors.

A good example to illustrate this point is the role of the bicycle in the wave of women's emancipation at the end of the 19th century. The bicycle enjoys a widespread reputation as having been instrumental in this social, cultural and political change, and to be sure, the bicycle *was* highly appreciated by women activists of the time because of the new possibilities to increase the individual freedom of movement (Herlihy, 2004, p. 266). However, in general the new technology of cycling was adapted in such a way as to suit the existing social norms and gender divisions, rather than the other way around. Tandems became popular at the time because they allowed for combined travel of men and women under the direction of men, with the man sitting behind, but still in control of the steering. More importantly, a bicycle frame that was designed specifically for women quickly became dominant for female users: the step-through frame was technically inferior and usually heavier than the diamond frame of men's bicycles, but fitted in better with existing expectations about women's behavior and dress. In general, historical research has established that the bicycle brought less change in gender roles than that its use was adapted to conform to existing norms and practises (Bleckmann, 1999; Mackintosh and Norcliffe, 2007; Oddy, 1995).

Returning to the constructivist view in general, we may quote anthropologist Vivanco who has summarized the main point succinctly in his analysis of diverging bicycle cultures around the globe: "bicycles are heterogeneous, multidimensional, and contextual objects, enmeshed in specific technological conditions, practices of life, social relations, cultural meanings, and political-economic dynamics. [...] these conditions help produce important variations across cities, countries, and social groups in how people think about and interact with bicycles in their everyday lives" (Vivanco, 2013, pp. xx–xxi).

Consequently, questions of technology are inherently connected with questions of culture (understood as a web of collectively shared meanings and practices). Not the technical characteristics as such are decisive for the decision to use the bicycle, but the perception of these characteristics (as well as of other, non-technical aspects of cycling). This perception is not truly an individual evaluation of cycling as a mode of transport: it is pre-formed through collective cultural connotations, that exist *before, between* and *outside* individuals (in the form of texts, images and objects). Cultures of cycling are as much part of the context individuals find themselves in as the material bicycle facilities that they are confronted with (or not). These cultures of cycling exists on different levels. While many studies of contemporary bicycle use focus on local case studies, historical research shows that *national* cultures of cycling should not be ignored: they are influential and resilient, because national societies for so long have been relatively independent and powerful communicative unities, with their own nation-wide media, associations, institutions, lobby groups and laws (Ebert, 2010; Kuipers, 2013; Oosterhuis, 2019). I will return to this point at the end of this chapter.

This chapter aims to show the interactions between the technology and the cultures of cycling, by discussing the perceptions and practices linked to the technical properties of the bicycle. The results are a number of common characteristics associated with the bicycle, some of which can become more prominent or more appreciated than others in a particular context, situation or social group. The chapter is based on existing historical research on bicycle use and concerns a varied but limited number of countries. The idea is to produce insights based on a few different cases, rather than to try to provide an all-encompassing overview of facts. The chapter aims to convince the readers of the arguments presented above by discussing examples from historical research that together may help to demonstrate that it is of crucial importance to involve questions of (national, local and group) culture in the analysis of cycling—not only for those aiming to understand and to explain, but also for those who are involved in planning and changing transport behaviors.

2. Defining the bicycle

A recent Dutch book publication on the ethics and politics of traffic policies challenged the readers on the first page to draw a bicycle from memory and reserved a blank space in the book for readers to record their effort (Verkade and Te Brömmelstroet, 2020). The gimmick was meant to demonstrate how little people actually know about the bicycle (and cycling), even in a country that has more bicycles than citizens. However, even if we start looking closely it is not that easy to say what defines a bicycle and to determine its main characteristics. In the first instance, the answer seems simple enough: if we ignore additional accessories, a bicycle basically consists of two equally sized wheels in a row, a steering bar connected to the front wheel, in the middle a saddle and pedals, and a chain allowing the pedals to drive the back wheel.

While this description is probably recognizable to most people, individual bicycle designs in past and present can deviate from this description in almost every aspect. At present, there is a huge diversity of bicycle designs commercially available, to a level perhaps equaled only during the pioneering age of bicycle innovations around 1890; that is, before the mass produced bicycle came to dominate during most of the 20th century (see Sharp, 1896). Since the 1990s, we have entered a new period, a period of "global flexibilization" of the bicycle, in which innovative production techniques and globalization of production facilities make it commercially feasible to produce specific designs for relatively small market segments (Rosen, 2002, pp. 119–154). While during the first post-war decades the bicycle increasingly was viewed as out-of-date and outliving the end of its technical development, since a few decades the bicycle is again considered a vehicle worthy of R&D (Stoffers, 2019). At the same time and notwithstanding the design diversity that characterizes the bicycle market today, it should be noted that today's bicycle is to a relatively high extent a "modular product," characterized by many standardized components (and standardized "interfaces" between components), whose production is dominated by "mega-suppliers" Shimano and SRAM (Mari, 2021, pp. 8–34).

When speaking about the present design diversity, I am not just referring to the differences between road (racing) bikes, urban bicycles, tourist models and mountain bikes, but also to variations in basic lay-out. The chain may drive the front wheel instead of the back wheel, or it may be replaced by a belt or a shaft, or it can be absent altogether (as in the first pedal driven bicycles from the 1860 to 70s). The wheels can be extra small (as in many folding bicycles), they can be of different size, and there can be three instead of two, effectively creating a tricycle—popular in cargo cycles and so-called "pedicabs." The pedals can be placed before the front wheel instead of between the wheels (as on many feet-forward recumbent bicycles), they can also be replaced by levers (replacing circular motion with linear movement), or be completely absent, creating a walking or balance bike, like the first bicycle ever. There usually is one rider per bike, but there can be also two (as in tandems) or even more (as in triplets etc.). The pedals are usually driven by the strongest muscles in humans, to be found in the legs.

But there are also handcycles, driven by arm muscles, or rowing bike designs combining arms, back and legs. Since a decade or so, the addition of electric pedal assist motors has become popular, strongly reducing the required physical effort to cycle. The saddle can be replaced by a seat (extending to the back) or even a small hammock. The frame connecting all these elements was first made from wood, then from steel and nowadays it is often built from aluminum, but it can also be made from carbon fiber, titanium, or again wood. The frame may also fold, for easy storage. Usually, the rider is unprotected against the elements, but there are bicycles and tricycles available with some sort of cover or fairing—to protect the rider from the weather or because of the aerodynamic effect. Finally, for most bicycles nothing but the pneumatic tyres smooth down the ride, but some bicycles are equipped with additional forms of (frame) suspension.

Considering this design diversity, can we say at all what defines a bicycle? The question seems all the more problematic if we consider the fact that different users (and non-users) will characterize the bicycle in different ways. Some of these characterizations have to do with the bicycle's perceived technical qualities, while others are unrelated to technology. The bicycle can be seen—and actually has been seen—as a modern or as an out-dated mode of transport, as a white elitist status symbol or as an outdated vehicle of necessity for the poor, as slow or fast, as a sports vehicle or a utility vehicle, as exhausting or relaxing, as a male adventure vehicle or a vehicle for the emancipation for women, as exposed to the elements or "a feast for the senses," as a signifier of a sub- or counter-cultural life-styles or as part of a national habit. For both reasons (the technical and the cultural diversity) the seemingly simple question what a bicycle is, is not answered in the same way everywhere.

In the following I will discuss a number of technical characteristics seen in most bicycles, and the implications these characteristics have for the practices and the perceptions of cycling. I suggest that three characteristics are the most relevant. These three are the single-track design, the self-moving principle, and the extraordinary efficiency of the bicycle (that is: the increase of the speed and range of travel without extra energy consumption). After discussing these three (and their implications for the use and perception of the bicycle) in detail, I will conclude by addressing some limitations of this analysis and point to perceptions of the bicycle that are *not* related to its technology or design but that still are important cultural determinants of bicycle use.

3. The single-track design

The first word used for a bicycle of sorts was *Laufmaschine*, German for running machine. It was the term used by the German inventor Karl Drais (1785–1851), whose brilliance in 1817 it was to imagine the feasibility of a self-propelled vehicle with two wheels behind one another (Hadland and Lessing, 2014; Lessing, 2003). The first and perhaps decisive element in Drais' invention was that the vehicle had a single track only, with both wheels placed in tandem. Even if the "draisine" did not yet have pedals, the single-track design was crucial for the ensueing development of the bicycle. It is difficult for us to conceive of the creative imagination and boldness required to think that this arrangement was at all possible, let alone that it would bring any advantages. In the case of the *Laufmaschine* the vehicle was additionally balanced by the feet of the rider on either side of the machine, which in an alternate rhythm similar to ice-skating would touch the ground and push the bicycle forward. Successful users however quickly discovered the unimaginable: that even without any feet touching the ground, the machine would not fall sideways while moving forward.

The single-track design of the bicycle brought—and still brings—many advantages: it saves weight, reduces mechanical friction and aerodynamic drag, and it reduces the space needed for traveling and parking to a minimum. Where space is scarce, as on busy streets, cyclists claim significantly less space than car drivers. Furthermore, as Drais himself already pointed out, on a single-track vehicle it is much easier to choose the best way on an uneven surface—a characteristic that both everyday cyclists avoiding potholes and mountain bikers still exploit to their benefit. Although nineteenth-cyclists became leading proponents for the improvement of roads before the advent of the car, the bicycle's initial success did not depend on it, as for instance Fitzpatrick's groundbreaking research of 19th-century cyclists in rural Australia demonstrates: "the bicycle's real serviceability lay in its versatility over a variety of surfaces" (Fitzpatrick, 1980, p. 99). The inherent agility of the bicycle makes it possible to navigate the narrowest of single trails, a factor which together with the bicycle's silence, became instrumental in the military successes of Viet Minh and Viet Cong jungle-warfare (Fitzpatrick, 2011, pp. 175–203). It is telling that the earliest mountain bikes in the 1970s and 80s were nothing but modified old "clunkers"; only later, extra suspension was added to navigate otherwise inaccessibly rough terrain (Buenstorf, 2003; Berto, 1999; Hadland and Lessing, 2014, pp. 433–444).

The success of the latest fashion in sports cycling, the "gravel bike" (basically a racing bike with drop bars, no added suspension and only slightly fatter tyres), is another indication that the basic design of the bicycle is well suited for many off-road uses.

The single-track design of the bicycle also brings disadvantages. The fact that it took some time before American law unequivocally acknowledged the bicycle as a "vehicle" with similar rights to the road as other vehicles has undoubtedly something to with its unusual single-track design (Longhurst, 2015, pp. 22–50). The single-track design also makes cycling a balancing act, that can be easily disturbed by impacts from outside. Still, since the development of the "safety bicycle" the most serious danger for cyclists does not come from some inherent unsafety in the bicycle's design but from the co-existence with much broader, heavier and faster vehicles. Accordingly, perceptions of the "unsafeness" of bicycles vary according to the measure in which cyclists feel protected from other traffic.

4. The self-moving principle and its consequences

The second characteristic of Drais' invention that was essential to him was that his machine was self-propelled, meaning that it didn't require animal labor: the driver-rider is the passenger is the engine. To this day, the Chinese and Japanese words commonly used to designate the bicycle, zixingchē and jitensha, emphasize that a bicycle is self-propelled. The title of a recent book publication on the cycling history of Austria's capital Vienna puts it aptly: *Motor bin ich selbst* ("I am the motor"; Hachleitner et al., 2013).

From the 1960s onward, the self-propelled aspect of cycling received renewed positive attention, but now no longer to distinguish the bicycle from animal-dependent transport, but to distinguish it from cars and other motorized vehicles. At a time people started to realize that increasing energy consumption was quickly becoming problematic for the planet, the bicycle was discovered to be "the most benevolent of machines" (Stoffers, 2016; Wilson, 1973). The act of cycling causes no air pollution and although cyclists still produce CO_2—after all they have to eat and breathe, and bicycles have to be produced before they can be used—estimates suggest that the total CO_2 cost per kilometer of cycling is less than 10% compared to car driving (Blondel, 2011). The discursive "greening of the bicycle" was of course part of the rise of the environmentalist movement to prominence:

since the 1960s the bicycle has become to ever more people a "vehicle of sustainability" (Horton, 2006). Typical for this renewed emphasis on the cyclist as "self-mover," was the new umbrella term "human-powered vehicle," introduced by MIT-professor David Gordon Wilson in the 1960s and consequently embraced by an international movement of engineers, who aimed to innovate the bicycle and make it a closer competitor to motorized transport (Stoffers, 2019).

The fact that the cyclist is a self-mover has two interlinked consequences for the characteristics of the bicycle: firstly, riding a bicycle requires physical effort, and secondly, for that reason it needs to be a lightweight construction. Both characteristics have a number of further consequences for the practice and perception of cycling.

To start with the second characteristic, because there is a natural limit to the weight on wheels an unassisted human can comfortably accelerate or push upward, it is crucial to keep the bicycle's weight low. The search for ever lighter bicycle designs and materials is therefore not a racers' fad, but an essential driving force in bicycle innovation since the very beginning. Indeed, design historians not only consider the bicycle an early example of the modernist "aesthetics of the ephemeral," but also a forerunner of modern lightweight construction principles (Krausse, 1986, pp. 59–72). Drais' 1817 machine, built from wood, may not have looked so ephemeral, but it weighed about 20 kg, equal to or even less than many later steel versions (Besse, 2008).

The need for a lightweight construction sets limits to the sturdiness of bicycles: compared to driving vehicles with a motor (which can be built in a heavier and sturdier way), bicycle riding inevitably comes with more frequent wear and tear—just think of punctured tyres, rusting chains, worn-out brake pads, broken lighting cables. Even though in the last few decades many improvements have been made in this respect (such as more puncture resistant tyres), the bicycle remains a high-maintenance machine that requires a minimum level of DIY-mentality from its regular user. It is no coincidence that the saddle bag with repair set is a common bicycle accessory.

The need to keep the weight as low as possible is also an important factor in the bicycle's "openness": enclosing the cyclist comes at a weight penalty (and additionally creates stability issues for single-track vehicles). The minimalist bicycle is a skeleton without a body, and cyclists sit on it, rather than in it. This means that they are exposed, unprotected against the elements.

To some, in some weather conditions, this is considered a major disadvantage, others celebrate cycling as a feast for the senses, even in climates as tough as in Iceland (Haraldsson, 2010, pp. 116–118). Already in the 19th century cyclists favorably compared the openness of cycling to enclosed train travel. "The locomotive has pulled man away from nature," one Dutch bicycle brochure from 1897 claimed—not only because of its straight lines and its high speed, but also because passengers are put away "behind small windows" (Gink, 1897, p. 21; cf Schivelbusch, 1989, pp. 52–61). By contrast, the bicycle restored the contact of travelers with their surroundings. Similar praise of the openness of cycling was again voiced in 1960s and '70s counter-culture (and can still be heard today), contrasting bicycles with cars rather than with trains, and emphasizing the bicycle as a "tool for conviviality" which enables travelers to stay in contact with fellow-humans in a way impossible to encapsulated car drivers (Horton, 2006; Illich, 1973, 1974).

The need for a lightweight construction is, as mentioned before, a consequence of the physical effort that riding a bicycle requires. The physical effort required is obviously also crucial for the bicycle's prominent quality as a sports and leisure instrument, associated with exercise and athleticism. Its attraction in this respect is closely related to the rise of modern society characterized by an increasingly inactive life style. As early as 1837 the health benefits of cycling for sedentary city dwellers were highlighted (Hadland and Lessing, 2014, p. 25)—and this aspect has remained an important (and perhaps the most constant) theme in the discourses on cycling. The health benefits of cycling were for instance widely discussed in the decades around 1890 when cycling started to spread beyond the initial small group of the well-to-do. Especially by middle-class users, cycling was seen as a way to prepare body and mind for the exacting requirements of modern times (Ebert, 2010, pp. 55–90; Friss, 2015, pp. 117–143). The combination of physical and mental abilities needed for cycling made that the bicycle was perceived as an instrument suitable to recover and develop one's true (individual) nature in an increasingly unnatural society.

Related yet different was the early popularity of the bicycle as a sports vehicle. Races on bicycles were held from the 1860s onward and were especially popular among young males, driven by the urge to show off their physical prowess. In the course of the 19th century bicycles races became the first instances of mass spectator sport (Holt, 1981, pp. 81–103; Rabenstein, 1996). The fact that cycle races from the beginning were performed not only on closed circuits, but also on public roads made competitive cycling into a public spectacle with strong effects on public perceptions of cycling. In the first half of the 20th century in many countries in Europe, including France, Italy and Belgium, a strong worker's culture of bicycle racing developed that contributed to defining cycling as in the first place a sport activity (Rabenstein, 1996; Thompson, 2006, Ch. 4; Vanysacker, 2000; Knuts, 2014). By contrast, in the Netherlands, where road racing was banned since 1905, the public image of cycling as a sport remained secondary to cycling as transport (Ebert, 2010).

Since the 1960s, with ever increasing numbers of people leading increasingly sedentary lifestyles, there is again a growing appreciation of the health benefits of cycling, both among medical experts, policy makers and cyclists themselves. As a consequence more people choose to cycle for recreational purposes, to relax and stay fit. In the US, for instance, the percentage of people who participated in cycling for recreation more than tripled from 1960 to 1982 (Cordell et al., 1999, p. 235). At the same time, cycling as a sport, during much of in the 20th century an almost exclusively European activity, has become more global. Since the 1980s and '90s, American and British competitive cycling has risen to prominence, partly as a result of the renewed scientific study of cycling linked to the human powered vehicle movement (Stoffers, 2019, pp. 212–213). By now, cycling races on all continents are organized, including an increasing number of professional races for women—making cycling more of a global sport than ever. In some countries or regions "cycling" is predominantly framed as a sporting activity—an image that is not necessarily conducive to its use for everyday transport. In fact, it may be no coincidence that several countries where cycling is strongly associated with sport, including France, Italy and the United Kingdom, do not have strong cultures of cycling for transport. For policy makers it is important to realize that cycling as a sport and leisure activity and cycling as transport constitute different practices, that are not necessarily linked by spill-over effects. Nor do both have the same impact on the environment: while cycling for transport usually implies a reduced use of motorized vehicles, cycling for leisure and sport often leads to more motorized traffic by cyclists who use cars to travel to environments attractive to cycling.

We cannot conclude this discussion of the cyclist as a self-mover without stating the obvious: the quality of the "motor" of the bicycle is different from one cyclist to the other (even if the bicycles themselves are identical). This quality (or "fitness") depends on genetic constitution, age and frequency of use, making cycling more agreeable to some than to others and the easier the more one cycles. It is also clear that while cycling obviously takes effort and energy, exactly for this reason it can result in a sense of accomplishment, wellbeing and fulfillment that is not provided by using motorized forms of transport. Maybe the present success of the pedal-assisted e-bike can at least partly be explained by the fact that it reduces the effort required to ride a bicycle while at the same time providing the satisfaction of self-moving, even if this self-moving is partially illusionary.

5. Efficiency, speed and range of travel

By calling his bicycle a running *machine* Drais framed it as a modern product linked to technical progress and efficiency. At least until the end of the 19th century the word "machine" was fondly used by many cyclists all over Europe and the US to designate their vehicle and during this whole period the bicycle was widely considered both a symbol and advancer of modernity. Its modernism was the reason why it was criticized by the likes of John Ruskin, who in 1888 wrote that he was "quite prepared to spend all [his] best 'bad language' in reprobation of the bi-, tri-, and 4-5-6 or 7 cycles, and every other contrivance and invention for superseding human feet on God's ground" (as quoted in Davis, 2015, p. 170). A similar anti-modern ethos one can still sometimes be observed in complaints of hikers about the intrusion of mountain bikers in their favorite stretch of nature (see, e.g., Cessford, 2003).

The progress the "running machine" promised was increased speed and, with that, an increased range of travel—without major increase in energy consumption compared to walking. Drais emphasized speed as a central characteristic of his invention by giving his vehicle the name "vélocipède" when he introduced it in France, referring to the Latin words for speed and feet, and related to the German expression "schnellfüssig": moving lightly and quickly (cf Hadland and Lessing, 2014, pp. 20–41). Until at least the 1880s "vélocipède" became the general word for bicycles all over Europe and in the US. Even now it is in one of its derivative forms—including velosiped in Russia, sepeda in Indonesia, and vélo in France, Luxembourg and Switzerland—the common word for bicycle in a range of countries. Also the enigmatic Dutch word for bicycle, *fiets*, not derived from velocipede but probably from a dialect verb meaning "to move quickly," emphasized speed as an essential characteristic of the bicycle (Sanders, 1996). Typically, in France "vélo" is used to indicate a racing bicycle in contrast to the utilitarian "bicyclette" (Fournel, 2008, pp. 29–30).

Already Drais' still primitive running machine made it possible to outperform pedestrians as well as horse-drawn carriages without too much effort. With the addition of pedals in the 1860s, the speed of cyclists increased substantially: in 1869, in the earliest French road race ever the winner could sustain an average speed of 11.52 kph over 123 km of ordinary roads. Soon, specialized racing bicycles were developed: the high wheeler (Hadland and Lessing, 2014, p. 97). In 1883 the hour record on a high wheeler on a bicycle track was 33 km. More stunning perhaps was the 24 h world record on a similar bike by Dutch cyclist Johan Faber over ordinary roads a few years later, in 1887, covering 406 km in 19.5 h and sustaining an average speed of 21 kph (Hogenkamp, 1916, pp. 92–93). With the introduction of the safety bicycle the efficiency of the two-wheeler improved again substantially, and at present the 24 h record is above 1000 km. In 19th-century advertising the effortless speed of the bicycle was one of the commonly claimed characteristics, as demonstrated by the frequent association of cycling with flying, both in advertising posters and literary fiction (see, e.g., Besse, 2002; Schenkel, 2008, pp. 80–88). Hyperbole and sales talk, sure, and hilariously mocked by writer Jerome K. Jerome in his 1900 novel *Three men on the Bummel* ("few bicycles do realize the poster"). Still, apart from the actual flying, the claims about effortless speed weren't all that far-fetched: scientists maintain that the bicycle provides more efficient propulsion than any other machine or indeed any moving creature on earth (Wilson, 1973, 2004, p. 161).

Increased speed made it possible to cover stunning distances using nothing but human power. The famous French dictionary by Littré noted in 1874 as a defining feature of cyclists that "a trained *vélocipédiste* can, on a well maintained road and in a moderately hilly country, cover a daily distance of 80–100 km for several consecutive days" (Littré, 1874, p. 2434). Many ultralong-distance tours by bicycle, including the first bicycle tour around the world, were already undertaken in the 1880s. Cyclists riding the 1893 Vienna-Berlin long-distance race took less than half the time of the military horse riders the year before to cover the distance of 580 km, and did this with far less exhaustion. Of the 200 participating horses about 30 died from the physical effort. Among the cyclists there were no casualties (Ebert, 2010, pp. 192–197).

But the extended range the bicycle provided was obviously not only conducive to such record attempts, it also and more importantly changed everyday life. The bicycle reduced the distance between the city and the surrounding countryside, and thus not only made the city more easily accessible to people in the surrounding area, but conversely also became an important factor in the touristic development of the countryside (Holt, 1985; Bertho Lavenir, 1999). Furthermore, the bicycle made it possible to live further away from work, substantially increasing the range of places where one could work or live, but also where one could shop or recreate (see, e.g., Friss, 2015, 148ff; Norcliffe, 2001, pp. 211–235).

The technical qualities of the bicycle created an hitherto unknown freedom of movement for individuals. The first successful safety bicycle, Starley's Rover (1885), got its name exactly from this capacity to go wherever one wanted (and "rower" is still the common word for bicycle in Polish). That this freedom could actually be enjoyed by ever more people was related to the bicycle's relatively low cost—another consequence of it being a human-powered and slim construction. Even in the 19th century, when the bicycle still was an expensive hand-built product, it was cheap compared to keeping a horse, the only alternative for individual travel beyond walking and hardly quicker. All well-to-do could buy a bicycle, but not all could keep a horse. This alone created a strong increase of people who could move around faster and further at will. With the lowering of the prices for bicycles in the era of the mass-produced bicycle, these new possibilities became within reach of those to whom this level of independent movement had been denied before (or who could not afford it previously): middle class men, women, workers, youth.

These qualities of the bicycle have not disappeared; they are just as real now, as they were in the 19th century. Cycling is still an extraordinarily efficient way of traveling, multiplying the speed and range of travel of humans *without* substantial increases of energy consumption. Of course, with the rise of automobility, the bicycle was out-performed in terms of speed and range of transport (although in most western countries it would take at least until mid-century before car drivers actually out-numbered cyclists) (Oldenziel et al., 2016). But what really changed was the *appreciation* of the speed of the bicycle. In some countries (such as the Netherlands) cyclists were officially designated as "slow traffic," in many others cyclists were lumped together with the three to four times slower pedestrians in the category "non-motorized traffic." Gradually, especially since the 1990s this perspective has started to change again and the relative speed of cycling for transport is increasingly appreciated. Paradoxically, the most important factor in this development has been the utter success of the car: ever increasing car numbers have made congestion a serious problem in many cities and this has slowed down the door-to-door speed of cars on short trips considerably. According to a EU handbook for local decision makers cycling is generally faster than car driving on trips fewer than 5 km (Dekoster and Schollaert, 1999). In line with this statement, surveys show that speed is again one of the most appreciated characteristics of the bicycle in urban contexts (see, e.g., Börjesson and Eliasson, 2012, p. 253). The increasing popularity of the e-bike and the speed-pedelec will undoubtedly strengthen this renewed appreciation of the speed of the bicycle in urban transport.

6. Concluding remarks

This chapter has discussed a number of technical qualities of bicycles and the effects these qualities have for the practice and appreciation of cycling. We have defined the single-track design, the self-moving principle and the increased speed and range of travel without increased energy consumption as core characteristics of the bicycle. These qualities have led us to consider a number of other, inter-connected characteristics, such as the bicycle's spatial efficiency and agility, its minimalist and lightweight construction, and its "openness." In passing, we have also noted the bicycle's silence and affordability as additional consequences of its basic technical characteristics. To what extent these qualities are appreciated or considered important depends on the various cultures of cycling, which can differ substantially not only from one time to another, but also from one social group to another, and from one country to another.

A number of limitations of this analysis should be noted. Not all the characteristics that have been mentioned, are shared by all cycles that you can see on the road. Tricycles are not as agile and space-efficient as bicycles and they are usually heavier—but they do not require to balance and are (therefore) more suitable for carrying heavy loads (including children). Velomobiles (faired recumbent bicycles or tricycles) do not have the "openness" of ordinary bicycles, but they can attain and maintain higher speeds thanks to the aerodynamic qualities of their fairings. Electric bicycles are just as agile as fully human-powered bicycles and they certainly provide effortless speed, but they are usually heavier and they are not in the strict sense self-powered—reducing both the costs and the benefits of this characteristic of non-motorized bicycles discussed above.

There is further diversity that should be noted. Some bicycles are designed as sports vehicles for high speeds on the road or for negotiating steep and rough offroad terrain, others are designed as utility vehicles for everyday urban use. Every bicycle design comes with its own distinct (im)practicalities. However, this diversity is not evident to all users, thus limiting their conceptions of what a bicycle is and can be. To give just one example, according to a recent historical study of American bicycle use in the 1890s the predominance of bicycle designs for recreation instead of for utility was a major factor in the early demise of cycling in the United States (Friss, 2015, p. 201). For most of the 20th century, the majority of bicycles in America remained children's bicycles, and when adult bicycles finally returned as a substantial market segment in the 1970s, these were again mainly bicycles designed for recreation, not for everyday practical use (Berto et al., 2009, p. 225). All in all, in the American case the most common bicycles were never practical vehicles for everyday transportation. In the Netherlands, by contrast, after the Dutch bicycle manufacturers managed to gain full control of the internal market after World War I, the dominant national bicycle design became a rather heavy and slow, upright urban bicycle, designed for everyday use in all weather conditions, keeping the rider's clothes clean and allowing them to transport moderate loads (Ebert, 2009). Even in the present time of "global flexibilization" of the bicycle we can still notice the legacy of the mass produced bicycle in the dominance of certain bicycle designs in the different countries, that are suited for some purposes more than for others and may not all be suitable for everyday use.

Finally, it should be noted that the technical characteristics of the bicycle discussed above may not be the ones that are decisive for its (non-) appreciation. One of the recurring topics in historical analyses of bicycle use is its ever changing social status: the extent to which the bicycle is being seen as signifying a specific group identity. Historical research is unanimous in suggesting that a major aspect of the decline of cycling in 20th century Europe was that elites turned their back on the bicycle after the car became available to them and the bicycle spread among the working classes. The bicycle no longer provided social distinction (in a positive way) and became a vehicle of necessity for those who could not afford a car, and thus a signifier of being poor. This was a strong disincentive to use the bicycle, and as soon as people could afford it, they would turn to other forms of transportation. The strength of the social stigma associated with the bicycle as a vehicle of the poor, can, according to Vivanco, today still be seen in the Bolivian capital Bogotá: despite policies and facilities designed to encourage cycling, the image of the bicycle as a vehicle of the poor strongly limits its use (Vivanco, 2013, pp. 76–83).

There are other group identities the bicycle is (or has been) associated with and that hinder its use by other groups. In the United States this applies to the strong link between cycling and childhood, that recent historical research has shown was strongly affected by advertising campaigns of

American bicycle manufacturers in the first half of the 20th century. The result was that for much of the 20th century the bicycle was considered unsuitable as transportation for responsible and "masculine" adults (Turpin, 2018). Again, in the 1970s, in many Western countries the bicycle was strongly pushed by counterculture movements, for whom the bicycle was a "vehicle of opposition" to the dominant capitalist order (Horton, 2006; Furness, 2005; Lambert, 2004). Consequently, in countries where these groups were able to substantially influence the collective image of cycling, such as the US and the UK, the bicycle became less attractive to those who did not identify with these movements.

As a final example of the importance of group identities for cycling let's turn once more to the Dutch, known for the universality of their bicycle use. In her fascinating 2010 comparative analysis of German and Dutch cycling history until 1940, historian Anne-Katrin Ebert has demonstrated how the continuing popularity of the bicycle in the Netherlands can be explained by the fact that cycling became associated not so much with distinct groups within society as with conceptions of the national community as a whole—not unlike the position of the car in the United States. It was exactly the association of the bicycle with Dutch national identity that made that Dutch elites did not fully turn their back on the bicycle in the 20th century, even when it spread to the working classes and no longer provided social distinction. Riding a bicycle became and remained a way to be a decent, hard-working and self-disciplined Dutch citizen, irrespective of income or social status (Ebert, 2010). To this day Dutch elites, including leading politicians and members of the royal family, reproduce this national culture of cycling by purposefully presenting themselves to the public riding their bicycles. As a recent historical analysis of Dutch bicycle policies in the 20th century shows, the continued appreciation of the bicycle by Dutch elites also extended to subaltern policy makers and traffic engineers, making them receptive to pleas and demands by bicycle advocates (Dekker, 2021, pp. 340–341). All in all, in the Dutch case the bicycle is at the same time completely common and highly valued, creating ideal circumstances for the appreciation of the bicycle in all its qualities.

References

Bertho Lavenir, C., 1999. La roue et le stylo. Comment nous sommes devenus touristes. Editions Odile Jacob, Paris.

Berto, F.J., 1999. The Birth of Dirt. Origins of Mountain Biking. Van der Plas Publications, San Francisco.

Berto, F., et al., 2009. The Dancing Chain: History and Development of the Derailleur Bicycle, third ed. Cycle Publishing/Van der Plas Publications, San Francisco.
Besse, N. (Ed.), 2002. Voici des ailes: affiches de cycles. Musée d'art et d'industrie de St Étienne, Paris.
Besse, N. (Ed.), 2008. The Velocipede, a modern object, 1860–1870—Le vélocipède, objet de modernité 1860–1870. Silvana Editoriale/Musée d'Art et d'Industrie, Saint-Étienne.
Bijker, W.E., 1995. Of Bicycles, Bakelites and Bulbs: Towards a Theory of Sociotechnical Change. M1T Press, Cambridge, MA, and London.
Bleckmann, D., 1999. Wehe wenn sie losgelassen! Über die Anfänge des Frauenradfahrens in Deutschland. Maxime Verlag, Gera-Leipzig.
Blondel, B., 2011. Cycle more Often 2 Cool Down the Planet! Quantifying CO_2 Savings of Cycling. ECF, Brussels.
Börjesson, M., Eliasson, J., 2012. The benefits of cycling. Viewing cyclists as travellers rather than non-motorists. In: Parkin, J. (Ed.), Cycling and sustainability. Bingley, Emerald, pp. 247–268.
Buenstorf, G., 2003. Designing clunkers. Demand-side innovation and the early history of the mountain bike. In: Metcalfe, J.S., Cantner, U. (Eds.), Change, Transformation and Development. Physica, Heidelberg, pp. 53–70.
Burri, M., 1998. Das Fahrrad: Wegbereiter oder überrolltes Leitbild? Eine Fussnote zur Technikgeschichte des Automobils. ETH/Institut für Technikgeschichte, Zürich.
Cessford, G., 2003. Perception and reality of conflict: walkers and mountain bikes on the Queen Charlotte Track in New Zealand. J. Nat. Conserv. 11 (4), 310–316.
Cordell, H.K., et al., 1999. Outdoor recreation participation trends. In: Cordell, H.K., McKinney, S.M. (Eds.), Outdoor Recreation in American Life: A National Assessment of Demand and Supply Trends. Sagamore Publishing, Champaign, IL, pp. 219–321.
Cox, P., Van de Walle, F., 2007. Bicycles don't evolve—velomobiles and the modelling of transport technologies. In: Horton, D., Rosen, P., Cox, P. (Eds.), Cycling and Society. Ashgate, Aldershot, pp. 113–131.
Davis, A., 2015. Technology. In: O'Gorman, F. (Ed.), The Cambridge Companion to John Ruskin. Cambridge University Press, Cambridge, pp. 170–186.
Dekker, H.-J., 2021. Cycling Pathways. The Politics and Governance of Dutch Cycling Infrastructure, 1920–2020. Amsterdam University Press, Amsterdam.
Dekoster, J., Schollaert, U., 1999. Cycling. The Way Ahead for Towns and Cities. European Commission, Luxembourg.
Ebert, A.-K., 2009. Nationales Design? Auf der Suche nach dem "Holland-Rad", 1900–1940. Technikgeschichte 76 (3), 211–231.
Ebert, A.-K., 2010. Radelnde Nationen. Die Geschichte des Fahrrads in Deutschland und den Niederlanden bis 1940. Campus Verlag, Frankfurt.
Edgerton, D., 2006. The Shock of the Old: Technology and Global History since 1900. Profile, London.
Filarski, R., 2004. The Rise and Decline of Transport Systems: Changes in a Historical Context. Ministry of Transport and Public Works, Rotterdam.
Fitzpatrick, J., 1980. The Bicycle and the Bush. Man and Machine in Rural Australia. Oxford University Press, Oxford.
Fitzpatrick, J., 2011. The Bicycle in Wartime, An Illustrated History, Rev. ed. Star Hill Studio, Kilcoy, QLD.
Fournel, P., 2008. Méli-Vélo. Abecedaire amoureux du vélo. Seuil, Paris.
Friss, E., 2015. The Cycling City. Bicycles and Urban America in the 1890s. The University of Chicago Press, Chicago and London.
Furness, Z.M., 2005. Put the Fun between Your Legs! The Politics and Counterculture of the Bicycle. Ph.D. thesis, University of Pittsburgh.

Gink van, Ott Bultman & Co, 1897. De natuur terug gevonden. Aangeboden door de Rijwiel–en Machinefabriek "De Hinde". Van Gink, Ott Bultman & Co, Amsterdam.
Hachleitner, B., Marschik, M., Müllner, R., et al. (Eds.), 2013. Motor bin ich selbst. 200 Jahre Radfahren in Wien. Metroverlag, Vienna.
Hadland, T., Lessing, H.-E., 2014. Bicycle Design: An Illustrated History. MIT Press, Cambridge, MA.
Haraldsson, R.H., 2010. Philosophical lessons from cycling in town and country. In: Ilundáin-Agurruzza, J., Austin, M.W. (Eds.), Cycling Philosophy for Everyone. A Philosophical Tour de Force. Wiley-Blackwell, Chichester, pp. 112–122.
Herlihy, D.V., 2004. Bicycle: The History. Yale University Press, New Haven and London.
Hogenkamp, G.J.M., 1916. Een halve eeuw wielersport. Amsterdam.
Holt, R., 1981. Sport and Society in Modern France. Macmillan, Londen, Oxford.
Holt, R., 1985. The bicycle, the bourgeoisie and the discovery of rural France, 1880-1914. Int. J. Hist. Sport 2, 127–139.
Horton, D., 2006. Environmentalism and the bicycle. Environ. Polit. 15, 41–58.
Illich, I., 1973. Tools for Conviviality. Marion Boyars Publishers, London.
Illich, I., 1974. Energy and Equity. Harper & Row Publishers, New York, Evanston.
Knuts, S., 2014. Converging and Competing Courses of Identity Construction: Shaping and Imagining Society through Cycling and Bicycle Racing in Belgium before World War Two. PhD dissertation, KU Leuven.
Krausse, J., 1986. Versuch, auf's Fahrrad zu kommen. Zur Technik und Ästhetik der Velo Evolution. In: Neyer, H.J. (Ed.), Zwischen Fahrrad und Fließband. Absolut modern sein: culture technique in Frankreich 1889–1937. Elefanten Press, Berlin, pp. 59–74.
Kuipers, G., 2013. The rise and decline of national habitus: Dutch cycling culture and the shaping of national similarity. Eur. J. Soc. Theory 16 (1), 17–35.
Lambert, B., 2004. Cyclopolis, ville nouvelle. Contribution à l'histoire de l'écologie politique. Editions Médecine & Hygiène, Genève.
Lessing, H.-E., 2003. Automobilität: Karl Drais und die unglaublichen Anfänge. Maxime-Verlag, Leipzig.
Littré, É., 1874. Dictionnaire de la langue française. 4 Librairie Hachette, Paris.
Longhurst, J., 2015. Bike Battles. A History of Sharing the American Road. University of Washington Press, Seattle and London.
Mackintosh, P.G., Norcliffe, G., 2007. Men, women and the bicycle: gender and social geography of cycling in the late 19th century. In: Horton, D., Rosen, P., Cox, P. (Eds.), Cycling and Society. Ashgate, Aldershot, pp. 153–177.
Mari, C., 2021. A Business History of the Bicycle Industry. Shaping Marketing Practices. Palgrave Macmillan, New York.
Norcliffe, G., 2001. The ride to modernity. The bicycle in Canada, 1869–1900. University of Toronto Press, Toronto, Buffalo, London.
Oddy, N., 1995. The bicycle: an exercise in gendered design. Cycle Hist. 5, 37–44.
Oldenziel, R., Emanuel, M., Albert de la Bruhèze, A.A., et al. (Eds.), 2016. Cycling Cities: The European Experience: Hundred Years of Policy and Practice. Foundation for the History of Technology, Eindhoven.
Oosterhuis, H., 2019. Entrenched habit of fringe mode; comparing national bicycle policies, cultures and histories. In: Männistö-Funk, T., Myllyntaus, T. (Eds.), Invisible Bicycle: Parallel Histories and Different Timelines. Technology and Change in History, vol. 15. Brill, Leiden, London, pp. 48–97.
Rabenstein, R., 1996. Radsport und Gesellschaft: Ihre Sozialgeschichtlichen Zusammenhänge in Der Zeit Von 1867 Bis 1914, second ed. Weidmann, Hildesheim, München, Zürich.

Radkau, J., 1995. Das Fahrrad in den Technikvisionen der Jahrhundertwende, oder: das Erlebnis in der Technikgeschichte. In: Briese, V., Matthies, W., Renda, G. (Eds.), Wege zur Fahrradgeschichte. BVA Bielefelder Verlag, Bielefeld, pp. 9–32.
Rosen, P., 2002. Framing Production: Technology, Culture, and Change in the British Bicycle Industry. MIT Press, Cambridge, MA.
Sanders, E., 1996. Fiets: de geschiedenis van een vulgair jongenswoord. SDU, s-Gravenhage.
Schenkel, E., 2008. Cyclomanie. Fahrrad und Literatur. Edition Isele, Eggingen.
Schivelbusch, W., 1989. Geschichte der Eisenbahnreise: Zur Industrialisierung von Raum und Zeit im 19. Jahrhundert. Fischer, Frankfurt.
Sharp, A., 1896. Bicycles & Tricycles: An Elementary Treatise on Their Design and Construction. Longmans, London.
Stoffers, M., 2016. The politics of bicycle innovation: comparing the American and Dutch human-powered vehicle movements, 1970s—present. In: Oldenziel, R., Trischler, H. (Eds.), Cycling and Recycling. Histories of Sustainable Practices. Berghahn, New York, Oxford, pp. 33–57.
Stoffers, M., 2019. Modernizing the bicycle: the international human-powered vehicle movement and the "bicycle renaissance" since the 1970s. In: Männistö-Funk, T., Myllyntaus, T. (Eds.), Invisible Bicycle: Parallel Histories and Different Timelines. Technology and Change in History, vol. 15. Brill, Leiden, London, pp. 180–214.
Stoffers, M., Oosterhuis, H., Cox, P., 2010. Bicycle history as transport history: the cultural turn. In: Mom, G. (Ed.), Mobility in history: themes in transport. T2M yearbook 2011. Éditions Alphil-Presses universitaires suisses, Neuchâtel, pp. 265–274.
Thompson, C.S., 2006. The Tour de France: A Cultural History. University of California Press, Berkeley, CA.
Turpin, R., 2018. First Taste of Freedom: A Cultural History of Bicycle Marketing in the United States. Syracuse University Press, New York.
Vanysacker, D., 2000. Koersend door een eeuw Italiaanse en Belgische geschiedenis. De Italo-Belgische connectie in en rond het wielerpeloton. Acco, Leuven, Den Haag.
Verkade, T., Te Brömmelstroet, M., 2020. Het recht van de snelste. Hoe ons verkeer steeds asocialer werd. S.l.: De correspondent.
Vivanco, L.A., 2013. Reconsidering the Bicycle. An Anthropological Perspective on a New (Old) Thing. Routledge, New York, London.
Wilson, S.S., 1973. Bicycle technology. Sci. Am. 228 (3), 81–91.
Wilson, D.G., 2004. Bicycling science, 3rd. The MIT Press, Cambridge (Mass.), London.

CHAPTER THREE

The rise of the electrically assisted bicycle and the individual, social and environmental impacts of use

Jessica E. Bourne[a,*], Paul Kelly[b], and Nanette Mutrie[b]
[a]Centre for Exercise, Nutrition and Health Sciences, School of Policy Studies, University of Bristol, Bristol, United Kingdom
[b]Physical Activity for Health Research Centre, Institute for Sport, Physical Education and Health Sciences, University of Edinburgh, Edinburgh, United Kingdom
*Corresponding author: e-mail address: jessica.bourne@bristol.ac.uk

Contents

Advances in Transport Policy and Planning, Volume 10
ISSN 2543-0009
https://doi.org/10.1016/bs.atpp.2022.04.003

Abstract

Since the mid-2000s there has been a substantial increase in electric bicycle related research seeking to answer a variety of questions in domains ranging from engineering to health. This chapter explores several of these questions, bringing together information on electric bicycle usage and sales, literature examining the demographics of electric bicycle users and the impact of electric bike use on transport, the environment, health, and safety. The chapter also highlights how e-bikes are being promoted across the world and identifies future research priorities.

Keywords: Electrically assisted pedal cycling, E-bike, Pedelec, Active travel, Health, Environment, User demographics

1. Introduction

With increased interest in cycling and advances in the technology of batteries, motors and product weight, electric bicycles have become increasingly popular over the past 20-years. With increased purchasing and use there has been an increase in electric bicycle related research across domains ranging from engineering to health. This chapter explores some of the questions researchers have sought to answer, examines how electric cycling has been promoted and identifies future research priorities.

2. Definitions and electric bicycle sales

2.1 What is an electric bicycle?

The term electric bicycle or e-bike does not have a specific definition and there are a wide variety of e-bikes available on the market with differences in motor size, maximum speed available from the electrical assistance and the main method of control (i.e., throttle control or pedal assistance). Fishman and Cherry (2016) make the distinction between *bicycle-style e-bikes* in which the bicycle has functional pedals but is assisted by an electric motor, these bicycles can be solely electric powered or require pedaling for electrical assistance to be provided, and *scooter-style e-bikes*, in which pedals are present for regulatory purposes but rarely provide a function.

In Europe, North America and Australia the term e-bike predominantly refers to bicycle style e-bikes (Fishman and Cherry, 2016). These bicycles are predominantly pedal assisted electric bicycles and are sometimes referred to as pedelecs or electric pedal-assisted cycles. The electrical assistance is provided by the motor when sensors detect pedaling speed and force.

Pedelecs are legally classified as bicycles in most countries with motors ranging from 250 to 750 W and top speeds of between 25 and 32 km/h. In the EU and the UK, the maximum power output for a pedelec is 250 W with a top speed of 25 km/h.

Recently, North America and Europe, predominantly Switzerland, have seen a rise in speed-pedelecs, with a maximum speed of 45 km/h. In the USA these speed-pedelecs are legally classified as bicycles, as with regular pedelecs, and do not require a driving license, although users must be over 17-years of age. In the EU, the speed pedelec falls under different regulations to pedelecs. Specifically, users of speed pedelecs are required to wear a helmet, need a driving and operating license and must be insured with a license plate. Speed pedelecs in Europe and North America are not allowed to use protected bike lanes or bike paths.

In China, the common style of e-bike is a scooter style bike which uses a throttle to provide power and does not require pedaling (Fishman and Cherry, 2016). Pedals are present at the point of sale for regulatory purposes and are often removed by the consumer. Until 2019 all e-bikes were classified as bicycles and a driving license was not required for operation. As such, e-bike related literature did not distinguish between scooter style and bicycle style e-bikes. In April 2019 China implemented new rules stating that electric bicycles should be limited to 25 km/h and the weight could not surpass 55 kg (Yang, 2019). Furthermore, to qualify as an electric bicycle the bike must have functional pedals and the motor power must not exceed 400 W. Vehicles that do not meet these requirements are classified as electric motorcycles requiring license plates and drivers licenses to operate. The aim of these new standards are to improve the safety of e-bikes and provide more opportunities for e-bike share systems.

In Japan and Israel electric bicycle motors cannot exceed 250 W or speeds over 24/25 km/h. Terminology and regulations of e-bikes in South America, Africa and the rest of Asia is unclear due to limited research in these areas.

Given the extensive difference between types of e-bikes we propose a taxonomy of bicycles including clear distinctions between the different types of electric bicycle as shown in Fig. 1. We encourage future researchers to be clear about the type of e-bike to which they are referring to enable fair comparisons on health, transport & safety data between countries. The current chapter focuses on e-bikes that require pedaling for assistance to be provided (i.e., pedelecs or speed pedelecs) and will here on in be referred to as e-bikes. The majority of authors do not distinguish between e-bike models. However, in Europe, North America and Australia the

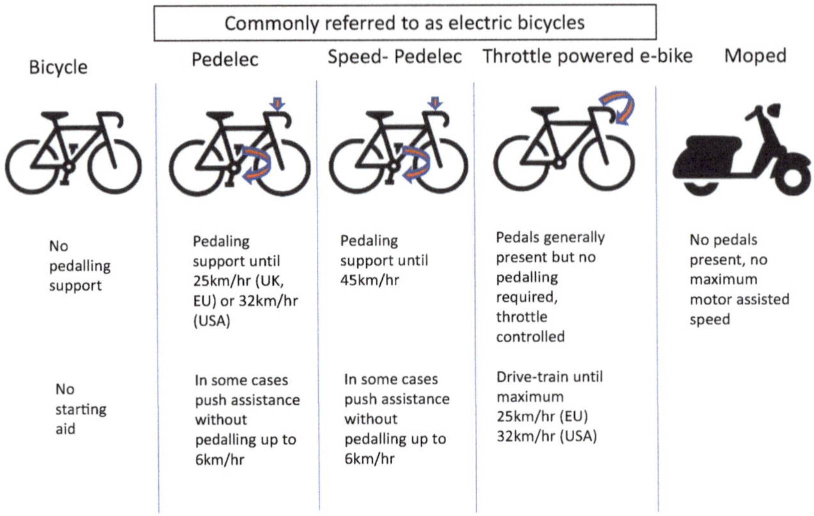

Fig. 1 Proposed taxonomy of bicycles. Distinction between conventional bicycles, pedelecs, throttle powered e-bikes and moped. *Adapted from Panwinkler, T., Holz-Rau, C. 2021. Causes of pedelec (pedal electric cycle) single accidents and their influence on injury severity. Accid. Anal. Prev. 154.*

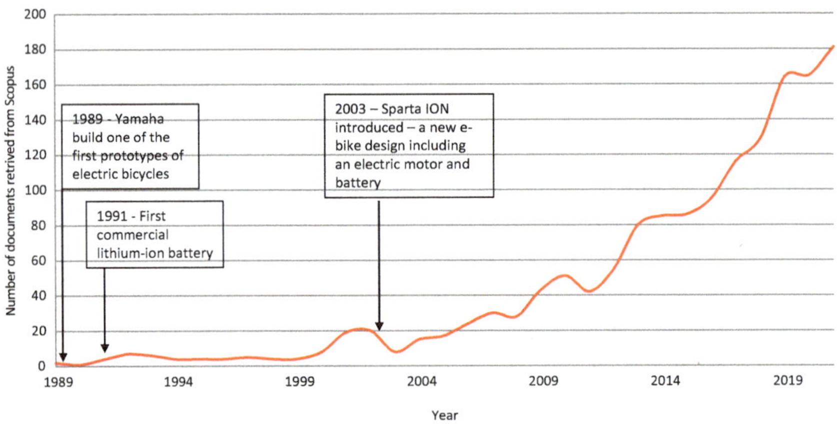

Fig. 2 Documents retrieved from Elsevier's Scopus database with e-bike related terms in the title from 1973 to 2021. The search terms included: *"pedelec," "e-bike," "electrically assisted bicycle," "electrically assisted cycle," "electrically assisted bike," "pedal-assist," "electric bicycle," "electric bike," "electric cycle."*

predominant e-bike is a pedelec. As such, in the current chapter when reviewing the literature on user demographics and the impact of e-bikes on health, transport and safety, data from Asia are excluded due to the focus on pedelecs (Fig. 2).

2.2 How have e-bike sales changed over the years?

Commercially available e-bikes originated in Japan in the 1980s but became increasingly popular in the early 2000s with technological advances in the batteries and motors and reduced weight of the bikes (Salmeron-Manzano and Manzano-Agugliaro, 2018). The market for electric bicycles, as a collective and in regard to total number of units sold, has been dominated by China (Fishman and Cherry, 2016). With just over 40-million e-bikes sold worldwide in 2015, 90% were sold in China, 5% in Europe and 0.7% in the USA (Salmeron-Manzano and Manzano-Agugliaro, 2018).

Across Europe sales of e-bikes, primarily pedelecs, have been growing at a faster rate than conventional bicycles. Specifically, conventional bicycle sales in the EU decreased by 5% between 2010 and 2016, from 19,873,000 to 18,873,000, while e-bike sales grew by 284% for the same period from 588,000 to 1,667,000 (CONEBI, 2017). Furthermore, between 2016 and 2019, e-bikes sales in Europe doubled with Germany, the Netherlands, Belgium, France and Italy accounting for the majority of these e-bike sales (Mordor Inelligence., 2020). Specifically, in the Netherlands in 2018, 40% of all new bicycles sold were e-bikes (Stichting BOVAG-RAI Mobiliteit., 2019). In Switzerland, in 2006 1% of all bicycles sold were e-bikes, compared to 36% in 2019 (Velosuisse, 2020). While in Germany annual growth rates of more than 39% in the number of e-bikes were recorded (ZIV, 2020).

Sales of e-bikes in the UK have been slower than in Europe. However, there has been consistent year on year growth as e-bikes have become more mainstream and in 2017 e-bikes accounted for 2% of all bicycle sales in the UK (CONEBI, 2017). Similar to the UK, e-bike sales in Australia, New Zealand and North America are growing but slower than the growth seen in Europe. However, tracking e-bikes sales has been reported to be difficult. In North America a large portion of conventional bikes have been converted to e-bikes using at home kits (MacArthur et al., 2014). Furthermore, in the USA, Australia and New Zealand there is no systematic tracking of the number of e-bikes being sold (Johnson and Rose, 2013; MacArthur et al., 2018b; Wild and Woodward, 2019). Best estimates of customs data suggest that e-bike imports more than doubled from 2016 to 2018 in New Zealand (Downard-Wilke, 2020). In Canada e-bike sales also appear to be on the rise and between 2014 and 2016 retailers in Vancouver reported increases in e-bike sales of between 100% and 500% (Shore, 2016).

The COVID-19 pandemic significantly impacted bicycle and e-bike sales around the world. The start of the pandemic saw sales of e-bikes drop due to cities imposing lockdown restrictions. However, once stores were allowed to reopen there were sudden bursts in sales in several western countries. Sales data from Halfords UK showed that in 2020 24% of all bikes purchased during the pandemic were electric (Halfords, 2021), while in the USA e-bike sales grew by 145% between 2019 and 2020 (The NPD Group, 2020). In Australia, 2019/2020 sales of e-bikes reached 48,000 and e-bike imports have tripling over the past 3 years (Kennedy, 2019; Spence, 2021). In December 2020, three European cycling associations released new forecasts for the cycling sector based on current trends, COVID-19 impacts and government announcements about future cycling investments. The report predicted sales of e-bikes to grow from 2.7 million bikes sold in 2019 to 17 million in 2030 (Heinrich-Böll-Stiftung European Union, 2021).

3. Demographics of e-bike users and reasons for use

3.1 Does e-cycling increase the diversity of individuals riding?

The demographics of conventional cyclists and determinants of use are discussed in chapters "A global overview of cycling trends" by Buehler and Goel and "Cycling and socioeconomic (dis)advantage" by Vidal Tortosa. Chapter "A global overview of cycling trends" by Buehler and Goel shows that older adults and women are often found to cycle less in countries with low levels of cycling. E-cycling may have the ability to reduce demographic specific barriers and increase the diversity of individuals cycling due to the electrical assistance provided. Preliminary studies exploring the demographic characteristics of e-bike users reported that e-cyclists were primarily older white males (Hendriksen et al., 2008; MacArthur et al., 2014; Popovich et al., 2014; Wolf and Seebauer, 2014). While it has been argued that these "early adopters" may differ from those who engage in e-cycling as it becomes more mainstream, recent research suggests that the propensity to own and use an e-bike remains higher among older adults across countries with both high and low rates of cycling (de Haas et al., 2021; Kroesen, 2017; MacArthur et al., 2018b; Melia and Bartle, 2021). However, there is some evidence that younger adults are beginning to adopt e-bikes. A recent study in Belgium reported that while the overall modal share of e-cycling was 2.9%, the e-cycling share among adults aged

45–54 was 3.8% (Janssens et al., 2020). In addition, data from the Dutch National Mobility Survey showed that in 2013 54% of e-bike kilometers traveled were made by adults aged 65 or over, while in 2017 this share decreased to 46%, indicating that younger age groups are adopting e-bikes (Statistics Netherlands (CBS), 2017).

There appears to be a difference in the gender distribution of e-bike users between countries with high versus low levels of cycling, similar to that seen among conventional bike use. Specifically, countries with high rate of cycling such as the Netherlands, Denmark and parts of Belgium report similar rates of e-cycling between men and women (Kroesen, 2017; Rérat, 2021), and in some cases higher rates of e-cycling among women than men (Cappelle et al., 2003; de Haas et al., 2021). In contrast, in countries with low rates of cycling, such as Australia, the USA and the UK, men outnumber women in regard to e-bike use (Johnson and Rose, 2013; MacArthur et al., 2014, 2018a, 2018b; Melia and Bartle, 2021). However, more women appear to be adopting e-bikes in countries with low cycling rates. Specifically, a 2014 survey of e-bike owners in the USA reported 15% of the sample were female (MacArthur et al., 2014). When the survey was repeated in 2018, 28% of the sample were female (MacArthur et al., 2018a). The authors note that neither survey utilized random sampling and therefore the results may not indicate an increase in riders within these groups.

A recent qualitative study with e-bike users and stakeholders (i.e., retailers, cycling planners and policy makers) in New Zealand found that e-cycling had the potential to empower women to cycle by enabling them to transport their children and shopping with reduced physical exertion and associated perspiration. Furthermore, e-cycling increased women's confidence to ride and enabled women with lower fitness to engage in cycling (Wild et al., 2021). Among older adults e-bikes enable individuals to ride with less effort and cover longer distances than a conventional bicycle (Jones et al., 2022; Van Cauwenberg et al., 2018).

Studies exploring the income and education level of e-bike users have reported mixed results. In the USA, Australia and the UK e-bike owners have been reported to have a higher income and/or level of education than the general population. (Johnson and Rose, 2013; MacArthur et al., 2014, 2018a; Melia and Bartle, 2021; Popovich et al., 2014). In the Netherlands, Kroesen (2017) reported that e-bike owners were more likely to have lower levels of education, but higher than average household incomes. However, in Austria e-bike owners were found to be of lower education and income levels than the general population (Wolf and Seebauer, 2014). In Switzerland Rérat (2021) reported a portion of e-bike owners to be of low income. This could potentially be due to advancing age and associated retirement. Melia and Bartle (2021) note a negative correlation with age and income in their sample of e-bike users with 53% of those aged 60 or younger having a household income of more than £55,000, compared with only 23.5% of the over-60s. This suggests that older, retired individuals on lower incomes are not discouraged from purchasing an e-bike due to their cost. In addition, e-bikes may offer a cheaper mode of transport than running a motorized vehicle with additional health benefits that maybe of interest to older adults.

Regarding the health of e-bike users, a recent survey of 14,000 bicycle owners in Switzerland, of which 2000 were e-bike owners, found that e-bike owners reported lower levels of physical fitness than conventional bike users (Rérat, 2021). In addition, e-bike users have been found to have a higher body mass index (BMI) than conventional cyclists or public transport users (Castro et al., 2019; Dons et al., 2018). The higher BMI likely reflects the appeal of e-bikes to help overcome the physical burden of conventional bicycles, rather than the impact of lower physical exertion required for e-cycling.

3.2 Are there differences in the purpose of e-bike use based on demographics?

The purpose for which e-bikes are used varies between age groups. Specifically, there is evidence that e-bikes are primarily used for commuting for individuals $\leq$55 years of age, while older adults use e-bikes primarily for recreational purposes but also for shopping and visiting people (Bourne et al., 2020). Whether e-bikes are used primarily for recreation or running errands in older adults varies across studies. In an exploration of different e-bike user groups from the Dutch National Mobility Survey, de Haas et al. (2021) report that the fastest growing e-bike user group is part-time working women with children, for transport and escorting. While the share of e-bike use among retired older people, who use the e-bike primarily for leisure purposes, is decreasing.

Few studies have explored differences in use based on gender. One observational study among older adults reported that women used the e-bike more for making social visits than men (Van Cauwenberg et al., 2018). Similarly, among individuals with type 2 diabetes mellitus (T2DM) the co-authors own research found that women used the e-bike more for connecting with friends and family either through visiting or riding together, while men preferred to cycle alone for exercise (Bourne, 2021). We are aware of no studies that have explored differences in e-bike use or purpose of use based on ethnicity.

3.3 What motivates people to purchase and use e-bikes and how is e-cycling perceived?

Retrospective surveys and qualitative investigations with e-bike owners and small-scale trials have been conducted to explore individuals' perceived benefits and barriers to e-cycling as well as motivation for use and purchasing. Motivation for e-bike use and the benefits associated with use are commonly reported in relation to overcoming the barriers to conventional cycling. Specifically, the electrical assistance allows individuals to maintain speed with less effort, enabling users to overcome topographic obstacles, carry a heavy load and allowing those with reduced physical fitness or other health conditions to ride a bicycle (Bourne et al., 2020; de Geus and Hendriksen, 2015; Jones et al., 2016b; MacArthur et al., 2018a). Furthermore, the electrical assistance enables individuals to complete longer and/or faster journeys (Boland, 2019; Dill and Rose, 2012; Fyhri et al., 2017a; Johnson and Rose, 2015; Jones et al., 2016b; Melia and Bartle, 2020; Popovich et al., 2014; Shimano Steps, 2021).

These motivational factors and perceived benefits vary based on age. In general, younger adults are motivated to e-cycle due to environmental concerns, to reduce car use and to save money. In addition, reduced travel time in comparison to a conventional bike and a car, providing more predictable journey times and the ability to carry shopping, children and other items are important motivational factors for younger adults (Bourne et al., 2020; Eddeger et al., 2012; Edge et al., 2018; Kairos Impact Research and Development, 2010; Shimano Steps, 2021). In comparison, despite the reduced physical effort compared to conventional cycling, older adults are motivated to e-cycle as a means of maintaining or increasing their physical activity and fitness. Furthermore, cycling is frequently viewed as a means of continuing to cycle despite physical limitations that negatively impact conventional cycling (Johnson and Rose, 2015; Leger et al., 2019; Spencer et al., 2019; Van Cauwenberg et al., 2018), thereby extending the cycling careers of individuals who would otherwise cease cycling. In addition, e-cycling removes some of the differences in riding abilities due to fitness or physical limitations, enabling individuals to ride with friends and family (Johnson and Rose, 2015; Leger et al., 2019). Interestingly, the reduced physical effort associated with e-cycling is reported as a barrier to e-cycling in younger individuals (Edge et al., 2018).

Clinical populations may also present unique motivations for engaging in e-cycling. Specifically, among individuals with T2DM the primary motivation to e-cycling was to improve health, with little consideration for the environmental impact. Furthermore, individuals felt that e-cycling was an easier way of managing their diabetes than dieting or other types of exercise, largely due to enjoyment (Bourne, 2021). Motivators for e-cycling have not yet been explored in other clinical populations.

The enjoyment associated with e-cycling is the most commonly reported benefit of e-cycling and a key motivator to maintaining riding (Bourne et al., 2020). The heightened enjoyment is believed to come from the reduced physical effort which enables individuals to overcome the many barriers to conventional cycling (Spencer et al., 2019). A qualitative study of 21 inactive adults who were loaned an e-bike for 8 months reported that initial motivation for e-cycling was to increase physical activity and improve health. However, sustained e-cycling was associated with the enjoyment experienced while riding, suggesting a shift from more external motivation for riding (i.e., to improve health) to more autonomous, internal motivation (i.e., enjoyment) (Mildestvedt et al., 2020). Among older adults e-bikes enabled users to travel further distances and explore their surroundings, something that they would not have thought possible on a conventional bicycle, and bought significant enjoyment (Leger et al., 2019; Melia and Bartle, 2021; Spencer et al., 2019; Van Cauwenberg et al., 2018). There is a substantial body of literature which demonstrates that positive enjoyment during exercise is associated with greater future engagement (Rhodes and Kates, 2015). This enjoyment is a unique aspect of e-cycling over other forms of active travel such as running or conventional cycling.

While perceived as enjoyable, some studies report user safety concerns, although findings are inconsistent. Specifically, in some studies individuals report feeling safer riding an e-bike on busier streets in comparison to a conventional bike due to the ability to keep up with traffic and accelerate faster at traffic lights (Dill and Rose, 2012; Edge et al., 2018; MacArthur et al., 2017). Conversely other studies report users feeling unsafe riding in traffic due to the potential for collisions with motor vehicles for fear of road users being unable to differentiate between conventional bicycles and e-bikes and underestimating the speed of the e-bike (Haustein and Møller, 2016; Jones et al., 2016b; Popovich et al., 2014).

In addition to fear of conflict with motor vehicles there are several factors that deter e-cycling, largely related to the e-bike itself and/or the environment (Bourne et al., 2020). A lack of appropriate cycling infrastructure including segregated cycle paths, conflict with pedestrians and conventional bike users, lack of charging and/or parking facilities and fear of theft all negatively impact riding. These environmental barriers differ across countries. In the Netherland conflict with other cyclists is a barrier to e-cycling, while in the UK the lack of cycling infrastructure and poor parking facilities are more commonly reported (Jones et al., 2016b). Regarding the e-bike itself, concerns about battery range and the weight of the e-bike negatively impact riding. Specifically, the weight of the e-bike makes it difficult to lift into cars and onto public transport or make repairs. This appears to be of greater concern for women, older adults and clinical populations (Bourne, 2021; Bourne et al., 2020). The cost of purchasing an e-bike and associated maintenance is a commonly reported barrier to several e-bike users, particularly younger adults (Bourne et al., 2020; Melia and Bartle, 2021; Shimano Steps, 2021).

The factors associated with e-bike purchasing and use among current e-bike users or following an e-bike trial have been used to infer the potential of e-bike adoption. However, there do appear to be some differences in e-bike perceptions between users and non-users. There has been a general perception that e-bikes are for lazy, overweight, or unfit individuals (Jones et al., 2016b; Plazier et al., 2017b; Popovich et al., 2014). Conversely, in a study with older adults e-bikes were reported as being for young, active individuals (Cappelle et al., 2003). The stigma associated with e-cycling is present in countries with both high and low levels of conventional cycling (Shimano Steps, 2021). This suggests that even in areas with a positive cycling culture, such as the Netherlands, this positive perception of cycling may not currently extend to e-bikes.

Comparing the perceived e-cycling benefits of non-e-bike users with e-bike users, Simsekoglu and Klöckner (2019) found that non-users were more concerned about safety and the e-bikes weight and battery range which negatively related to intention to buy. In addition, non-users were less optimistic of the health and mobility benefits of e-bikes than current users. However, these perceptions are malleable, with experimental studies reporting that attitudes towards e-bikes become more positive with increased use (Drage and Pressl, 2012; Edge et al., 2018; Plazier et al., 2017b; Sustrans, 2013). Trialing an e-bike is positively associated with e-bike purchasing (Ton and Duives, 2021), while e-bike purchasing is positively associated with e-bike use (Fyhri and Sundfør, 2020; Ton and Duives, 2021). Simsekoglu and Klöckner (2019) also reported that familiarity with e-bikes increased intention to buy. As such, as e-bikes become more common place in the transport system we will likely see a shift in perceptions from non-users. Since 2017 e-bikes have received considerable attention in the USA, Australia and the UK and findings from a European survey revealed that there was an 11% increase in the percentage of individuals likely to purchase an e-bike from 2019 to 2020 (Shimano Steps, 2021).

4. The impact of e-cycling on transport mode use, the environment and health

4.1 What is the impact of e-cycling on the frequency and duration of cycling?

Qualitative studies, conducted primarily in Europe and North America, consistently report perceived increases in the frequency and duration of cycling following the acquisition of an e-bike (Dill and Rose, 2012; Fyhri et al., 2017a; Kroyer and Johansson, 2013; MacArthur et al., 2018a). Similar findings are reported in studies utilizing surveys and/or travel diaries. Specifically, survey data collected across seven European countries found that the average daily distance cycled by commuters on an e-bike was 8.0 km compared to 5.3 km on a conventional bike (Castro et al., 2019). In addition, individual trip distances and duration of rides on e-bikes are reported to be longer than those completed on a conventional bike (Castro et al., 2019; Mobiel 21, 2014).

Cross-sectional data from 3 years of the Dutch National Mobility Survey revealed that e-bike users cycled 3.0 km a day, compared to 2.6 km a day for conventional cyclists (Kroesen, 2017). Building on this, Sun et al. (2020) examined the travel patterns of people who bought an e-bike between two data collection periods of the same survey, creating a prospective study design. The authors found that while the share of conventional cycling decreased, the total amount of cycling increased among e-bike users. Using an experimental design Fyhri and Fearnley (2015) loaned 66 individuals an e-bike for up to 4 weeks. Using travel diaries before and after e-bike acquisition the authors found that e-bike users substantially increased their total bicycle use from an average of 4.8 (±8.1) km per day to 10.3 (±12.2) km per day compared to a reduction in bicycle use in the control group (4.1 [±8.6] to 3.0 [±6.4] km per day). Increases in cycling trip frequency from 0.9 to 1.4 per day were reported in the e-bike group. Recent research by the same group reported that individuals who purchased an e-bike increased their average daily cycling from 2.1 to 9.2 km per day with no changes in cycling behavior in a control group (Fyhri and Sundfør, 2020).

In a randomized cross-over study in which participants were assigned a conventional bike then an e-bike in a random order for 3 months each, Bjørnarå et al. (2019) reported that e-cycling led to the greatest amount of cycling both in regard to distance cycled and duration with minimum variability in use (Median km per week [IQR][a]: 20.2[24.8], Median minutes per week [IQR]: 62.7 [68.5]) compared to conventional cycling (Median km per week [IQR]: 11.9[21.2], Median minutes per week [IQR]: 51.1 [84.7]). Furthermore, over the course of the intervention individuals reduced their cycling more rapidly in the conventional cycling period than during the e-cycling period suggesting that e-cycling enabled individuals to maintain their motivation for cycling. Collectively, this research suggests that e-bike use increases the total frequency and distance traveled by bicycle and promotes longer individual cycle trips, compared to a conventional bicycle.

4.2 What is the impact of e-cycling on travel behavior?

Globally, e-bikes have been reported to substitute for between 23% and 72% of conventional bike journeys and 20% to 86% of private car journeys (Bourne et al., 2020). There is also evidence that e-bikes substitute for public transport but little evidence that they substitute for walking. Importantly the extent to which e-bikes substitute for other transport modes depends on local context and the primary transport mode prior to the introduction of an e-bike. For example Castro et al. (2019) reported that in Antwerp e-bikes primarily substituted for conventional cycling (34%) and private car journeys (38%) while in Zurich, the e-bike primarily substituted for public transport journeys (22%).

As such, the degree to which e-bikes increase cycling frequency and substitute for cycling may also relate to cycling modal share. In countries with high rates of cycling, such as Europe, e-bikes appear to replace conventional bicycles to a greater extent than in regions with low rates of cycling such as the UK or the USA (Bourne et al., 2020). A survey of 27 e-bike owners in the USA found that 20 individuals reported using their car less since purchasing an e-bike (Popovich et al., 2014), while a longitudinal survey of 60 e-bike owners in Belgium reported that a substantial portion of conventional bicycle journeys were replaced with the e-bike in addition

[a] A measure of dispersion of the data representing the middle 50% of the data.

to also substituting for some car and public transport trips (Astegiano et al., 2018).

To date, most studies examining substitution effects have relied on retrospective reports or cross-sectional data making it difficult to determine within person changes in travel behavior. Using 4 years of data from the Dutch National Mobility Survey, Sun et al. (2020) found that purchasing an e-bike significantly reduced conventional cycling as well as car, walking and public transport use although to a lesser extent. Using 5 years of data from the same survey de Haas et al. (2021) reported differences in substitution effect based on the purpose of trips. Specifically, for commuting, the e-bike acted as a replacement for both the conventional bicycle and the car, while for leisure and shopping trips the e-bike only substituted for the conventional bicycle. The authors raise concerns about whether the promotion of e-cycling has a positive effect on the environment, road congestion and health. However, in the Netherlands cycling plays an important role in daily mobility, with one in every four trips being made by bicycle. As such, these results may not generalize to countries with low rates of cycling. It is encouraged that cities and countries consider the current mobility patterns prior to determining the appropriateness of e-bike initiatives. De Haas et al. (2021) also point out that the substitution effects may change over time as more people purchase e-bikes.

It is also important to acknowledge that there may be differences in the substitution effect based on demographics (de Haas et al., 2021; Sun et al., 2020). This area requires further investigation to understand where best to target e-bike promotion schemes in order to have the greatest impact on individual health and the environment. Among older adults it appears that there is greater substitution of conventional bikes in favor of the e-bike (Johnson and Rose, 2015; Van Cauwenberg et al., 2018). Qualitative research suggests that older adults and those with physical limitations often switch to e-cycling from conventional cycling due to health concerns or feeling that conventional cycling is too hard (Bourne et al., 2020; Jones et al., 2016a). As such, in this respect e-cycling maybe serving to prolong their cycling careers.

4.3 What is the environmental impact of e-cycling?

With the worldwide acknowledgement of the need for more sustainable mobility the electrification of motorized vehicles has become a priority in recent years. However, shifting from motorized to electric vehicles alone will not be sufficient to diminish the environmental impact of the transport system (Creutzig et al., 2018). Substituting motorized vehicles for active travel modes is a more rapid approach to reducing transport related greenhouse gas emissions. Both scenario/modeling research (Goodman et al., 2019; Lovelace et al., 2011; Rojas-Rueda et al., 2016; Tainio et al., 2017; Woodcock et al., 2018) and empirical data (Brand et al., 2021a) suggest that active travel can reduce transport-related greenhouse gas emissions. Furthermore, e-bikes may have the potential to replace motorized vehicle use to a greater extent than conventional cycling or walking due to the electrical assistance provided which increases the distance people are willing to travel by bicycle (Bourne et al., 2020; Pooley et al., 2011).

Brand et al. (2021b) examined the extent to which active travel, including e-cycling, was associated with lower carbon emissions from daily travel activity using primary data from seven European cities. Using pooled data from e-cyclists and conventional cyclists the authors reported that cyclists had 84% lower life cycle CO_2 emissions[b] than non-cyclists. Furthermore, for every additional cycling trip made there was a decrease of 14% in life cycle CO_2 emissions. The authors reported that the average person 'shifting modes' from car (three to two trips a day) to bike (zero to one trip a day) would decrease emissions by 3.2 (95%CI 2.0–5.2) $kgCO_2$ per day (Brand et al., 2021a). Using longitudinal data from the same study Brand et al. (2021b) found that an increase in cycling or walking consistently and independently decreased mobility-related lifecycle CO_2 emissions, suggesting that active travel substituted for motorized travel rather than just leading to added travel over and above motorized travel. To illustrate this, an average person cycling one trip/day more and driving one trip/day less for 200 days a year would decrease mobility-related lifecycle CO_2 emissions by about 0.5 t over a year. A limitation of these studies is the pooling of data from cyclists and e-cyclists making it impossible to assess the independent impact of e-cycling on transport related greenhouse gas emissions. This distinction is important given the increase in modal share of e-bikes and their ability to support more frequent and longer trips than conventional cycling.

Modeling research, conducted by the Centre for Research into Energy Demand Solutions at the University of Leeds found that e-bikes, if used to replace car travel, have the capability of cutting CO_2 emissions in England by up to 50% (about 30 million tonnes per year) (Philips et al., 2020).

[b] The overall greenhouse gas impact of the mode of transport from production, use and disposal.

Specifically, the researchers reported that if each person used an e-bike to replace as many car journeys as possible they would be able to reduce their CO_2 emissions by 0.7 t per year. As well as reducing CO_2 levels, e-bike use has other benefits including improving local air quality due to less traffic on the road.

It is however important to acknowledge that although there are no emissions while using the e-bike, there are charging-related emissions, making the e-bike less environmentally friendly compared to the conventional bicycle (Otten et al., 2015). In addition, if considering the full life cycle impact of e-bikes there are emissions associated with the maintenance of the bikes, the cost of manufacturing batteries and motors as well as getting rid of the bike. The European Cyclists' Federation estimated that e-bikes have a higher average manufacturing carbon footprint than conventional bikes, at 134 kg CO_{2e}[c] per e-bike compared to 96 kg for a conventional bike (European Cyclists' Federation., 2011). They also estimate that e-bikes use 23 Wh of electricity per km traveled. Based on the average amount of CO_{2e} produced per watt hour of electricity in Europe in 2006 it is estimated that e-bikes lead to 9 g of CO_{2e} per km traveled. This is believed to be a high estimate with others suggesting emissions from charging maybe as low as 1.5 g of CO_{2e} per km traveled based on battery range (Stott, 2020). Furthermore, it has been argued that e-bikes have a lower carbon footprint than conventional cycling because fewer calories are consumed per kilometer, despite the greater emissions from battery manufacturing and electricity use. The European Cyclists' Federation assumes that an average 70 kg cyclist on an e-bike will burn 4.4 extra calories per km over and above the amount used when not exercising (compared to 11.0 for a conventional bicycle). However, this does assume that for every extra calorie burned another calorie is consumed through diet and this may not be the case (Elder and Roberts, 2007).

Overall e-bikes have the potential to significantly reduce transport related CO_2 emissions while also reducing congestion. While the CO_2 emissions savings may not be as substantial as switching to a conventional bicycle people are willing to travel further on an e-bike and therefore willingness to make modal shifts maybe greater for electric bicycles.

[c] Carbon dioxide equivalent (CO_{2e}) is used to describe different greenhouse gases in a common unit. It describes the number of metric tons of CO_2 emissions with the same global warming potential as one metric ton of another greenhouse gas.

4.4 What is the intensity of activity associated with e-cycling and the impact on physical activity?

Several studies have explored the intensity of activity associated with e-cycling to understand the potential of e-cycling to accrue health benefits. Some studies have compared the physiological responses of e-cycling to traditional modes of active travel including conventional cycling and walking (Berntsen et al., 2017; Gojanovic et al., 2011; Hansen et al., 2017; Langford et al., 2017), while others have compared the physiological responses to different levels of e-cycling assistance (e.g., e-cycling on high assistance vs low or no assistance) (Bini et al., 2019; La Salle et al., 2017; Louis et al., 2012; Meyer et al., 2014; Simons et al., 2009; Sperlich et al., 2012).

These studies have used a variety of different research designs, explored rides on different topographies and terrains and reported different physiological measures of intensity. Despite methodological differences the evidence consistently suggests that e-cycling, even at a high assistance level, is performed at a moderate intensity, with mean estimated METs[d] while riding an e-bike at a self-selected intensity ranging from 4.9 to 8.3 METs (Alessio et al., 2021; Bourne et al., 2018). Similarly, relative physiological outcomes show that the percentage of maximum heart rate while e-cycling ranges from 67.1 to 79.1 and the percent of $VO_{2peak/max}$[e] ranges from 51 to 75. Among individuals with T2DM e-cycling elicited an average heart rate of 75% of maximum during riding (Cooper et al., 2018). These physiological values exceed the proposed minimum intensity thresholds required for improvements in cardiorespiratory fitness in adults (Garber et al., 2011; Haskell et al., 2007; Swain and Franklin, 2002) and as such suggest that engagement in e-cycling may lead to sufficient intensity of activity to positively impact health in both inactive and clinical populations.

E-cycling elicits slightly higher (Cooper et al., 2018; Langford et al., 2017) or similar (Gojanovic et al., 2011) physiological responses to walking. While in comparison to conventional cycling, e-cycling leads to similar or sometimes lower physiological markers of intensity (Bourne et al., 2018) as shown in Fig. 3. Specifically, Alessio et al. (2021) reported that conventional cycling was associated with a mean MET value of 6.5 on a flat 3-mile loop compared to 5.6 and 4.6 while e-cycling on low and high assistance respectively on the same loop.

---

[d] The ratio of the rate at which a person expends energy, relative to the mass of the person, while performing a specific activity, commonly set at 3.5 mL of oxygen per kg per minute which is considered the energy expended at rest.

[e] The maximum amount of oxygen an individual can use during maximal exercise.

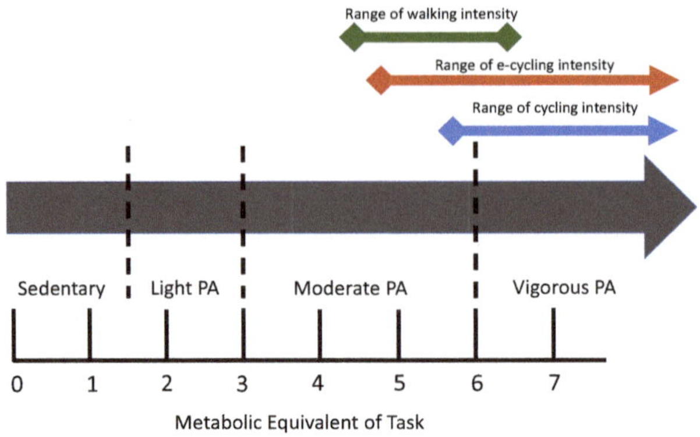

Fig. 3 Intensity of active travel modes. *Data taken from Bourne, J.E., Sauchelli, S., Perry, R., Page, A., Leary, S., England, C., et al., 2018. Health benefits of electrically-assisted cycling: a systematic review. Int. J. Behav. Nutr. Phys. Act. 15, 116. doi:10.1186/s12966-018-0751-8.*

The differences in physiological responses to e-cycling and conventional cycling are more pronounced on uphill segments of rides with conventional cycling being significantly more intense than e-cycling (Berntsen et al., 2017; Gojanovic et al., 2011; Langford et al., 2017). This is most likely due to individuals being less able to control their pace on inclines, while on the flat, when able to self-select their pace, individuals self-select to cycle at a pace that elicits a moderate intensity activity regardless of the mechanical assistance provided (Bourne et al., 2018). This may explain the similar physiological outcomes between conventional cycling and e-cycling which become more pronounced on hills. In support of this when Gojanovic et al. (2011) asked individuals to maintain a cycling cadence of 60 rpm while riding, there were significant differences in oxygen uptake and heart rate between e-bikes and conventional bikes compared to studies in which individuals were able to self-selected their pace and intensity (Berntsen et al., 2017; Hansen et al., 2017; La Salle et al., 2017). Similarly, when instructed to complete 60-m of riding in 10-s for a total of 30-min the reported relative VO_{2max} was 29 mL/min/kg for e-cycling and 37 mL/min/kg for conventional cycling (Theurel et al., 2012). This suggests that performing the same amount of work requires more effort on a conventional bike than an e-bike, but that human beings reduce the amount of work conducted on a conventional bike, through choosing a slower speed, to account for the increase in expended effort.

Using data from a smartphone application and a chest strap for recording heart rate, Stenner et al. (2020) explored e-bike and conventional bike use in an everyday setting using a randomized crossover design. The researchers found that e-cycling was associated with a lower mean heart rate han conventional cycling (109 ± 14 bpm, vs. 118 ± 17 bpm), though both elicited heart rates in the moderate intensity zone. However, total riding time was reduced for individuals in the e-cycling condition. Similarly, when comparing the same routes, researchers report that the travel time on an e-bike is significantly reduced compared to a conventional bike (Berntsen et al., 2017; La Salle et al., 2017). Specifically, Berntsen and colleagues found that e-cycling reduced travel times by 35% on hilly routes and 15% on flat routes (Berntsen et al., 2017). This reduced travel time associated with e-cycling will therefore lead to reduced total energy expenditure in comparison to conventional cycling over the same distance.

However, e-cycling has been associated with greater weekly energy expenditure when compared to conventional cycling potentially due to the reduced physical effort required which encourages more frequent and/or longer rides. Stenner et al. (2020) reported that the weekly energy expenditure for those e-cycling was 717 (±652) MET min/week compared to 484 (±557) in the conventional cycling condition based on heart rate recorded while cycling. Furthermore, Castro et al. (2019) reported that physical activity was 4463 (95% CI 3999, 4926) MET min/week among e-cyclists compared to 4085 (95% CI 3978, 4191) among conventional cyclists. In addition, e-cyclists engaged in longer individual trip distances and daily travel distances compared to conventional bike users. In Norway, a longitudinal questionnaire reported an increase of 353.5 min of self-reported physical activity per week following the provision of an e-bike (Sundfør and Fyhri, 2017), while in the UK, the provision of an e-bike led to a perceived increase in physical activity (Cairns et al., 2017).

4.5 Are there long-term physical health benefits of e-cycling?

The above section highlights that engaging in e-cycling provides at least a moderate-intensity dose of physical activity. Given the wealth and strength of evidence linking engagement in physical activity with improved health, engaging in e-cycling will incur health benefits. However, from an advocacy perspective it is also important to explore the long term health benefits of e-cycling, which takes into account the behavioral impact.

Intervention studies have shown that e-cycling has the potential to increase individuals' physical fitness. Specifically, when setting weekly riding goals of at least three times per week studies among inactive adults report increases in VO_{2peak} of up to 10% (de Geus et al., 2013; Höchsmann et al., 2017; Peterman et al., 2016). Höchsmann et al. (2017) reported that 4 weeks of e-cycling, with the target of cycling on 3 days per week, led to an increase in VO_{2peak} of 3.6 mL/kg/min in the e-cycling group compared to 2.2 mL/kg/min in the conventional cycling group.

In the absence of setting weekly e-cycling targets Lobben et al. (2019) reported a 7.7% increase in VO_{2peak} (2.4 mL/min/kg) in a group of 25 inactive adults following up to 8 months of e-cycling. Among individuals with T2DM, Cooper et al. (2018) found that 5 months of e-cycling led to increases in maximum power output of 16.8 W. A recent pilot randomized controlled trial among the same population reported that self-selected engagement in e-cycling for 3 months led to a 10.7% (2.08 mL/kg/min) increase in VO_{2peak} and 10.8% (15.95 W) increase in maximum power, compared to a 1.9% (0.43 mL/kg/min) increase in VO_{2peak} and 3.6% (−6.72 W) decrease in power output in the control group (Bourne, 2021). These results suggest that under free living conditions (i.e., not setting e-cycling goals) both inactive individuals and clinical populations engage in e-cycling and this can lead to improvements in fitness.

Beyond physical fitness few studies have explored the impact of e-cycling on physical health. Peterman et al. (2016) reported a decrease in 2 hour post plasma glucose following an oral glucose tolerance test after 4 weeks of e-cycling among inactive adults. No other metabolic changes were seen. Among individuals with T2DM, Bourne (2021) reported that e-cycling had a favorable impact on weight, waist circumference, fasting measures of glucose and insulin and dynamic measures of insulin resistance which were not seen in the control condition. While underpowered to make definitive statements about effectiveness, these findings suggest that more research is warranted into the physical health benefits of e-cycling particularly among clinical populations.

Qualitative work reveals that middle and older aged adults and those with T2DM report that e-cycling has a positive impact on their physical health primarily through increased physical activity (Jones et al., 2016b; Mildestvedt et al., 2020; Searle et al., 2019; Spencer et al., 2019).

4.6 Are there mental health benefits of e-cycling?

Few studies have quantitatively explored the impact of e-cycling on psychological health. In an 8 week e-cycling intervention among older adults (aged 50–83) engagement in e-cycling (instructed at three times per week for

30-min in duration) was associated with improvements in mental health quality of life as assessed using the 36-item short form quality of life survey (SF-36) compared to a group of non-cycling controls (Leyland et al., 2019), though no differences in physical quality of life were reported. Among individuals with T2DM engaging in e-cycling for 12-weeks led to a clinically meaningful increase in both physical and mental health related quality of life as reported by the SF-36 with increases of 6.6% and 5.3% respectively, compared to a 2.6% and 1.1% decrease in physical and mental health quality of life respectively in the control group (Bourne, 2021).

These findings are supported by qualitative studies in which both regular e-bike users and individuals participating in intervention research consistently report e-cycling as having a positive impact on well-being (Boland, 2019; Mildestvedt et al., 2020; Plazier et al., 2017a; Popovich et al., 2014; Searle et al., 2019; Spencer et al., 2019; Wild and Woodward, 2019). Using focus group interviews with 21 inactive Norwegian individuals who were loaned an e-bike for three to 8 months engaging in e-cycling led to improved feelings of well-being and enjoyment (Mildestvedt et al., 2020). Furthermore, participants commonly reported the benefit of being able to breathe fresh air and being closer to nature as what made e-cycling enjoyable. This ability of e-cycling to enable individuals to connect with nature is echoed by Spencer et al. (2019). E-cycling has also been reported to be satisfying and rewarding (Bourne, 2021; de Kruijf et al., 2019; Kairos Impact Research and Development., 2010). It is likely that the reduced physical effort, in comparison to a conventional bicycle, is what makes e-cycling enjoyable and satisfying while still provided participants with physical activity that is seen as rewarding.

4.7 What is the impact of e-bikes on incident risk and severity?

Concerns have been raised about e-cycling leading to more traffic incidents, of greater severity, than conventional cycling (Schepers et al., 2014; Weber et al., 2014). Specifically, analysis of emergency department (ED) injury treatment data from 13 Dutch hospitals found that e-bikes users were more likely to be involved in a crash that required ED treatment than conventional bike users after controlling for age, gender and cycling frequency (Schepers et al., 2014). A 2018 replication of this study (Schepers et al., 2018) reported similar findings with the odds of being treated in the ED following a crash being greater among e-bike users than conventional bike users (OR [95%CI] 1.24[1.03, 1.48]). However, when additionally controlling for distance traveled per year by bicycle (i.e., the amount of exposure to risk) the difference in ED treatment between the two bike types was minimal (OR [95%CI] 1.01[0.83, 1.22]). This is an important finding given that individuals report e-cycling for longer than they do a conventional bicycle. A survey of Norwegian cyclists reported no differences in crash severity between e-bike and conventional bike users after controlling for exposure (Fyhri et al., 2019).

Interestingly, there was no difference in the likelihood of being admitted to hospital for treatment following a crash on an e-bike compared to a conventional bicycle (Schepers et al., 2014; Schepers et al., 2018). Similarly, Verstappen et al. (2020) reported no difference in the severity of injuries between e-bike and conventional bike incidents as assessed through medical records at an ED in the Netherlands. In Switzerland, Weber et al. (2014) found that after controlling for age there were no differences in crash severity between electric bicycles and conventional bicycles as determined from police-recorded accidents.

Regarding incident risk, after controlling for exposure, e-bike users were no more frequently involved in incidents than conventional bike users (Schepers et al., 2018). Fyhri et al. (2019) found that e-bike users were more likely to have an incident than conventional bike users, however, this difference was attenuated once controlling for the impact of gender. Specifically, female e-cyclists were more likely to be involved in a crash than female conventional cyclists (Fyhri et al., 2019). Similarly, Schepers et al. (2020) found that older female e-cyclists were more likely to be involved in a crash that required treatment at the ED than those on a conventional bicycle. These differences were not seen in male cyclists or younger female cyclists. Furthermore, among those treated at the ED for a bicycle crash, the odds of sustaining a severe injury were significantly higher among older female e-cyclists than among older female conventional cyclists (Schepers et al., 2020).

Many of the incidents experienced on an e-bike are single-vehicle crashes (i.e., just involving the e-cyclist) (Hertach et al., 2018; MacArthur et al., 2014; Popovich et al., 2014; Schepers et al., 2014, 2018). These incidents have been reported to be due to mounting and dismounting issues (Schepers et al., 2018), potentially associated with that the weight of the e-bike (Twisk et al., 2017). While Twisk and colleagues highlight that older females may struggle more with these factors than men, Schepers et al. (2018) reported that after controlling for age, gender, bicycle use and health factors, individuals were equally as likely to fall on an e-bike as on a conventional bike. Furthermore, Fyhri et al. (2019) found no interaction between bicycle type, gender and age and difficulties mounting the e-bike.

Some of the increased incident risk among females has been attributed to lack of familiarity with the bicycle (Fyhri et al., 2019), which may disproportionally affect e-bike statistics given that e-cycling attracts more novice users to cycling, particularly women (Fyhri et al., 2017a). Notably, while e-bike users report more chronic disease, medication use and have a higher body mass index (BMI) than conventional bike users, these factors are not associated with increased accident risk or severity (Fyhri et al., 2019; Haustein and Møller, 2016; Schepers et al., 2020; Van Cauwenberg et al., 2018). As such, e-cycling appears to be an appropriate physical activity promotion approach in older adults and those in poor health with no differences in incident risk and crash severity compared to a conventional bicycle. More research is needed to explain why women, particularly older women are at an increased risk of e-bikes crashes and more severe crashes.

5. E-bike promotion schemes

5.1 How is e-bike use being encouraged?

There are a number of barriers to e-bike use including costs, fear, low confidence, lack of access or lack of awareness. As such strategies to encourage and incentivize uptake have been explored in several countries.

In 2016 the European Cyclists' Federation identified subsidy schemes at national and regional levels in Austria, Belgium, France, Germany, Italy, the Netherlands and Spain (Holger, 2016). In 2019 Newson and Sloman (2019) reviewed the impact of a range of e-bike subsidy schemes across Europe. Specifically, in Guernsey in 2018, a subsidy offering a 25% discount on e-bikes up to £1500 was found to be highly successful with the allocated budget for the scheme being spent within the first month of launching and 366 e-bikes being sold (Brehaut, 2018; GOV.GG, 2018). Of those that purchased an e-bike 51% stated they would not have purchased it without the subsidy. In Oslo, Norway in 2016, residents were offered a 20% reduction in the cost of an e-bike. Overall, 88% of individuals who applied for the scheme stated their decision to purchase an e-bike was based on the scheme (Fyhri et al., 2017b). While in Sweden a 25% e-bike grant was reported to be effective at reducing driving by car (The Swedish Transport Administration., 2019).

While some countries have directed grants to individuals, others have offered grants at an organizational level (Newson and Sloman, 2019). For example, in Scotland in 2018, an e-bike grant fund put out a call to local authorities, public sector agencies, community organizations, colleges and universities to encourage e-bike adoption with matched funding expected by the organization (Scottish Government News., 2018). They expected that these funds would enable the development of e-bike pools, secure cycle parking and safety equipment. Newson and Sloman's, 2019 review concluded that while many European countries reported a rise in e-bike popularity and sales prior to incentive schemes, the introduction of such incentives served to further uplift e-bike sales. Furthermore, subsidy schemes were reported to be most effective when run as a campaign, with fresh promotion to renew initiatives at different time periods.

In the USA and Canada few subsidies currently exist. In British Columbia, Canada the SCRAP-IT scheme offers individuals a \$750 incentive for purchasing an e-bike when scraping a motorized vehicle (Scrap-It, 2015). While in California, USA, the Clean Cars 4 All program enables individuals to trade in their old motorized vehicle for an e-bike with subsidies up to \$7500 (California Air Resources Board, 2018). In the USA, a 2019 policy briefing called for state level financial incentives to help individuals purchase e-bikes (Fitch, 2019), while recently one senator has called for a refundable tax credit worth 30% of a new e-bikes purchase price, capped at \$1500 (Hawkins, 2021).

In the UK, the government funded Cycle to Work scheme enables employed individuals, whose organizations participate in the scheme, to save up to 40% of the cost on a new bike. In 2019 the value of a bike that could be purchased on the scheme increased from £1000 to £2500 with the aim of enabling more individuals to purchase an e-bike. While positive, this scheme is only open to employees of participating organizations and those wishing to cycle to work. The UK governments November 2020 'Gear change' document (Department for Transport, 2020c) included a promise of the development of a national e-bike support program, anticipated to include e-bike interest free loans and subsidies. However, 1 year on few developments to this program have been released. Based on incentive schemes offered in other European countries Newson and Sloman (2019) concluded that an e-bike grant of £250 would be sufficient to increase e-bike purchasing in the UK.

Interest free loans which enable individuals to spread the cost of an e-bike over several months may also serve to increase uptake. In

January 2020 the Dutch government launched an interest free loan (https://www.rijksoverheid.nl/onderwerpen/fiets/fiets-van-de-zaak). Similarly in Scotland residents can obtain an interest free loan to support the purchase of e-bikes, e-cargo bikes or adaptive e-bikes with a four-year repayment plan (https://energysavingtrust.org.uk/grantsand-loans/ebike-loan/).

Finally, e-bike share schemes and loans may serve to increase e-bike uptake. These schemes provide increased awareness of e-bikes and make them a potentially viable means of public transport while removing barriers of cost and accessibility (Handy and Fitch, 2020). They may also act as a gateway for individuals to discover e-cycling and as such an incentive to seek out e-bike purchasing. The Department for Transport, UK (2020b) found that 29% of all shared e-bike users reported that they would like to buy an e-bike. For those wishing to trial an e-bike for a longer period, e-bike loans should be made available. In January 2020, the Dutch government announced a scheme in which employees could lease an e-bike for around seven euros a month, with potential reimbursement for business mileage traveled by bike. While in Scotland, the Energy Savings Trust, who administer the organizational level e-bike subsidy scheme, allocated £100,000 to enable members of the public to test ride e-bikes through Home Energy Scotland advice centers, active travel hubs and community centers.

Collectively, publicly funded schemes can help incentivize individuals to purchase an e-bike and may help to alter users travel behavior, including reduced car use and increased active travel. As such, this policy tool should be used to increase e-bike awareness and will enable countries to achieve their sustainability goals. This is particularly true in countries with low cycling rates which report having subsidy schemes for electric cars.

6. E-bike research, current research gaps and priorities

6.1 How has e-bike related literature changed over the years?

With the huge growth in e-bike sales since the early 2000s there has been continuing growth in e-bike related research. Salmeron-Manzano and Manzano-Agugliaro (2018) reported increases in published documents from 19 in 2008 to around 130 in 2017 with China and the USA leading these research efforts. The authors proposed that this is due to China having a large population and long tradition of e-bikes as a means of transport, while in the USA e-bike research has focused on e-cycling as a sustainable form of transport. The majority of this research has been conducted within the engineering domain while 15% of the research has explored e-cycling in the context of social science and medicine. Fig. 2 illustrates the number of documents found by searching Elsevier Scopus that include electric bike related terms. While the total number of publications on most topics has increased in real terms, this graph demonstrates that the absolute number of documents relating to e-cycling has increased, suggesting greater number of research endeavors to answer e-cycling related questions.

6.2 What are the current research gaps and future priorities?

Several priorities for research and policy exist and are summarized in Table 1. In the UK, the latest walking and cycling strategy released by the Department for Transport sets the target of doubling cycling by 2025. However, no specific targets for increasing e-bike use have been set (Department for Transport, 2020a). Similarly, the EU states a goal of pushing and promoting e-mobility, including e-bike use, however it provides no estimates as to by how much or when (Niestadt and Bjornavold, 2019). This means there is no clear guidance or incentives to focus e-bike initiatives. There needs to be clarity from governments on the role of e-bikes in transport policy through the development of e-bike use targets, distinct from cycling. Data on the prevalence of e-cycling and its impact on mobility patterns is required to set such targets and provide insight into the effectiveness of e-cycling promotion campaigns and purchasing. However, conventional bicycles and electric bicycles are currently not distinguished in the UK or other national travel surveys and we know of no plans to distinguish between the two. Alternatively, e-cycling could be monitored using health surveys to assess e-bike use and the impact on health, wellbeing, and physical activity.

Without widespread collection of data pertaining to e-bike use it is hard to recognize the potential of e-cycling to impact transport and health. This information is important at a policy level to provide evidence to guide investment. The Netherlands has been collecting data on e-bike use since 2013 and this data is being used to map changes in e-bike use over time and across different user groups. The data reveals large increases in e-bike use for commuting and education purposes (de Haas et al., 2021). Other countries are encouraged to follow suit and begin the process of monitoring e-bike use.

Furthermore, modeling the health and environmental implications of switching from different modes of travel to e-cycling is difficult without data on the prevalence of e-bike use. Scenario modeling in the UK estimated

Table 1 Future priorities.

Future priorities for research and policy makers	Why required
Researchers are encouraged to clearly identify the specific style of electric bicycle to which they are referring in their research.	This will enable the comparison of findings across similar models of electric bicycles and ensure unfair comparisons are not being made.
The inclusion of e-cycling as a standalone category in National Travel Surveys across countries or inclusion in health surveys.	Without the inclusion of e-cycling as a standalone category it will be hard to fully comprehend the extent to which e-cycling substitutes for other transport modes, the impact on health and the associated cost and benefits of e-cycling. Furthermore, this data will give us more information on the demographic characteristics of e-bike users versus non-users.
Inclusion of specific e-cycling targets in active travel strategies.	Clear e-cycling targets will provide guidance that will help to focus national and local e-bike initiatives.
Longitudinal research to examine the causal impact of individual, social and physical determinants associated with e-bike use and travel behavior.	Current evidence provides a qualitative understanding of potential determinants of e-cycling. No studies have examined the individual, social and physical factors directly associated with e-bike use and travel behavior through quantitative estimates. This information is important for future e-bike promotion strategies.
Research to examine the effect of e-bike availability on travel behavior by age, sex, ethnicity and socio-economic status.	Few studies have examined the impact of demographic outcomes on e-bike use, travel behavior or the purpose of use. This information is important to identify where it maybe most appropriate to target e-bike initiatives.
Experimental research to examine effects of e-bike availability on travel behavior in individuals less familiar with e-cycling.	Most of the research to date has been conducted with e-bike owners or those familiar with cycling. Individuals unaccustomed to e-cycling will likely display different patterns of use and possess different attitudes and experiences of e-cycling.

Continued

Table 1 Future priorities.—cont'd

Future priorities for research and policy makers	Why required
Randomized controlled trials exploring the impact of e-cycling on a range of health and behavioral outcomes in a range of populations using objective measures.	Much of the research to date has used qualitative research designs or single group designs making it hard to determine the impact of e-cycling on health and behavior.
Research to examine the potential of e-bikes to serve as company vehicles and replace cars or light goods vehicles for deliveries. In addition, individuals barriers and facilitators to the use of e-bikes in the workplace should be explored.	This is an important area of research as 36% of all car journeys made in England in 2017 were for commuting or business purposes and light commercial vehicles were the faster growing motor vehicle in the UK in the last 25 years.
Evaluation of the addition of e-bikes to bike share systems and their impact on alternative transport.	It is important to ascertain whether the provision of e-bikes into bike share systems is an effective method of increasing e-bike access and subsequent use.
Longitudinal research exploring the impact of switching from other modes of transport specifically to e-cycling.	No primary data currently exists exploring the environmental impact of transport related greenhouse gas emissions associated with switching to e-cycling from other transport modes. This information will be important to transport and city planners.
Objective measures of e-bike use and travel behavior using GPS or smartphone tracking prior to and during e-bike access to quantify the impact of e-bikes on travel behavior.	Current evidence relies primarily on self-report, retrospective measures of travel behavior.

that if 25% of the English population became regular cyclists and all new cyclists had access to e-bikes, reductions in years of life lost due to premature mortality would be 93,000 and reductions in CO_2 emissions due to reduced car miles would be approximately 2.7% (Woodcock et al., 2018). However, this data was based on the Dutch National Travel Survey, a nation with high rates of cycling.

Much of the research reporting on travel behavior, including e-bike use uses retrospective surveys or qualitative methods. Device-based measures of e-bike use and travel behavior will increase our understanding of the impact of e-bike access on travel behavior. In addition, to understand the impact of e-cycling on physical and mental health fully powered definitive trials among different populations are needed.

Future research should also explore the differences between injury risk and crash severity based on the type of e-bike. Specifically, speed pedelecs, which support human pedaling up to 45 km/h have been found to be much faster than conventional bicycles (speed differences of over 10 km/h) compared to regular pedelecs which support human pedaling up to a speed of 25 km/h and have a speed difference of between 2 and 4 km/h with a conventional bicycle (Twisk et al., 2021). Speed pedelecs vary their speed to a greater extent and brake more harshly and more frequently than conventional bicycles, while no differences are seen between regular pedelecs and conventional bicycles (Twisk et al., 2021). A survey of 3600 Swiss e-bikes users found that approximately a third of respondents rode a speed pedelec (Hertach et al., 2018). Given their increased popularity, the differential impact of regular and speed e-bikes should be explored.

Finally, as we strive for a more carbon neutral world, it is important to establish how e-bikes fit into the workplace and bikeshare domain. To date the majority of research has explored the perceptions and motivators of e-bike use and impact on travel behavior from the perspective of personal e-bike use. Little research has explored how e-bikes are perceived in the workplace, an important component of the transport section. What has been done suggests that e-cycling in the workplace is perceived as providing greater autonomy regarding journeys in comparison to public transport or carpooling with easy city access and the avoidance of parking complications (Kroyer and Johansson, 2013; Prill, 2015). Bike share services have rapidly expanded in cities worldwide. They have the potential to offer a healthier and more environmentally sustainable mobility option. Limited research has explored how e-bikes fit into the bike share system and the impact that their presence has on travel behavior. Furthermore, little work has explored how e-bikes are perceived by policy makers, active travel practitioners or city planners.

7. Conclusion

This chapter has shown how e-bike sales have increased dramatically over the past two decades. With increased purchasing and use e-bike related research has shown a dramatic rise across a range of disciplines. Research suggests that e-cycling is performed at a moderate intensity with the potential to increase levels of physical activity and improve long term health. E-cycling is appealing to a wide variety of populations and may serve to prolong the cycling careers of older adults. E-cycling has the potential to substitute for alternative modes of transport including motorized vehicles, and in some cases to a greater extent than conventional cycling as individuals are willing to ride more frequently and further on an e-bike. Furthermore, despite initial concerns there appears to be minimal differences in the severity and risk of incidents between e-bikes and conventional bikes. The enjoyment commonly associated with e-cycling is believed to be one of the primary factors that may encourage long term engagement in this behavior making it more sustainable than traditional modes of active travel. As such, encouraging engagement in e-cycling is warranted, with the potential for positive environmental consequences through the reduction of transport related emissions and improvements in air quality. One effective way through which to promote e-bike use is through subsidy schemes which should be implemented at national level, particularly in countries with low cycling and high motorized vehicle rates.

References

Alessio, H.M., Reiman, T., Kemper, B., von Carlowitz, W., Bailer, A.J., Timmerman, K.L., 2021. Metabolic and cardiovascular responses to a simulated commute on an E-bike. Transl. J. Am. Coll. Sports Med. 6 (2), e000155. https://doi.org/10.1249/TJX.0000000000000155.

Astegiano, P., Fermi, F., Martino, A., 2018. Investigating the impact of e-bikes on modal share and greenhouse emissions: a system dynamic approach. In: 21st EURO Working Group on Transportation Meeting, EWGT 2018, Braunschweig, Germany.

Berntsen, S., Malnes, L., Langaker, A., Bere, E., 2017. Physical activity when riding an electric assisted bicycle. Int. J. Behav. Nutr. Phys. Act. 14 (1), 55. https://doi.org/10.1186/s12966-017-0513-z.

Bini, R., Wundersitz, D., Kingsley, M., 2019. Biomechanical and physiological responses to electrically assisted cycling during simulated mail delivery. Appl. Ergon. 75, 243–249. https://doi.org/10.1016/j.apergo.2018.11.004.

Bjørnarå, H.B., Berntsen, S., te Velde, S.J., Fyhri, A., Deforche, B., Andersen, L.B., Bere, E., 2019. From cars to bikes—the effect of an intervention providing access to different bike types: A randomized controlled trial. PLoS One 14 (7), e0219304. https://doi.org/10.1371/journal.pone.0219304.

Boland, P., 2019. An Exploration of the Barriers and Enablers of Using Electrically Assisted Bikes (e-Bikes) in the Development of a Stroke Intervention for People After Stroke. University of Central Lancashire. http://clok.uclan.ac.uk/29319/.

Bourne, J.E., 2021. The Use of Electrically Assisted Bicycles for Promoting Active Transport and Health. University of Bristol, UK.

Bourne, J.E., Sauchelli, S., Perry, R., Page, A., Leary, S., England, C., Cooper, A.R., 2018. Health benefits of electrically-assisted cycling: a systematic review. Int. J. Behav. Nutr. Phys. Act. 15 (116). https://doi.org/10.1186/s12966-018-0751-8.

Bourne, J.E., Cooper, A.R., Kelly, P., Kinnear, F.J., England, C., Leary, S., Page, A., 2020. The impact of e-cycling on travel behaviour: a scoping review. J. Transp. Health 19, 100910. https://doi.org/10.1016/j.jth.2020.100910.

Brand, C., Dons, E., Anaya-Boig, E., Avila-Palencia, I., Clark, A., de Nazelle, A., Gascon, M., Gaupp-Berghausen, M., Gerike, R., Götschi, T., Iacorossi, F., Kahlmeier, S., Laeremans, M., Nieuwenhuijsen, M.J., Pablo Orjuela, J., Racioppi, F., Raser, E., Rojas-Rueda, D., Standaert, A., Stigell, E., Sulikova, S., Wegener, S., Int Panis, L., 2021a. The climate change mitigation effects of daily active travel in cities. Transp. Res. D: Transp. Environ. 93. https://doi.org/10.1016/j.trd.2021.102764, 102764.

Brand, C., Götschi, T., Dons, E., Gerike, R., Anaya-Boig, E., Avila-Palencia, I., de Nazelle, A., Gascon, M., Gaupp-Berghausen, M., Iacorossi, F., Kahlmeier, S., Int Panis, L., Racioppi, F., Rojas-Rueda, D., Standaert, A., Stigell, E., Sulikova, S., Wegener, S., Nieuwenhuijsen, M.J., 2021b. The climate change mitigation impacts of active travel: evidence from a longitudinal panel study in seven European cities. Glob. Environ. Chang. 67, 102224. https://doi.org/10.1016/j.gloenvcha.2021.102224.

Brehaut, A.J., 2018. E-Bike Subsidy Is Spent in Less than a Month.

Cairns, S., Behrendt, F., Raffo, D., Beaumont, C., Kiefer, C., 2017. Electrically-assisted bikes: potential impacts on travel behaviour. Transp. Res. A: Policy Pract. 103 (Suppl. C), 327–342. https://doi.org/10.1016/j.tra.2017.03.007.

California Air Resources Board, 2018. Clean Cars 4 All. http://ww2.arb.ca.gov/sites/default/files/movingca/vehiclescrap.html.

Cappelle, J., Lataire, P., Timmermans, J., Maggetto, G., Van den Bossche, P., 2003. Electrically assisted cycling around the world. In: Report from the European ETour (Electric Two Wheelers on Urban Roads) Project. https://etec.vub.ac.be/publications/paperEVS-20.pdf.

Castro, A., Gaupp-Berhausen, M., Dons, E., Standaert, A., Laeremans, M., Clark, A., Anaya, E., Cole-Hunter, T., Avila-Palencia, I., Rojas-Rueda, D., Nieuwenhuijsen, M., Gerike, R., Panis, L.I., de Nazelle, A., Brand, C., Raser, E., Kahlmeier, S., Götschi, T., 2019. Physical activity of electric bicycle users compared to conventional bicycle users and non-cyclists: insights based on health and transport data from an online survey in seven European cities. Transp. Res. Interdiscip. Perspect, 100017. https://doi.org/10.1016/j.trip.2019.100017.

CONEBI, 2017. European Bicycle Market 2017 edition.

Cooper, A., Tibbitts, B., England, C., Procter, D., Searle, A., Sebire, S., Ranger, E., Page, A., 2018. The potential of electric bicycles to improve the health of people with type 2 diabetes: a feasibility study. Diabet. Med. 35 (9), 1279–1282. https://doi.org/10.1111/dme.13664.

Creutzig, F., Roy, J., Lamb, W.F., Azevedo, I.M.L., Bruine De Bruin, W., Dalkmann, H., Edelenbosch, O.Y., Geels, F.W., Grubler, A., Hepburn, C., Hertwich, E.G., Khosla, R., Mattauch, L., Minx, J.C., Ramakrishnan, A., Rao, N.D., Steinberger, J.K., Tavoni, M., Ürge-Vorsatz, D., Weber, E.U., 2018. Towards demand-side solutions for mitigating climate change. Nat. Clim. Change 8 (4), 268–271. https://doi.org/10.1038/s41558-018-0121-1.

de Geus, B., Hendriksen, I., 2015. Cycling for transport, physical activity and health: what about Pedelecs? In: Gerike, R., Parkin, J. (Eds.), Cycling Futurs: From Research into Practice, first ed. Routledge.

de Geus, B., Kempenaers, F., Lataire, P., Meeusen, R., 2013. Influence of electrically assisted cycling on physiological parameters in untrained subjects. Eur. J. Sport Sci. 13 (3), 290–294. https://doi.org/10.1080/17461391.2011.606845.

de Haas, M., Kroesen, M., Chorus, C., Hoogendoorn-Lanser, S., Hoogendoorn, S., 2021. E-bike user groups and substitution effects: evidence from longitudinal travel data in the Netherlands. Transportation. https://doi.org/10.1007/s11116-021-10195-3.

de Kruijf, J., Ettema, D., Dijst, M., 2019. A longitudinal evaluation of satisfaction with e-cycling in daily commuting in the Netherlands. Travel Behav. Soc. 16, 192–200. https://doi.org/10.1016/j.tbs.2018.04.003.

Department for Transport, 2020a. Cycling and Walking Investment Strategy. https://assets.publishing.service.gov.uk/government/uploads/system/uploads/attachment_data/file/936926/cycling-and-walking-investment-strategy-report-to-parliament-document.pdf.

Department for Transport, 2020b. Future of Transport: User Study. https://assets.publishing.service.gov.uk/government/uploads/system/uploads/attachment_data/file/937918/Future-of-Transport-User-Study-accessible.pdf.

Department for Transport, 2020c. Gear Change. A Bold Vision for Cycling and Walking. https://assets.publishing.service.gov.uk/government/uploads/system/uploads/attachment_data/file/904146/gear-change-a-bold-vision-for-cycling-and-walking.pdf.

Dill, J., Rose, G., 2012. Electric bikes and transportation policy. Transp. Res. Rec 2314, 1–6. https://doi.org/10.3141/2314-01.

Dons, E., Rojas-Rueda, D., Anaya-Boig, E., Avila-Palencia, I., Brand, C., Cole-Hunter, T., de Nazelle, A., Eriksson, U., Gaupp-Berghausen, M., Gerike, R., Kahlmeier, S., Laeremans, M., Mueller, N., Nawrot, T., Nieuwenhuijsen, M.J., Orjuela, J.P., Racioppi, F., Raser, E., Standaert, A., Int Panis, L., Götschi, T., 2018. Transport mode choice and body mass index: cross-sectional and longitudinal evidence from a European-wide study. Environ. Int. 119, 109–116. https://doi.org/10.1016/j.envint.2018.06.023.

Downard-Wilke, A., 2020. Predicting e-Bike Sales in NZ. https://viastrada.nz/index.php/e-bike-sales.

Drage, T., Pressl, R., 2012. Pedelec-Test (in Andritz) in The Context of the European Union Project Active Access. https://www.eltis.org/sites/default/files/case-studies/documents/aktive_access_pedelec_test_12.pdf.

Eddeger, C., Lewis, T., Ditrich, J., Kubova, M., Daude, P., Forderer, W., Acunzo, N., Simeone, M., Daggers, T., Ditewig, R., 2012. Best Practices With Pedelecs, Go Pedelec! www.gopedelec.eu/bestpractices.

Edge, S., Dean, J., Cuomo, M., Keshav, S., 2018. Exploring e-bikes as a mode of sustainable transport: a temporal qualitative study of the perspectives of a sample of novice riders in a Canadian city. Can. Geogr. 62 (3), 384–397. https://doi.org/10.1111/cag.12456.

Elder, S.J., Roberts, S.B., 2007. The effects of exercise on food intake and body fatness: a summary of published studies. Nutr. Rev. 65 (1), 1–19. https://doi.org/10.1111/j.1753-4887.2007.tb00263.x.

European Cyclists' Federation, 2011. Cycle More Often 2 Cool Down the Planet: quantifying CO_2 Savings of Cycling.

Fishman, E., Cherry, C., 2016. E-bikes in the mainstream: reviewing a decade of research. Transp. Rev. 36 (1), 72–91. https://doi.org/10.1080/01441647.2015.1069907.

Fitch, D., 2019. Electric Assisted Bikes (E-bikes) Show Promise in Getting People out of Cars. https://escholarship.org/uc/item/3mm040km#main.

Fyhri, A., Fearnley, N., 2015. Effects of e-bikes on bicycle use and mode share. Transp. Res. D Transp. Environ. 36, 45–52. https://doi.org/10.1016/j.trd.2015.02.005.

Fyhri, A., Sundfør, H.B., 2020. Do people who buy e-bikes cycle more? Transp. Res. D Transp. Environ. 86, 102422. https://doi.org/10.1016/j.trd.2020.102422.

Fyhri, A., Heinen, E., Fearnley, N., Sundfør, H.B., 2017a. A push to cycling—exploring the e-bike's role in overcoming barriers to bicycle use with a survey and an intervention study. Int. J. Sustain. Transp. 11 (9), 681–695. https://doi.org/10.1080/15568318.2017.1302526.

Fyhri, A., Sundfør, H.B., Weber, C., 2017b. Effect of Subvention Program for e-Bikes in Oslo on Bicycle Use, Transport Distribution and CO_2 Emissions. TOI Report 1498/2016.

Fyhri, A., Johansson, O., Bjørnskau, T., 2019. Gender differences in accident risk with e-bikes—survey data from Norway. Accid. Anal. Prev. 132, 105248. https://doi.org/10.1016/j.aap.2019.07.024.

Garber, C.E., Blissmer, B., Deschenes, M.R., Franklin, B.A., Lamonte, M.J., Lee, I.-M., Nieman, D.C., Swain, D.P., 2011. Quantity and quality of exercise for developing and maintaining cardiorespiratory, musculoskeletal, and neuromotor fitness in apparently healthy adults: guidance for prescribing exercise. Med. Sci. Sports Exerc. 43 (7), 1334–1359. https://doi.org/10.1249/MSS.0b013e318213fefb.

Gojanovic, B., Welker, J., Iglesias, K., Daucourt, C., Gremion, G., 2011. Electric bicycles as a new active transportation modality to promote health. Med. Sci. Sports Exerc. 43 (11), 2204–2210. https://doi.org/10.1249/MSS.0b013e31821cbdc8.

Goodman, A., Rojas, I.F., Woodcock, J., Aldred, R., Berkoff, N., Morgan, M., Abbas, A., Lovelace, R., 2019. Scenarios of cycling to school in England, and associated health and carbon impacts: application of the 'propensity to cycle tool'. J. Transp. Health 12, 263–278. https://doi.org/10.1016/j.jth.2019.01.008.

GOV.GG, 2018. https://www.gov.gg/article/164563/ECycle-subsidy-announced.

Halfords, 2021. The Great Bike Boom Continues: A State of the Nation Look at the Explosion of Cycling. https://washford.a.bigcontent.io/v1/static/9.%20HAM46582%20CYCLING%20REPORT%20PR%20March%202021%20Landscape_1.

Handy, S.L., Fitch, D.T., 2020. Can an e-bike share system increase awareness and consideration of e-bikes as a commute mode? Results from a natural experiment. Int. J. Sustain. Transp. 1-16. https://doi.org/10.1080/15568318.2020.1847370.

Hansen, D., Soors, A., Deluyker, V., Frederix, I., Dendale, P., 2017. Electrical support during outdoor cycling in patients with coronary artery disease: impact on exercise intensity, volume and perception of effort. Acta Cardiol. 1-8. https://doi.org/10.1080/00015385.2017.1385153.

Haskell, W.L., Lee, I.-M., Pate, R.R., Powell, K.E., Blair, S.N., Franklin, B.A., Macera, C.A., Heath, G.W., Thompson, P.D., Bauman, A., 2007. Physical activity and public health: updated recommendation for adults from the American College of Sports Medicine and the American Heart Association. Med. Sci. Sports Exerc. 39 (8), 1423–1434. https://doi.org/10.1249/mss.0b013e3180616b27.

Haustein, S., Møller, M., 2016. E-bike safety: individual-level factors and incident characteristics. J. Transp. Health 3 (3), 386–394. https://doi.org/10.1016/j.jth.2016.07.001.

Hawkins, A.J., 2021. The Senate's E-BIKE Act Could Make Electric Bikes a Lot Cheaper. The Verge. https://www.theverge.com/2021/7/24/22590792/ebike-act-senate-brian-schatz-tax-credit-infrastructure.

Anon., 2021. European Mobility Atlas: Facts and Figures about Transport and Mobility in Europe. Heinrich-Böll-Stiftung European Union.

Hendriksen, I., Engbers, L., Schrijver, J., Gijlswijk, R.v., Weltevreden, J., Wilting, J., 2008. Elektrisch Fietsen: marktonderzoek en verkenning toekomstmogelijkheden (9789059862876) http://resolver.tudelft.nl/uuid:6f24f885-cdb8-403b-bad8-2ded79395f38.

Hertach, P., Uhr, A., Niemann, S., Cavegn, M., 2018. Characteristics of single-vehicle crashes with e-bikes in Switzerland. Accid. Anal. Prev. 117, 232–238. https://doi.org/10.1016/j.aap.2018.04.021.

Höchsmann, C., Meister, S., Gehrig, D., Gordon, E., Li, Y., Nussbaumer, M., Rossmeissl, A., Schäfer, J., Hanssen, H., Schmidt-Trucksäss, A., 2017. Effect of E-bike versus bike commuting on cardiorespiratory fitness in overweight adults: a 4-week randomized pilot study. Clin. J. Sport Med. 28 (3), 255–265. http://journals.lww.com/cjsportsmed/Fulltext/publishahead/Effect_of_E_Bike_Versus_Bike_Commuting_on.99449.aspx.

Holger, H., 2016. Electromobility for all.

Janssens, D., Paul, R., Wets, G., 2020. Onderzoek verplaatsingsgedrag Vlaanderen 5.5 (2019-2020). Tabellenrapport. https://assets.vlaanderen.be/image/upload/v1597749512/ovg51-tabellen-globaal_noscoi.pdf.

Johnson, M., Rose, G., 2013. Electric bikes—cycling in the New World City: an investigation of Australian electric bicycle owners and the decision making process for purchase. In: Australasian Transport Research Forum, ATRF 2013—Proceedings.
Johnson, M., Rose, G., 2015. Extending life on the bike: electric bike use by older Australians. J. Transp. Health 2 (2), 276–283. https://doi.org/10.1016/j.jth.2015.03.001.
Jones, T., Chatterjee, K., Spinney, J., Street, E., Van Reekum, C., Spencer, B., Jones, H., Leyland, L.A., Mann, C., Williams, S., Beale, N., 2016a. cycle BOOM. Design for Lifelong Health and Wellbeing. Summary of Key Findings and Recommendations.
Jones, T., Harms, L., Heinen, E., 2016b. Motives, perceptions and experiences of electric bicycle owners and implications for health, wellbeing and mobility. J. Transp. Geogr. 53, 41–49. https://doi.org/10.1016/j.jtrangeo.2016.04.006.
Jones, T., Spencer, B., Beale, L., Leyland, L.-A., van Reekum, C.M., 2022. "You can go out 14 miles away with the knowledge that you've got the battery to help you back if you need it!" Narratives of ranging behaviour and wellbeing in diaries of e-bike trial participants. Active Travel Stud. 1 (1), 1–28. https://doi.org/10.16997/ats.1046.
Kairos Impact Research & Development, 2010. Landrad—Neue Mobilität Für Den Alltagsverkehr in Vorarlberg. Endbericht. https://repository.difu.de/jspui/handle/difu/186405.
Kennedy, E., 2019. E-bikes surge in popularity in Australian cities but experts warn of risks. The Guardian. https://www.theguardian.com/lifeandstyle/2019/nov/06/e-bike-surge-in-popularity-in-australian-cities-but-experts-warn-of-risks.
Kroesen, M., 2017. To what extent do e-bikes substitute travel by other modes? Evidence from the Netherlands. Transp. Res. Part D: Trans. Environ. 53, 377–387. https://doi.org/10.1016/j.trd.2017.04.036.
Kroyer, H., Johansson, K., 2013. Elfordon i Malmö i familjen och på arbetet: erfarenheter av elbilar, elmopeder och elcyklar. Lunds universitet.
La Salle, D.T., Shute, R., Heesch, M., Slivka, D., 2017. Demands of simulated commuting using an electrically assisted bicycle. Int. J. Exerc. Sci. 10 (3), 454–464. https://www.ncbi.nlm.nih.gov/pmc/articles/PMC5421980/pdf/ijes.10.03.454.pdf.
Langford, B.C., Cherry, C.R., Bassett, D.R., Fitzhugh, E.C., Dhakal, N., 2017. Comparing physical activity of pedal-assist electric bikes with walking and conventional bicycles. J. Transp. Health 6, 463–473. https://doi.org/10.1016/j.jth.2017.06.002.
Leger, S.J., Dean, J.L., Edge, S., Casello, J.M., 2019. "If I had a regular bicycle, I wouldn't be out riding anymore": perspectives on the potential of e-bikes to support active living and independent mobility among older adults in Waterloo, Canada. Transp. Res. Part A: Policy Pract. 123, 240–254. https://doi.org/10.1016/j.tra.2018.10.009.
Leyland, L.-A., Spencer, B., Beale, N., Jones, T., van Reekum, C.M., 2019. The effect of cycling on cognitive function and well-being in older adults. PLoS One 14 (2), e0211779. https://doi.org/10.1371/journal.pone.0211779.
Lobben, S., Malnes, L., Berntsen, S., Tjelta, L.I., Bere, E., Kristoffersen, M., Mildestvedt, T., 2019. Bicycle usage among inactive adults provided with electrically assisted bicycles. Acta Kinesiologiae Universitatis Tartuensis 24, 60–73.
Louis, J., Brisswalter, J., Morio, C., Barla, C., Temprado, J.J., 2012. The electrically assisted bicycle: an alternative way to promote physical activity. Am. J. Phys. Med. Rehabil. 91 (11), 931–940. https://doi.org/10.1097/PHM.0b013e318269d9bb.
Lovelace, R., Beck, S.B.M., Watson, M., Wild, A., 2011. Assessing the energy implications of replacing car trips with bicycle trips in Sheffield, UK. Energy Policy 39 (4), 2075–2087. https://doi.org/10.1016/j.enpol.2011.01.051.
MacArthur, J., Dill, J., Person, M., 2014. Electric bikes in North America. Transp. Res. Rec. 2468, 123–130. https://doi.org/10.3141/2468-14.

MacArthur, J., Kobel, N., Dill, J., Mumuni, Z., 2017. Evaluation of an Electric Bike Pilot Project at Three Employment Campuses in Portland, Oregon. https://pdxscholar.library.pdx.edu/cgi/viewcontent.cgi?article=1126&context=trec_reports.
MacArthur, J., Harpool, M., Scheppke, D., Cherry, C., 2018a. Electric Boost: Insights from a National E-bike Owner Survey. Project Brief NITC-RR-1041. https://pdxscholar.library.pdx.edu/cgi/viewcontent.cgi?article=1062&context=trec_briefs.
MacArthur, J., Harpool, M., Scheppke, D., Cherry, C., 2018b. A North American Survey of Electric Bicycle Owners. https://pdxscholar.library.pdx.edu/trec_reports/161/.
Melia, S., Bartle, C., 2020. Who Uses e-Bikes in the UK and why?
Melia, S., Bartle, C., 2021. Who uses e-bikes in the UK and why? Int. J. Sustain. Transp. 1-13. https://doi.org/10.1080/15568318.2021.1956027.
Meyer, D., Steffan, M., Senner, V., 2014. Impact of electrical assistance on physiological parameters during cycling. Proc. Eng. 72, 150–155. https://doi.org/10.1016/j.proeng.2014.06.026.
Mildestvedt, T., Hovland, O., Bernsten, S., Bere, E., Fegran, L., 2020. Getting physically active by E-bike: an active commuting intervention study. Phys. Act. Health 4 (1), 120–129. https://doi.org/10.5334/paah.63.
Mobiel 21, 2014. Het e-fietspotentieel Aanbevelingen voor beleid en bedrijven.
Mordor Inelligence, 2020. Sample Industry Report: E-bike market 2020-2025.
Newson, C., Sloman, L., 2019. A Case for a UK Incentive for e-Bikes.
Niestadt, M., Bjornavold, A., 2019. Electric Road Vehicles in the European Union Trends, Impacts and Policies. https://www.europarl.europa.eu/RegData/etudes/BRIE/2019/637895/EPRS_BRI(2019)637895_EN.pdf.
Otten, M., Hoen, M.T., Boer, L.D., 2015. STREAM passenger transport 2014 version 1.1; Study on Transport Emissions of All Modalities Emission Key Figures. 2011 emission figures.
Peterman, J.E., Morris, K.L., Kram, R., Byrnes, W.C., 2016. Pedelecs as a physically active transportation mode. Eur. J. Appl. Physiol. 116 (8), 1565–1573. https://doi.org/10.1007/s00421-016-3408-9.
Philips, I., Anable, J., Chatterton, T., 2020. e-Bike Carbon Savings—How Much and Where? CREDS Policy Brief 011. https://www.creds.ac.uk/publications/e-bike-carbon-savings-how-much-and-where/.
Plazier, P.A., Weitkamp, G., van den Berg, A.E., 2017a. "Cycling was never so easy!" An analysis of e-bike commuters' motives, travel behaviour and experiences using GPS-tracking and interviews. J. Transp. Geogr. 65 (Suppl. C), 25–34. https://doi.org/10.1016/j.jtrangeo.2017.09.017.
Plazier, P.A., Weitkamp, G., van den Berg, A.E., 2017b. The potential for e-biking among the younger population: a study of Dutch students. Travel Behav. Soc. 8, 37–45. https://doi.org/10.1016/j.tbs.2017.04.007.
Pooley, C., Tight, M., Jones, T., Horton, D., Scheldeman, G., Jopson, A., Mullen, C., Chisholm, A., Strano, E., Constantine, S., 2011. Understanding Walking and Cycling: Summary of Key Findings and Recommendations.
Popovich, N., Gordon, E., Shao, Z., Xing, Y., Wang, Y., Handy, S., 2014. Experiences of electric bicycle users in the Sacramento, California area. Travel Behav. Soc. 1 (2), 37–44. https://doi.org/10.1016/j.tbs.2013.10.006.
Prill, T., 2015. Pedelecs als Beitrag für ein nachhaltiges Mobilitätssystem? Eine Analyse zur Akzeptanz, Nutzung und Wirkung einer technologischen Innovation Goethe. Universität Frankfurt am Main.
Rérat, P., 2021. The rise of the e-bike: towards an extension of the practice of cycling? Mobilities 1-17. https://doi.org/10.1080/17450101.2021.1897236.

Rhodes, R.E., Kates, A., 2015. Can the affective response to exercise predict future motives and physical activity behavior? A systematic review of published evidence. Ann. Behav. Med. 49 (5), 715–731. https://doi.org/10.1007/s12160-015-9704-5.

Rojas-Rueda, D., de Nazelle, A., Andersen, Z.J., Braun-Fahrländer, C., Bruha, J., Bruhova-Foltynova, H., Desqueyroux, H., Praznoczy, C., Ragettli, M.S., Tainio, M., Nieuwenhuijsen, M.J., 2016. Health impacts of active transportation in Europe. PLoS One 11 (3), e0149990. https://doi.org/10.1371/journal.pone.0149990.

Salmeron-Manzano, E., Manzano-Agugliaro, F., 2018. The electric bicycle: worldwide research trends. Energies 11 (7), 1894–1909. https://doi.org/10.3390/en11071894.

Schepers, J.P., Fishman, E., den Hertog, P., Wolt, K.K., Schwab, A.L., 2014. The safety of electrically assisted bicycles compared to classic bicycles. Accid. Anal. Prev. 73, 174–180. https://doi.org/10.1016/j.aap.2014.09.010.

Schepers, P., Wolt, K.K., Fishman, E., 2018. The Safety of E-Bikes in the Netherlands. In. International Transport Forum, Paris, France.

Schepers, P., Klein Wolt, K., Helbich, M., Fishman, E., 2020. Safety of e-bikes compared to conventional bicycles: what role does cyclists' health condition play? J. Transp. Health 19, 100961. https://doi.org/10.1016/j.jth.2020.100961.

Scottish Government News, 2018. £1.3m for Electric Bike Revolution in Scotland. https://www.gov.scot/news/gbp-1-3m-for-electric-bike-revolution-scotland/.

Scrap-It. (2015). Retrieved 11th November from https://scrapit.ca/.

Searle, A., Ranger, E., Zahra, J., Tibbitts, B., Page, A., Cooper, A., 2019. Engagement in e-cycling and the self-management of type 2 diabetes: a qualitative study in primary care. BJGP Open 3 (2), 1–9. https://doi.org/10.3399/bjgpopen18X101638.

Shimano Steps, 2021. State of the Nation Report: Examining Attitudes towards e-Bike Usage in 11 European Countries.

Shore, R., 2016. E-Bike Sales Accelerating as Riders Seek an Added Spark for Hilly Routes.

Simons, M., Van Es, E., Hendriksen, I., 2009. Electrically assisted cycling: a new mode for meeting physical activity guidelines? Med. Sci. Sports Exerc. 41 (11), 2097–2102. https://doi.org/10.1249/MSS.0b013e3181a6aaa4.

Simsekoglu, Ö., Klöckner, C., 2019. Factors related to the intention to buy an e-bike: a survey study from Norway. Transp. Res. Part F 60, 573–581. https://doi.org/10.1016/j.trf.2018.11.008.

Spence, A., 2021. Boomers supercharge electric bike boom. In: Daily. https://indaily.com.au/news/2021/03/04/boomers-supercharge-electric-bike-boom/.

Spencer, B., Jones, T., Leyland, L.-A., van Reekum, C.M., Beale, N., 2019. 'Instead of "closing down" at our ages … we're thinking of exciting and challenging things to do': older people's microadventures outdoors on (e-)bikes. J. Adventure Educ. Outdoor Learn 19 (2), 124–139. https://doi.org/10.1080/14729679.2018.1558080.

Sperlich, B., Zinner, C., Hebert-Losier, K., Born, D.P., Holmberg, H.C., 2012. Biomechanical, cardiorespiratory, metabolic and perceived responses to electrically assisted cycling. Eur. J. Appl. Physiol. 112 (12), 4015–4025. https://doi.org/10.1007/s00421-012-2382-0.

Statistics Netherlands (CBS), 2017. Netherlands Travel Survey (OViN 2013–2016—Data Adapted by KiM) in KiM (2017). Mobiliteitsbeeld (Mobility Report 2017).

Stenner, H.T., Boyen, J., Hein, M., Protte, G., Kück, M., Finkel, A., Hanke, A.A., Tegtbur, U., 2020. Everyday Pedelec use and its effect on meeting physical activity guidelines. Int. J. Environ. Res. Public Health 17 (13). https://doi.org/10.3390/ijerph17134807.

Stichting BOVAG-RAI Mobiliteit, 2019. Fietsen in de statistiek 2011–2018 Nederland.

Stott, S., 2020. How Green is Cycling? Riding, Walking, Ebikes and Driving Ranked. Retrieved 11th November 2021, from https://www.bikeradar.com/features/long-reads/cycling-environmental-impact/.

Sun, Q., Feng, T., Kemperman, A., Spahn, A., 2020. Modal shift implications of e-bike use in the Netherlands: moving towards sustainability? Transp. Res. Part D: Transp. Environ. 78, 102202. https://doi.org/10.1016/j.trd.2019.102202.

Sundfør, H.B., Fyhri, A., 2017. A push for public health: the effect of e-bikes on physical activity levels. BMC Public Health 17 (1), 809–820. https://doi.org/10.1186/s12889-017-4817-3.

Sustrans, 2013. Cairngorms Electric Bicycle Network Pilot Project.

Swain, D.P., Franklin, B.A., 2002. VO2 reserve and the minimal intensity for improving cardiorespiratory fitness. Med. Sci. Sports Exerc. 34 (1), 152–157. https://journals.lww.com/acsm-msse/Fulltext/2002/01000/V_O2_reserve_and_the_minimal_intensity_for.23.aspx.

Tainio, M., Monsivais, P., Jones, N.R.V., Brand, C., Woodcock, J., 2017. Mortality, greenhouse gas emissions and consumer cost impacts of combined diet and physical activity scenarios: a health impact assessment study. BMJ Open 7 (2), e014199. https://doi.org/10.1136/bmjopen-2016-014199.

The NPD Group, 2020. Plot Twist: U.S. Performance Bike Sales Rise in June, Reports the NPD Group. https://www.npd.com/news/press-releases/2020/plot-twist-u-s-performance-bike-sales-rise-in-june-reports-the-npd-group/.

The Swedish Transport Administration, 2019. Elcykeltrenden fortsätter att öka (The electric bicycle trend continues to increase). https://www.trafikverket.se/om-oss/pressrum/pressmeddelanden/Nationellt/2019/2019-06/elcykeltrendenfortsatter-att-oka/.

Theurel, J., Theurel, A., Lepers, R., 2012. Physiological and cognitive responses when riding an electrically assisted bicycle versus a classical bicycle. Ergonomics 55 (7), 773–781. https://doi.org/10.1080/00140139.2012.671964.

Ton, D., Duives, D., 2021. Understanding long-term changes in commuter mode use of a pilot featuring free e-bike trials. Transp. Policy 105, 134–144. https://doi.org/10.1016/j.tranpol.2021.03.010.

Twisk, D.A.M., Platteel, S., Lovegrove, G.R., 2017. An experiment on rider stability while mounting: comparing middle-aged and elderly cyclists on pedelecs and conventional bicycles. Accid. Anal. Prev. 105, 109–116. https://doi.org/10.1016/j.aap.2017.01.004.

Twisk, D., Stelling, A., Van Gent, P., De Groot, J., Vlakveld, W., 2021. Speed characteristics of speed pedelecs, pedelecs and conventional bicycles in naturalistic urban and rural traffic conditions. Accid. Anal. Prev. 150, 105940. https://doi.org/10.1016/j.aap.2020.105940.

Van Cauwenberg, J., De Bourdeaudhuij, I., Clarys, P., de Geus, B., Deforche, B., 2018. E-bikes among older adults: benefits, disadvantages, usage and crash characteristics. Transportation 46, 2151–2172. https://doi.org/10.1007/s11116-018-9919-y.

Velosuisse, 2020. Sales in 2020. https://www.velosuisse.ch/en/neuverkaeufe-2020/.

Verstappen, E.M.J., Vy, D.T., Janzing, H.M., Janssen, L., Vos, R., Versteegen, M.G.J., Barten, D.G., 2020. Bicycle-related injuries in the emergency department: a comparison between E-bikes and conventional bicycles: a prospective observational study. Eur. J. Trauma Emerg. Surg. https://doi.org/10.1007/s00068-020-01366-5.

Weber, T., Scaramuzza, G., Schmitt, K.U., 2014. Evaluation of e-bike accidents in Switzerland. Accid. Anal. Prev. 73, 47–52. https://doi.org/10.1016/j.aap.2014.07.020.

Wild, K., Woodward, A., 2019. Why are cyclists the happiest commuters? Health, pleasure and the e-bike. J. Transp. Health 14, 100569. https://doi.org/10.1016/j.jth.2019.05.008.

Wild, K., Woodward, A., Shaw, C., 2021. Gender and the E-bike: exploring the role of electric bikes in increasing women's access to cycling and physical activity. Active Travel Stud. 1 (1). https://doi.org/10.16997/ats.991.

Wolf, A., Seebauer, S., 2014. Technology adoption of electric bicycles: a survey among early adopters. Transp. Res. Part A 69 (Suppl. C), 196–211. https://doi.org/10.1016/j.tra.2014.08.007.

Woodcock, J., Abbas, A., Ullrich, A., Tainio, M., Lovelace, R., Sá, T.H., Westgate, K., Goodman, A., 2018. Development of the Impacts of Cycling Tool (ICT): A modelling study and web tool for evaluating health and environmental impacts of cycling uptake. PLoS Med. 15 (7), e1002622. https://doi.org/10.1371/journal.pmed.1002622.

Yang, Y., 2019. New national standards on electric bicycles take effect. China Daily. https://www.chinadaily.com.cn/a/201904/16/WS5cb5858da3104842260b6805.html.

ZIV, 2020. Figures—Data—Facts About the German Bicycle and e-Bike Market 2019. https://www-ziv- -zweirad-de.translate.goog/presse-medien/pressemitteilungen/detail/article/zahlen-daten-fakten-zum-deutschen-fahrrad-und-e-bike-markt-2020/?_x_tr_sl=de&_x_tr_tl=en&_x_tr_hl=en&_x_tr_pto=nui,sc.

CHAPTER FOUR

Street level design for cycling

Marc Schlossberg*
City and Regional Planning, University of Oregon, Eugene, OR, United States
*Corresponding author: e-mail address: schlossb@uoregon.edu

Contents

Abstract

This chapter focuses on street-level designs that support cycling as a primary transport mode for most people for most everyday trips. Having a high rate if cycle use is critical for cities that are serious about addressing household affordability (combined housing plus transportation costs), climate change, public health, and more, like happiness, social trust, and freedom and independence, to name a few. In the end, there is clear consensus in how to achieve these objectives as it includes only two elements: (1) make cycling direct, safe, comfortable, and coherent, throughout the community; and (2) make it harder to drive and park private vehicles. This chapter focuses on high quality street-level design practices for making cycling safe and comfortable for the widest range of users, from children to seniors. And while every community considers itself unique, no community needs to reinvent what to do regarding cycling because some cities have been experimenting and perfecting what to do for the last 50 years. Thus, while it is great to be unique community, in terms of cycling infrastructure, the time for experimenting is largely over because it is likely that even the most unique circumstances have been addressed somewhere else.

Note: the term "bicycle" or "bike" will be used throughout this chapter, though it really is shorthand for a range of related transportation vehicles such as tricycles, tandems, cargo bikes, electronic versions of each, and increasingly also for other forms of motorized micro-mobility like scooters, one-wheels, and other similar small footprint, low or no carbon, point-to-point mobility tools.

Keywords: Bicycle, Cycle track, Protected bike lane, Advisory bike lane, Neighborhood greenway, Bicycle boulevard, Sustainable transport

Advances in Transport Policy and Planning, Volume 10
ISSN 2543-0009
https://doi.org/10.1016/bs.atpp.2022.04.004

1. Introduction

The focus of this chapter is on urbanized areas (as opposed to rural areas) and the normal, everyday trips that people make to live their lives. Urbanized areas come in all types of sizes and densities and the focus of this chapter applies across the transect from dense cores to more sprawling suburbs and all the shifting patterns in between and throughout.

The good thing about redesigning streets for cycling is that it is mostly only a political problem at this point rather than a technical one since some cities around the world have spent the last 50 years figuring out what to do and many other cities have taken those lessons and adapted that knowledge for their own context. And while every community thinks of themselves as somehow unique and special, there are some universal principles and designs to draw from.

2. Creating priority networks with busy streets

Busy roads tend to be the most direct path for longer trips in most communities and given the policies of auto-centric infrastructure and street design of the last 70 years, these streets tend to be almost entirely dedicated to the movement of cars. Not only is bicycle infrastructure usually not included on these streets, local engineers and planners are often loathe to allocate space for cycling either because they do not want to "take space" from car usage or such streets feel too busy and therefore complicated or unsafe to try to integrate cycling.

Yet, it is precisely due to the extreme auto-centricity of such streets that the proper mindset of transport designers and policymakers must be that streets with high speed and volume of motorized vehicles demand better bicycling infrastructure. The key to integrating bicycle infrastructure in such spaces that a broad spectrum of the population would actually use is to create space between the cyclist and motor traffic as it is the differential in speed and mass in such areas that creates risk and discomfort for users. There are three key designs that achieve this separation goal on these busier streets: protected lanes, lanes with differential height, and buffered lanes.

2.1 Protected lanes

Protected lanes have a physical barrier between the bike and motor vehicle lanes. The most robust versions have either a concrete barrier (see Fig. 1A–C) or parked cars (1d) as that physical barrier (see Fig. 1).

(a) Eugene, Oregon (USA) (b) *Vancouver (Canada)*

(c) *Copenhagen (Denmark)* (d) *New York City, New York (USA)*

Fig. 1 Curb and parking protected bike lanes (images by Marc Schlossberg).

With these physical barriers, cyclists need to expend little energy worrying about what car traffic is doing, especially when a system of such lanes exist, and intersections are designed at a consistent and appropriate level of quality and comfort. When such lanes exist throughout a city on most, if not all, busy streets, then cycling through a city is more akin to riding on a separated path along the beach or a river, than defensively moving throughout a congested city of cars.

Curb-protected lanes like the Eugene (A) example above take up relatively limited space, but create an important barrier between bike and car. When designed properly, they should be high enough to cause a visual and physical deterrent to motorists, though should be permeable for cyclists to enter and exit practically "at will." This permeability could be through a rounded barrier that cyclists can transcend (yes, motorists can too, but the barrier is like that of a sidewalk curb—permeable for its primary user and still a deterrent to motorists for all but extreme and rare cases) or through enough curb gaps to allow cyclists to enter and exit the bike lane easily and efficiently (the above execution is not a great example as it requires cyclists to come to a near stop to enter or exit). Alternatively, the curb can be small enough to easily roll over on bike, yet still provide a visible, notable and physical deterrent toward cars doing the same thing. The Vancouver (B) example above uses planter boxes as the physical barrier, adding an opportunity to bring beauty and ecology into the urban hardscape and create a more enjoyable environment. The Copenhagen (C) example above demonstrates an even more robust and comprehensive approach by creating both a curb protected bike lane and a pedestrian boarding and alighting zone for busses, eliminating the need for large transit busses to cross or "park" in a bike lane to pick up and drop off passengers (pedestrians have the right of way when a bus arrives).

Parking protected bikeways are another way to create that physical separation, though without the need to construct anything new. In many locations, the bike lane and the parking lane just need to be flipped so that the bike lane is against the main street curb rather than parked cars. Adding 2–3 ft of a painted buffer area, or door zone, allows a parked car's door to open without impeding the bike lane. For this design, in addition to adding the physical barrier, flipping the bike lane and the parking lane typically results in a bike lane that is adjacent to a car's passenger door rather than a driver-side door, significantly reducing conflict given that all car trips have drivers, but many if not most do not have passengers (at least in a US context). (The New York image above (C) is a somewhat unique example where creating a parking protected bike lane actually puts cyclists closer to the driver-side door, and hence the use of the buffer, as this is a one-way street with the bike lane on the less typical side of the street.) Swapping parking and bike lanes is a strategy that cities that already have bike lanes can do with relative ease, low cost, much less political friction given parking supply is not reduced, and can do quickly. The improvement of experience for cyclists can be quite dramatic and this approach can be a potentially good interim measure given it is increasing bicycle access without reducing motor vehicle access.

2.2 Lanes with differential height

Another approach to creating physical separation between cyclists and motorists is by differentiating the height of the bike lane relative to lanes for cars and trucks, and possibly pedestrians. This differential height is the preferred method in Copenhagen, one of Europe's top cycling cities where around 50% of all trips are done by bike and this special infrastructure makes cycling the expected modes for commutes up to 7-miles. (For comparison, almost the entire 200,000 person Eugene-Springfield (USA) metropolitan area is within seven miles of the University of Oregon, the region's largest employer; using the Copenhagen model, nearly all 40,000 university attendees would be considered within the bicycle commute shed of the University, yet the bicycle mode share for work trips is about 6%.)

As can be seen in the images in Fig. 2, raised lanes look very similar to "regular" bike lanes and often exist without additional buffers or barriers between the cyclist and motorist. Yet, the height differential makes a difference for all road users in terms of understanding which mode belongs in which space and reduces the fear of cars encroaching into cyclists' space. Typically, these Copenhagen-styled raised lanes are around 3 in (7.5 cm) higher than the main road height and another half inch (1.3 cm) below the sidewalk. These relatively small differences in height maximize the permeability for cyclists, allowing them to join or leave the lane at any given location as appropriate to their journey, yet the curb is a strong visual and physical signal to motorists (and pedestrians) about road space that is off-limits to them. At certain key locations where cyclists tend to enter or exit the raised bike lane, it is possible to make low-cost, low-engineered asphalt access ramps, per the lower-right image (d), adding comfort to cyclists and responding to user-defined travel patterns not always anticipated by professional transport planners.

(a) (b) (c) (d)

Fig. 2 Examples of raised bike lanes in Copenhagen, Denmark.

2.3 Buffered lanes

A more compromised approach toward protected bike lanes that is increasingly common in the U.S. context is the buffered bike lane. In this case, there is generally not a physical barrier like a curb or parked cars, but there is extra paint demarcating extra, otherwise unused, road space between the space for cyclists and motorists. This extra space increases the distance between cyclists and motor vehicles, which increases the comfort and safety for people on bike.

While the buffered bike lane is inferior to a curb or barrier-protected lane, it is significantly better than a bike lane without the buffer and this approach may have some attraction for cities that do not have money or political will, yet, to invest in curb-protected lanes. These buffered spaces can serve as a type of land bank and can be upgraded toward more robust physical protection as budgets and priorities allow.

Fig. 3 shows four examples of buffered bike lanes. In the first Eugene example (A), when the two-way bike lane is buffered, more space on this

(a) *Buffered, 2-way bike lane in Eugene, Oregon (USA)*

(b) *Buffered lane on 1-way street in New York City (USA)*

(c) *Buffered 2-way, center-of-the-street lanes in Washington DC (USA)*

(d) *Buffered bike lane with plastic bollards in Eugene, Oregon (USA)*

Fig. 3 Buffered bike lanes.

street cross-section is allocated to the bike than to cars and trucks. This overall design allows for social or two abreast riding—people on bike next to each other, talking—while retaining space for someone to pass on bike in either direction. The buffer adds additional comfort in such circumstances and clearly communicates to motorists that cycling is equally entitled to and supported on this particular street. In the New York example above (B), the buffer adds just enough spatial separation to improve the cycling situation. However, without the physical barrier, and especially in a busy city like New York, there is a high frequency of vehicles using the bike lane as a parking lane (quick image searches on-line will show just how prevalent this violation is, including by police and school busses, in addition to delivery vehicles, taxis/ridehail drivers, and more). The Washington DC example (C) is unique in that the buffered bike lanes are in the middle of a wide street cross-section. The buffer area helps clarify to all road users, by expanding the user space, that cyclists are a key road user. The final image (D) shows the addition of plastic bollards to the buffered area; this creates an additional visual barrier that is relatively inexpensive, though often adds an unattractive element to the public sphere. Bollard alternatives such as large reflectors, which are low to the ground offer a hybrid approach between the curb protected bikeway and the buffered bike lane.

2.4 Advisory bike lanes

A newer approach toward elevating bicycle infrastructure space in urban areas for many communities is the advisory bike lane. This approach from the Netherlands is more commonly known as a very good re-design of narrower rural roads or skinnier residential streets, but can also be applied to busier urban spaces once: (1) bicycle volumes start crossing tipping points, (2) more road space is needed to rightfully prioritize for bikes in ways that more standard bike lanes do not allow due to space limitations of the right of way, and (3) the volumes of cyclists or the political will are not yet great enough to commit to removing all bike infrastructure because the street has essentially turned into a bicycle priority street simply by user volume.

The basic design, as highlighted in the rural example in Fig. 4, is to remove the center line, create bike lanes on either side of an existing road such that the space remaining for cars cannot fit two vehicles passing one another without one vehicle moving into the bike lane. This purposeful design takes advantage of the low volume of vehicles and low volume of bikes such that it would be extremely rare for two vehicles to meet at the same time while a cyclist was present in each bike lane, making the free flow

Fig. 4 Rural Advisory Bike Lane (Netherlands).

(a) (b)

Fig. 5 Urban advisory bike lane in Utrecht (Netherlands).

of all modes easy. In the rare instance of conflict, priority is given to cyclists and drivers must slow down sufficiently so that one driver finds a gap and can move safely into the bike lane temporarily.

The urban version of the advisory bike lane is the same, but with wider bike lanes to handle increased cyclist volumes. The center "car lane" should still be narrower than it takes for two vehicles to pass each other, thereby forcing drivers to pay extra attention, slow down, and defer to the presence of the preferred road user: the cyclist. Fig. 5 shows an example of the advisory bike lane in an urban setting. Note that in this image there is two-way car travel, bike lanes on either side, on-street car parking, and a decent intensity in land use—familiar conditions to most urban streets. The difference is in the relative allocation of space and the hierarchy of road user priority with cycling explicitly designed as a more important urban road user. Also note the creative use of different materials in the street to demarcate space in addition to the painted dashed line. This is an excellent approach to re-allocating existing street right-of-way to significantly elevate the needs, comfort, and safety of people on bike.

3. Creating priority networks with residential streets

While busier streets tend to have many of the destinations we try to reach, many homes and apartments—trip origins—are located on quieter residential streets. Making changes to these streets are often one of the easiest and most comprehensive ways to build or enhance a bicycle transportation system. Often referred to as bicycle boulevards, traffic calming zones, or neighborhood greenways, the basic approach is to make small changes to the streets that allow full system connectivity for people on bike, but disrupt connectivity for car drivers. Accessing an individual address by car is usually not impeded; streets are redesigned to encourage local car usage only. The result, however, is lower car traffic and more continuous bicycle access on specific corridors, which increases both comfort and travel time for cyclists.

Fig. 6 shows two typical examples of how very simple, low-cost changes to a residential street or intersection can radically alter the cycling experience. These approaches prioritize connectivity for cyclists while essentially removing non-local car traffic by disrupting connectivity for drivers. In the intersection example (A), two corners on a four-way intersection are extended toward the center of the intersection, pinching the space previously available to about the width of a vehicle. To make it impossible, or unlikely, for a car to

(a) (b)

Fig. 6 Residential street prioritization for cycling in Eugene, Oregon (USA).

travel through the remaining space, a small island with a reflective bollard was placed in the middle, leaving enough room for cyclists traveling through the intersection from any direction to easily move about without obstruction. Cars wanting to travel through this intersection cannot and instead need to turn, likely making their route more indirect and therefore less preferred. Emergency vehicles, however, can simply go through the intersection in this design as bollards in such a design typically are collapsible.

In the other example (B), entrance to the neighborhood by car is prohibited, but not by bike. Drivers are allowed on the street and can exit the neighborhood at this location, but can only access the neighborhood by a less direct approach. Cyclists, on the other hand, have direct access.

There are often further enhancements to a bike-prioritized residential street like this that reinforce bicycle comfort and restrict car access other than to residents or visitors to addresses on the street itself. For example, on a residential bicycle corridor, if stop signs are used in the neighborhood, all such signs should be pointed toward the users of the perpendicular streets and not on the corridor itself. The restricted access points as shown in Fig. 6 can be used to limit car traffic, making a stop-sign-free corridor available essentially to both local and through-cyclists, but available only to local drivers, thus reducing the speed and size differential conflict between cars and people on bike.

Due to the low infrastructure cost and high quality of the result in terms of cyclist user experience, these types of neighborhood greenway designs can be implemented quickly to create comprehensive, connected bicycle transportation systems. Often, creating a system of these types of streets can serve as an initial infrastructure investment to build bike usage and momentum given that these types of street redesigns can be directly adjacent to where many people live. It is also critically important that a system of neighborhood greenways is not the only street-level designs taken up by local municipalities as eventually people will want to access more than just residential streets and will want and need the same level of access and comfort when turning onto busier streets where many of our goods, services, and jobs are located.

4. Conclusion

In the end, there is actually a vast array of experience and evidence on how to design or re-design a city so that cycling becomes a regular, widely-used, normal mode of transport for most people doing most things in their daily lives. There really are only two main ingredients: (1) create bike infrastructure that helps people feel safe to use it; and (2) make it harder to drive. Building the right infrastructure is no longer a technical challenge because there are cities that have figured it out through 50 years of experimentation and evolution. For any city serious about either shifting car trips to bike, or substantially increasing modal share of bikes, it is impossible to do so simply by making non-car modes easier to use; it must also become less attractive to drive. Thus, the challenge for cities is purely political—are they willing to put knowledge into practice to address some of the most pressing environmental, social, and economic challenges of our time or are they too embedded into a status quo that survives on inertia and not much else?

The key for policy makers, designers, and transport agency leaders to truly understand how straightforward the calculus is to transform from a car-dependent society to one of freedom and independence provided by the bicycle is to understand the basic formula that every transportation mode follows: build it and they will come. Cities that build systems of high-quality bicycle infrastructure get more people biking just as cities that add more frequent, rapid transit get more transit users just as cities that build more highways and lanes and parking get more car users. It is a relatively simple formula that has been significantly skewed over the last 70 years via policy and public investments toward making car driving easier. Simply adding non-car infrastructure without reducing the ease of driving will yield changes that are insignificant to individual, family, community and society needs. Based on the experience in some of the world's top cycling cities, however, once a city is transformed such that half of all trips (work and non-work) are done by bike, the city may actually be easier to drive on for those who really do need a car as their transport tool because there will be so few vehicles on the road.

In the end, the bicycle promises tremendous opportunity for real mobility in most communities and offer a flexibility that most other modes do not. Bikes are point-to-point transportation that can span low, medium, and high-density areas in ways that both walking and transit cannot. Cycling is low cost, is accessible as independent mobility for people from childhood to old age, and can be part of the solution toward the crises of household affordability where housing plus transportation costs create real cost burdens for many households. As the most efficient human invention ever created, cycling is also good environmentally and for personal health.

And the key to unlocking all of this goodness is simply to create protected bike lanes on all of a city's busiest streets and connect them to a network of minimally altered residential streets that create bicycle priority and directness. For most communities, the cost of doing all of this equates to the building of one highway overpass.

CHAPTER FIVE

Network level design for cycling

Regine Gerike[a,*], Simone Weikl[b], Caroline Koszowski[a], and Klaus Bogenberger[b]

[a]"Friedrich List" Faculty of Transport and Traffic Sciences, Technische Universität Dresden, Dresden, Germany
[b]Department of Mobility Systems Engineering, Technische Universität München, München, Germany
*Corresponding author: e-mail address: regine.gerike@tu-dresden.de

Contents

Abstract

This chapter provides an overview of existing approaches for cycle network planning in research and in practice. First, main requirements for cycle networks are described, which are safety, cohesion, directness, comfort, attractiveness and adaptability. Second, an overview of traditional and emerging data sources for cycle network planning is presented and compared with the initially formulated requirements. Third, two approaches for the multi-modal functional classification of street networks including cycling are introduced, followed by a presentation of specific guidance for

Advances in Transport Policy and Planning, Volume 10
ISSN 2543-0009
https://doi.org/10.1016/bs.atpp.2022.04.005

developing cycle networks and related academic studies. Three approaches for cycle network design are described. (1) The development of cycle networks based on desire lines and cycle routes connecting relevant origins and destinations as suggested by most guidelines is a suitable basis for cycle network design. (2) It should be combined with data-driven demand-focused approaches in order to optimally adjust the cycle networks with user patterns and preferences. (3) Optimization concepts and network growth strategies help to prioritize investments. The main challenge that is hardly addressed in any of the identified references is the coordination of cycle network development with the other transport modes and street functions. We therefore propose an integrated multi-modal approach for cycle network design, an approach that considers all transport modes, street users, street functions and usages and is also coordinated with street design and space availability.

Keywords: Cycle networks, Cycle facilities, Urban street design, Cycle network optimization, MCDA

1. Introduction

The strategic development of cycle networks is the "most abstract and at the same time most essential activity entailed in the design of cycle-friendly infrastructure" (CROW, 2016, p. 61). Clearly defined hierarchic strategic cycle networks are fundamental for the successful provision and promotion of cycling. They set out main connections between relevant origins and destinations for providing accessibility and high levels of service. They ensure that consideration is given to cycling within transport planning and policy making from the very beginning. They should be the basis for prioritization in investment programs, and for informing street design teams about the routes likely to carry higher volumes of cycle traffic. They can promote the bicycle mode among those who do not yet use the bicycle for daily transport and exploit all modal shift potentials from other modes to bicycle, e.g., by also enabling trips with (e)-bike-friendly distances from or to suburban areas. (Cycle) network analysis and the identification of gaps and deficits at network level are the basis for evidence-based and efficient transport policy making. For example, small measures that close gaps in networks and thus have a major impact on the quality of the overall cycle provision, can be identified and can be implemented with highest priority.

The core outcome of cycle network planning is a hierarchical network of preferred routes. In combination with standards for the design and operation for the different levels in the hierarchy of the cycle network, strategic network development directly provides guidance for designing specific elements of the street network.

Current and potential future cyclists are in the focus of cycle network planning, including all types of cyclists from the "strong and fearless" to the "interested but concerned" (Geller, 2009). Cycle network planning should follow a process of thinking about the people who actually make trips or those who want to make trips, the places that they go to and the purposes of their journeys; it should be done together with all the relevant stakeholders from the very beginning.

The literature is consistent in that high quality cycle networks need to be safe, coherent, direct, comfortable and attractive (CROW, 2016). There is consistent evidence in the literature that cities with high cycling levels also have extensive networks of separate cycle facilities and traffic-calmed streets (Buehler and Dill, 2016; Mueller et al., 2018). Caulfield (2014) finds stated preferences for continuous or connected cycle facilities compared to cycle facilities in general. Titze et al. (2008) find a significant relationship between self-reported measures of the bicycling environment and cycling levels. Schepers et al. (2013), based on the example of Dutch urban street networks, demonstrate convincingly that unbundling vehicular and cycle traffic increases road safety and bicycle usage. Schoner and Levinson (2014) find, based on bicycle commuting data for 74 US cities, that the density of the overall bikeway network including all types of cycle facilities had the largest effect on cycling levels, this effect was larger than the combination of the network variables connectivity, fragmentation and directness. Further studies report significant associations between a wider range of built environment attributes including population density, land use mix and street connectivity (Koohsari et al., 2020). Only few studies examine the shape of the relationship between built-environment variables and cycling. Mueller et al. (2018) find the following for 167 European cities: a non-linear relationship between the lengths of the cycling network and the cycling mode share; there seems to be a saturation, meaning a threshold of cycle network length above which the gradient gets flatter. Similar findings are reported in Kerr et al. (2016) and Koohsari et al. (2020).

Overall, evidence for cyclists' preferences for certain types of cycle facilities and at the level of single street sections including their perceived safety is more reliable compared to the network level. However, findings from the existing studies are consistent in that coherent and dense cycle networks positively impact cycling levels (Buehler and Dill, 2016).

Two main types of material are relevant for network level design for cycling. First, ministries, expert organizations, NGOs and further mainly non-academic institutions provide guidance on how to design for cycling

(ASTRA, 2008; CROW, 2016; DfT, 2020; FGSV, 2010; FSV, 2014; Gerike et al., 2019; Parkin, 2018c; TfL, 2016). Second, academic studies develop approaches for optimizing cycle networks, based on often innovative data sources such as trajectory data or data from bike share systems and based on different criteria for the optimization (Duthie and Unnikrishnan, 2014; Lin and Yu, 2013; Liu et al., 2018; Mauttone et al., 2017; Mesbah et al., 2012; Plumed et al., 2016).

Guidance on (cycle) network design mainly follows a supply-side approach. Cycle networks should be designed in a way that allows cyclists to reach all relevant destinations safely and comfortably. Only some guidelines recommend the consideration of current or potential cycle demand for supporting prioritization in network development. Academic studies, on the other hand, are data-driven. They either follow a demand-side approach (cycle facilities should correspond to cyclists' revealed or stated desire lines), a supply-side approach (cycle networks should be designed in a way that allows cyclists to reach all relevant destinations while at the same time minimizing costs) or a mixture of both. Both approaches have strengths and weaknesses, supply-side approaches might ignore important (potential) cycle flows and might choose insufficient widths or types of cycle facilities as a consequence. Purely data-driven approaches might ignore suppressed cycle traffic at routes with low current cycling levels, for example due to deficient cycle facilities, but high future cycling potential, for example due to cycle-affine origins and destinations adjacent to a route.

Besides these mode-specific studies, guidance on the multi-modal functional classification of road networks is also relevant as these should implicitly or explicitly consider cycling as one of the various transport modes to be taken into account (FGSV, 2008; Jones et al., 2008). Only few of such multi-modal approaches for road network development exist, these focus on motorized traffic and are hardly useful for the development of cycle networks (Gerike et al., 2019). This is not conducive, the ambitious goals in transport policy making such as the reduction of greenhouse gas emissions can only be reached with integrated approaches that jointly optimize the mode-specific networks. These are the only way to use the scarce space and also time (e.g., in signaling schemes) efficiently, particularly within urban areas where it is hardly possible to accommodate all street user needs already today and where new functions and requirements arise constantly, e.g., for climate adaption or water management.

This chapter argues that cycle network planning should be undertaken as part of a multi-modal travel planning exercise, not limited by city boundaries, and closely coordinated with spatial planning. The aim of this chapter is to set out such an integrated approach to strategic multi-modal transport network development and street design, in its wider transport and land use context. For meeting this ambition, this chapter draws on both groups of relevant references as introduced above, that is, guidance material for (cycle) network design and academic studies on network optimization.

This chapter first introduces the main requirements for cycle networks, which form the basis for any activity in developing cycle networks. Second, an overview of traditional and emerging data sources for cycle network planning and for monitoring the requirements is provided. Third, an overview is given of guidance on the multi-modal functional classification of road networks including all street user groups and usages, followed by a presentation of specific guidance for developing cycle networks and related academic studies. Based on this overview of the state-of-the-art, we develop an integrated approach for cycle network design that considers all transport modes, street users, functions and usages and that is also coordinated with street design and available space. The chapter concludes with an outlook for further research and for policy making.

2. Requirements for cycle networks

The following five main requirements for cycle networks are consistently formulated in the researched guidelines: safety, cohesion, directness, comfort and attractiveness (CROW, 2016; DfT, 2017, 2020; Godefrooij et al., 2009; Highways England, 2021; Parkin, 2018a; Sustrans, 2014; TfL, 2016). They are consistent with cyclists' preferences as identified in the literature and also with normative goals in policy making. They form the basis and are the benchmark for successful cycle network planning. Adaptability is added as a sixth criterion that came up recently in response to the high dynamics in cycle volumes and types of bicyclists and bicycles (TfL, 2016).

2.1 Safety

Safety first, this holds for planning at the street level and also at the network level. Most cyclist-related collisions happen at the intersections, which are mainly collisions related to conflicts in turning maneuvers but also while crossing and single-bicycle accidents (Liu and Marker, 2020; Reynolds et al., 2009). At street sections, single-bicycle accidents are also a problem, together with conflicts at entrances to adjacent properties, bus or tram stops, with parked vehicles and also with pedestrians (Thomas and DeRobertis, 2013). The cycle network requirement safety is operationalized first with the degree to which design standards are met, this relates for example to sufficient sight distances and appropriate types of cycle facilities compared to motor traffic volumes and speed (TfL, 2016). ASTRA (2008) additionally uses at the network level the indicators of uniformity and continuity of the types of cycle facilities (these should not change too often), the number of particularly dangerous locations (e.g., missing cycle facilities, unprotected turning maneuvers, insufficient sight distances or poorly visible obstacles) and perceived safety. The latter is measured based on expert assessments of each location using criteria such as social surveillance and liveliness, visibility and lighting. Godefrooij et al. (2009) adds the separation of cyclists from motorized vehicles but also from other street users such as pedestrians as an important determinant of objective and perceived safety.

2.2 Cohesion

Cohesion (also called coherence) means that all parts of the cycle network should be well connected to each other; the cycling infrastructure should form a coherent whole and should be readily accessible by proper interconnections. ASTRA (2008) formulates the goal that relevant destinations should not be further away from the cycle network than 200 m (within built-up areas) or 500 m (outside built-up areas). Recommended grid sizes of cycle networks as the distance between more or less parallel connections in a network differ in the literature. CROW (2016) states 300–500 m within built-up areas (1000–1500 m outside), TfL (2016) 400 m, ASTRA (2008) 200–250 m and Sustrans (2014) suggests a basic network with a mesh grid of 250 m. FSV (2014) recommends grid sizes of 500–1000 m for the main cycle network within built-up areas but these should be complemented by lower level cycle routes in distances of 200–250 m. FGSV (2010) comes with the lowest values of 100–200 m grid size for the main cycle network, related to the ambition that 90% of residents should live at a maximum distance of 200 m from the main cycle network. CROW (2016) states that 70% of cycle route kilometers should be covered through the main cycle network. Cohesion also includes connections to the other transport modes (e.g., by providing parking facilities at appropriate locations) and wayfinding (Godefrooij et al., 2009; TfL, 2016). Cohesion and high network connectivity also contribute to low-stress cycling and thus increase the attractiveness of cycling networks (Furth et al., 2016).

2.3 Directness

Directness means minimizing detours in terms of distance and time losses, e.g., due to waiting times at junctions, crossing at street sections or other disruptions. Detour factors are the commonly used indicators, they are defined as the ratio between the shortest distance in the real network and the distance as the crow flies. The same detour factor is less problematic for short distance trips because the absolute detour is smaller than for longer trips. CROW (2016) states a detour factor of 1.27 for a perfect rectangular network and suggests that well-designed cycle networks should have lower detour factors. FGSV (2010) recommends maximum detour factors of 1.2 compared to the shortest possible route and maximum 1.1 compared to parallel main streets, and there should be no additional slope for the cycle route. ASTRA (2008) considers the distance and the difference in altitude for computing the detour factor and requests a detour factor of 1.2 for reaching the highest level of directness but allows for higher values for the subsequent quality levels, for routes with mainly leisure cycling and outside built-up areas. Mean detour factors for networks can be computed as the mean value of detour factors for a sample of randomly selected origin-destination pairs. The literature consistently shows that detour factors are a significant determinant of bicyclists' route choices (Broach et al., 2012; Winters et al., 2010).

2.4 Comfort

The criterion comfort addresses all nuisances and delays caused by bottlenecks and shortcomings in cycle facilities which require additional physical effort as well as any discomfort of vibration due to poor or inappropriate surfaces (Godefrooij et al., 2009). ASTRA (2008) allows for a maximum of one disruption per 500 m within built-up areas (2000 m outside) for the highest level of comfort and assesses surface quality based on the proportion of the cycle route that is covered with asphalt or concrete. CROW (2016) names appropriate widths of cycle facilities, surface quality, smooth longitudinal vertical profiles, the absence of any instantaneous changes in vertical level such as Krebs, minimum number of stops, optimized wayfinding, comprehensibility, a limited amount of turning-off maneuvers and minimized bendiness (no necessity of sudden reactions or changes of direction or speed) as further indicators for the criterion comfort (see also DfT, 2020; Parkin, 2018c).

2.5 Attractiveness

Cyclists are more directly exposed to the environment than drivers of motorized vehicles, they therefore particularly value attractive routes (e.g., through parks or at waterfront locations) and well-designed streets and places (DfT, 2020). "Cycle infrastructure shall be designed with appropriate character and quality resonant with the environment through which it passes" (Parkin, 2018c, p. 41). The attractiveness of cycle routes is also about low noise exposure and air pollution, streets should be well maintained and free from litter or broken glass (DfT, 2020). Cycle routes should preferably pass through lively and well-lit areas in order to minimize concerns about personal security. Cycle routes with stimulating environments, e.g., with restaurants, window shopping, greenery or street furniture are more attractive, facilities for resting are valued. Shade and shelter should be provided if possible, for example against wind with the help of trees or greenery.

2.6 Adaptability

Seeing the rapidly growing cycle volumes in London, TfL (2016) suggests adaptability as the sixth requirement for cycle networks (see also Sustrans, 2014). Considerations should be given to the ability to accommodate any future changes in cycle demand or further framework conditions and particularly large increases in use. This criterion might also be extended to a wider range of bicycle types and other micro vehicles that might use cycle facilities in the future.

2.7 Discussion

Most references use the first five main requirements with few exemptions. ASTRA (2008) for example works only with three main requirements, which are: safe, attractive and seamless. The indicators used for operationalizing each of these criteria, however, cover most aspects of the five main requirements introduced above. Godefrooij et al. (2009) stress that these requirements can be and should be applied for all levels from whole cycle networks down to specific street sections and intersections. This characteristic is a strength of these requirements and makes them suitable for integrated approaches that optimize strategic networks and specific street design and operation at the same time.

Furth (2021) works with a different approach, he introduces "low-stress connectivity" as an umbrella high-level requirement for cycle networks that is operationalized by 5-s-level requirements: (1) separation from traffic stress,

(2) pleasant, well-lit, and low-crime surroundings, (3) smooth, well-maintained pavement, (4) avoiding long, steep climbs, (5) connected and direct. These requirements can be well matched to the ones introduced above, they are a mixture of the above criteria themselves (connected and direct) and the criteria used for operationalizing the above requirements. For example, "avoiding long, steep climbs" could be assigned to the comfort requirement. Bicycle Level-of-Service/Safety measures are suitable criteria for operationalizing the different requirements (Carter et al., 2007; LaMondia and Moore, 2015).

The main requirements introduced above are suitable for utilitarian and also for leisure cycle networks, only the priorities differ. For example, directness is more important for utilitarian cycling whereas attractiveness is more important for leisure cycling. Leisure cycle routes can be upgraded by particularly nice surroundings that make cycling an experience, by supplementary products and branding, by marketing activities such as information, campaigns, events or specific route planners as well as by supplementary facilities such as resting places or accommodation (CROW, 2016). These things are less relevant for utilitarian networks.

Various interdependencies and overlaps between the individual requirements exist. For example, lighting supports attractiveness and also safety; the uniformity and continuity of cycle facilities are listed as criteria for safety and also for cohesion; delays are named as criterion for comfort but also support directness. If purposefully considered, these interdependencies can help to maximize synergies and efficiency in developing successful cycle networks.

3. Data for cycle network planning

Data is needed for cycle network planning in order to assess current and future cycle demand, cycle facilities and networks, land use and also the degree to which the above introduced requirements are met: safety, cohesion, directness, comfort, attractiveness and adaptability. We summarize the suitability of different data sources for cycle network development and for measuring the requirements of cycle networks. Table 1 gives an overview on the different data needs for cycle network planning and for measuring the six-cycle network requirements. Table 2 indicates which data sources are suitable to fulfill these data needs.

Measuring safety requires data on collisions and near-misses, infrastructure characteristics (e.g., sight distances, types of cycle facilities, conflict zones with other modes), street user behavior (e.g., speed), perceived safety

Table 1 Data needs for cycle network planning and for measuring the requirements of cycle networks.

	Data needs	Cycle network requirements					
		Safety	Cohesion	Directness	Comfort	Attractiveness	Adaptability
1	Accidents	X					
2	Near-accidents (e.g., interactions, conflicts)	X					
3	Dangerous locations/situations (e.g., low sight distance)	X					
4	Number of turning movements	X			X		
5	Number of crossings	X			X		
6	Conflict zones with other modes (e.g., at intersections, bus stops, vehicle parking, footways)	X					
7	Speed (bicycle and other modes)	X			X	X	
8	Traffic volume (bicycle and other modes)	X			X	X	
9	Number of vehicle lanes	X			X	X	
10	Road functional class	X					
11	Origins, destinations		X	X			
12	Supply of other transport facilities		X				
13	Willingness for detours			X			
14	Detour factor of cycle routes			X			
15	Waiting times (e.g., at traffic signals and signs)			X	X		

16	Type of cycle facility (cycle lane/track/street, one-way/ bidirectional, etc.)	X	X		
17	Width of cycle facility	X	X		
18	Surface type	X	X		
19	Perceived shortcomings in cycle infrastructure	X	X	X	
20	Vibrations	X	X		
21	Slopes	X	X		
22	Lighting	X	X	X	
23	Perceived comfort/stress	X	X		
24	Cycle parking		X		
25	Noise level			X	
26	Air pollution level			X	
27	General environment (presence of trees/green space, etc.)			X	
28	Cleanliness			X	
29	Potential/future demand				X

Table 2 Data sources for measuring the requirements of cycle networks.

	Covered data needs
Household travel surveys	11, 13, 23, 29
Manual or automated traffic counts	8, 29
Safety reports	1
GPS-tracking apps (exact routes)	2[a], 4, 5, 11, 13, 15, 20[a], 21, 23[a]
Activity-tracking apps (aggregated street-link-based traffic volumes)	11, 13[b], 15[b], 29
Bikeshare data	4[b], 5[b], 11, 13[b], 15[b], 29
Imagery (e.g., Google street view, Mapillary)	3, 4, 5, 6, 9, 12, 16, 17, 18, 22, 24, 27, 28
Online participation platforms	1, 2, 3, 6, 19, 23
Network data (e.g., Open Street Map)	4, 5, 6, 7, 9, 10, 12, 16, 17[c], 18, 21[c], 22[c], 24, 27
Social media	1, 2, 3, 19, 23
Floating car data	7, 11, 29
Mobile cell phone data (aggregated data)	7, 8, 11[d], 13[d], 29
Vehicle trajectories (e.g., public transport agencies, navigation system providers)	7, 8
General Transit Feed Specification (GTFS)	12
Digital elevation models (e.g., EU-DEM, Google elevation API)	21
Noise mapping	25
Data on air quality (measurement stations or computation)	26

[a]If combined with physiological/acceleration sensors.
[b]If disaggregated data is provided.
[c]Depending on the data quality.
[d]For bicycles, if mode classification is possible.

and particularly also on traffic volumes for cyclists and for the (potentially) conflicting other modes. Measuring cohesion and directness mainly requires data on bicyclists' origins and destinations, infrastructure supply for interconnections including also data on the number of stops and waiting times. Measuring comfort mainly requires data on the surface type and quality, vibrations (e.g., caused by potholes), cycle way type, cycle lane width and slopes. For measuring attractiveness, data on cleanliness and the general environment including, e.g., the presence of trees and green space are needed, data on noise and air pollution levels is beneficial. Adaptability requires data on potential and future cycle demand including origin-destination pairs with high modal shift potential from the car to the bicycle. Some data needs are relevant for multiple cycle network requirements. The immense diversity of the mentioned (and maybe not even complete) required information shows the necessity of diverse data sources for cycle network planning.

Alattar et al. (2021) (see also Nelson et al., 2021; Olmos et al., 2020; Willberg et al., 2021) provide comprehensive overviews of traditional and emerging bicycle data sources including their attributes, access options, spatial-temporal coverage, limitations, data biases and applications. Data on bicycle traffic is traditionally collected by manual traffic counts (e.g., video recordings, surveys, handheld counters, ride-along observations) or automated traffic counts (e.g., pneumatic tubes, infrared sensors, magnetometers, video data with automated image processing). Both manual and automated traffic counts have low spatial-temporal coverage as measurements are only conducted at a few locations at specific times (except for permanent bike counters) due to high maintenance costs and labor-intensity. With the exception of surveys, very little background information (e.g., socio-demographic data) is collected. Surveys are error-prone (e.g., sampling bias) and challenging due to high sample collection costs and decreasing response rates. Crash data is traditionally provided by police safety reports or insurance reports, underreporting is an issue.

The emergence of smartphones, wearables and location-based services paved the way for new data collection methods. Tracking data from smartphones or further wearable devices with exact routes are increasingly generated, e.g., in campaigns like bicycle reward systems. Activity tracking data is produced also by social fitness networks like Strava or bicycle navigation apps (Francke and Lißner, 2017). This data holds a great potential for cycle network planning by delivering real-time and permanent information on who (e.g., age and gender) cycles where (network-wide link-based traffic volumes and eventually OD matrices), when (high temporal granularity), why (e.g., commuting versus leisure) and how (speed, route choice and waiting times at nodes). App-generated activity tracking data provide a great estimate on spatial-temporal bicycle exposure and therefore are of great importance for future cycle network planning. If the devices used for tracking were also able to measure noise, physiological changes and acceleration, additional questions could be answered. For example, Nuñez et al. (2018) analyze the influence of noise, vibration, cycle paths and period of day on cyclists' stress levels using similar data.

Besides the data mentioned above, bikeshare data particularly from dockless systems could also be used for cycle network planning. This data includes at least the time and location of trip start and end times and sometimes also demographic data such as age and gender. Other useful data sources are imagery (e.g., Google street view or aerial imagery) for environmental information, Open Street Map (OSM) for network data, online participation platforms where citizens can report safety issues and concerns, as well as geotagged digital footprints on social media. In addition to the mentioned bicycle-specific data sources, mode-unspecific data sources could be helpful for estimating potential demand. These data sources are, for instance, floating vehicle data and origin-destination matrices calculated from mobile cell phone data (e.g., by commercial providers like Teralytics). For the latter, it must be noticed that until now mode detection only works well for distances >30 km but not for smaller distances (Thust and Franceschina, 2020). Data from Geographic Information Systems (GIS) on points of interest, census data on residents and employment and further geo-located statistical data on the built-environment and land use provides information on the location and characteristics of relevant origins and destinations. GIS data inventories kept by governments are often not complete in terms of data needed for cycle network development. For example, data on parking is rarely available but of high relevance for cyclists' safety.

None of the various possible data sources cover all requirements on their own, it becomes clear that evidence-based cycle network planning requires a combination of different data sources. Some requirements are hardly covered by any of the possible data sources. Further data, e.g., from environmental planning departments is needed in order to close these gaps.

4. Guidelines for intermodal street network planning

Only few guidelines for intermodal street network classification could be identified in the literature research, which are mainly the German "Guidelines for Integrated Network Design" (RIN) (FGSV, 2008; Gerike et al., 2011) and the "Link and Place" approach (Jones et al., 2008). FGSV (2008) develops a two-dimensional functional classification for road and rail networks which is based on the spatial planning principle of giving prime importance to central locations. Each link in a network first gets assigned a "connector function" and second a "road category". The connector function is mode-specific, it rises with a higher importance and hierarchy level of the central locations that are connected by each specific link. The road category describes all road functions beyond connecting central locations, it considers the road type (motorways, country roads, urban roads), location (outside built-up areas, bordering built-up areas, within built-up areas), type of adjoining land-use (non-built-up, built-up) and whether the street section is a main or access road. With this two-dimensional approach, the RIN covers networks for individual motorized vehicles, public transport, cycling, walking and interchange points.

Jones et al. (2008) develop the "Link and Place" approach (also called "Movement and Place") for road network planning, this is another two-dimensional system including the following two primary functions for each single element of the network:

- Link: A link function is assigned to each street section acknowledging that streets serve as conduits for through movement for different road users: pedestrians, cyclists, public transport and individual motorized transport. These movements should be safe, convenient, seamless and quick. The general goal is to minimize travel times for the link users. For one street section, the link function might differ for the different transport modes.
- Place: Streets are destinations in their own right, as public spaces and for providing access to adjoining frontages. The place function aims to encourage users to stay in the street, for example to shop, work, rest, eat, talk or wait and to enjoy the surroundings. Besides these activities, the place function includes the following traffic and transport activities: loading/unloading, access for serving, vehicles dropping off and picking up passengers, parking, buses and trams stopping to drop off/pick up passengers, taxis waiting for customers, and pedestrians strolling. One success criterion for the place function is to maximize the dwell time spent by people taking part in activities on or adjacent to the street (place users).

Both approaches consider for each street section the two main functions (1) of moving people and vehicles and (2) of being places on their own. Thanks to mode-specific connector and link functions, both approaches are generally suitable for consistent intermodal network design including cycling as an important transport mode. The strength of the German RIN approach is its direct connection with spatial planning, the connector function is assigned based on the importance of the central locations to be connected, this is less clear for the link function in the "Link and Place" approach. The RIN approach is focused on connections between municipalities and central locations, it is less suitable for inner-municipal network classification which is, however, the focus for cycle network design. The place function in the "Link and Place" approach is far more detailed compared to the road category in the RIN, this is a strength of the "Link and Place" approach. It is better suitable to consider the variety of place functions in the network classification. Both approaches aim at intermodal street network classification but only the "Link and Place" approach provides detailed guidance on how to solve problems of space scarcity when link and place functions for the different transport modes are combined in specific street sections.

5. Guidelines for cycle network planning

Table 3 gives an overview of approaches and steps for cycle network planning in the international guidance material. Hardly any of the guidelines require the formulation of objectives for cycle network planning, most references begin directly with the analysis. The analysis always includes the identification of relevant origins and destinations, most guidelines also recommend analyzing the current cycle network, fewer guidelines call for the analysis of current and/or future cycling demand. For example, FGSV (2010) is very clear that cycle network planning is supply-side planning, and that suitable connections should be provided between all relevant origins and destinations regardless of current and future cycle flows (see FSV, 2014 for a similar approach).

In most guidelines, the next step is to generate desire lines that connect relevant origins and destinations by straight lines and then to convert these desire lines into routes at the physical street network. DfT (2017, 2020) is one example guideline that does not work with desire lines. Instead, current and future cycling patterns are directly converted into a network of cycle routes, this is used as the basis for identifying deficits and necessary improvements in the existing cycle network. TfL (2016) follows a similar approach and also focusses mainly on improvements of the specific elements of the cycle network based, e.g., on mesh density analysis. Such "mesh concepts" are suitable for high numbers of relevant origins and destinations, they presuppose and support the aim to cycle from everywhere to everywhere.

Only CROW (2016) and FGSV (2010) confront the generated cycle routes with the networks for the other modes of transport: "in practice it

Table 3 Stages of cycle network planning.

	Objectives, scope	Analysis	Desire lines	Network concept	Other users	Cycle facilities	Measures	Implementation	Monitoring
ASTRA (2008)		Map existing network, identify origins, destinations, potential demand	Generate desire lines	Convert desire lines into routes, define network sections for appraisal, identify gaps and problems in the network, appraisal of variants, check transition between network sections			Assess the urgency of measures at problematic locations, develop and assess variants, select measures		
CROW (2016) (main cycle network)		Identify origins, destinations and links	Generate desire lines	Convert desire lines into routes	Confront routes with infrastructure for other modes				
DfT (2017, 2020) (walking and cycling)	Determine scope (geographical extent, governance, timescale)	Identify existing patterns and potential new journeys, origins and destinations, cycle flows		Convert flows into a network of routes and determine the types of improvements required			Prioritize improvements, develop a phased plan for future investment	Integrate outputs into current policies and strategies	
FGSV (2010)	Define planning area, analyze current status of network planning	Identify origins and destinations, quality of existing network (including safety), current cycle demand	Generate desire lines	Convert desire lines into routes, assignment to network levels	Coordination with other network concepts		Solutions for deficits and gaps in the network, list with measures, prioritization, timeline for implementation, funding	Appraisal, decision, implementation	Monitoring
FSV (2014)	Define planning area, objectives	Analysis of current situation and comparison with objectives	Generate desire lines	Convert desire lines into routes		Choice of cycle facilities	Prioritization, choice of measures for implementation	Implementation	Monitoring

Continued

Table 3 Stages of cycle network planning.—cont'd

	Objectives, scope	Analysis	Desire lines	Network concept	Other users	Cycle facilities	Measures	Implementation	Monitoring
Godefrooij et al. (2009)		Map land use, origins and destinations, existing facilities, routes, cycling-related accidents, cycle trip purposes, missing connections, barriers, assess and understand potential demand	Generate desire lines	Define and establish the priorities for a bicycle network structure using qualitative or quantitative methods					
Parkin (2018b)	Define objectives	Map existing and proposed land use, existing cycle routes and facilities, cycle volumes, cycling-related collisions, predict potential demand				Identify priority locations/ constraints, identify network improvements	Prioritize and select schemes	Implement schemes	Monitor, assess operation
Sustrans (2014)		Identify main trip attractors, assess demand (existing and potential), review existing routes, parking, barriers and options for improvement	Identify desire lines	Develop a prioritized costed network development plan, marketing					Monitor and review
TfL, (2016)		Review of existing conditions, mesh density analysis, accessibility classification audit, porosity analysis, cycling level of assessment	Look for desire lines			Based on the analysis, networks and cycle facilities should be adapted			

turns out that relatively little attention is given to the confrontation between the cycle network and the networks for other modes of transport" (CROW, 2016, p. 73). This holds also for the feedback loop with street design, only two references include the step of checking the feasibility to actually accommodate cycle facilities that meet the required standards with the available street space (CROW, 2016; FGSV, 2010). The selection, appraisal and prioritization of possible network modifications is considered as the next planning step in most guidelines, only Parkin (2018c) specifically recommends to model future cycling demand for the different possible network modifications. The cycle network planning process concludes with the implementation and the monitoring phases leading ideally directly into the next round of cycle network planning. Godefrooij et al. (2009) focus strongly on stakeholder engagement from the analysis phase, Sustrans (2014) even lists the engagement with stakeholders as an own planning phase.

The types of origins and destinations considered for cycle network planning are quite similar in the different guidelines (see, e.g., CROW, 2016; Godefrooij et al., 2009; Sustrans, 2014). They include all functions, buildings, facilities and activities that attract cyclists: shopping areas, city/town/district centers, buildings with important public functions, schools and universities, health and sports facilities, focal points for jobs, public transport hubs, tourist attractions and natural areas, activities such as markets, leisure and entertainment facilities such as theaters or cinemas. Special attention should be given to the edges of the planning region and to the points of connection with the neighboring (regional) cycle network. Future changes in land use should be anticipated whenever possible.

The recommended number of hierarchy levels differ between the guidelines. CROW (2016) distinguishes between the basic structure, the main cycle network and bicycle highways. Guidance focusses on the main network and bicycle highways. The basic network includes the remaining parts of the whole street network, which should also meet the design standards and provide accessibility to the higher level networks. TfL (2016) follows this approach. Cycle networks in FGSV (2010) consist of four levels within and three levels outside built-up areas, these are distinguished by their connector function assigned based on the RIN categories (FGSV, 2008). ASTRA (2008) distinguishes international, national, regional and local cycle routes, FSV (2014) distinguishes main routes, connector/collector routes and basic routes. Only CROW (2016) provides specific recommendations for design standards for the different hierarchy levels.

6. Academic approaches for supporting and optimizing cycle network planning

This section gives an overview of academic approaches to supporting and optimizing cycle network planning. These approaches can be subdivided into three main research directions:

1. Multi-criteria assessment approaches
2. Optimization-based approaches
3. Data-driven network growth strategies

6.1 Multi-criteria assessment approaches

The general goal of multi-criteria assessment approaches, which are also called multi-criteria decision analysis (MCDA) approaches, in cycle network planning is the numerical analysis, assessment and prioritization of cycle network improvement plans considering multiple planning objectives (criteria) and priorities of different stakeholders (e.g., bicyclists, non-bicyclists, investors, the public, transport planners, transport experts). According to Pardalos et al. (2000) (see also Zuo and Wei, 2019), MCDA techniques include three basic steps: (1) the determination of relevant alternatives and criteria, (2) the attachment of numerical measures to the relative importance of the criteria and to the impacts of the alternatives on these criteria, and (3) the calculation of the numerical values to determine the ranking of each alternative. Standardization and weighting of the diverse criteria is done based on mathematical methods such as the analytical hierarchy process or based on stakeholder surveys.

Within the literature on GIS-based MCDA approaches in cycle network planning, so-called suitability or preference maps are used in order to visualize spatially where cycle facilities are suitable or preferred from the stakeholders' individual or combined (weighted) perspective (Terh and Cao, 2018). This is done on different levels of detail, e.g., on the neighborhood level, grid cell level or cycle facility level. The maps can be compared with planned cycle networks. Rybarczyk and Wu (2010) highlight that for a comprehensive cycle network planning approach both supply- and demand-based criteria should be considered in order to account for potential dilemmas in bicycle network planning. For instance, local roads that have a good bicycle level of service (BLOS) on the supply side might have low potential on the demand side.

Table 4 gives an overview on GIS-based MCDA approaches for cycle network planning in relevant academic references. For each approach, we

Table 4 Literature overview of multi-criteria assessment approaches for cycle network planning.

Reference	Supply-side criteria	Demand-side criteria	Cycle network requirements not covered
Rybarczyk and Wu (2010)	Bicycle level of service (BLOS) based on traffic counts, heavy truck volumes, parking lane widths, number of vehicle lances, lane widths	Potential demand based on businesses, schools, recreation areas, parks, population, crime	Directness, attractiveness
Hsu and Lin (2011)	Traffic volumes, curb lane widths, sidewalk widths, speed limit, pavement quality, curb activity disturbance	–	Cohesion, directness, attractiveness, adaptability
Larsen et al. (2013)	Discontinuities in the cycle network, bicycle-vehicle collisions	Observed bicycle trips, potential bicycle (short car) trips, priority bicycle segments identified in cycling survey	Comfort, directness, attractiveness
Lowry et al. (2016)	Number of lanes, speed limit, types of cycle facility	Bicycling stress	Comfort, directness, connectivity
Guerreiro et al. (2018)	Network characteristics (e.g., network length, number of intersections, number of turns)	Criteria related to the exact survey-based geographical locations of real and potential users and trip generators (trip distance to/from network, OD coverage, population coverage etc.)	Safety, directness, attractiveness
Saplıoğlu and Aydın (2018)	Accident prone areas, bus lanes, road side car park, bicycle parks, road grade, signalization, traffic capacity, connected bike lanes, separated bike lanes	–	Cohesion (only interconnections with other modes), directness, attractiveness, adaptability
Terh and Cao (2018)	Slope, pedestrian traffic, distance from major roads	Proximity to potential destinations for short-distance trips or last-mile commute (education, retail, employment, community amenities, MRT/LRT stations, bus stops)	Comfort, directness, attractiveness, adaptability
Zuo and Wei (2019)	Goal: Increase bicycle connectivity and bicycle-transit connection with minimized impacts on motor vehicles and costs Performance criteria: fraction of bike-sharing stations connected to all possible destinations by cycle network, fraction of population with access to transit by cn, fraction of bike-sharing stations connected to transit by cn	Proportion of trips connected by the cycle network, automobile traffic delay, capital costs	Safety, comfort, directness, attractiveness, adaptability

highlight the applied supply- and demand-side assessment criteria. The criteria only partially cover all the above introduced six requirements for successful cycle networks. In general, within GIS-based MCDA approaches a set of pre-defined alternatives for cycle network improvements can be evaluated. Depending on the completeness and quality of these alternatives, the final recommendations might not be optimal from a network-wide planning perspective. Optimization-based approaches address this gap by developing optimal cycle networks in terms of pre-defined optimization criteria from scratch.

6.2 Optimization-based approaches

Designing networks for cars and public transport is associated with solving the problem of user equilibrium. According to Duthie and Unnikrishnan (2014), this is not necessary for cycle network planning, bicyclists can just be assigned to the "best" path because bicycle congestion is rarely a problem. Therefore, researchers have developed optimization-based approaches for cycle network planning that find these "best" paths using objective functions under constraints resulting in suggested locations of cycle facilities within the street network.

The previously presented MCDA approaches evaluate and rank a set of pre-determined alternatives for cycle network adjustments based on defined criteria. In comparison, optimization-based approaches consider the whole solution space of all alternatives and thus aim to deliver the globally optimal solution under the network perspective. The objective functions and constraints represent the trade-offs between different stakeholders (mostly bicyclists, car drivers, planners). As outlined above, bicyclists want to travel on safe, coherent, comfortable, direct and attractive paths that are adaptable for future demand. So far, all optimization-based approaches found in the literature only focus on a small subset of these requirements. None of the approaches incorporate more than three requirements. Most approaches consider the cohesion requirement. Few approaches also include the safety, comfort, directness or adaptability requirements. None of the approaches consider the attractiveness requirement. Compared to these user requirements, planners have to keep specific budget limits for cycle network improvements or do not want to deteriorate the situation for other modes. The budget constraint is included in almost all approaches. Most approaches use traditional data sources such as potential origins and destinations or OD matrices whereas a few approaches also use emerging data sources such as bike share trajectories or floating vehicle data in order to estimate potential demand. Table 5 gives an overview on optimization-based approaches

Table 5 Overview of optimization-based approaches for cycle network planning.

Reference	Objectives	Constraints	Cycle network requirements not covered	Data used
Mesbah et al. (2012)	Upper level (system optimum): maximize total travel distance on bicycle lanes, minimize car travel times Lower level: traffic assignment for bikes and cars with user-equilibrium hypotheses	Budget, cohesion	Safety, directness, comfort, attractiveness, adaptability	OD matrices (bicycle and car)
Smith (2011)	Minimize bicycle travel distance, maximize bicycle level of service	Budget, cohesion	Safety, directness, attractiveness, adaptability	OD matrix (bicycle)
Lin and Yu (2013)	Minimize safety risk, maximize comfort, maximize coverage, minimize traffic impacts	Budget, cohesion	Directness, attractiveness, adaptability	Potential bicycle origins and destinations (no traffic flows)
Duthie and Unnikrishnan (2014)	Minimize costs	Cohesion (including maximum accepted length), comfort (suitable level for biking for all OD path segments)	Safety, attractiveness, adaptability	Potential bicycle origins and destinations (no traffic flows)
Bao et al. (2017)	Maximize coverage, maximize continuity of road segments along routes	Budget, cohesion (max. k components)	Safety, directness, comfort, attractiveness, adaptability	Station-less bike share trajectory data (Mobike, Shanghai)
Mauttone et al. (2017)	Minimize bicycle travel cost (distance or time)	Budget, cohesion (addressed algorithmically in the solution method)	Safety, comfort, attractiveness, adaptability	OD matrix

Continued

Table 5 Overview of optimization-based approaches for cycle network planning.—cont'd

Reference	Objectives	Constraints	Cycle network requirements not covered	Data used
Akbarzadeh et al. (2018)	Minimize bicycle travel cost (distance or time), minimize network length	Coverage, cohesion (but not globally), adaptability (indirectly via detection of communities with more significant travel connections and optimal cycle networks connecting the key nodes with highest potential within each community)	Safety, comfort, attractiveness	Taxi trips in Isfahan city, Iran
Caggiani et al. (2019)	Minimize equity differences in bikeway accessibility (spatial, social) among different population groups, maximize cohesion	Budget	Safety, directness, comfort, attractiveness, adaptability	Share of disadvantaged individuals for each district
Liu et al. (2018)	Maximize coverage, maximize cohesion, minimize travel time (indirectly via utility function)	Budget	Safety, directness, comfort, attractiveness, adaptability	Station-less bike share trajectory data (Mobike, Shanghai)

for cycle network planning including objectives, constraints and data used. The table also indicates for each approach, which cycle network requirements were not covered.

Optimization-based approaches rarely involve stakeholder engagement and might therefore lead to suggested cycle networks that cannot be realized, for instance due to legal or structural limitations. Moreover, computational problems might occur. Akbarzadeh et al. (2018) de-composed the optimization problem into sub-problems within network communities to tackle these problems. For the budget constraints, more research is required for determining the cost functions and considering the substantial differences in infrastructure costs depending on local circumstances (Duthie and Unnikrishnan, 2014). In order to incorporate the adaptability constraint, potential (not yet realized) demand has to be included into the optimization models. Akbarzadeh et al. (2018) is the only reference that considers potential demand by finding optimal cycle networks that connect so-called key nodes with the highest rates of short-range trips <4km. Another option would be to weigh origins and destinations in the objective functions and constraints based on their potential for bicycle trips. Due to the budget constraints, the developed approaches should be supplemented by prioritization methods for individual parts of the cycle network in order to put improvements in the right order and to finally achieve the optimal target network.

6.3 Data-driven network growth strategies

Olmos et al. (2020) and Szell et al. (2021) recently opened up a third category of academic approaches for cycle network planning: data-driven growth strategies. Olmos et al. (2020) estimate potential bike demand based on trips that could be done by bicycle. These trips are filtered via a rejection-sampling algorithm from a phone-based overall OD matrix by a bicycle distance distribution emulated from a biking app in Bogotá. The authors apply percolation theory for identifying the minimal connected bike-path network that (1) covers the entire city and (2) is composed of the links with the highest bicycle flows. Their approach covers the cohesion and adaptability requirements of successful cycle networks.

Szell et al. (2021) develop a similar open-source approach based on points of interest for growing synthetic bicycle networks in arbitrary cities that could be used as initial visions of a cohesive bicycle network. The authors compare different growth strategies and conclude that the random strategy (which is often predominant in cycle network planning) needs at least three times the investments than the other strategies to reach the critical threshold for cohesion. Besides cohesion, no other cycle network requirements are considered.

7. Strengths and weaknesses of current methods for designing cycle networks

The overall goal of cycle network planning is to promote cycling as an attractive and safe mode of transport and as one core backbone of future sustainable transport systems. The different identified approaches in research and practice have strengths and weaknesses compared to this overall ambition. Clear goals are often missing; these might for example include modal split shares for cycling or other modes at city-level, for specific areas or person groups, hierarchies of transport modes, specific targets for each of the requirements or design standards. Optimization methods set targets and constraints that mainly focus on financial budgets and travel times. So far, they do not succeed in covering all requirements for cycle networks and ambitions in transport policy making comprehensively.

Proposed cycle networks rarely have a clear hierarchy. This is a shortcoming of increasing relevance seeing the growing variety of bicycle types and of further emerging micro vehicles and the related need for longer-distance bicycle highways in addition to "traditional cycle networks". No clear design standards are formulated for different levels of cycle network hierarchies and hardly any feedback loops are considered between cycle network development and street design including all street user groups and usages. CROW (2016) as the only exemption provides design standards for the two higher levels in the cycle network hierarchy, this is the main cycle network and the bicycle highways. For the lowest hierarchy level, the basic cycle network, no specific recommendations are provided besides that safe cycle facilities should be planned in each and every part of the overall street network. Together with the target for the main cycle network to carry about 70% of cycle traffic, this Dutch approach seems very suitable for integrating network development and street design for cycling and for making sure (with the help of the basic network) that appropriate cycle facilities are provided in each and every segment of a street network and not only in dedicated cycle networks.

Similar to the other references, CROW (2016) does also not explicitly address the intermodal perspective and does not account for the potential negative multimodal impacts when taking away space from other modes to build cycle facilities. Feedback loops in the guidance material would be needed to address this issue and scientific approaches for cycle network planning should also incorporate constraints or criteria that check for multimodal feasibility. The Network Robustness Index (NRI) developed by Burke and Scott (2016) could be used for this purpose.

The combination of guidelines and academic approaches holds a substantial potential for optimizing future cycle networks and for prioritizing investments into cycle facilities. Guidelines with their so far mainly supply-side approaches ensure that all relevant origins and destinations get systematically connected. Data-driven demand based academic approaches help to prioritize and to optimize. For example, origins and destinations might be prioritized based on current and future mode-specific demand in order to design cycle networks that exploit the full demand for cycling including also trips that are done today with other modes, to other destinations or not at all.

8. Development of an integrated multi-modal approach for network level planning for cycling

Based on the insights gained so far, we now develop an integrated multi-modal network and facility planning approach as shown in Fig. 1. Clear strategic goals are the basis for planning networks and facilities, further inputs include constraints, deficits in the existing street network and leverage points. Based on these inputs, mode-specific hierarchic street networks are developed for cycling but also for walking, public transport and further vehicular traffic in passenger and freight. These networks are developed with a combination of the approaches described in the guidelines and academic references. Guidelines come with a supply-side focus, cycle networks should mainly connect all relevant origins and destinations. Optimization approaches help to find the best routes for specific desire lines, to take decisions based on multi-criteria assessments and to prioritize investments. Data-driven results based on academic methods with a focus on demand and supply-side planning results complement each other. Their comparison and combination optimize the mode-specific target networks that are translated into mode-specific link functions enriched by mode-specific place functions.

Mode-specific network development should include all steps up to the selection of design elements for specific street sections. The selection of target facilities on the street level should also be supported by data-driven

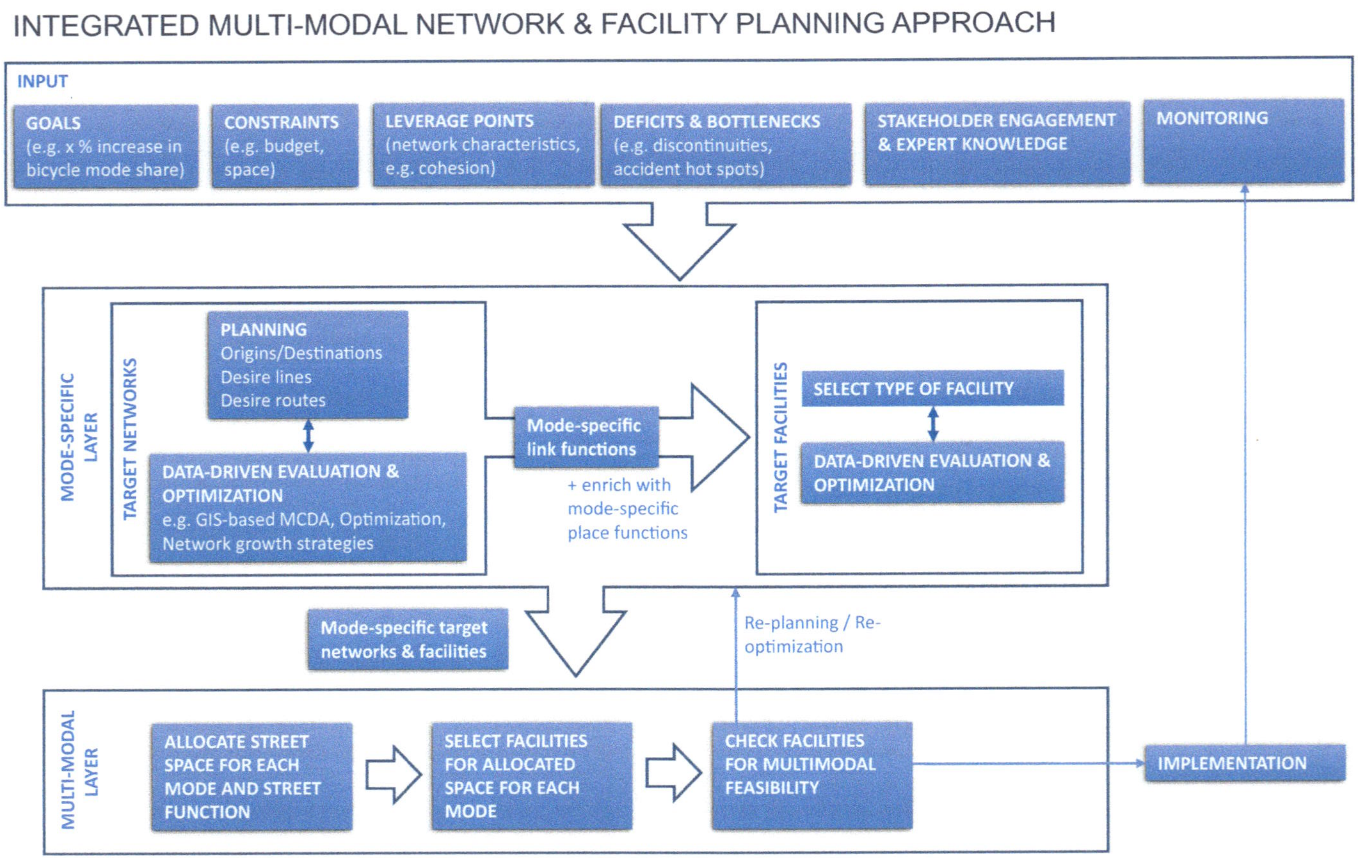

Fig. 1 Integrated multi-modal network and facility planning approach.

approaches. The superposition of the mode-specific solutions and possible re-planning or re-optimization are the next steps ensuring that developed mode-specific solutions are actually feasible within the available time and space. The finally chosen solutions then need to be implemented; analytic growth strategies might help to find sequences and priorities for investments. Monitoring is key for understanding the effects of the implemented measures but also of changes beyond, e.g., in user preferences or behavior, therefore it directly feeds into the next planning loop as one core input.

9. Conclusions

This chapter has provided an overview of existing approaches for cycle network planning in research and in practice. Various approaches were identified; their application in practice in many cities and regions worldwide is one driver of the advancements in cycling provision and promotion in recent years. Developing cycle networks based on desire lines and cycle routes connecting relevant origins and destinations as suggested by most guidelines is a suitable basis for cycle network design and requires the least resources and knowledge. It could be combined with data-driven demand-focused approaches in order to optimally adjust the cycle networks with user patterns and preferences. Optimization concepts and network growth strategies help to prioritize investments.

The main challenge that is hardly addressed in any of the identified references is the coordination of cycle network development with the other modes and street functions. We argue that successful cycle network planning can only be achieved in a multi-modal approach that is well coordinated with spatial planning, that jointly balances all street users' needs and that does not only optimize cycle networks on their own.

Future dynamics in the types, dimensions and characteristics of vehicles for bicycles, micro vehicles but also for all other possible vehicle types should get more attention, we recommend to add adaptability as a fixed sixth requirement for cycle network design to the existing ones, which are safety, cohesion, directness, comfort and attractiveness.

Whenever possible, cycle network planning should always be done "from scratch" and for the whole network, as if a new network was to be planned. Such an approach minimizes the risk to only remove local deficits in the cycle network, to overlook changes in behavior and demand and to inefficiently prioritize investments into cycle facilities. The integration of network planning for all modes and street functions is paramount for efficiently using the available resources, the same holds for the integration with further (transport) policy measures beyond cycle network development. Emerging data sources and increasingly pro-bike attitudes in all relevant stakeholder groups including travelers, policy makers and planners hold promise for increased opportunities for future cycle promotion and provision including cycle network development. The balance between what is theoretically possible thanks to novel data and data science methods on the one hand and what is accepted and feasible in practice on the other hand has to be found anew for each new planning task. The demonstration of efficiency gains thanks to systematic optimization approaches and growth-strategies can help to widen and to intensify their application.

References

Akbarzadeh, M., Mohri, S.S., Yazdian, E., 2018. Designing bike networks using the concept of network clusters. Appl. Netw. Sci. 3 (1), 12.

Alattar, M.A., Cottrill, C., Beecroft, M., 2021. Sources and applications of emerging active travel data: A review of the literature. Sustainability 13 (13), 7006.

ASTRA, 2008. Planning Cycling Routes [Online]. Bundesamt für Straßen. Available at https://www.newsd.admin.ch/newsd/message/attachments/11128.pdf. (Accessed 5 January 2022).

Bao, J., He, T., Ruan, S., Li, Y., Zheng, Y., 2017. Planning bike lanes based on sharing-bikes' trajectories. In: New York, NY. Proceedings of the 23rd ACM SIGKDD International Conference on Knowledge Discovery and Data Mining. Halifax, NS, Canada, 13.08.2017–17.08.2017. ACM, USA, pp. 1377–1386.

Broach, J., Dill, J., Gliebe, J., 2012. Where do cyclists ride? A route choice model developed with revealed preference GPS data. Transp. Res. A Policy Pract. 46 (10), 1730–1740.

Buehler, R., Dill, J., 2016. Bikeway networks: A review of effects on cycling. Transp. Rev. 36 (1), 9–27.

Burke, C.M., Scott, D.M., 2016. The space race: A framework to evaluate the potential travel-time impacts of reallocating road space to bicycle facilities. J. Transp. Geogr. 56, 110–119.

Caggiani, L., Camporeale, R., Binetti, M., Ottomanelli, M., 2019. An urban bikeway network design model for inclusive and equitable transport policies. Transp. Res. Proc. 37 (2), 59–66.

Carter, D.L., Hunter, W.W., Zegeer, C.V., Stewart, J.R., Huang, H., 2007. Bicyclist intersection safety index. Transp. Res Rec. J. Transp. Res. Board 2031 (1), 18–24.

Caulfield, B., 2014. Re-cycling a city—examining the growth of cycling in Dublin. Transp. Res. A Policy Pract. 61, 216–226.

CROW, 2016. Design Manual for Bicycle Traffic. Ede, Crow.

DfT, 2017. Local Cycling and Walking Infrastructure Plans: Technical Guidance for Local Authorities [Online]. Department for Transport, London. Available at https://www.gov.uk/government/publications/local-cycling-and-walking-infrastructure-plans-technical-guidance-and-tools. (Accessed 5 January 2022).

DfT, 2020. Cycle Infrastructure Design: Local Transport Note 1/20 [Online]. Department for Transport, London. https://www.gov.uk/government/publications/cycle-infrastructure-design-ltn-120. (Accessed 5 January 2022).

Duthie, J., Unnikrishnan, A., 2014. Optimization framework for bicycle network design. J. Transp. Eng. 140 (7), 4014028.
FGSV, 2008. Guidelines for Integrated Network Design (RIN) [Online]. Forschungsgesellschaft für Straßen- und Verkehrswesen, Cologne.
FGSV, 2010. Guidelines for Cycling Facilities (ERA) [Online]. Forschungsgesellschaft für Straßen- und Verkehrswesen, Cologne.
Francke, A., Lißner, S., 2017. Big Data in Bicycle Traffic [Online]. TU Dresden. Available at https://nbn-resolving.org/urn:nbn:de:bsz:14-qucosa-233278. (Accessed 5 January 2022).
FSV, 2014. RVS 03.02.13—Bicycle Traffic [Online]. Österreichische Forschungsgesellschaft Straße-Schiene-Verkehr, Vienna. Available at http://fsv.at/cms/default.aspx?ID=9815dd09-f5a8-41a8-9fb5-b1197ffb1cd2. (Accessed 5 January 2022).
Furth, P., 2021. Bicycling infrastructure for all. In: Buehler, R., Pucher, J. (Eds.), Cycling for Sustainable Cities [Online]. MIT Press, Cambridge, pp. 81–102. https://ebookcentral.proquest.com/lib/kxp/detail.action?docID=6454637.
Furth, P.G., Mekuria, M.C., Nixon, H., 2016. Network connectivity for low-stress bicycling. Transp. Res Rec. J. Transp. Res. Board 2587 (1), 41–49.
Geller, R., 2009. Four Types of Cyclists [Online]. Portland Bureau of Transportation, Portland, OR. Available at https://www.portlandoregon.gov/transportation/44597?a=237507. (Accessed 9 March 2022).
Gerike, R., Gerlach, J., Rau, A., 2011. Accessibility standards—discussion of their necessity with the example of the German 'guidelines for integrated network design' (RIN). In: Button, K.J., Reggiani, A. (Eds.), Transportation and economic development challenges [online]. Edward Elgar, Cheltenham, U.K, Northampton, Mass., USA, pp. 121–143. Available at http://www.elgaronline.com/view/9781849801676.xml.
Gerike, R., Dean, M., Koszowski, C., Schröter, B., Wittwer, R., Weber, J., Jones, P., 2019. Urban Corridor Road Design: Guides, Objectives and Performance Indicators: Deliverable D1.2, Multimodal Optimisation of Roadspace in Europe [Online]. Available at https://www.roadspace.eu. (Accessed 5 January 2022).
Godefrooij, T., Pardo, C., Sagaris, L., 2009. Cycling-Inclusive Policy Development: A Handbook [Online]. Available at https://bicycleinfrastructuremanuals.com/manuals4/Cycling-inclusive-Policy-Development-Handbook.pdf. (Accessed 5 January 2022).
Guerreiro, T.D.C.M., Kirner Providelo, J., Pitombo, C.S., Antonio Rodrigues Ramos, R., Rodrigues da Silva, A.N., 2018. Data-mining, GIS and multicriteria analysis in a comprehensive method for bicycle network planning and design. Int. J. Sustain. Transp. 12 (3), 179–191.
Highways England, 2021. CD 195—Designing for Cycle Traffic [Online]. Available at. https://www.standardsforhighways.co.uk/dmrb/search/4b59ebc3-065b-467f-8b43-09d2802f91c8. (Accessed 5 January 2022).
Hsu, T.P., Lin, Y.T., 2011. A model for planning a bicycle network with multi-criteria suitability evaluation using GIS. In: Management of Natural Resources, Sustainable Development and Ecological Hazards III, Malaysia, 13.12.2011–15.12.2011. WIT Press, Southampton, UK, pp. 243–252.
Jones, P., Marshall, S., Boujenko, N., 2008. Creating more people-friendly urban streets through "link and place" street planning and design. IATSS Res. 32 (1), 14–25.
Kerr, J., Emond, J.A., Badland, H., Reis, R., Sarmiento, O., Carlson, J., Sallis, J.F., Cerin, E., Cain, K., Conway, T., Schofield, G., Macfarlane, D.J., Christiansen, L.B., van Dyck, D., Davey, R., Aguinaga-Ontoso, I., Salvo, D., Sugiyama, T., Owen, N., Mitáš, J., Natarajan, L., 2016. Perceived neighborhood environmental attributes associated with walking and cycling for transport among adult residents of 17 cities in 12 countries: the IPEN study. Environ. Health Perspect. 124 (3), 290–298.

Koohsari, M.J., Cole, R., Oka, K., Shibata, A., Yasunaga, A., Hanibuchi, T., Owen, N., Sugiyama, T., 2020. Associations of built environment attributes with bicycle use for transport. Environ. Plan. B Urban Anal. City Sci. 47 (9), 1745–1757.
LaMondia, J.J., Moore, N., 2015. Using bicycle level of service for decision making' transportation research record. J. Transp. Res. Board 2520 (1), 123–131.
Larsen, J., Patterson, Z., El-Geneidy, A., 2013. Build it. But where? The use of geographic information systems in identifying locations for new cycling infrastructure. Int. J. Sustain. Transp. 7 (4), 299–317.
Lin, J.-J., Yu, C.-J., 2013. A bikeway network design model for urban areas. Transportation 40 (1), 45–68.
Liu, P., Marker, S., 2020. Evaluation of contributory factors' effects on bicycle-car crash risk at signalized intersections. J. Transp. Safe. Secur. 12 (1), 82–93.
Liu, S., Shen, Z.-J.M., Ji, X., 2018. Urban bike lane planning with bike trajectories: models, algorithms, and a real-world case study. SSRN Electron. J. 21 (3), 18.
Lowry, M.B., Furth, P., Hadden-Loh, T., 2016. Prioritizing new bicycle facilities to improve low-stress network connectivity. Transp. Res. A Policy Pract. 86 (10), 124–140.
Mauttone, A., Mercadante, G., Rabaza, M., Toledo, F., 2017. Bicycle network design: model and solution algorithm. Transp. Res. Proc. 27 (2), 969–976.
Mesbah, M., Thompson, R., Moridpour, S., 2012. Bilevel optimization approach to design of network of bike lanes. Transp. Res Rec. J. Transp. Res. Board 2284 (1), 21–28.
Mueller, N., Rojas-Rueda, D., Salmon, M., Martinez, D., Ambros, A., Brand, C., de Nazelle, A., Dons, E., Gaupp-Berghausen, M., Gerike, R., Götschi, T., Iacorossi, F., Int Panis, L., Kahlmeier, S., Raser, E., Nieuwenhuijsen, M., 2018. Health impact assessment of cycling network expansions in European cities. Prev. Med. 109, 62–70.
Nelson, T., Ferster, C., Laberee, K., Fuller, D., Winters, M., 2021. Crowdsourced data for bicycling research and practice. Transp. Rev. 41 (1), 97–114.
Nuñez, J., Teixeira, I., Silva, A., Zeile, P., Dekoninck, L., Botteldooren, D., 2018. The influence of noise, vibration, cycle paths, and period of day on stress experienced by cyclists. Sustainability 10 (7), 2379.
Olmos, L.E., Tadeo, M.S., Vlachogiannis, D., Alhasoun, F., Espinet Alegre, X., Ochoa, C., Targa, F., González, M.C., 2020. A data science framework for planning the growth of bicycle infrastructures. Transp. Res. C Emerg. Technol. 115, 102640.
Pardalos, P.M., Hearn, D., Triantaphyllou, E., 2000. Multi-Criteria Decision Making Methods: A Comparative Study. Springer US, Boston, MA.
Parkin, J. (Ed.), 2018a. Designing for Cycle Traffic: International Principles and Practice [Online]. ICE Virtual Library. Available at https://www.icevirtuallibrary.com/isbn/9780727763495. (Accessed 5 January 2022).
Parkin, J., 2018b. Planning for cycle traffic. In: Parkin, J. (Ed.), Designing for Cycle Traffic: International Principles and Practice [Online]. ICE Virtual Library, pp. 13–34. Available at https://www.icevirtuallibrary.com/isbn/9780727763495. (Accessed 5 January 2022).
Parkin, J., 2018c. Principles of design for cycle traffic'. In: Parkin, J. (Ed.), Designing for Cycle Traffic: International Principles and Practice [Online]. ICE Virtual Library, pp. 35–62. Available at https://www.icevirtuallibrary.com/isbn/9780727763495. (Accessed 5 January 2022).
Plumed, M.F., Ramírez, F.C., Ochando, C.L., 2016. Cycling Network Projects: A Decision-Making Aid Approach: CEUR Workshop Proceedings [Online]. Available at. http://hdl.handle.net/10251/87734. (Accessed 5 January 2022).
Reynolds, C.C.O., Harris, M.A., Teschke, K., Cripton, P.A., Winters, M., 2009. The impact of transportation infrastructure on bicycling injuries and crashes: a review of the literature. Environ. Health Glob. Access Sci. Sour. 8, 47.
Rybarczyk, G., Wu, C., 2010. Bicycle facility planning using GIS and multi-criteria decision analysis. Appl. Geogr. 30 (2), 282–293.

Saplıoğlu, M., Aydın, M.M., 2018. Choosing safe and suitable bicycle routes to integrate cycling and public transport systems. J. Transp. Health 10 (5), 236–252.
Schepers, P., Heinen, E., Methorst, R. and Wegman, F. (2013) 'Road safety and bicycle usage impacts of unbundling vehicular and cycle traffic in Dutch urban networks [Online]', Eur. J. Transp. Infrastruct. Res. (EJTIR), vol. 13, no. 3, pp. 221–238 doi:10.18757/ejtir.2013.13.3.3000 (Accessed January 5, 2022).
Schoner, J.E., Levinson, D.M., 2014. The missing link: bicycle infrastructure networks and ridership in 74 US cities. Transportation 41 (6), 1187–1204.
Smith, H., 2011. A Mathematical Optimization Model for a Bicycle Network Design Considering Bicycle Level of Service: PhD thesis [Online]. University of Maryland. Available at http://hdl.handle.net/1903/14759. (Accessed 5 January 2022).
Sustrans, 2014. Handbook for Cycle-Friendly Design [Online], Bristol. Available at. https://www.essexdesignguide.co.uk/media/1790/sustrans_handbook_for_cycle-friendly_design_11_04_14.pdf. (Accessed January 5, 2022).
Szell, M., Mimar, S., Perlman, T., Ghoshal, G., Sinatra, R., 2021. Growing Urban Bicycle Networks [Online]. Available at. http://arxiv.org/pdf/2107.02185v2. (Accessed 5 January 2022).
Terh, S.H., Cao, K., 2018. GIS-MCDA based cycling paths planning: a case study in Singapore. Appl. Geogr. 94 (1), 107–118.
TfL, 2016. London Cycling Design Standards [Online]. Transport for London. Available at https://tfl.gov.uk/corporate/publications-and-reports/streets-toolkit. (Accessed 5 January 2022).
Thomas, B., DeRobertis, M., 2013. The safety of urban cycle tracks: a review of the literature. Accid. Anal. Prev. 52, 219–227.
Thust, M., Franceschina, L., 2020. Modal OD matrices derived from mobile network data. In: European Transport Conference 2020 [Online]. Available at https://trid.trb.org/view/1770202. (Accessed 5 January 2022).
Titze, S., Stronegger, W.J., Janschitz, S., Oja, P., 2008. Association of built-environment, social-environment and personal factors with bicycling as a mode of transportation among Austrian city dwellers. Prev. Med. 47 (3), 252–259.
Willberg, E., Tenkanen, H., Poom, A., Salonen, M., Toivonen, T., 2021. Comparing spatial data sources for cycling studies: a review. In: Mladenović, M.N., Toivonen, T., Willberg, E., Geurs, K.T. (Eds.), Transport in Human Scale Cities [Online]. Edward Elgar Publishing, Northampton, pp. 169–187. Available at https://www.elgaronline.com/view/edcoll/9781800370500/9781800370500.xml. (Accessed 5 January 2022).
Winters, M., Teschke, K., Grant, M., Setton, E.M., Brauer, M., 2010. How far out of the way will we travel? Transp. Res Rec. J. Transp. Res. Board 2190 (1), 1–10.
Zuo, T., Wei, H., 2019. Bikeway prioritization to increase bicycle network connectivity and bicycle-transit connection: a multi-criteria decision analysis approach. Transp. Res. A Policy Pract. 129 (2), 52–71.

CHAPTER SIX

Tools and processes for practitioners

John Parkin*
University of the West of England, Bristol, United Kingdom
*Corresponding author: e-mail address: john.parkin@uwe.ac.uk

Contents

Abstract

The purpose of this chapter is to discuss guidance and tools for decision-making and planning. The discussion starts with methods to assess policy, strategy and program level development. This is followed by the technical processes that include mode and route choice modeling that feed into network planning. Design and operational appraisal tools are then considered and they include visualization tools, the modeling of interactions and the operation of the network. As part of a discussion of scheme appraisal, the important topic of the evaluation of health benefits is considered,

Advances in Transport Policy and Planning, Volume 10
ISSN 2543-0009
https://doi.org/10.1016/bs.atpp.2022.04.006

after which there is a discussion of the generic cost-benefit analysis and multicriteria analysis methodologies. Level of service assessment and auditing is considered before finally turning to monitoring and evaluation.

Keywords: Planning, Design, Operational appraisal, Scheme appraisal, Auditing, Evaluation

1. Introduction

Transport planning practitioners create and prosecute policy, plans, and programs. They are involved in the development of schemes and projects, including the assessment of need (demand), the shape of proposals (e.g., networks), and their appraisal and design. These activities include auditing for level of service and safety, and monitoring and evaluation.

Extensive listings of tools exist, and perhaps the most extensive is the CIVITAS Urban Mobility Tool Inventory (CIVITAS, 2021), an on-line database of over 200 "guidelines, software, manuals, mobile apps, games, and planning approaches, ... from scenario building and measure selection to implementation and evaluation." Seventy-four of those tools relate to cycling.

The following sections summarize tools under the following headings: Section 2, Policy, strategy and program level plan development; Section 3, Modeling and network planning; Section 4, Design and operational appraisal; Section 5, Scheme appraisal; Section 6, Level of service assessment and auditing; Section 7, Monitoring and evaluation. This order broadly follows the order of first planning a scheme, with then the monitoring and evaluation occurring post-implementation. Finally, a summarizing conclusion is presented.

2. Policy, strategy and program level development

A transport policy will usually communicate a political idea (or vision, or aims, or ambition) about the future of transport, identify problems to be solved, define outcomes and impacts in broad terms, and outline general principles to be applied. A strategy is the next level of detail and will apply that political idea, define more detailed principles and objectives, and broad programs of activity. It may also define levels of investment, and targets for outcomes and impacts. A program level plan will detail budgets and the outputs from that investment, and the timing within the program of individual projects at different locations.

Strategies and plans will focus on responsibilities, resources and actions to deliver them, including institutional arrangements and funding. The time period for a policy and strategy is usually longer than for a plan. Building infrastructure and changing people's travel behavior can be a lengthy process, so this allows enough time for change.

More general transport policies, strategies and plans may omit, or merely pay lip-service, to cycling (and walking). This may be because the general plan is at a regional level, whereas cycling is seen as a local transport issue. However, cycling needs to be considered in all transport policy, strategy and plans for several reasons. Cycling needs to claim funding from general transport budgets, acts as a feeder mode for public transport, and is not just local, especially with the advent of e-cycles. It contributes to climate change policies and health and wellbeing.

Specifically in relation to low resource countries, but with worldwide application, the World Cycling Alliance and the European Cyclist Federation (European Cyclists' Federation, 2017) suggest the Sustainable Development Goals are a sound basis for developing, and measuring actions relating to cycling.

The *Bicycle Policy Audit tool* (BYPAD, 2021) tool was developed as part of a European Union funded project to evaluate cycling policy quality by assessing strengths and weaknesses. BYPAD is a self-evaluation method that brings together the assessments of politicians, administrators and users. The focus of the method is to set up a structured communication to improve cycling policy. The process develops an action plan with recommendations for improvement. The so-called quality chain comprizes of nine domains grouped in three ways:

- user needs, leadership and co-ordination, policy on paper, means and personnel;
- infrastructure and safety, information and education, promotion and partnerships, complementary actions; and
- evaluation and effects.

The process has been applied in nearly 250 cities, regions and towns in 25 countries. The processes are comprehensive, but time consuming to carry out, the need to undertake such an audit must be perceived as being core to policy development, otherwise it is unlikely that a planning authority will engage in such a process.

The Dutch "Cycle balance" or *Fietsbalans project* (Broer, 2008) surveyed municipalities using an instrumented bicycle to determine features relevant to the comfort and attractiveness of cycling. Data connected with the propensity to cycle (e.g., socio-demographics) and policy and policy satisfaction of the population were also collected. These data are used at the strategic level to determine the municipal wide level of service offered to cycling. This sort of discrete, well executed project, in this case carried out by cycle advocacy organizations, is the sort of approach that should form a core part of transport planning for cycle traffic. Its value is in linking data and an evaluation of policies which may positively influence trajectories in that data (e.g., mode share).

The *Place Based Carbon Calculator* (PBCC, 2021) estimates the per capita carbon footprint at the level of the Lower Super Output Area (a geographic area for reporting statistics and with populations of 1500 to 3000 in England). The tool is designed to provide easily understandable comparative data on the mass of emissions of carbon dioxide equivalent per person per year, disaggregated to include estimates for car and van driving. It is accessed via an interactive map and allows policy makers and communities to understand the scale of the issue. Several community groups have used the tool to formulate plans and advocate for local change. Transport authorities are using the models ability to produce lines of equal travel time from an origin and the tool it being developed to estimate whole life carbon emissions of proposed transport infrastructure. As, finally, the issue of carbon emissions appear to be taken more seriously in transport planning, such a tool will be valuable in understanding the current aggregate transport carbon emissions by presenting quantitative data usable as a basis for planning (and see the HEAT and IHTIM tool later for appraisal).

3. Modeling and network planning

Mode and route choice modeling may be undertaken with either aggregate or disaggregate models. Typically, such modeling for cycle traffic is not undertaken in practice, and simplified methods of creating desire lines and route assignments for network planning are adopted. This section considered mode and then route choice modeling, which are further expanded on in chapter "Innovations in data collection and research methods" by Griffin. The final section describes some common methods for network planning.

3.1 Mode choice

Aggregate models estimate the contribution to mode choice of transport system, geographic and socio-economic variables. They remain popular (for example, Wang et al., 2020), and exploit available sources of revealed preference secondary data, but the challenge is to demonstrate that a significant correlation represents a causal mechanism.

Disaggregate modeling (at the level of the individual traveler) can explain choice in terms of socio-economic and household characteristics; trip characteristics; built environment; natural environment; and cycling facilities (Muñoz et al., 2016). In addition, subjective variables can be modeled including perceptual indicators of environmental and cycling facilities (e.g., hilliness or risk) and psychological indicators including satisfaction, perceptions of comfort, convenience, social norms, perceived controls on behavior (i.e., physical constraints on being able to cycle), habit, experiences, and preferences.

Instead of the full complexity of using a modeling approach, it may often be the case in practice that simplified methods of assessing demand for cycling scheme proposals are adopted. One common method is the use of diversion factors (or abstraction rates). These may be determined from surveys of cyclists on new schemes for future use. At the other extreme, it may be that cycling is fully accounted for in the strategic model for a city. An example is Budapest, which has modeled its cycle share scheme within a strategic transport demand model (FLOW, 2017). In passing, it should be noted that the design of such cycle hire schemes in low resource countries may serve different markets and need to be established in different ways than in developed countries (ITDP, 2013).

3.2 Route choice

Route choice modeling for motor vehicles is a mature discipline. Demand is defined by a matrix of origin and destination pairs and routing across the network is estimated by accounting for the capacity of a route which varies as a result of the volume of traffic it carries. Wardrop (1952) was the first to consider criteria for distributing traffic across alternative routes and suggested two different optima: (1) User Equilibrium, "no driver can reduce his (sic) journey time by choosing a new route" (p. 345); and (2) System equilibrium, the average journey time across the network is a minimum. The choice in assignment models is based on the cost made up of time-based costs estimated using a value of time, and vehicle operating costs.

Cycle traffic routing usually takes account of factors linked with the comfort and attractiveness of a route, and the inverse of those, the perception of risk. A number of studies of route choice have been undertaken and many revealed preference studies are usefully summarized by Pritchard (2018). The majority of studies use GPS data, with re-call-based studies being the next most prevalent. Other recent studies include children's route choice (Dessing et al., 2016), and qualitative approaches to understanding route choice (Desjardins et al., 2021). Factors relevant in route choice include distance and directness, number of intersections (and their type of priority or control and the type and number of the turns), degree of protection from motor traffic on links, route signing, hilliness, attractiveness and quality of the route.

While researchers have developed a high level of understanding on route choice criteria, none have been converted into validated route choice models for planning purposes. Advocacy groups have web-based tools to allow the population to plan cycling journeys based on algorithms roughly based on routes that are either being a fast route, a quiet route or a balanced route (e.g., Cycle Streets, 2021), and these are embedded in planning tools discussed in the following section.

3.3 Accessibility and network planning

The methods described in this section are confined to tools specifically for accessibility and network planning according to a range of attributes relevant to creating comfortable and attractive cycle networks. Many further tools are more targeted to assessing the nature of the design features of routes and these are dealt with in Section 6.

Braess et al. (2005) demonstrated that adding a link to a congested network could increase overall journey time in a network, and this has become known as Braess's paradox. The implied corollary is that traffic speeds can be increased when links are removed. Motivated by Braess, Bagloee et al. (2016) investigated the use of what they called "latent misutilized capacity" in the highway network to offer as exclusive space for cycle traffic. They found that the conversion to cycle tracks of 30 road lengths totaling 2.77 km would enhance the capacity of the road network. This finding is challenging from the point of view that such a conversion would potentially make driving relatively still more attractive than riding.

Similarly focussed as much on the network as the demand, is the open source Propensity to Cycle Tool which has been developed over a number of years (Woodcock et al., 2021). Using census data, demand for cycle commutes in England and Wales are estimated based on distance to work, hilliness, age, gender, ethnicity, car ownership and area level deprivation. The assignment of the demand to routes uses an open-streets network based cycle planning tool (Cycle Streets, 2021). However, the tool is used by practitioners to inform network development at area and route level. For example, the Hereford Case Study (Propensity to cycle tool, 2021) shows how the tool identifies cycle desire lines (crow-fly lines between origins and destinations) and the level of flow on routes that would be used by all origin-destination pairs aggregated together. This allows for the routes that will be in most demand to be identified for improvement and investment. In a similar fashion Zuidgeest and Brussel (2012) report a model for Pune in India which shows the change in accessibility a result of a proposed cycle network for access to employment and educational.

An extension to the Propensity to Cycle Tool, the Cycling Infrastructure Prioritization Toolkit (CyIPT, 2018) considers existing road types and motor traffic flows and speeds limits to suggest appropriate types of cycle infrastructure. It then aggregates individual route recommendations to create programs of work, estimate construction costs and benefits, and hence value for money.

The Department for Transport (2017) Local Cycling and Walking Infrastructure Plan technical guidance provides planners with a five-step process to follow to plan cycle networks. The key, third, step of network planning is split into the three phases of estimating cycle trip generation, determining desire lines and assigning that demand to routes. The Propensity to Cycle Tool is the core method identified for this purpose. The desire lines are needed to assist in identifying missing links in a current network of routes, i.e., where the current route adds significant distance as compared with the desire line.

Decisions about when and how to separate routes for cycle traffic from the carriageway are made using a Route Selection Tool which scores current and possible future improved routes for the following attributes: directness, gradient, safety, connectivity and comfort. The scoring is automated based on data lying within predetermined range, but neither the ranges, the scoring nor the weightings used in aggregation are built on any validated measures linked to route choice. The tools value is in its ability to make broad comparisons both between a route before and after intervention, and between different options for improvement. Si milar and related approaches are prescribed in the Welsh Government (2021) Design Guidance Active Travel (Wales) Act 2013.

4. Design and operational appraisal

Once a network has been planned, a route, and individual junctions along that route, will need to be designed to handle the volumes of cycle traffic that are estimated. This section deals with these types of tools, which include visualization tools, and tools for understanding the interactions between different types of user.

4.1 Visualization tools

The following summarize one physical and two virtual street visualization tools.

- The Canadian Complete Streets Game (Centre for active transportation, 2019) has images of different parts of a street cross-section on 110 magnetic pieces which can be used with professionals and communities to collaboratively re-imagine streets, help visualize opportunities and options, and build consensus. Images include true to scale representations of bike lanes, sidewalks, bus lanes, vehicular travel lanes, trees, and benches.
- Streetplan (n.d.) is an on-line drag and drop tool for visualizing streets. It provides the user with a red / amber /green rating of the completed design relative to American standards and it has compliant templates as a starting point.
- Streetmix (n.d.) is an open source on-line international resource emanating from the United States which allows streets to be designed visually. Updates and expansion to new territories and languages take place on a continuous basis.

The value of such tools is to generate ideas and consensus, but the tools' value will be limited beyond the point where the design needs to be confirmed to a buildable level of detail within existing urban constraints, and these will likely vary along a route.

4.2 Modeling interactions and operation

The operational appraisal of junctions has typically been undertaken only with motor traffic in mind. Analyses have been focussed on assessing the operation of the junction to minimize delay and maximize capacity. Little consideration has been given to the delay caused to cycle traffic either within the carriageway, or on cycleways (or pedestrian routes) intersecting with the junction.

Increasingly, consideration has been given to appropriate design for junctions and crossings to properly accommodate cycle traffic. Many of the developments in junction design have used the principles that are evident in design in North European countries, particularly, the Netherlands (CROW, 2017). In low resource countries, the guidance provided by IDTP (2011) may be more relevant. These enhanced designs result in a need for designers to be able to understand the operations of the junction, particularly in relation to interactions between different users and types of user. As a result of the focus being less on assessing capacity and more on interactions, modeling approaches that focus on individual users and the way they interact are of the greatest value.

Microsimulation-based models have been used extensively in assessing motor traffic at junctions. They have the advantage that they are also able to be used as route choice models. There are a number of proprietary pieces of software including, for example, PTV Vissim, Caliper Transmodeler, Sumo, TSS Aimsun, and Paramics. Being based in motor traffic modeling, the default methodology has been based on the car following model (Wiedemann, 1991). A number of parameters including desired driving speed, the time gap to a preceding vehicle when a driver slows, following distance, and braking characteristics are variables which are stochastically adjusted to mimic natural variance in driver behavior.

Again, there are developments being made in research in relation to microsimulation modeling (see chapter "Innovations in data collection and research methods" by Griffin, and usefully reviewed by Twaddle et al., 2014). There are also many developments in relation to cellular automata modeling and the use of the Social Force Model (Helbing and Molnar, 1995).

There are many working in practice who are now modeling cycling using microsimulation. As an example, and as part of the European Union project FLOW (FLOW, 2017), Gdynia in Poland has extended its microsimulation model to include pedestrian and cycle traffic to assess the beneficial impact of walking and cycling on congestion reduction.

5. Scheme appraisal

Appraisal comprises of the processes leading to a decision about whether to built a scheme or not. Schemes will commonly use national or local funding and as a result it is usually governments and authorities which define appraisal processes. Hence, they are country specific.

Typically, these will involve measuring the scheme against the objectives through a process of estimating its benefits (to users and the economy and society more generally) and comparing them to its disbenefits. Processes broadly fall into three categories: Cost-Benefit Analysis (CBA), Multi-Criteria Analysis (MCA), and more specifically Environmental Impact Assessment (EIA) and Health Impact Assessment (for a full discussion see Mouter, 2020). Methods associated with and sometimes supporting CBA include Balance Sheet Calculations (BSC) and Cost-Effectiveness Analysis (CEA, Ruffino and Jarre, 2020). The health impacts of cycling are important, and specific tools have been developed to analyze these.

This section first considers tools that specialize in appraising health impacts. This is followed by a discussion of CBA (and its associated methods of BSC and CEA) and then MCA. Environmental impacts are considered within these latter two sections.

5.1 Health impact appraisal

Modern western lifestyles are predominantly sedentary and many people do not undertake enough physical activity. Cycling is a way of being active as part of everyday life. As a consequence, and at a population level, the benefits to health of the physical activity of cycling are considerable. The link between physical activity and health, including impacts on non-communicable diseases such as diabetes, depression and cancers, is well established (De Nazelle et al., 2011).

The World Health Organisation (2021) has developed a *Health Economic Assessment Tool (HEAT)*, now in its fifth version and with extended applicability worldwide. The tool estimates habitual behavior amongst adults at the population level, but is not suitable for populations with already very high average levels of walking or cycling. The impacts on health of physical activity, traffic injury, and air quality are estimated, although impacts resulting from changed air quality cannot be made in locations with very high levels of air pollution. Typically, the tool would be used to compare a current with a future proposed scenario. Inputs include estimates of the change in the number of people regularly cycling as the result of a scheme, and all-cause mortality. The tool estimates the health and carbon impacts and the order of magnitude of monetary value of the benefit based on a willingness to pay to secure a marginal reduction in the risk of premature death.

The *Integrated Transport and Health Impact Modeling tool* (ITHIM, 2021) combines estimated weekly mean travel times undertaking physical active travel with the Metabolic Equivalent of Task (MET, the ratio of a person's energy expenditure for a task relative to their mass). Injury, exposure to air pollution and physical activity changes are combined to estimate a health benefit in disability-adjusted life-years (DALY) and number of deaths attributable to the activity.

Interestingly, it is the benefit of a "healthy" modes that is appraised in analyses such as these, rather than the negative effects on health of a sedentary lifestyle. Arguably, analyses that focus on the disbenefits of, for example, driving, should be undertaken and they would demonstrate significant negative impacts on health at the population level. It would then be for policy makers to generate a wide range of interventions, which may include driver time charging (as opposed to road use charging) as well as active travel and other interventions, to reduce car travel and hence reduce these disbenefits. It is thought-provoking to wonder how an inversion in appraisal practice may influence policy.

5.2 Cost-benefit analysis

Balance Sheet Calculations, or Financial Cost-Benefit Analysis, is a limited form of appraisal which considers the only financial costs and returns. There needs to be some form of user payment for this approach to be adopted, which may be relevant for bicycle sharing schemes and bicycle parking (Ruffino and Jarre, 2020). The analysis will determine whether the income covers the set-up and running costs of the life of the scheme. It may form a part of a wider CBA which would include the user payments when assessing wider user benefits (e.g., health benefits) and non-user benefits (e.g., reduction in car use).

Cost-benefit analysis compares a proposed scheme with a scenario where nothing is done (do-nothing) or a scenario where some minimum necessary intervention is going to have to be carried out to solve a particular issue (do-minimum). The cause of any change in benefit is a changed pattern of travel. This changed pattern of use includes people switching from other modes to cycling thereby creating benefits for themselves, the environment and non-users. It will also include benefits to people already cycling, for example, in terms of reduced collision risk. The core requirement is to convert every benefit into a monetary value. The benefits over the life of the scheme are then discounted to a base year, as are the costs. The net (benefits minus costs) present (i.e., at the assumed base year) monetary value (Net Present Value) of the scheme can then be estimated. This may be expressed as a ratio of the benefit to the cost (BCR). Table 1 summarizes the typical sources of benefit and comments on the monetization of these benefits (Department for Transport, 2020a).

Similar listings of impacts are used in the Dutch (Decisio, 2017) and the Danish (COWI and City of Copenhagen, 2008) approaches to appraisal. The Department for Transport (2020b) has developed a tool to assist appraisers in assessing the CBA of cycling schemes to account for the impacts noted in Table 1. Inputs include the number of cycle trips for the do-nothing or do-minimum and for the proposed scheme.

Cost effectiveness analysis is used to investigate the ratio between costs and some specific measure of interest. For example, this could be the

Table 1 Impacts of cycling interventions and their monetization.

Impact	Monetization method
Noise	Valuation of Number of Disability-Adjusted Life Years (DALYs) lost (or gained) based on assessment to the population effected and the level of change in noise
Local Air Quality	Options include abatement cost approach, damage cost approach, impact pathways approach (identifying number of receptors affected), with different valuations used depending on whether mean limit threshold limits are exceeded
Greenhouse Gases	Abatement costs per ton of carbon dioxide equivalent applied to the change in emissions based on estimates of change in energy consumption
Journey Quality	Valuations of different types of comfort and attractiveness of routes
Physical Activity	Through use of the HEAT tool or equivalent
Traffic Injuries	Willingness to pay to avoid pain, grief and suffering, loss of economic output due to injury, and medical costs estimated for a changed number of fatalities, serious injuries and slight injuries
Economic efficiency for users	Valuation of time used to estimate benefits from reduced journey times on quicker routes
Economic efficiency for non-users	Decongestion benefits (journey time, infrastructure, accident, local air quality, noise, greenhouse gas, and indirect taxation changes) to those who remain motor vehicle users

accessibility change as a result of a cycling network (Ruffino and Jarre, 2019). The approach may also be used assist with sensitivity testing of options against subcriteria within the wider framework of CBA.

5.3 Multicriteria analysis

Multicriteria analysis can include quantitative and qualitative indicators of impact, and therefore this approach presents a wider range of impact factors within the framework of an appraisal than is possible by using solely impacts to which monetary values can be associated. The challenge relates to how the different non-commensurable factors are weighted in an analysis. The methodology may suffer from assessor subjectivity in defining both the level of the impacts and the way in which they are combined. To overcome potential biases, Macharis and Bernardini (2015) urge that weightings should be decided by a wide group of stakeholders. A case can be made for decisions being made without the use of weightings based on the strong logic of an argument.

Wider impacts include impacts on landscape, townscape, the historic environment, biodiversity, water environment, personal security, and severance, and accessibility. Consideration may also be given to the distribution of the social and monetary impacts across different groups in society.

The European Union FLOW project (FLOW, 2017) developed a multicriteria Congestion Assessment Tool which assesses together the quantitative benefits of congestion reduction from cycling interventions and the wider environmental social and economic benefits. The Impacts of Cycling Tool (ICT, Woodcock et al., 2018) visualizes for the user the impacts of different levels of uptake of cycling at the level of England, or the regions of England, in terms of change in journey time, miles cycled, proportion of the population that meets WHO physical activity guidelines and reduction in life years lost, car miles driven and carbon emissions.

6. Level of service assessment and auditing

Assessments and audits may be used to determine the fitness-for-purpose, quality and safety of existing infrastructure to determine whether improvements need to be made. They may also be used as part of the process of planning and designing schemes with the audit process sometimes occurring more than once during design development. For example, safety auditing may take place at the preliminary and detail stages of design development and pre-opening (National Highways, 2020).

Whether they use quantitative data or qualitative data, audits should be reliable and valid. However, as Parkin (2018) has pointed out, there are many cycling related audit methodologies that are not validated against, for example, user perception data, and rely to a great or lesser extent solely on the judgment of the person carrying out the audit. This section considers level of service assessment in Section 6.1, street and route auditing in Section 6.2 and, safety auditing in Section 6.3.

6.1 Level of service auditing

The concept of level of service is borrowed from analysis of traffic flow where its use was limited to considerations relating to the level of free-flow of a motor traffic stream. The concept has been expanded for cycle traffic to include features of the environment and geometry which affect the cyclist, as summarized below:

- Motor traffic: flow, composition by vehicle type and speed
- Carriageway features: number of lanes and their width, presence of a median island, presence of parking, traffic calming features
- Separation: whether cyclists are separated from motor traffic, and the degree and type of separation (e.g., kerb separation)
- Geometry: width, gradient, sight lines
- Other features: frontage activity and land use intensity, presence of driveways, bus stops and bus lanes, lighting, direction signing, presence of green space

Table 2 summarizes some of these models.

The only models operationalized for use by practitioners are the models from the United States and Australia. Dependent variables are variously based on stated preferences or scores from cyclists and would-be cyclists who have either ridden the route for which objective measurements have been taken, or been shown video of the route.

Most models deal predominantly with conditions on sections of route between junctions, while some deal explicitly with junctions. Where a model deals only with junctions, consideration is given to the scale of conflicting flows, the form of the junction (priority, roundabout or signal control) and its geometry. Some models (Parkin et al., 2007 and the USA Level of Stress model) provide a measure for whole route, while most models create a score for individual links or junctions. Pritchard et al. (2019) summarizes these and other models in more detail and tests some of them against student route choice in Trondheim.

Table 2 Summary of level of service assessment methods.

Country	References	Name and description
UK	Guthrie et al. (2001)	Cyclability Index of individual rural road segments
UK	Parkin et al. (2007)	Risk and route acceptability covering a route including links and junctions
Australia	Munro (2013)	Level of service based on stated preference with an added focus on routes shared with pedestrians
USA	Transportation Research Board (2016)	Level of service (build on a long stream of work, including Sprinkle Consulting (2007) and Landis et al. (1997)
USA	Mekuria et al. (2012)	Level of traffic stress across networks (For a link to a web-based tool, see Alta Planning, 2017)
Denmark	Jensen (2007) and Jensen (2013)	Level of service for junctions and (separately) links
India	Beura et al. (2018)	Level of service

The Cycle Level of Service tool recommended in the United Kingdom (Department for Transport, 2017) for route improvement considers the Dutch design principles of directness, safety, connectivity and comfort and gradient. The assessor inputs a range of measured (ratio) data and each attribute is then allocated an (ordinal) score from 1 to 5. Results for each attribute for both the current situation and a design solution are compared on a spider diagram. The (unvalidated) scores for the input data bear no relation to potential cyclists' perceptions, but the method provides a way of approximately estimating the level of improvement and can be used to compare different levels of improvement.

6.2 Street and route audits

Audit tools may be used on existing streets to understand their fitness for purpose and also during design development of new streets and street adaptations. Table 3 summarizes USA and UK audit tools.

The audit process may collect a range of both qualitative and quantitative data. However, the main feature of such tools, especially in relation to design, is that they rely for their use on an auditor who is experienced and can form judgments which integrate findings from data collection as part

Table 3 Audit tools.

Name	Country	References	Comment
Systematic Pedestrian and Cycling Environmental Scan (SPACES) Instrument	USA	Pikora (n.d.)	The SPACES instrument measures the physical environmental factors that influence walking and cycling in local neighborhoods. The instrument is used in combination with additional tools based on Geographical Information Systems (GIS)
Quality audit	UK	Department for Transport (2011)	Used in the street design process to achieve balance between place and movement functions, enable access for all users; cater for through movement, ensure quality of the public realm, meet local needs, ensure safety and security, consider quality of appearance, durability and maintenance requirements
Healthy street audit	UK	Transport for London (2017)	Indicators of a healthy street are pedestrians from all walks of life; people choosing to walk, cycle and use public transport; clean air; people feeling safe; quiet environment, easy to cross the carriageway, places available to stop and rest, provision of shade and shelter, people feeling relaxed, and availability of things to see and do
New cycling route quality criteria	UK	*Transport for London* (2019)	Consideration given to the following: degree of separation from motor traffic, speed of motor traffic, appropriate width provided, collision risk minimized, minimal kerbside activity, minimal interaction with heavy goods vehicles

of an audit process. A major potential disadvantage of some more prescriptive audit processes is that they may become a "tick box exercise." This can be avoided if the methodology is one of asking open questions and providing prompt notes to the auditor.

Audits tools will also generally need to be country, state or city specific as a result of different regulatory, design and environmental factors. Tools may or may not be validated against, for example, user perceptions. Data may be collected from audits within the street, virtually using Google Streetview or using secondary data (Pliakas et al., 2017).

6.3 Safety auditing

Safety auditing may be undertaken on exiting routes with a view to introducing remedial measures to counter any identified risk issues. These approaches may be termed collision investigations (Chartered Institution of Highways and Transportation, 2007). Such auditing may be for more general purposes linked with the initial stages of the development of proposals for new routes, or changes to existing routes.

It is recognized that the collision record typically underestimates the numbers of collisions, and therefore injuries to cyclists. This is especially the case where the injury may have been sustained where no other vehicle was involved. Data beyond what is available in the official record may often therefore need to be supplemented with additional sources of data, and interpretations of the environment which can lead to heightened risk.

Such additional data collection may include the collection of so-called near-miss data from participants in surveys which can reveal locations and types of risk (Aldred, 2016; Aldred and Crosweller, 2015). Objective measures of near-misses may also be derived from observational studies (e.g., Laureshyn and Várhelyi, 2018). Table 4 summarizes safety data types and sources that are drawn from, or disseminated to, the traveling public.

More in depth and participatory methods may also be used, such as the Bike Barometer, which is a web-based platform where school pupils can evaluate cycling safety along their route from home to school (https://fietsbarometer.ugent.be). The Bike Barometer contains teaching material for three geography lessons. Their contributions provide an additional source of information for cycle planning.

General road safety audits (e.g., National Highways, 2020 and as supplemented by Chartered Institution of Highways and Transportation (2021) are a typically multistep processes at each stage of the design to examine the potential risks as a result of design decisions. Again, the approach and governance of the process will be country specific.

There are audit tools available specifically in relation to cycling (e.g., FHWA, 2012). These would usually provide an overview of basic principles

Table 4 Safety data types and sources.

Type	Location	References	Comment
Public perception data	International map based	https://bikemaps.org/	Uses local knowledge of cycling safety, hazards, and cycle theft to identify hot spots.
Public dissemination	New Orleans	https://www.saferstreetspriorityfinder.com/	Allows users to understand local safety data
On-cycle collection	UK	https://seesense.cc/	GPS tracking with ability to provide comments for a ride to a central data base
Infrastructure deficiency data	UK	https://www.cyclinguk.org/campaign/fill-hole	Mobile phone app to send information about road surface deficiencies to the highway authority
Infrastructure deficiency data	UK	https://www.fixmystreet.com/	As above but for more general problems, including littering and street lighting
Infrastructure deficiency data	Austria	https://www.radkummerkasten.at/	As above, for Vienna, Austria

of the safety of cyclists and potential issues affecting cyclists by describing safety considerations. As noted above, these approaches need to avoid prescriptive tick box approaches so that the auditor considers the situation in the round. Open ended question, qualitative responses, and prompt lists are the most effective form of creating useful audits.

7. Monitoring and evaluation

Schemes sponsors may want to be assured of the contribution of a scheme to its original objectives. Monitoring and evaluation of the impacts of a scheme will provide that assurance. Monitoring is the process of collecting data about the outcomes of a scheme and these may include, for example, counts of cycles. Her Majesty's Treasury (2020) defines evaluation as "a systematic assessment of the design, implementation and outcomes of an intervention. It involves understanding how an intervention is being, or has been, implemented and what effects it has, for whom and why. It identifies what can be improved and estimates its overall impacts and cost-effectiveness." A comprehensive evaluation will typically consist of one or more of the following:

- A Process Evaluation to analyze the implementation of an intervention. It is likely to involve interviews or focus groups with those who have been involved with scheme delivery.
- An Impact Evaluation to analyze changes that have occurred, their scale, and the extent to which they are attributable to the scheme. In the context of cycling, this includes cycle counts and mode shares, attributing changes in cycle use to the scheme (e.g., change in number on a new route), and the socio-economic distribution of impacts.
- A Value-for-money evaluation which compares the costs with the benefits post-hoc (see also Section 5)

These standard processes of evaluation are applied extensively to schemes post-opening in the United Kingdom. By contrast, the Netherlands finds it unimportant either undertake pre-scheme cost-benefit analysis for cycling investment, or to monitor a scheme's impacts.

Cycling policy interventions occur over a period of time in the real world and are not to susceptible to evaluation through experimental design, which would include approaches such as randomized control trials. With suitable data, however, quasi-experimental methods can be used to evaluate cycle schemes (e.g., sequencing, Goodman et al., 2016; time series, Heinen et al., 2017; difference-in-difference, Goodman et al., 2013).

More often than not so-called theory based evaluations are commonly used in transport evaluations, including evaluations of cycling investment. This type of evaluation attempts to identify evidence to support chains of cause and effect; for example, the introduction of cycle parking on a high street has the effect of increasing the number of shopping trips by bicycle. The theory-based approach will be driven by a logic map which identifies the causal links and the relevant factors are classified as follows:

- Inputs: the resources committed and the activities undertaken; for example, the costs of the scheme
- Outputs: what has been created or delivered; for example, length of cycle route number of cycle training events)
- Outcomes: the resulting observed change as a result of the scheme; for example, number of additional kilometers cycled in a town
- Impacts: the resulting wider changes; for example, reduced greenhouse gas emissions.

Sloman et al. (2017) provides an example of a meta-analysis of evaluations of investment in sustainable transport investment in 12 English urban areas. Scheme outputs included length of new or upgraded cycle route, number of new or upgraded cycle parking spaces, number of adults taking up services to encourage them to cycle and the number of children receiving cycle training. Outcomes were measured using household surveys for mode share and cycle counts at cordons and at key locations. Qualitative evidence linked the outputs to the outcomes.

8. Concluding summary

So far as policy making is concerned, processes and tools are needed which allow decision makers to understand the current position with clearly presented data, against which they can then set their policy agenda. Ideally such agendas will be then benchmarked against the policies of other areas.

Mode and route choice estimation for cycling has received a lot of research attention in recent years. However, in practice, mode choice estimation may be carried out typically using simplified methods such as diversion factors, and route choice may be based on algorithms that are not linked to evidence about cyclists' actual preferences. Ideally, network planning tools need to be developed further to ensure they use relevant mode and route choice variables and validated parameters. However, the cost of deriving these and using them in modeling is likely to be disproportionate to the value and extent of cycle infrastructure schemes.

Tools to assist in designing and understanding the operation of a network are at the two ends of a spectrum of complexity. On the one hand, visualization tools have some value to begin to generate conceptions about what a scheme may look like, but will have limited value when more detailed stages of design are reached. On the other hand, tools for modeling operations are necessarily complex and usually rely on microsimulation models.

Appraisal has a focus on the impacts of cycling which accrue from enhanced physical activity levels. Arguably, policy makers ought to be assessing the risks to health posed by modes such as motor traffic and developing policies to limit these modes. In so doing, there would likely be a significant suppressed demand for cycling generated. The choice between cost-benefit analysis and multi-criteria analysis in appraisal is usually determined by the funding agency. Arguably better decisions are made when the full range of factors, including those without monetary values, are considered. The challenge with the approach is avoiding bias during such an assessment.

As with mode and route choice modeling, there are many sophisticated level of service models that have been developed by researchers. Few are used in practice, and often the approaches that are taken are based on crude scoring mechanisms which do not fully use the detail in the data available. Audits can be used for a variety purposes including street design and quality, and safety. The best audit methodologies will cover all the necessary features of a route which affect cycling, and be performed by trained practitioners considering issues in an holistic way.

There are well established methods for transport planning which have been refined over many years. These are applied in often stripped-down ways to cycling, and this results from a need to keep the costs of the planning and design stages in proportion to the overall scheme costs. However, the knowledge and understanding that is available from research is often not used to best effect in many of the tools that are applied to carry out these planning processes.

Acknowledgments

Sien Benoit, Ghent University; Malcolm Morgan, Leeds University; Karl Reiter, Institut für Verkehrspädagogik; Christian Brand, Oxford University; Paul Kelly, University of Edinburgh; James Woodcock, Cambridge University; Kees van Ommeren, Decisio.

References

Aldred, R., 2016. Cycling near misses: their frequency, impact, and prevention. Transp. Res. A: Policy Pract. 90, 69–83.

Aldred, R., Crosweller, S., 2015. Investigating the rates and impacts of near misses and related incidents among UK cyclists. J. Transp. Health 2 (3), 379–393.

Alta Planning, 2017. Level of Traffic Stress — What it Means for Building Better Bike Networks. (Available at https://blog.altaplanning.com/level-of-traffic-stress-what-it-means-for-building-better-bike-networks-c4af9800b4ee. Accessed 29/11/2021).

Bagloee, S.A., Sarvi, M., Wallace, M., 2016. Bicycle lane priority: promoting bicycle as a green mode even in congested urban area. Transp. Res. A 87, 102–121.

Beura, S.K., Manusha, V.L., Chellapilla, H., Bhuyan, P.K., 2018. Defining bicycle levels of service criteria using Levenberg–Marquardt and self-organizing map algorithms. Transp. Dev. Econ. 4, 11.

Braess, D., Nagurney, A., Wakolbinger, T., 2005. On a paradox of traffic planning. J. Transp. Sci. 39, 446–450 (Translated from the original: Braess D (1968) Über ein Paradoxon aus der Verkehrsplanung. Unternehmensforschung 12: 258–268 [In German]).

Broer, K. (2008) Fietsbalans II: competitiveness bicycle greatly improved. Fietsverkeer nr. 20. Fietsberaad. Available at https://www.fietsberaad.nl/Kennisbank/Fietsbalans-II-Concurrentiepositie-van-fiets-flink Accessed on 29/11/2021.

BYPAD, 2021. Bicycle Policy Audit. (Available at: http://www.bypad.org/ [Accessed 14th October 2021).

Centre for active transportation, 2019. Complete Streets Game 3.0. (Available at https://www.tcat.ca/resources/complete-streets-game/. (Accessed on 1/11/2021).

Chartered Institution of Highways and Transportation, 2007. Collision Prevention and Reduction. Chartered Institution of Highways and Transportation, London.

Chartered Institution of Highways and Transportation (2021) CIHT SoRSA Road Safety Audit Guidelines 2021. Available at https://www.ciht.org.uk/sorsa/manual-home/. Accessed on 1/12/2021.

CIVITAS, 2021. Urban Mobility Tool Inventory. (Available at: https://civitas.eu/tool-inventory [Accessed on 25th October 2021).

COWI & City of Copenhagen, 2008. Economic Evaluation of Cycle Projects - Methodology and Unit Prices. Available at: https://fietsberaad.nl/Kennisbank/Economic-evaluation-of-cycle-projects-methodology. Accessed on 23/11/2021.

CROW, 2017. Design Manual for Bicycle Traffic. Centre for research and contract standardisation in civil engineering, Ede, The Netherlands.

Cycle Streets, 2021. CycleStreets Cycling intelligence for the UK. Available at https://www.cyclestreets.net/. (Accessed 1/11/2021).

CyIPT, 2018. Cycling Infrastructure Prioritisation Toolkit. (Available at https://www.cyipt.bike/ [Accessed on 25th October 2021).

De Nazelle, A., Nieuwenhuijsen, M.J., Antó, J.M., Brauer, M., Briggs, D., Braun-Fahrlander, C., Cavill, N., Cooper, A.R., Desqueyroux, H., Fruin, S., 2011. Improving health through policies that promote active travel: a review of evidence to support integrated health impact assessment. Environ. Int. 37 (4), 766–777.

Decisio, 2017. Waarderingskengetallen MKBA Fiets. https://www.rwseconomie.nl/binaries/rwseconomie/documenten/rapporten/2017/12/20/waarderingskengetallenfiets/171215+Waarderingskengetallen+MKBA+Fiets_definitief.pdf. Accessed on 23/11/2021.

Department for Transport, 2011. Quality Audit in the Street Design Process. Traffic Advisory Leaflet 2/11. Department for Transport, London (Available at https://www.gov.uk/government/publications/quality-audit. Accessed on 1/12/2021).

Department for Transport, 2017. Local Cycling and Walking Infrastructure Plans: Technical Guidance for Local Authorities. Department for Transport, London (Available at https://assets.publishing.service.gov.uk/government/uploads/system/uploads/attachment_data/file/908535/cycling-walking-infrastructure-technical-guidance-document.pdf [Accessed on 25th October 2021).

Department for Transport, 2020a. Transport Appraisal Guidance (TAG) Unit A5.1 Active mode appraisal. (Available at https://www.gov.uk/government/publications/tag-unit-a5-1-active-mode-appraisal. Accessed on 23/11/2021).

Department for Transport, 2020b. Active Mode Appraisal Toolkit. Department for Transport (Available at https://assets.publishing.service.gov.uk/government/uploads/system/uploads/attachment_data/file/888754/amat-user-guidance.pdf. Accessed on 23/11/2021).

Desjardins, E., Apatu, E., Razavi, S.D., Higgins, C.D., Scott, D.M., Páez, A., 2021. "Going through a little bit of growing pains": a qualitative study of the factors that influence the route choice of regular bicyclists in a developing cycling city. Transp. Res. F: Traffic Psychol. Behav. 81, 431–444.

Dessing, D., de Vries, S.I., Hegeman, G., Verhagen, E., van Mechelen, W., Pierik, F.H., 2016. Children's route choice during active transportation to school: difference between shortest and actual route. Int. J. Behav. Nutr. Phys. Act. 13 (1), 48.

European Cyclists' Federation, 2017. Cycling delivers the global goals. European Cyclists' Federation (Available at https://ecf.com/sites/ecf.com/files/The%20Global%20Goals_internet.pdf. Accessed on 3rd January 2022).

FHWA, 2012. Bicycle Road Safety Audit Guidelines and Prompt Lists. US Department of Transportation Federal Highway Administration. Available at https://safety.fhwa.dot.gov/ped_bike/tools_solve/fhwasa12018/ (Accessed on 1/12/2021).

FLOW (2017) Putting walking and cycling on an equal footing http://h2020-flow.eu. Accessed on 23/11/2021.

Goodman, A., Panter, J., Sharp, S.J., Ogilvie, D., 2013. Effectiveness and equity impacts of town-wide cycling initiatives in England: a longitudinal, controlled natural experimental study. Soc. Sci. Med. (1982) 97, 228–237.

Goodman, A., van Sluijs, E.M.F., Ogilvie, D., 2016. Impact of offering cycle training in schools upon cycling behaviour: a natural experimental study. Int. J. Behav. Nutr. Phys. Act. 13 (1), 34.

Guthrie, N., Davies, D.G., Gardner, G., 2001. Cyclists' Assessments of Road and Traffic Conditions: The Development of a Cyclability Index. TRL Report 490, Transport Research Laboratory, Crowthorne.

Heinen, E., Harshfield, A., Panter, J., Mackett, R., Ogilvie, D., 2017. Does exposure to new transport infrastructure result in modal shifts? Patterns of change in commute mode choices in a four-year quasi-experimental cohort study. J. Transp. Health 6, 396–410.

Helbing, D., Molnar, P., 1995. Social force model for pedestrian dynamics. Phys. Rev. E 51 (5), 4282–4286.

Her Majesty's Government, 2020. Magenta Book: Central Government Guidance on Evaluation. Her Majesty's Treasury, London (Available at https://assets.publishing.service.gov.uk/government/uploads/system/uploads/attachment_data/file/879438/HMT_Magenta_Book.pdf).

IDTP, 2011. Better Streets, Better Cities: A Guide to Street Design in Urban. Institute for Transportation and Development Policy, New York (Available at India http://itdp.in/wp-content/uploads/2014/04/07.-Better-Streets-Better-Cities-EN.pdf. Accessed on 3rd January 2022).

ITDP, 2013. Bike sharing planning guide. Institute for Transportation and Development Policy, New York (Available at https://3gozaa3xxbpb499ejp30lxc8-wpengine.netdna-ssl.com/wp-content/uploads/2014/07/ITDP_Bike_Share_Planning_Guide.pdf. Accessed on 3rd January 2022).

ITHIM, 2021. Integrated Transport and Health Impact Modelling Tool. MRC Epidemiology Unit, University of Cambridge (Available at: https://www.mrc-epid.cam.ac.uk/research/research-areas/public-health-modelling/ithim/. Accessed on 23/11/2021).

Jensen, S., 2007. Pedestrian and bicyclist level of service on roadway segments. Transp. Res. Rec. 2031, 43–51.

Jensen, S., 2013. Pedestrian and bicycle level of Service at Intersections, roundabouts and other crossings. In: 92nd Annual Meeting of the Transportation Research Board, Washington, DC.

Landis, B.W., Vattikuti, V.R., Brannick, M.T., 1997. Real-time human perceptions toward a bicycle level of service. Transp. Res. Rec. 1578.

Laureshyn, A., Várhelyi, A., 2018. The Swedish Traffic Conflict Technique observer's Manual. Lunds Tekniska Högskola, Lund, Sweden (Available at https://www.bast.de/EN/Traffic_Safety/Subjects/InDeV/Documents/pdf/TCT-OM.pdf?__blob=publicationFile&v=2#:~:text=According%20to%20the%20Swedish%20TCT,start%20taking%20an%20evasive%20action. Accessed on 1/12/2021).

Macharis, C., Bernardini, A., 2015. Reviewing the use of multi-criteria decision analysis for the evaluation of transport projects: time for a multi-actor approach. Transp. Policy 37, 177–186.

Mekuria, M., Furth, P., Nixon, H., 2012. MTI Report 11–19. Low-Stress Bicycling and Network Connectivity. Mineta Transportation Institute. Available online: https://transweb.sjsu.edu/sites/default/files/1005-low-stress-bicycling-network-connectivity.pdf. Accessed on 29/11/2021.

Mouter, N. (Ed.), 2020. New Methods, Reflections and Application Domains in Transport Appraisal. Elsevier.

Muñoz, B., Monzon, A., Daziano, R.A., 2016. The increasing role of latent variables in modelling bicycle mode choice. Transp. Rev. 36 (6), 737–771.

Munro, C., 2013. Level of Service Model for Bicycle Riders. (Prepared for Australian Road Research Board and Queensland Department of Transport and Main Roads. Australian Bicycle Council and CDM research).

National Highways, 2020. GG119 Road Safety Audit, in Design Manual for Roads and Bridges. (Available at https://www.standardsforhighways.co.uk/dmrb/. Accessed on 29/11/2021).

Parkin, J., 2018. Designing for Cycle Traffic: International Principles and Practice. ICE Publishing, London.

Parkin, J., Wardman, M., Page, M., 2007. Models of perceived cycling risk and route acceptability. Accid. Anal. Prev. 39 (2), 364–371.

PBCC, 2021. Place Based Carbon Calculator. (Available at: https://www.carbon.place/).

Pikora, T (n.d.) Systematic Pedestrian and Cycling Environmental Scan Spaces Instrument. (Available at https://activelivingresearch.org/systematic-pedestrian-and-cycling-environmental-scan-spaces-instrument. (NB url not working, reference to be update when reply to email received).

Pliakas, T., Hawkesworth, S., Silverwood, R.J., Nanchahal, K., Grundy, C., Armstrong, B., Casas, J.P., Morris, R.W., Wilkinson, P., Lock, K., 2017. Optimising measurement of health-related characteristics of the built environment: comparing data collected by foot-based street audits, virtual street audits and routine secondary data sources. Health Place 43, 75–84.

Pritchard, R., 2018. Revealed preference methods for studying bicycle route choice—a systematic review. Int. J. Environ. Res. Public Health 15 (3), 470.

Pritchard, R., Frøyen, Y., Snizek, B., 2019. Bicycle level of service for route choice—a GIS evaluation of four existing indicators with empirical data. ISPRS Int. J. Geo Inf. 8 (5), 214.

Propensity to cycle tool, 2021. Using the PCT to Help Identify a Priority Cycle Network in Small Cities. (Available at https://npct.github.io/pct-shiny/regions_www/www/static/03b_case_studies/hereford-case-study.pdf [accessed on 25th October 2021).

Ruffino, P., Jarre, M., 2019. Valutazione dei Costi e dei Benefici della Mobilita' Attiva. Caso di San Donato Milanese. (Available at https://www.comune.sandonatomilanese.mi.it/wp-content/uploads/2020/02/Report_CBA_SdM_Final.pdf. Article accessed 23/11/2021 (In Italian).

Ruffino, P., Jarre, M., 2020. Appraisal of cycling and pedestrian projects. In: Mouter, N. (Ed.), New Methods, Reflections and Application Domains in Transport Appraisal. Elsevier. Chapter 7. Also available at https://www.ncbi.nlm.nih.gov/pmc/articles/PMC7553907/.

Sloman, L., Cairns, S., Goodman, A., Hopkin, J., Taylor, I., Hopkinson, L., Ricketts, O., Hiblin, B., Dillon, M., 2017. Meta-Analysis of Outcomes of Investment in the 12 Local Sustainable Transport Fund Large Projects. (Final Report to Department for Transport. Available at https://assets.publishing.service.gov.uk/government/uploads/system/uploads/attachment_data/file/738267/meta-analysis-of-lstf-large-projects-final-report.pdf. Accessed on 26/11/2021).

Sprinkle, 2007. Bicycle Level of Service Applied Model. Sprinkle Consulting Inc. (Available at https://nacto.org/docs/usdg/bicylce_Level_of_service_model_sprinkle_consulting.pdf. Accessed on 28th January 2018).

Streetmix (n.d.) Streetmix. (Available at streetmix.net (accessed 1/11/2021).

Streetplan (n.d.) Streeplan. Available at streetplan.net (accessed 1/11/2021).

Transport for London, 2017. Healthy Streets for London: Prioritising Walking, Cycling and Public Transport to Create a Healthy City. Transport for London, London (Available at http://content.tfl.gov.uk/healthy-streets-for-london.pdf. Accessed on 1/12/2021).

Transport for London, 2019. New Cycling Street Quality Criteria. Transport for London (Available at https://tfl.gov.uk/corporate/publications-and-reports/cycling. Accessed on 1/12/2021).

Transportation Research Board, 2016. Chapter 18 Urban Street Segments. In: Highway Capacity Manual: A Guide for Multimodal Mobility Analysis. Transportation Research Board of the National Academies, Washington, DC, USA (ISBN 978-0-309-44148-3).

Twaddle, H., Schendzielorz, T., Fakler, O., 2014. Bicycles in urban areas: review of existing methods for modeling behavior. Transp. Res. Rec. 2434, 140–146.

Wang, K., Akar, G., Lee, K., Sanders, M., 2020. Commuting patterns and bicycle level of traffic stress (LTS): insights from spatially aggregated data in Franklin County, Ohio. J. Transp. Geogr. 86, 102751.

Wardrop, J.G., 1952. Some theoretical aspects of road traffic research. Proc. Inst. Civ. Eng. 1 (3), 325–362.

Welsh Government, (2021). Active Travel Act Guidance. The Welsh Government, Cardiff, UK. https://gov.wales/active-travel-act-guidance (accessed 29/4/2022).

Wiedemann, R., 1991. Modelling of RTI-elements on multi-lane roads. In: Advanced Telematics in Road Transport edited by the Commission of the European Community, DG XIII, Brussels.

Woodcock, J., Abbas, A., Ullrich, A., Tainio, M., Lovelace, R., Sá, T.H., Westgate, K., Goodman, A., 2018. Development of the impacts of cycling tool (ICT): a modelling study and web tool for evaluating health and environmental impacts of cycling uptake. PLoS Med. 15 (7), e1002622.

Woodcock, J., Aldred, R., Lovelace, R., Strain, T., Goodman, A., 2021. Health, environmental and distributional impacts of cycling uptake: the model underlying the propensity to cycle tool for England and Wales. J. Transp. Health 22, 101066.

World Health Organisation, 2021. Health Economic Assessment Tool (HEAT) for Cycling and Walking. World Health Organisation (Available at: https://www.euro.who.int/en/health-topics/environment-and-health/Transport-and-health/activities/guidance-and-tools/health-economic-assessment-tool-heat-for-cycling-and-walking. Accessed 23/11/2021).

Zuidgeest, M., Brussel, M., 2012. Cycling research in developing countries: context, challenges and policy relevant research. In: Parkin, J. (Ed.), Cycling and Sustainability. Emerald, Bingley (Chapter 8).

CHAPTER SEVEN

A global overview of cycling trends

Ralph Buehler[a,*] and Rahul Goel[b]
[a]Urban Affairs and Planning, Virginia Tech, Arlington, VA, USA
[b]Transportation Research and Injury Prevention Centre, Indian Institute of Technology Delhi, New Delhi, India
*Corresponding author: e-mail address: ralphbu@vt.edu

Contents

Abstract

During the last 30 years, many cities and countries have promoted cycling to increase livability and the sustainability of their transport systems. This chapter provides an overview of bicycling internationally, comparing differences in cycling levels, trends, distance, duration, speed, as well as gender and age of cyclists across countries and cities. The first part of the chapter focuses on traditional non-motorized bicycles. This is followed by a section summarizing the current spread and usage of electric bicycles (e-bikes). The goal of the chapter is to provide a global overview of cycling levels in countries and cities and to identify similarities and differences in trip making, trip distance as well as age and gender of cyclists internationally.

Keywords: Bicycling, Gender, Age, E-bikes, Europe, Americas, Australia, Asia, International comparison

Advances in Transport Policy and Planning, Volume 10
ISSN 2543-0009
https://doi.org/10.1016/bs.atpp.2022.04.007

1. Introduction

During the last 30 years many cities and countries have promoted bicycling for daily trips to increase livability and the sustainability of transport systems. Bicycling is a healthy, efficient, economical, and environmentally friendly mode of transport (Buehler and Pucher, 2021). Riding a bicycle produces virtually no local and global air pollutants. Even pedal assist e-bikes have much lower CO_2 emissions per kilometer when compared to automobiles with combustion or electric engines (Brand et al., 2021). The very energy needed to propel a bicycle burns calories and generates valuable physical activity leading to significant health benefits for the rider (Garrard et al., 2021). Bicycles are very space efficient, requiring only a fraction of the space needed to move and park automobiles. For individuals bicycling is much cheaper than owning and operating an automobile. For the public sector building bikeways and bicycle parking facilities only costs a fraction compared to the large expenses for building and maintaining roadway infrastructure and car parking structures (see for example: PBOT, n.d.).

This chapter provides an overview of bicycling internationally, comparing differences in cycling levels, trends, distance, duration, as well as gender and age of cyclists across countries and cities. We are relying on a uniquely internationally comparable dataset assembled by Goel et al. (2021). This information is supplemented with information and statistics on bicycling in countries and cities from other sources including Buehler and Pucher (2021). The first part of the paper focuses on traditional non-motorized bicycles. This is followed by a special section summarizing the current state of knowledge on electric bicycles (e-bikes). The goal of the chapter is to provide a global overview of cycling levels in countries and cities and to identify similarities and differences in trip making, trip distance as well as age and gender of cyclists internationally. As explained in the next section, the global reach of this chapter is limited by data availability and comparability.

2. Data sources and methods

The availability of travel survey datasets varies greatly across countries. Many high-income countries conduct national travel surveys (Kunert et al., 2002), while there are no low-and-middle income countries (LMICs) with such surveys at the national level. City- or regional-level surveys are more common, however, they are still scarce in most LMICs. Among LMICs, Latin American countries such as Argentina, Brazil, Chile (a high-income country) and Colombia have the most extensive data available for travel surveys of major cities or metropolitan areas. In India, cities conduct travel surveys infrequently for the purpose of transport planning and their datasets are often not available in the public domain.

We aimed to access travel survey datasets for countries to represent different world regions and per capita income levels. For the cities and regions in North and South America, we downloaded travel survey datasets from online portals. For Europe, we obtained access through online requests to the concerned authorities (e.g., England, Finland, Switzerland). For Japan, which does not permit data to be transferred outside the country, analysis was conducted by a researcher in Japan. Datasets for cities in African countries and India were obtained through local collaborators for a research project (Woodcock et al., 2017).

We present results at the city and country levels. For the latter, we present some analyses that represent the whole country and some that represent only urbanized areas. For the following countries national-level surveys are not available– Argentina, Australia, Brazil, and Chile. For these, we combined data from multiple individual cities or urban parts of the regions for our country-level analysis (see Table 1). The cities/regions included represent 53% of the urban population of Argentina, 35% in Australia, 18% in Brazil, and 65% in Chile.

Travel survey datasets typically report travel activities of sampled individuals using a travel diary. The duration of reporting is 1 day for most datasets.

Table 1 Cities or regions included in country-level analysis (countries for which dataset was combined from multiple cities/regions).

Country	Geographies included for country-level analysis
Argentina	Buenos Aires; Cordoba; Mendoza; Neuquén y Cipolletti; Posadas; Resistencia-Corrientes; Rosario; Salta; Tucuman
Australia	Cairns Region; Darling Downs and Lockyer; Gladstone; Gympie, Gayndah, Kingaroy and Tin Can Bay/Cooloola; Mackay; Rockhampton Region; South East Queensland; Townsville; Toowoomba region; Wide Bay Burnett; Victoria Region
Brazil	Belo Horizonte; Feira de Santana; Salvador; Sao Paulo
Chile	Antofagasta; Arica; Copiapo; Coquimbo-La Serena; Gran Valparaiso; Iquique; Puerto Montt; Santiago; Temuco-Padre Lascasas; Valdivia

The exceptions are country-level datasets of England and Germany where respondents reported their travel activities for a week. For the corresponding cities of the two countries included in city-level analysis (London, Berlin, Cologne, Hamburg, and Munich), we used different city-level datasets with a reporting duration of 1 day. The other exceptions are the US cities of Chicago, where a fraction of respondents were selected to report for 1 day and the rest for 2 days, and Seattle, where the reported data is a mix of 1 day for some respondents and a week for the rest.

The results presented here include either trips or the individuals who made those trips as units of analyses. For trips with multiple stages and multiple modes, we assigned main modes. For most datasets, this was already assigned. If not, we used stage-level data and assigned the mode used for the stage with the longest duration. If stage-level duration was not available, we used a hierarchy of modes (all modes except walking were assigned a higher level than cycling). We defined trip distance and duration as the total distance and duration, respectively, from origin to the destination of the trip including all stages. We defined trip purpose as a dichotomized variable—work and non-work. In work, we also included trips classified as work-related or business. We classified trips to work and the following trip back home as work trips, and a trip back home was classified as a work trip only if it immediately followed a trip to work. In some datasets, this classification was already available, and the country-level dataset of Germany used a different criterion. In that dataset, returning home trips were classified as work trips if there were a maximum of three trips away from the trip to work, therefore, allowing two trips between work and home. We present multiple metrics of cycling and overall travel behavior, using either trips or individuals as units of analysis. When available, we used trip weights or person weights to ensure analysis is representative of the population.

For the geographies that reported travel diaries for more than a day, we are more likely to capture cycling trips that are not made on a regular basis, which may bring some bias with respect to the geographies where only 1 day of travel is reported (Shaw et al., 2020). Further, travel surveys are better at reporting cycling to reach a destination than recreational cycling, though they do report the latter to some extent. Activity-diary surveys are likely to report both equally well. It is likely that recreational cycling may have a relatively significant share in cities with low levels of cycling, such as in the USA. Our definition of main mode also excludes cycling that is done for a part of the trip, for example, to access public transportation. Our analysis could not differentiate between age and cohort effect.

Many travel surveys do not differentiate between e-bikes and conventional cycles, though there are exceptions such as the Netherlands. As a result, much of the research related to demographic and trip characteristics of e-bike users is based on small-scale studies (Melia and Bartle, 2021). For e-bikes, we present results from this literature.

3. Cycling levels and trends

As shown in Fig. 1, the percentage of daily trips made by bicycle varies greatly between countries. At the high end, in the Netherlands more than one quarter of all daily trips (27%) are made by bicycle. In Denmark, Japan, and Germany over 10% of trips are by bicycle. Sweden (9%), Belgium (8%), Finland (8%), and Switzerland (7%) form the midfield, followed by Austria (6%) and Norway (5%). The lowest cycling levels are in England and Australia (~2% each) as well as in countries in the Americas: Argentina (4%), Chile (3%), Brazil (1%), and the United States (1%). Compared to countries in the Americas, England and Australia, cycling levels in more bicycling-oriented countries like Denmark, Japan, and Germany are 3–10 times greater and cycling levels in the Netherlands, the most bike oriented country, are 7–10 times greater.

Several countries, such as India, China, Ireland, or Canada do not have national household travel surveys that capture the percentage of daily trips

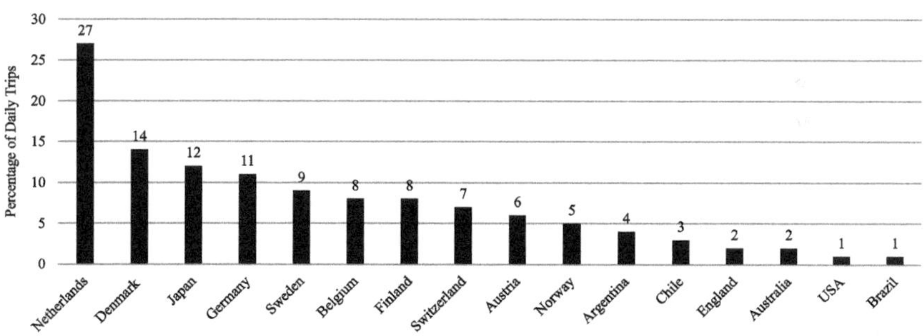

Fig. 1 Percentage of daily trips by bicycle in selected countries. *Based on data in Buehler, R., Pucher, J. (Eds.), 2021. Cycling for Sustainable Cities. MIT Press, Cambridge, MA; Goel, R., Goodman, A., Aldred, R., Nakamura, R., Tatah, L., Garcia, L., Diomedi-Zapata, B., et al., 2021. Cycling behaviour in 17 countries across 6 continents: levels of cycling, who cycles, for what purpose, and how far?. Transport Reviews doi:10.1080/01441647.2021.1915898 (Note: Data for Argentina, Japan, Chile, Australia, and Brazil in this figure are based on the authors' aggregation of travel surveys from large urbanized regions and reflect travel in metropolitan regions only.)*

made by bicycle. Some countries report this data for the commute to work based on national censuses–often only capturing the mode of transport to work used for the majority of weekdays. For example, in Canada between 1 and 2% of regular commuters ride a bicycle to work most days of the week compared to 3% in Ireland, and 20% in India (Buehler and Pucher, 2021). Other countries like China do not have a national travel survey nor national level data on commuting by bicycle.

Fig. 2 shows the percentage of daily trips made by bicycle for select cities in Europe, the Americas, Australia, Japan, India, China, and one city in Kenia. As was the case for cycling levels by country, there is great variability in bicycling mode share among cities. In general, levels of cycling in cities follow the nation-level pattern seen in Fig. 1–with more cycling in cities in countries with higher cycling levels. For example, Dutch cities like Zwolle (49%), Groningen (48%), and Amsterdam (36%) have among the highest mode shares, while Brazilian, Australian, and US cities have among the lowest shares of trips by bicycle–reflecting nationally low shares of trips by bicycle there.

However, there is considerable variability among cities within the same country. For example, the German cities of Muenster, (38%), Freiburg (34%), and Frankfurt (20%) have much higher bike shares of trips than the city of Stuttgart (6%). Similarly, in England, Oxford (19%) and Cambridge (30%) have much higher bicycle share of trips than London (2%). In Switzerland, Basel (17%) has much higher cycling levels compared to Zurich (6%)—only 100 km away. In the United States, Washington, DC (5.0%) has a roughly 4 to 5 times higher mode share for bicycling compared to New York City (1.3%), Los Angeles (1.2%), or Seattle (1.1%). Fig. 2 also indicates the great variability in bike mode share in Chinese cities with 10% of trips by bicycle in Beijing compared to 29% in Shanghai, and 34% in Tianjin. Similarly, Delhi in India had a bike mode share of all trips of 5% and 11% for the commute compared to 22% of bike mode share for the commute in Kolkata. The only African city in Fig. 2 is Kisumu, Kenya with a bike mode share of 4%.

These differences between cities reflect differences in policies and infrastructure that promote cycling and make it safer as well as policies that restrict car use by limiting car travel speed and volumes (Buehler and Pucher, 2021). Other factors, such as topography, climate, and socio-economic factors also moderate bicycle usage. However, none of these factors presents an absolute barrier to cycling. For example, in the United States, Minneapolis, MN is among the large cities with the highest bicycle share for commuting trips

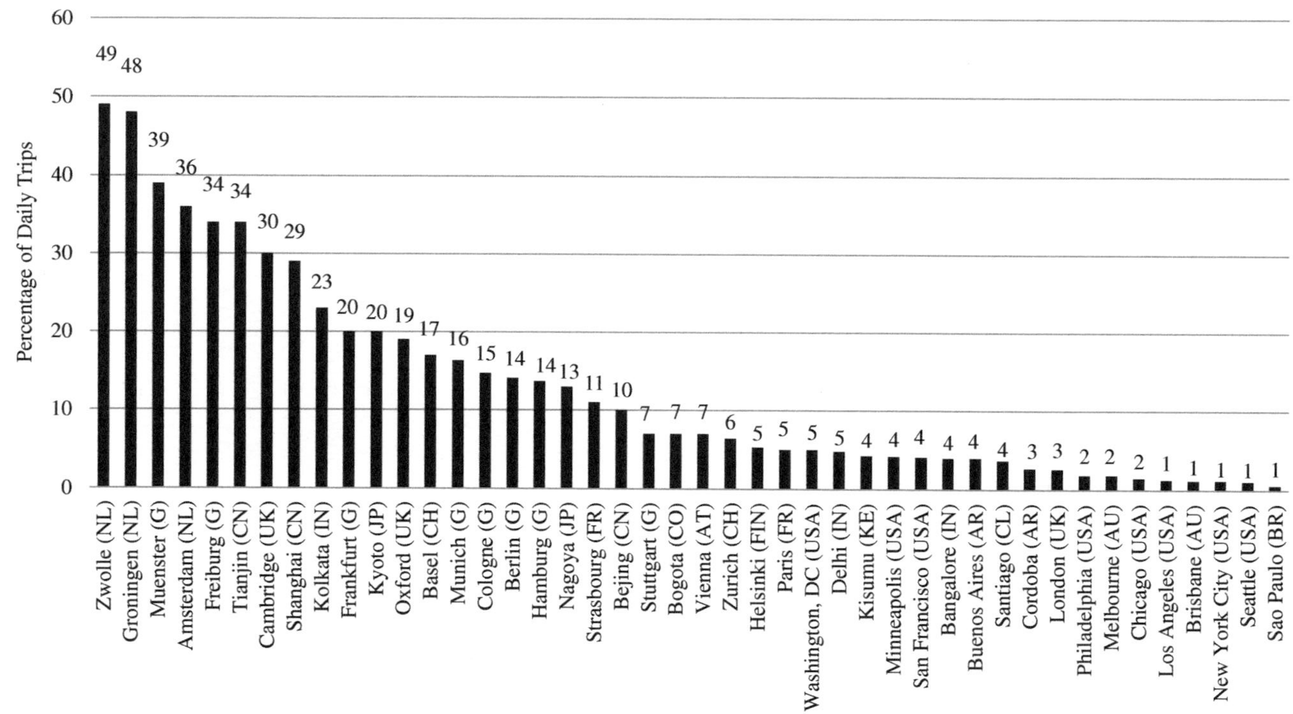

Fig. 2 Percentage of daily trips by bicycle in selected cities. *Source: Based on data in Buehler, R., Pucher, J. (Eds.), 2021. Cycling for Sustainable Cities. MIT Press, Cambridge, MA; Buehler, R., Teoman, D., Shelton, B., 2021. Promoting bicycling in car-oriented cities: lessons from Washington, DC and Frankfurt Am Main, Germany. Urban Science. 5 (3), 58. doi:10.3390/urbansci5030058; Goel, R., Goodman, A., Aldred, R., Nakamura, R., Tatah, L., Garcia, L., Diomedi-Zapata, B., et al., 2021. Cycling behaviour in 17 countries across 6 continents: levels of cycling, who cycles, for what purpose, and how far? Transport Reviews. doi:10.1080/01441647.2021.1915898. (Note: data originates from travel surveys for the individual cities. Methods and timing for the travel surveys are not entirely comparable; data for Minneapolis, San Francisco, and Kolkata are for regular commutes to work only.)*

to work (4.2%) in spite of its long and cold winters. Conversely, moderate climate does not guarantee high cycling levels. Similarly, San Francisco is among the top large US cycling cities (4.1% commute mode share) in spite of its many hills, while there are many topographically flat cities with low cycling levels. Lastly, cities with a high share of students often have high levels of cycling (like Oxford, Cambridge, or Freiburg), but high levels of students do not guarantee high cycling levels–as evidenced by many US college towns with low levels of cycling.

Bicycling levels also vary within cities and in metro areas. For example, in Amsterdam, the percentage of daily trips by bicycle in the most bicycle-oriented parts of the city was found more than twice (68% in the Centrum and 61% in the West) that in the least bicycle-oriented parts (26% in Zuidost and 27% in Noord) (Koglin et al., 2021). Similarly, an analysis of German speaking cities in Europe illustrates how bicycling mode share varies within urban regions (Buehler et al., 2017). In Berlin, bike mode share was highest in the city center (17%), fell to 11% in the rest of the city, but rose to 16% in inner suburban areas. In Hamburg, bike mode shares were comparable in the city center (13%), city areas outside of the center (11%), and inner suburban areas (12%). In Munich bicycle use was lowest in the city center (likely due to its large pedestrian-only area and dense light-rail network) at 10%, rose to 16% in the rest of the city and fell again to 12% in the inner suburban areas. Last, in Vienna, Austria, a city with a dense light-rail network and high levels of walking, cycling in the city center and inner suburban areas was 7%, but only 5% in the rest of the city.

Over time, trend data for the last 20 years indicate modest growth in the share of daily trips made by bicycle at the national level in several countries. The bicycle share of trips saw small increases in the Netherlands from 27% to 28% between 2005 and 2016, Norway (4–5%, 2001–2014), Austria (5–6%; 1995–2014), Switzerland (6–7%; 2000–2015), and Germany (9–11%, 2002–2017). In the United States (2001–2017) and Belgium (199–2012) the bicycle mode share did not change significantly, but bicycling declined in the northern European countries Denmark (18 to 14%, 2001–2018), Finland (11 to 8%; 1998–2018), and Sweden (10% to 8%, 2000–2018). Cycling levels and trends at the national level hide variability within countries and at the city level.

For some cities, data were available over time to document trends in bicycling levels. Fig. 3 shows trends in the percentage of trips by bicycle for 20 cities in Europe, the Americas, Australia, and China (sorted by magnitude of increase). With the exception of cities in China, bicycling levels

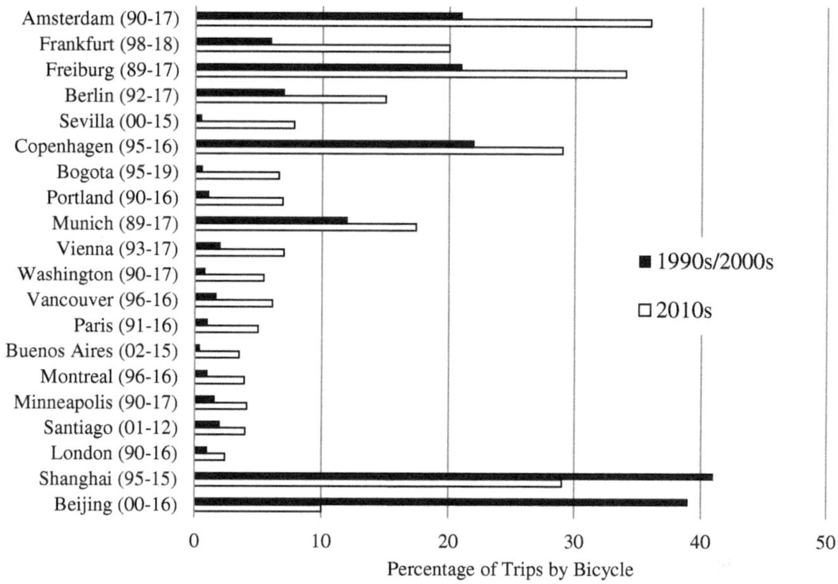

Fig. 3 Trend in percentage of daily trips by bicycle 1990s–2010s. *Based on data in Buehler, R., Pucher, J. (Eds.), 2021. Cycling for Sustainable Cities. MIT Press, Cambridge, MA. and Buehler, R., Teoman, D., Shelton, B., 2021. Promoting bicycling in car-oriented cities: lessons from Washington, DC and Frankfurt Am Main, Germany. Urban Science. 5 (3), 58. doi:10.3390/urbansci5030058 (Note: Mode shares for cities in the United States and Canada are for regular commutes to work only.)*

increased between the 1900s/2000s and 2010s. In Shanghai and Beijing cycling levels dropped sharply, as they did in many other Chinese cities. Moreover, data on bicycling in Chinese cities also include e-bikes which are often sit-down electric scooters without pedals (for details, see the section on e-bikes further below in this chapter). Thus, the decline in traditional pedal-based bicycling is likely even greater. Decreases in cycling in Chinese cities are likely related to growth in car ownership and use, automobile friendly policies, deconstruction of bikeway infrastructure, geographic expansion of cities and longer trip distances, as well as improved public transport systems (Pucher et al., 2021).

In spite of these declines, cycling levels in Chinese cities are still much higher than in many other parts of the world. In the United States and Canada, several cities saw strong increases in bike commuting from a very low level, such as a doubling in Minneapolis, a tripling in Vancouver, a 4-fold increase in Montreal, a 5-fold increase in Washington, DC, and a

7-fold increase in Portland. In South America, cycling levels increased 10-fold in Buenos Aires, doubled in Santiago and grew 7-fold in Bogota.

In Europe, several bike-oriented cities were able to increase cycling levels even further from already high levels, including Amsterdam and Freiburg (+15% and +13%) or Copenhagen (+7%). The strongest percentage increases, however, were in cities with low cycling levels and without recent history of bicycling, such as a doubling in London, a tripling in Vienna, a 5-fold increase in Paris, or an 8-fold growth in Seville. Frankfurt, Germany more than tripled its bike mode share from 6% to 20% (Buehler et al., 2021).

4. Characteristics of bicycle trips: Distance, duration, and speed

So far, we focused on the percentage of trips made by bicycle and its international variation. Another indicator for bicycle usage is distance cycled per inhabitant. National travel survey data on distance cycled per inhabitant per day reflect our discussion on differences in mode split above. In the Netherlands, inhabitants cycle about 3.2 km per day. Danes and Germans cycle only half the distance per day: 1.5 and 1.3 km respectively. As for the mode share data presented above, Switzerland (0.8 km), Austria (0.7 km), Finland (0.7 km), and Sweden (0.5 km) form the following group of countries. Last, reflecting their low bicycle share of trips, kilometers cycled per inhabitant per day is much lower in the UK (0.3 km) and the United States (0.1 km).

At the trip level, distance is an important determinant of bicycling. For very short trips walking may be the most attractive mode of transport. Unlocking and parking a bicycle may take too much time–making walking the fastest option. For longer trip distances, many may choose public transport or the automobile over traditional non-motorized bicycles because of actual or perceived physical exertion. In the following we report statistics for traditional non-motorized bicycles. In a section further below we discuss characteristics of trips by e-bikes.

Our analysis of household travel surveys shows that the median bike trip distances are typically between 2 and 3 km–implying that 50% of all bike trips are shorter than 2-3 km. Average bike trip distances are longer than median distances (3-5 km), due to long bicycle trips that pull the average above the median. In all countries average bike trip distance is at least 60% greater than median bike trip distance: Netherlands (median 2.0 km/average 3.4 km) and Germany (2.0/3.5), Switzerland (1.7/3.7), Finland (2/3.8), USA (1.9/4.3),

Australia (2.5/4.4), and England (3.2/5.2). Considering the distribution of all bike trip distances, in the Netherlands, Germany, Switzerland, Finland, and the United States roughly half of all bike trips are shorter than 2 km and about 80% of bike trips are shorter than 5 km. England and Australia report longer bike trips with 35% of bike trips shorter than 3 km and 70% shorter than 5 km. In all countries 90–95% of bike trips are shorter than 10 km (Goel et al., 2021).

Data for bike trip distances at the city level follow a similar pattern as national trips with median distances between 1.5 and 3 km: Chicago (1.5), Santiago (1.6), New York City (1.7), Zurich (1.8), London (1.9), Amsterdam (2), Munich (2), Cologne (2), Sao Paulo (2), Hamburg (2.2), Cordoba (2.2), Philadelphia, (2.3), Los Angeles (2.3), Berlin (2.5), Brisbane (2.8), Melbourne (2.9), Helsinki (3), Delhi (3), Bangalore (3), Seattle (3.1). Kisumu in Kenya is an outlier with a reported median bike trip distance of 5 km. Similar to the national-level data 40–60% of all bike trips in cities are shorter than 2 km, 80% are shorter than 5 km, and less than 10% of bike trips are longer than 10 km (Goel et al., 2021).

Duration of bike trips shows that typical bike trips are between 10 and 20 min long. Average trip duration ranged from 17 min in the Netherlands to 23 min in the United States and England. Median trip duration ranged from 10 min in the Netherlands, Germany, Switzerland, and Japan to 15 min in Australia, the United States, Argentina, and Finland and 20 min in Chile and Brazil. Again, city level data mirrored national level data ranging from a median of 10 min per bike trip in Amsterdam and Zurich to 20 min in Helsinki, Kisumu, Bangalore, Santiago, Melbourne, Los Angeles, and Sao Paulo. Delhi has the highest value in our dataset reporting 30 min median bike trip durations (Goel et al., 2021).

Combining aggregate distance and duration data at the city or country level, we were able to calculate average speeds for bicycle trips. Nationally, average reported speeds for bicycle trips are between 11 and 13 km/h. Similarly, at the city-level, average reported speeds for bicycle trips are between 9 and 13 km/h. Actual travel speeds while the bicycle is moving are likely higher, because average trip speeds include times when bicycles are stopped, such as waiting at traffic signals or intersections.

5. Demographics of cyclists: Gender and age

The percentage of bicycle trips varies between countries and among cities. In general, higher overall levels of bicycling are correlated with a higher share of bicycle trips made by women. Several studies indicate a greater aversion to traffic and other risks associated with cycling among women compared to men (e.g., Aldred et al., 2017). If countries and cities are to achieve a high level of bicycling, they need to create conditions for cycling that are attractive for men as well as women (Garrard, 2021).

Fig. 4 shows the percentage of bicycle trips made by women for countries and cities. Among countries, women account for less than 40% of bicycle trips in low cycling countries like Australia, England, and the Americas (Argentina, Brazil, the USA, and Chile). Conversely, more bike-oriented countries have higher shares of women riding bikes: 56% in Japan, 55% in the Netherlands, about 50% in Finland and Germany, and 46% in Switzerland. The share of bike trips made by women in cities follows the trends observed on the national levels with women in Dutch and German cities making about 50% of bicycle trips. In Sao Paulo, Melbourne, Seattle and Los Angeles women account for less than 30% of bicycle trips. The bicycle share of trips made by women is also very low in the two Indian cities Delhi and Bangalore—as documented elsewhere in the literature (Pucher et al., 2021).

Cycling levels also vary by age group. As Fig. 5 shows, in continental Europe and the United States cycling levels are highest for the age group 15 years and younger–with bicycles accounting for 36% of trips of those 15 and younger in the Netherlands, about 20% in Germany and Finland, 12% in Switzerland and 2% in the United States. In those countries cycling levels are lower for the mid-age group (16–59) and further decline for those 60 years and older. The Netherlands are an exception where cycling levels are slightly higher for the oldest age group compared to the mid age group. In England, Australia, the US and Japan, cycling levels are comparable for the youngest and middle age group, but decline for those 60 years and older. Contrary to the pattern observed so far, cycling levels for the 15 year and younger age group are lower than for the middle age group in the three South American countries included in the graph: Argentina, Chile, and Brazil. With the exception of the Netherlands, cycling levels are lowest for the oldest age group. In the Netherlands, those 60 years and older make over one quarter of their daily trips by bicycle.

At the city level (see Fig. 6), patterns discovered in aggregate national analysis hold. In general cities in the Netherlands have the highest level of cycling for each age group, followed by continental European and Japanese cities. By contrast, Australian cities and cities in the Americas have lower cycling levels for all age groups. Not shown in Figs. 5 and 6, several countries and cities have reported declining cycling levels for children and teenagers over the last decades, while young and mid-aged adults have increased their cycling level (Buehler et al., 2020; DTU, 2021; Rothman et al., 2018).

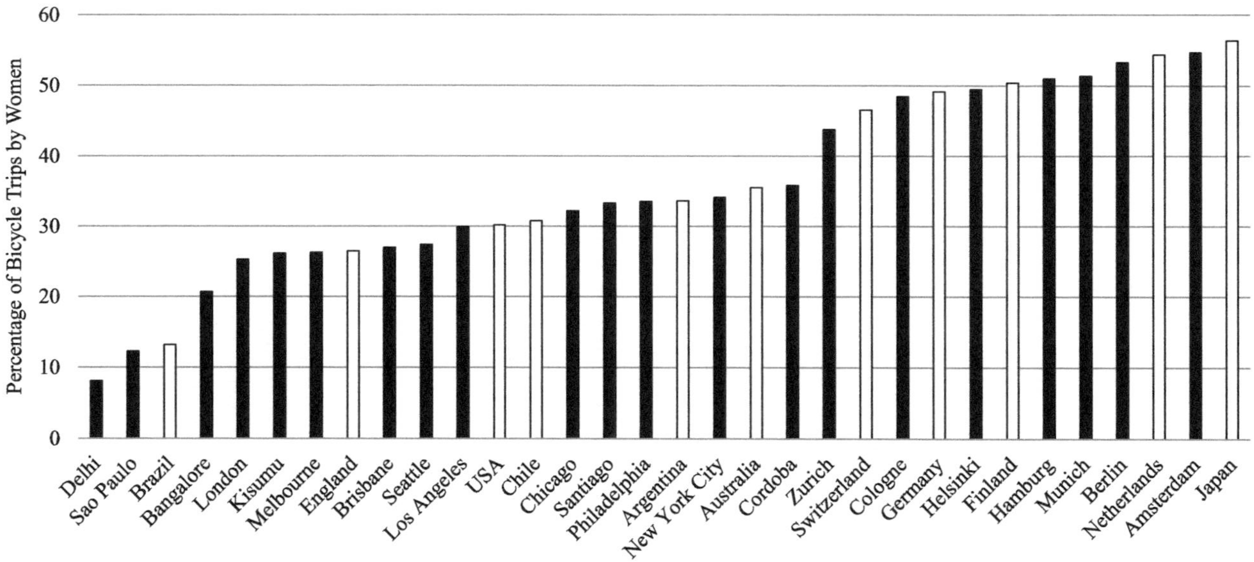

Fig. 4 Women's share of daily bicycle trips in select cities and countries. *Note: black bars represent cities; white bars represent countries. Source: Based on data in Buehler, R., Pucher, J. (Eds.), 2021. Cycling for Sustainable Cities. MIT Press, Cambridge, MA; Buehler, R., Teoman, D., Shelton, B., 2021. Promoting bicycling in car-oriented cities: lessons from Washington, DC and Frankfurt Am Main, Germany. Urban Science. 5 (3), 58. doi:10.3390/urbansci5030058; Goel, R., Goodman, A., Aldred, R., Nakamura, R., Tatah, L., Garcia, L., Diomedi-Zapata, B., et al., 2021. Cycling behaviour in 17 countries across 6 continents: levels of cycling, who cycles, for what purpose, and how far? Transport Reviews. doi:10.1080/01441647.2021.1915898 (Note: data originates from travel surveys for the individual cities. Methods and timing for the travel surveys are not entirely comparable.)*

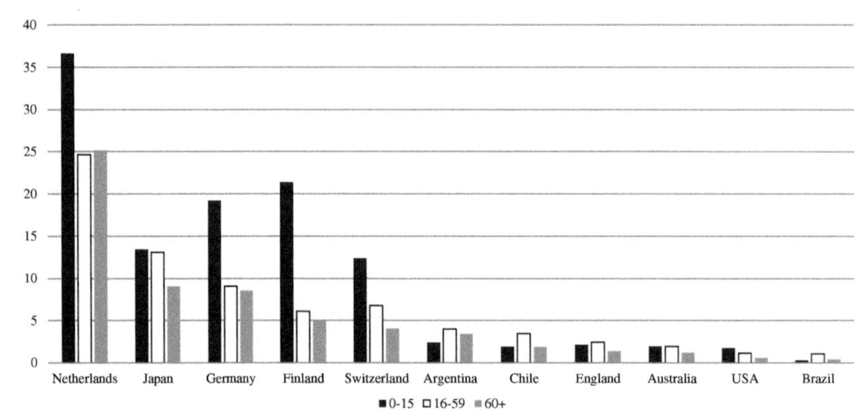

Fig. 5 Bicycle share of daily trips, by age group in select countries. *Figure created based on data from Goel, R., Goodman, A., Aldred, R., Nakamura, R., Tatah, L., Garcia, L., Diomedi-Zapata, B., et al. 2021. Cycling behaviour in 17 countries across 6 continents: levels of cycling, who cycles, for what purpose, and how far? Transport Reviews. doi:10.1080/01441647.2021.1915898.*

6. Electric bicycles (*E*-bikes)

6.1 Definition, growth and mode shift

There is a wide variety of electric powered two-wheelers that are classified as e-bikes depending on the country in which they are operated. In Australia, Europe, and North America, an e-bike is predominantly pedal-assist that uses both human and electric power to drive the wheels. Within these e-bikes, the maximum speed that can be reached with pedaling varies from 25 km/h (called pedelecs) and can be as high as 45 km/h (called S-pedelecs). The latter category may require additional licensing in Europe. Under naturalistic conditions, trips with pedelecs are about 2 km/h faster than conventional bicycles and trips with S-pedelecs are about 9 km/h faster (Schleinitz et al., 2017). A pedal-assist e-bike provides about 75% as much physical activity as a conventional bicycle for the same duration of usage (Castro et al., 2019). In China, until 2019, an e-bike did not require to have functional pedals, though the regulation (loosely enforced) controls the top speed (Fishman and Cherry, 2016). Such e-bikes do not provide any physical activity. However, a recent regulation classifies pedal-assist bicycles with a maximum speed of 25 km/h as e-bikes (Yang, 2019). In India also, e-bikes are not required to be pedal assist and are categorized based on the maximum power output and maximum speed (MORTH, 1989).

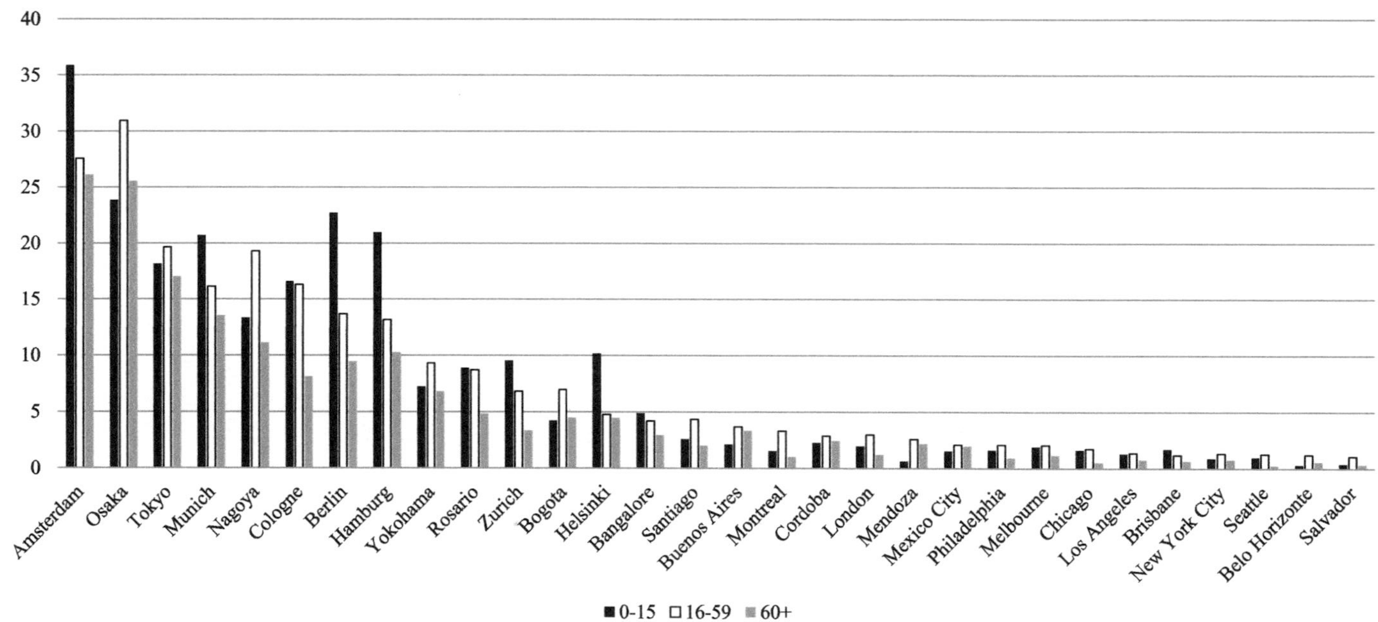

Fig. 6 Share of daily bicycle trips by age group in select cities. *Figure created based on data from Goel, R., Goodman, A., Aldred, R., Nakamura, R., Tatah, L., Garcia, L., Diomedi-Zapata, B., et al., 2021. Cycling behaviour in 17 countries across 6 continents: levels of cycling, who cycles, for what purpose, and how far?. Transport Reviews. doi:10.1080/01441647.2021.1915898.*

The literature has distinguished between the two categories of e-bikes—those that are pedal-assist and those that are fully throttle-powered. Studies from North America and Europe refer to the former category, while studies from Asia also include fully throttle-powered vehicles.

China is the largest market of e-bikes in the world followed by Germany, the Netherlands, the USA, Italy, and France (Bigazzi and Wong, 2020; Cherry and MacArthur, 2019). When expressed in terms of per capita annual sales of e-bikes, the Netherlands, Switzerland, Denmark, Austria, and Germany are the leading countries, in that order (Fishman and Cherry, 2016). In the Netherlands, e-bikes are a majority among new bikes sold. In Switzerland, the share of e-bikes among new bikes sold has grown rapidly from 1% in 2006 to 33% in 2019 (Rérat, 2021). During this period, the number of e-bikes across Europe has grown by more than 600% (Ebicycles, 2022).

In most countries, e-bike usage has only increased recently and this growth is a result of shifts from other modes. However, which modes are replaced by e-bikes differs across cities and countries and depends largely on the dominant modes of transport in the setting. According to a meta-analysis of mode shifts to e-bikes for cities and countries around the world, the median percent of e-bike trips that replaced public transport was the highest (33%), followed by those that replaced conventional bicycle trips (27%), and automobile trips (24%), with wide variation across the countries (Bigazzi and Wong, 2020). In the US, where car use is high, a major reason to buy e-bikes was to replace car trips, and a majority (60%) of e-bike trips replaced cars, followed by active travel or public transport (MacArthur et al., 2018). Similar mode shifts have been reported among older adults in Australia– another high car use country (Johnson and Rose, 2015). In the Netherlands and Denmark, with high levels of cycling, the majority of e-bike trips replaced conventional cycling and a slightly lower share of trips replaced cars. Public transport was also replaced by a high share of e-bike trips (Sun et al., 2020). In German cities, the mode shift from e-bikes was almost equally high from cars and conventional bicycles, and these accounted for a large majority of trips (Kämper et al., 2016). In Sweden, while cars were the main mode of transport that was replaced, e-bikes also replaced conventional cycles and public transport. In leisure trips, a significant share of conventional cycles was also replaced (Hiselius and Svensson, 2017). In Chinese cities, half of the e-bike users previously used the bus, 20–35% used conventional bicycles and about 10% were previously car users (Cherry et al., 2016; Cherry and Cervero, 2007).

6.2 Distance and trip purpose

Compared to conventional cycling, e-bikes are faster and need lower physical effort, which helps overcome some constraints such as hilliness and wind. As expected, e-bikes have been found to be used for longer distances than conventional cycling (Banerjee et al., 2021; Bourne et al., 2020; Castro et al., 2019). Studies have reported that total daily or weekly distance traveled by e-bikes are 50–70% greater than for conventional cycling (Bourne et al., 2020). This results from longer trips as well as a greater number of those. Sun et al. (2020) reported travel patterns of a set of Dutch individuals that adopted an e-bike. They compared their mode share by distance range before and after adoption of e-bike. Fig. 7 below shows that for every distance range, e-bike users traveled for a greater proportion of the trips compared to conventional cycles. While e-bikes replaced almost all the conventional cycle trips among e-bike users, they also replaced car, public transport, and walking trips. In the distance range of 10–15 km, the only significant mode shift to e-bikes was from cars, indicating that e-bikes have greater potential to replace car trips than conventional cycles (Kroesen, 2017). Similar trip distance distributions of the two types of bicycles have been reported for Denmark (Banerjee et al., 2021).

E-bikes are more frequently used for utilitarian purposes than for leisure (Bourne et al., 2020). In the Netherlands, for example, 67% of e-bikes trips were for commuting, shopping or transporting people or goods, and 26% for leisure (Sun et al., 2020). In China, more than half of the e-bike trips were

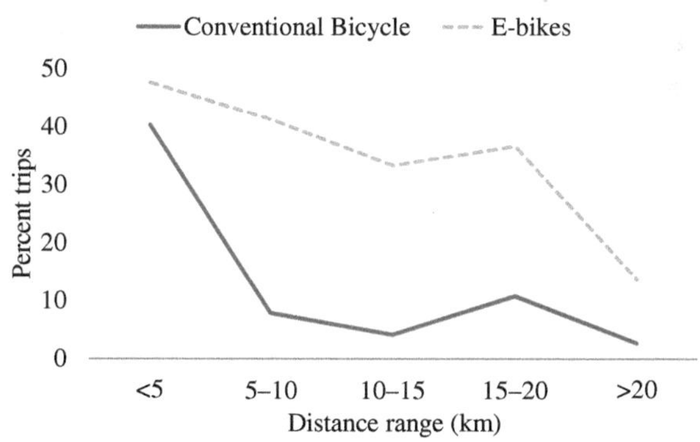

Fig. 7 Distance based mode share of conventional bicycles and e-bikes for individuals that adopted e-bikes. *Figure created based on data from Banerjee, A., Łukawska, M., Jensen, A.F., Haustein, S., 2021. Facilitating bicycle commuting beyond short distances: insights from existing literature. Transport Reviews, 1–25. doi:10.1080/01441647.2021.2004261.*

for commuting, followed by shopping. The use of e-bikes for 'entertainment' was rare (Cherry and Cervero, 2007). There are variations in the distribution of trip purposes by age. Across various settings in the US and Europe, e-bikes have been reported to be used primarily for commuting among populations aged 55 years or younger. It is used for leisure, visiting friends and for recreation by older adults and only rarely for commuting (Bourne et al., 2020).

6.3 Gender

The gender differences in uptake of e-bikes is largely a reflection of gender differences in overall cycling levels in the countries. In the Netherlands and Denmark where the majority of cyclists are females, e-bike users have a similar gender split as regular cyclists (Haustein and Møller, 2016; Melia and Bartle, 2021; Sun et al., 2020). In China also, conventional cycling as well as e-bike users have an even gender split (Cherry and Cervero, 2007). On the other hand, in Australia and the USA, with poor representation of females in overall cycling, they are a minority group among e-bike users as well (Melia and Bartle, 2021). Since e-bikes help overcome some of the barriers faced by conventional cyclists such as distance, hilliness and physical effort, e-bikes have shown the potential to have representation across a range of social groups (women, people over 40 years, and those with physical conditions) and to level some gender differences (Melia and Bartle, 2021; Rérat, 2021). For example, in Norway, ownership of e-bikes resulted in a greater increase in the number of cycle trips among females than males (Fyhri and Fearnley, 2015) and in the Netherlands, among those who shifted from conventional cycling to e-bikes, women increased their travel distance by a greater amount than did men. In Switzerland and New Zealand, women have greater representation among e-bike users than among conventional bicycle users (Rérat, 2021; Wild et al., 2021). However, such comparative data is not available in the literature for other settings to generalize these findings.

7. Conclusions

Over the last decades many cities and countries have promoted bicycling for daily trips as a healthy, efficient, economical, and environmentally friendly mode of transport. This chapter documented that there is great variability in cycling levels among countries and cities. Compared to countries in the Americas, England and Australia, cycling levels in more bicycling-oriented countries like Denmark, Japan, and Germany are 3–10 times greater and cycling levels in the Netherlands, the most bike oriented country, are 7–10 times greater. Among cities there was even greater variability in cycling levels with high cycling cities displaying a bicycle share of trips 40–50 times greater than in low cycling cities. While there was considerable variability within countries, in general, cities in high cycling countries had greater cycling levels than cities in low cycling countries. Our analysis shows that typical bicycle trip distances range between 2 and 3 km with an average duration of 10 and 20 min. Cyclists typically report riding speeds of 10–15 km/h.

During the last 20 years there were only small changes in the percentage of trips made by bicycle at national levels, but some cities were very successful at increasing cycling levels. This successful group included cities with traditionally higher cycling levels as well as newcomers to bicycling starting at very low cycling levels. One notable exception were Chinese cities that saw strong declines in bicycling. Countries and cities with higher cycling levels display lower or no inequalities in cycling use in terms of gender and age. Cycling conditions and cultures there may allow a larger share of society to ride bicycles and thus contributes to overall higher levels of cycling.

During the past decades or so, e-bike usage has grown rapidly in many Asian, European, and North American countries. In some western European countries, e-bikes account for a significant share among the new bicycles sold. With their ability to go faster with reduced physical effort, e-bikes can be used to travel longer distances, and provide ease while riding in windy conditions or on hilly roads. As a result, e-bikes have been reported to replace motorized modes (cars and public transport) for trips that may be too long for conventional cycling. Though, in this process, e-bike users are also replacing conventional cycling and this shift is of particular concern where baseline levels of conventional cycles are high (e.g., China, Denmark and Netherlands).

The preliminary evidence available from different settings suggests that e-bikes are being used primarily for commuting, though older adults are using them for non-utilitarian trips. This is beneficial as commuting trips are often longer than most other trips and for that reason are frequently made using motorized modes. With the ability of e-bikes to travel longer distances, these could be replaced. The trade-offs will differ if the shift is primarily from public transport that, unlike cars, also contribute to physical activity during last-mile access (Goel et al., 2022). However, going by the international evidence for conventional cycling (Goel et al., 2021), for e-bikes to achieve high levels of mode shares, it will need to cater to trips other than the commute to work. Benefits of e-bikes should also be seen from an equity perspective. Due to their ease of use compared to conventional bicycles, e-bikes are showing the potential to have greater representation from population sub-groups such as women, older adults and those with physical conditions that are often marginalized in conventional cycling.

Countries, especially in Asia, need to use caution as they push for electric two-wheeler policies. In China, until recently, e-bikes did not have to be pedal-assist and throttle-powered e-bikes are in high use. A recent course correction has made pedal-assist mandatory to classify as e-bikes in China. In India, regulations continue to permit the use of e-bikes that are fully throttle-powered, without any pedal-assist. While conversion to electric may reduce on-road emissions and limit top speed (if regulated), such vehicles do not provide any physical activity.

References

Aldred, R., Elliott, B., Woodcock, J., Goodman, A., 2017. Cycling provision separated from motor traffic: a systematic review exploring whether stated preferences vary by gender and age. Transp. Rev. 37 (1), 29–55.

Banerjee, A., Łukawska, M., Jensen, A.F., Haustein, S., 2021. Facilitating bicycle commuting beyond short distances: insights from existing literature. Transp. Rev. 1–25. https://doi.org/10.1080/01441647.2021.2004261.

Bigazzi, A., Wong, K., 2020. Electric bicycle mode substitution for driving, public transit, conventional cycling, and walking. Transp. Res. D Transp. Environ. 85. https://doi.org/10.1016/j.trd.2020.102412, 102412.

Bourne, J.E., Cooper, A.R., Kelly, P., Kinnear, F.J., England, C., Leary, S., Page, A., 2020. The impact of E-cycling on travel behaviour: a scoping review. J. Transp. Health 19, 100910. https://doi.org/10.1016/j.jth.2020.100910.

Brand, C., Goetschi, T., Dons, E., Gerike, R., et al., 2021. The climate change mitigation impacts of active travel: evidence from a longitudinal panel study in seven European cities. Glob. Environ. Chang. 67, 102224. https://doi.org/10.1016/j.gloenvcha.2021.102224.

Buehler, R., Pucher, J. (Eds.), 2021. Cycling for Sustainable Cities. MIT Press, Cambridge, MA.

Buehler, R., Pucher, J., Gerike, R., Goetschi, T., 2017. Reducing car dependence in the heart of Europe: lessons from Germany, Austria, and Switzerland. Transp. Rev. 37 (1), 4–28.

Buehler, R., Pucher, J., Bauman, A., 2020. Physical activity from walking and cycling for daily travel in the United States, 2001–2017: demographic, socioeconomic, and geographic variation. J. Transp. Health 16, 1405–2214, 100811. https://doi.org/10.1016/j.jth.2019.100811.

Buehler, R., Teoman, D., Shelton, B., 2021. 2021 promoting bicycling in Car-oriented cities: lessons from Washington, DC and Frankfurt Am Main, Germany. Urban Sci. 5 (3), 58. https://doi.org/10.3390/urbansci5030058.

Castro, A., Gaupp-Berghausen, M., Dons, E., Standaert, A., Laeremans, M., Clark, A., Anaya-Boig, E., Cole-Hunter, T., Avila-Palencia, I., Rojas-Rueda, D.,

Nieuwenhuijsen, M., 2019. Physical activity of electric bicycle users compared to conventional bicycle users and non-cyclists: insights based on health and transport data from an online survey in seven European cities. Transp. Res. Interdiscip. Perspect. 1, 100017.
Cherry, C., Cervero, R., 2007. Use characteristics and mode choice behavior of electric bike users in China. Transp. Policy 14 (3), 247–257. https://doi.org/10.1016/j.tranpol.2007.02.005.
Cherry, C., MacArthur, J.H., 2019. E-Bike Safety. A Review of Empirical European and North American Studies. Light Electric Vehicle Education and Research Initiative. https://wsd-pfbsparkinfluence.S3.Amazonaws.Com/Uploads/2019/10/EbikeSafety-VFinal.Pdf.
Cherry, C., Yang, H., Jones, L.R., He, M., 2016. Dynamics of electric bike ownership and use in Kunming, China. Transp. Policy 45, 127–135. https://doi.org/10.1016/j.tranpol.2015.09.007.
DTU, 2021. The Danish National Travel Survey. Technical University of Denmark, Copenhagen.
Ebicycles, 2022. E-Bike Facts & Statistics for 2022. eBicycles.com. Available at https://www.ebicycles.com/ebike-facts-statistics. (Accessed 4 January 2022).
Fishman, E., Cherry, C., 2016. E-bikes in the mainstream: reviewing a decade of research. Transp. Rev. 36 (1), 72–91. https://doi.org/10.1080/01441647.2015.1069907.
Fyhri, A., Fearnley, N., 2015. Effects of E-bikes on bicycle use and mode share. Transp. Res. D Transp. Environ. 36, 45–52. https://doi.org/10.1016/j.trd.2015.02.005.
Garrard, J., 2021. Women and cycling addressing the gender gap. In: Buehler, R., Pucher, J. (Eds.), Cycling for Sustainable Cities. MIT Press, Cambridge, MA, pp. 197–218.
Garrard, J., Rissel, C., Bauman, A., Giles-Corti, B., 2021. Cycling and health. In: Buehler, R., Pucher, J. (Eds.), Cycling for Sustainable Cities. MIT Press, Cambridge, MA, pp. 35–56.
Goel, R., Goodman, A., Aldred, R., Nakamura, R., Tatah, L., Garcia, L., Diomedi-Zapata, B., et al., 2021. Cycling behaviour in 17 countries across 6 continents: levels of cycling, who cycles, for what purpose, and how far? Transp. Rev. https://doi.org/10.1080/01441647.2021.1915898.
Goel, R., Oyebode, O., Foley, L., Tatah, L., Millett, C., Woodcock, J., 2022. Gender differences in active travel in major cities across the world. Transportation. https://doi.org/10.1007/s11116-021-10259-4.
Haustein, S., Møller, M., 2016. Age and attitude: changes in cycling patterns of different e-bike user segments. Int. J. Sustain. Transp. 10 (9), 836–846. https://doi.org/10.1080/15568318.2016.1162881.
Hiselius, L.W., Svensson, Å., 2017. E-bike use in Sweden—CO2 effects due to modal change and municipal promotion strategies. J. Clean. Prod. 141, 818–824. https://doi.org/10.1016/j.jclepro.2016.09.141.
Johnson, M., Rose, G., 2015. Extending life on the bike: electric bike use by older Australians. J. Transp. Health 2 (2), 276–283. https://doi.org/10.1016/j.jth.2015.03.001.
Kämper, C., Helms, H., Jöhrens, J., 2016. Modal shifting effects and climate impacts through electric bicycle use in Germany. J. Earth Sci. Geotech. Eng. 6, 331–345.
Koglin, T., teBroemmelstroet, M., van Wee, B., 2021. Cycling in Copenhagen and Amsterdam. In: Buehler, R., Pucher, J. (Eds.), Cycling for Sustainable Cities. MIT Press, Cambridge, MA, pp. 347–370.
Kroesen, M., 2017. To what extent do e-bikes substitute travel by other modes? Evidence from the Netherlands. Transp. Res. D Transp. Environ. 53, 377–387.
Kunert, U., Kloas, J., Kuhfeld, H., 2002. Design characteristics of national travel surveys: international comparison for 10 countries. Transp. Res. Rec. 1804 (1), 107–116.

MacArthur, J., Cherry, C.R., Harpool, M., Scheppke, D., 2018. A North American Survey of Electric Bicycle Owners. National Institute for Transportation and Communities (NITC).

Melia, S., Bartle, C., 2021. Who uses E-bikes in the UK and why? Int. J. Sustain. Transp. 1–13. https://doi.org/10.1080/15568318.2021.1956027.

MORTH, 1989. The Central Motor Vehicles Rules, New Delhi, India. https://morth.nic.in/sites/default/files/CMVR-chapter1_1.pdf.

PBOT. n.d. How Portland Benefits from Bicycle Transportation. City of Portland Bureau of Transportation, Portland, Oregon.

Pucher, J., Tiwari, G., Peng, Z., Cao, R., Gao, Y., 2021. Cycling in China and India. In: Buehler, R., Pucher, J. (Eds.), Cycling for Sustainable Cities. MIT Press, Cambridge, MA, pp. 281–300.

Rérat, P., 2021. The rise of the E-bike: towards an extension of the practice of cycling? Mobilities 16 (3), 423–439. https://doi.org/10.1080/17450101.2021.1897236.

Rothman, L., Macpherson, A., Ross, T., Buliung, R., 2018. The decline in active school transportation (AST): a systematic review of the factors related to AST and changes in school transport over time in North America. Prev. Med. 111, 314–322. ISSN 0091-7435 https://doi.org/10.1016/j.ypmed.2017.11.018.

Schleinitz, K., Petzoldt, T., Franke-Bartholdt, L., Krems, J., Gehlert, T., 2017. The German naturalistic cycling study—comparing cycling speed of riders of different e-bikes and conventional bicycles. Saf. Sci. 92, 290–297. https://doi.org/10.1016/j.ssci.2015.07.027.

Shaw, C., Russell, M., Keall, M., MacBride-Stewart, S., Wild, K., Reeves, D., Bentley, R., Woodward, A., 2020. Beyond the bicycle: seeing the context of the gender gap in cycling. J. Transp. Health 18, 100871.

Sun, Q., Feng, T., Kemperman, A., Spahn, A., 2020. Modal shift implications of E-bike use in the Netherlands: moving towards sustainability? Transp. Res. D Transp. Environ 78, 102202. https://doi.org/10.1016/j.trd.2019.102202.

Wild, K., Woodward, A., Shaw, C., 2021. Gender and the E-bike: exploring the role of electric bikes in increasing women's access to cycling and physical activity. Active Travel Stud. 1 (1).

Woodcock, J., Tainio, M., de Sa, T.H., de Nazelle, A., Goel, R., Gouveia, N., Tiwari, G., Verma, A., Miranda, J., Brage, S., 2017. Towards an integrated global transport and health assessment tool (TIGTHAT). J. Transp. Health 5, S99–S100.

Yang, Y., 2019. New National Standards on Electric Bicycles Take Effect. China Daily. Available at: https://www.chinadaily.com.cn/a/201904/16/WS5cb5858da310484226 0b6805.html. (Accessed 4 January 2022).

CHAPTER EIGHT

Modeling of cycling behavior

Danique Ton[a], Alexandra Gavriilidou[b], Yufei Yuan[b], Florian Schneider[c], Serge Hoogendoorn[b,*], and Winnie Daamen[d]

[a]NS Stations, Utrecht, The Netherlands
[b]Transport & Planning Department, Delft University of Technology, Delft, The Netherlands
[c]Freiburg, Germany
[d]Faculty of Civil Engineering and Geosciences, Department of Transport & Planning, Delft University of Technology, Delft, The Netherlands
*Corresponding author: e-mail address: s.p.hoogendoorn@tudelft.nl

Contents

Abstract

In this chapter, we focus on the modeling of the behavior of cyclists. This behavior encompasses different types of interconnected decisions: from the split-second decisions that cyclists make when they are riding their bike and are interacting with the road and other traffic participants to choices pertaining to the activities they want to perform and the locations where they can perform these activities. These different decisions are often related to different temporal (and spatial) scales. The detail in which these decisions need to be accurately modeled is often dependent on what the model is applied for, as will be explained in the ensuing of this chapter. Therefore, different (types of) models have been developed, as introduced in the last part of this chapter.

Keywords: Bicycle traffic flow operations, Bicycle route choice, Modal choice, Random utility models, Model identification, Impact assessment

Advances in Transport Policy and Planning, Volume 10
ISSN 2543-0009
https://doi.org/10.1016/bs.atpp.2022.06.001

1. Introduction

The commonly used definition of the term "model" is "a simplified representation of reality." We identify models for analysis of a problem, to achieve a better understanding of the main aspects and relations of importance of a specific process or phenomena. Models can be conceptual, relational, mathematical, or numerical. In this chapter, we focus on mathematical models. Computer implementations of these models often require translating mathematical constructs into discretized approximations of these models. We will refer to these computer implementations as (numerical) simulation models.

Models generally have *inputs* and *parameters or coefficients*. Parameters describe the (dynamic) behavior of a model. In the traffic and transportation domain, these parameters often have a physical or behavioral interpretation. Examples of parameters that will be discussed in the ensuing are the jam density of a cycle flow, or the personal characteristics of cyclists when choosing a route. Model inputs describe data that a model needs to determine a result. This could be a demand profile, a street layout, or the prevailing intersection control settings. In most cases, end users of commercial (simulation) models are expected to determine the input of a model before running their computations, while they usually do not change the model parameters (Brackstone et al., 2012). However, simulation guidelines as well as literature show that calibration and validation is not only necessary, but also a tedious part of a simulation study (Daamen et al., 2014).

1.1 Microscopic and macroscopic approaches

While model classifications can be made on many grounds two specific dimensions are very important for any transportation model, namely the way traffic is represented and how its behavior is described.

Traffic—in general—can be *represented* as individual particles (vehicles, bicycles, pedestrians). This representation is referred to as *microscopic*. Traffic can also be described in terms of its aggregate—often assumed continuous—characteristics (e.g., flows, densities, average speeds). This representation is referred to as *macroscopic* or *continuum* based on the analogy with how we represent continuum media such as fluids and gases. In some models, traffic is represented as *packets* (groups) or in terms of *distributions* (e.g., distribution of the speeds). Packets are generally not treated differently from individual particles (i.e., microscopically), while in many cases distributions are described via continuous variables (e.g., gas-kinetic models (Hoogendoorn and Bovy, 2001)).

Next to microscopic or macroscopic representations, we can describe the behavior of traffic in different ways. First, *behavioral rules* can express how individuals react to other traffic participants, the infrastructure and external conditions (think of weather, but also travel costs and time). These behavioral rules are typical *microscopic behavioral rules* that mathematically describe how we believe the cycling behavior of cyclists relate to the cycling behavior of other cyclists (e.g., see (Hoogendoorn et al., 2021)), but they can be interpreted broader than that. Second, we can also use—often empirically determined—descriptive relations. These *macroscopic* relations can be used to relate flow variables (e.g., the fundamental diagram describes the traffic flow as a function of the traffic density), or to relate the behavior of an individual to aggregate characteristics (e.g., the speed of a single cyclist is determined by the traffic density on the road she is traversing).

These two dimensions yield a matrix in which many of the modeling approaches that are used in the remainder can be classified. Table 1 visualizes this matrix and includes some examples of modeling approaches. For example, a microscopic model identifies individual cyclists (microscopic representation), and for each cyclist it determines the speed and acceleration based on the surrounding traffic and external conditions (microscopic behavioral rules). Another example is a traffic assignment model, which assigns flows (continuum representation) to a traffic network using the network topology, link characteristics and link performance functions (macroscopic relations).

1.2 Model validation

It is often said that "all models are wrong, but some are useful" (Box, 1976). The process of determining *how useful* is, in a way, related to the model quality: how accurate are the model predictions, how accurate does the model

Table 1 Traffic model classification and example modeling approaches.

	Microscopic representation	Continuum representation
Microscopic behavioral rules (predictive)	Microscopic models	Gas-kinetic models
Macroscopic relations (descriptive)	Particle models, route/mode choice models	Macroscopic models, assignment models

describe the real-world process. The process of improving the model quality generally consists of the following steps (Daamen et al., 2014):

1. *Verification* of a model is the step where a model developer checks if the (simulation) model behaves as expected and has been implemented correctly (e.g., in computer software). This step results in *construct* or *face validity*.
2. *Calibration or model estimation* is the step where a model is fitted to real data by tuning its parameters. If a model has been successfully calibrated, we say that it has *content validity* and is able to reproduce the data on which it has been calibrated.
3. *Validation* is the final step in the process where we assess the model using validation data (i.e., data that were not used for calibration). When a forecasting model is validated, we say it is *predictively valid*. For a causal model, this step describes how accurate the model is able to describe a situation for which it has not been developed.

Fig. 1 provides a schematic overview of these steps in developing, validating, and using a model. In both the calibration and validation steps, the definition of the Measure of Performance (MoPs, showing how well a model reproduces the data) is very important. Clearly, the data as well as the MoPs are determined by the intended model application. This also implies that in general, not all models are suitable for all applications, as will be explained in more detail in Section 2.

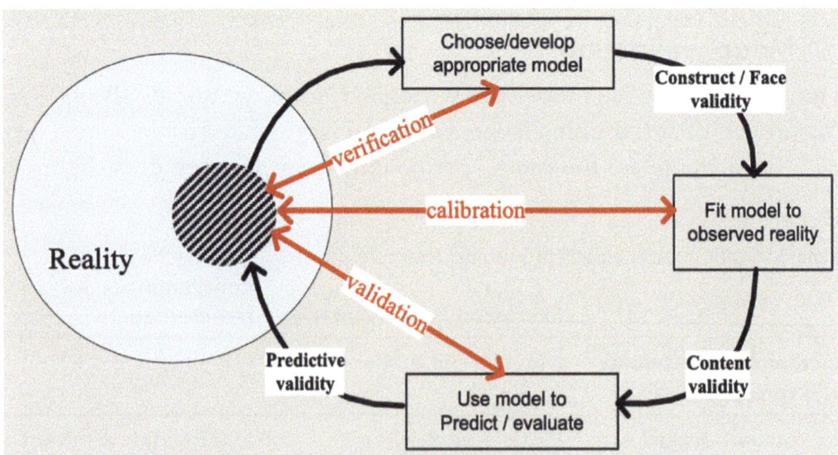

Fig. 1 Overview of different steps in model development and validation.

2. Bicycle modeling framework

The behavior of travelers in general manifests itself at *different temporal and spatial levels*. This also applies to cyclists. People decide if and if so, how often, they want or need to travel, where they want to go, which (combination of) travel mode(s) they will use, which route to use, when to leave, how to interact with other traffic participants, etc. Most of these decisions are not independent, but depend on previously taken decisions, e.g., someone can only use a bike if a bike is available to this person.

Fig. 2 shows an overview of the main behavioral levels that are often considered in travel and traffic modeling. Table 2 relates these different levels to different applications: it shows which levels are to be included in a model

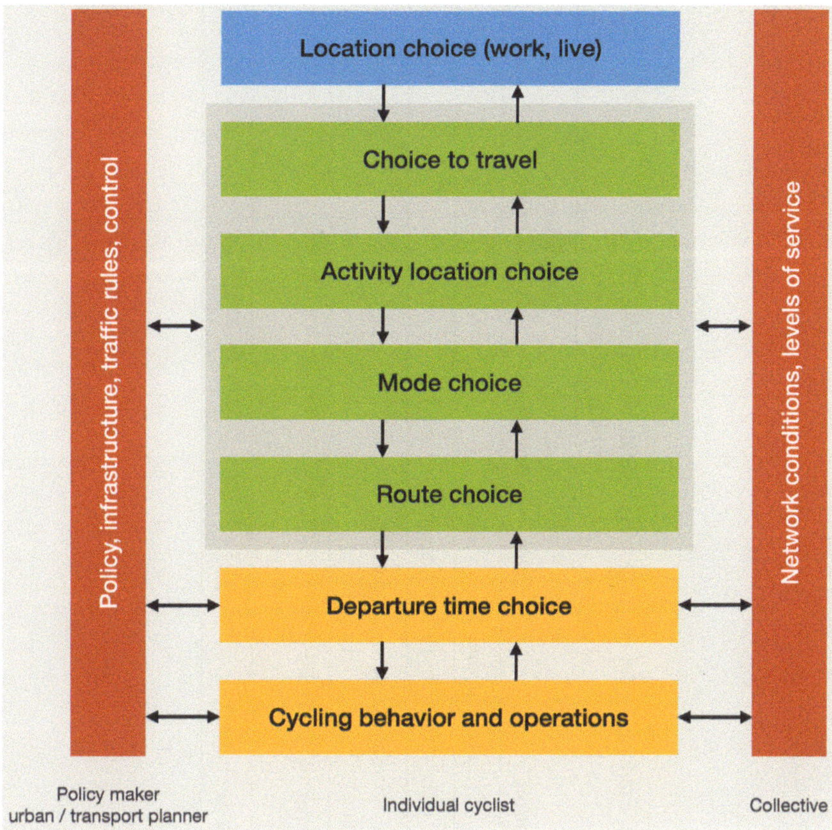

Fig. 2 Behavioral levels for bicycle travel in relation to policy, infrastructure, traffic regulations, and control, as well as to network conditions.

Table 2 Example model applications in relation to behavioral levels.

		Mobility behavior					
Application	**Scale**	**Cycling operations**	**Departure time choice**	**Route choice**	**Mode choice**	**Destination choice**	**Choice to travel**
Impact of travel subsidies	National		+	+	+	+	+
Impact of new bicycle path	Regional	+	+	+	+	+	
Design of intersection controller	Local	+		+			
Geometric design of bicycle path	Local	+					
Section in chapter:		5	4.2			3	

if the model has to be suitable for a specific type of application. For instance, if a policy maker aims to predict the impact of a subsidy on electric bicycles, she needs to be able to determine *if* this has impact on the frequency of travel, the locations people travel to, the mode choice, the route that people will use, and the times at which they will travel. However, when a transportation planner wants to determine the impact of a new control scheme for an intersection controller, she will likely be more interested in the local impacts on queuing, delays, etc. (i.e., cycling operations), and effects that these may have on for instance route choice. Note that Fig. 2 describes the generic choice processes. Models for each choice process will cover their specific behavioral rules as well as include the relevant influencing factors. For example, in the choice to travel also the travel frequency and trip chaining behavior (multiple destinations in a tour) may be included, in the mode choice model the availability of a bike or ebike and the use of the bike as access/egress mode may be included and instead of having separate models for mode and route choice, one can even considered a joint choice model.

There are few simulation packages that include high-fidelity and robust submodels for all of these levels. Often, strategic or planning models used by city planners or transportation analysts have relatively coarse descriptions of cycling operations, while detailed microscopic simulation models are often limited to modeling operations and route choice. In Section 6, we will discuss this issue in more detail.

3. Activity-travel modeling

Daily-life traveling is usually not a purpose on its own but a necessity to reach locations where people perform activities. The need for activity participation has to be reconciled with accessible activity locations. Consequently, activity-travel behavior can be conceptualized as a demand-supply problem (Schneider, 2021). A key mechanism to bring demand and supply in accordance is the activity location choice, see Fig. 3. In the following, the different elements of Fig. 3 will be described and discussed before concluding with some characteristics activity-travel behavior by bicycle.

The demand side is driven by the need for *activity participation*. *Activities* can be defined as actions that serve the satisfaction of personal or household needs (Mcnally and Rindt, 2007). For instance, most people work to have the financial resources to buy food, pay the rent or purchase other goods and services. While the needs can be very individual, corresponding activities are generally attributed to a few functional categories that recur in many

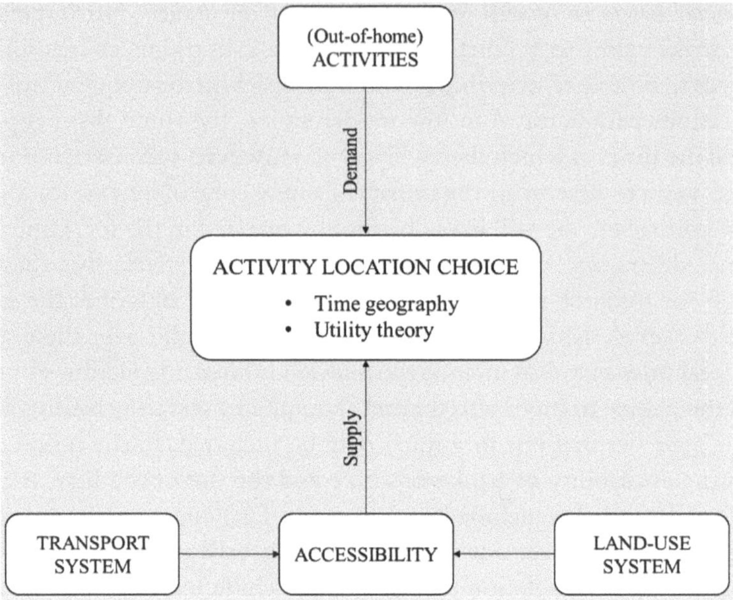

Fig. 3 Spatial activity-travel behavior. *Adapted from Schneider, F., 2021. Spatial Activity-Travel Patterns of Cyclists. Doctoral Dissertation, PhD Thesis, Delft University of Technology.*

daily-life schedules such as work, shop, leisure, etc. In addition, each activity is linked to the location where it is performed and a duration.

The supply side relates to the *accessibility* to corresponding activity locations. Accessibility describes in this context "the extent to which land-use and transport systems enable (groups of) individuals to reach activities or destinations by means of a (combination of) transport mode(s)" (Geurs and van Wee, 2013). The land-use component of this definition captures the spatial distribution of activity locations. The transport system component determines the burden of overcoming space between the different locations in the networks of the available travel modes. This burden or spatial resistance includes features such as travel costs, travel time and physical and psychological effort (Annema, 2013).

The key choice in the interplay between the need for activity participation and the accessibility to activity locations is the *activity location choice*. This choice dimension is of fundamental significance for several travel choices since it determines the locations of an origin and destination pair. Based on the spatial resistance between both locations for each travel mode, it will have, for instance, a strong impact on the mode choice. While the activity location choice conceptually precedes the mode choice, it must already include a rough feasibility analysis (also considering the available transport options).

A way to model the trade-off between activity participation and travel is based on *utility theory* (Fishburn, 1968). As said before, traveling is often a necessity for performing activities that comes with the burden of overcoming space. Consequently, activity participation is attributed a utility and travel a disutility. From a conceptual perspective, a person is supposed to make choices that maximize his or her utility. This representation means that a person would choose activity locations where the difference between the gained utility of activity participation and the disutility related to travel is largest. Translated into more practical terms, a person would usually look for the nearest or fastest to reach activity location and only travel further if this is related to a surplus of utility.

An important note on the presented framework is its dependence on some long-term choices. The residential *location choice* will determine the features of the surrounding land-use and transport system. Other long-term commitments, which are linked to a fixed location as well, such as work or education, will set further boundaries to the decision space of activity-travel behavior.

A further reflection on the presented framework concerns the *choice to travel*. It is obvious that only out-of-home activities induce individual travel. The distinction between typical home and out-of-home activities, however, is less straightforward than it used to be in the past. Due to several technical innovations (such as the widespread availability of fast internet), the increasing presence of social media as well as live chat and communication tools, the development of location-independent services (e.g., online fitness courses) and, not to forget, new regulations as a response to the pandemic, the freedom of choice has increased considerably. As a result, working from home is facilitated, people are enabled to have social interactions without any change of location and multifold products are delivered directly to home.

With regard to activity-travel behavior by bicycle, some mode-specific peculiarities need to be considered:

(i) Distance-sensitivity: In contrast to the motorized modes, locomotion by bicycle is based on a physical effort. For this reason, spatial resistance seems to be better captured by travel distance than by travel time (Schneider et al., 2021).

(ii) Utility and disutility: As described above, activity participation is usually related to utility and the corresponding travel to disutility. However, under certain conditions, riding a bicycle can also provide utility. This is the case when the bicycle ride directly satisfies a personal need, such as the need for physical exercise.

(iii) Further functional properties of the bicycle: The bicycle is a private means of transport with a high degree of temporal and spatial flexibility. Conversely, it is restricted (besides its limited spatial reach) about its capacity of transporting people and goods, its self-propulsion leads to lower attractiveness in case of hilly terrain and the fact that the cyclist is not well-sheltered, may lead to additional discomfort in case of adverse weather conditions (rain, wind, but also too high temperatures).

4. Mode and route choice modeling

In this section, we consider modeling of route choice and mode choice. We discuss the objectives of modeling, the determinants of the choices reported in literature, and the concept of choice sets.

4.1 Cycling mode choice

It is important to understand which factors influence an individual to use the bicycle for her trip. Discrete choice models are often used when investigating this type of research questions. These models require the identification of factors (attributes) to include in the model, and the relevant alternatives (cycling, walking, car, public transport, etc.) described in the choice set. Several categories of mode choice determinants are relevant for active mode choice: individual characteristics, household characteristics, season and weather characteristics, trip characteristics, built environment, and employment conditions (Ton et al., 2019). The most dominant categories of determinants for cycling are trip characteristics, built environment, and employment conditions.

- The individual characteristics entail for example socio-demographics. The socio-demographics have often been investigated; however mixed results are found. Often, literature claims that men cycle more often than women. Heinen et al. (2010) confirm this for countries with low cycling penetration, however in countries with high cycling penetration, such as the Netherlands and Denmark, women are found to cycle more often than men. Young people are often found to cycle more (Muñoz et al., 2016) and old people to cycle less (Fraser and Lock, 2011), Albeit the results are inconclusive. Often a higher education level is linked to lower cycling levels (Heinen et al., 2010), while again mixed results have been reported in the literature. In the Netherlands, socio-demographics have limited association with cycling (Ton et al., 2019), contrary to findings elsewhere (Vidal et al., 2022).

- Heinen et al. (2010) state that having no children increases the probability of cycling. Income is often identified as a determinant of cycling, however mixed results are reported regarding the directionality of the relationship (Heinen et al., 2010; Muñoz et al., 2016).
- Cyclists are more exposed to the seasonal and weather conditions than a person traveling by car or using public transport. Generally, summer and autumn are mentioned as the most favorable seasons (Heinen et al., 2010). Wang et al. (2016) report that environments with cold winters and warm summers are less attractive for active mode users. Temperature is found to have a non-linear effect, where cold and very hot weather are negatively associated with active mode use (Böcker et al., 2013). Season and weather are of limited influence in the Netherlands, which might be due to the relatively mild climate with frequent rain, which is considered normal to the Dutch (Ton et al., 2019).
- Distance is often investigated in cycling research (Fraser and Lock, 2011; Handy et al., 2014; Heinen et al., 2010; Ton et al., 2019). Heinen et al. (2010) suggest a non-linear relationship between distance and bicycle use, penalizing longer distances more adversely. Distance is related to the built environment, because land use and density of the built environment largely determine how far destinations are located in relation to residential areas (Handy et al., 2014). During weekdays the bicycle has a larger probability to be chosen (Hansen and Nielsen, 2014; Ton et al., 2019).
- Features of the built environment are explanatory variables of cycling. The presence, density, and continuity of active mode infrastructure (e.g., bicycle lanes, bicycle parking) is positively associated with cycling (Handy et al., 2014; Heinen et al., 2010). A mixed land use environment encourages active mode use, whereas low residential density discourages active mode use (Heinen et al., 2010; Muñoz et al., 2016). At a more aggregate level, small and medium size cities are positively correlated with bicycle use and the city center is more attractive for cycling compared to the suburbs (Heinen et al., 2010). In the Netherlands, however, the suburbs are found to be more attractive to cyclists compared to city centers or rural areas (Ton et al., 2019).
- Heinen et al. (2010) and Handy et al. (2014) state that the availability of facilities related to the car, for example (free) parking options, negatively

relate to the choice for cycling. Furthermore, Heinen et al. (2010) identify a positive relationship between facilities that are beneficial for cyclists, such as lockers or showers and bicycle choice. Providing incentives or reimbursement for the bicycle has a positive association with cycling (Handy et al., 2014; Ton et al., 2019). On the other hand, if the car is incentivized or reimbursed a negative association is found with bicycle use (Handy et al., 2014).

4.2 Cycling route choice

Research has identified a wide range of attributes that might influence the route choice behavior of cyclists, where the attributes selected for research mainly depend on the type of data used (RP or SP) and the availability of the data (in case of RP). Three categories of explanatory variables are identified: individual, network and contextual attributes.

- Individual attributes are commonly incorporated in SP studies, mainly as interaction terms, to identify differences in attitude between individuals with respect to network attributes. In the RP studies, Hood et al. (2011) have included gender and cycling experience in their model.
- Network attributes are most influential on route choice behavior. Distance, gradient and cycle path percentage are considered most important (e.g., Broach et al., 2012; Menghini et al., 2010; Ton et al., 2017, 2018). Distance or time can both be included in research. Most studies have used distance, but e.g. Björklund and Mortazavi (2013) studied cycle time. Regarding gradient different approaches are applied in literature. For example, Broach et al. (2012) divided sections of the route into different categories of up-slope, whereas Menghini et al. (2010) adopted the maximum gradient of the route. With respect to cycle paths, Furth (2012) identifies four categories: shared streets and lanes, cycling lanes, separate cycle paths and standalone paths.
- Contextual attributes are mostly found in SP studies, however also in RP studies trip purpose is found to be influential (e.g., Broach et al., 2012; Hood et al., 2011). Commuting cyclists tend to value distance more negative compared to other purposes (Ton et al., 2017).

5. Bicycle traffic operations modeling

As indicated in Section 2, we distinguish between microscopic models and macroscopic models. This section will introduce the microscopic theory and models in Section 5.1, while Section 5.2 introduced the macroscopic theory and models.

5.1 Microscopic theory and models

The term *microscopic bicycle traffic operations* refers to decisions and actions that individual cyclists take in a time horizon that is up to the order of seconds while they are riding. That is different from the horizon of milliseconds that is considered for the automatic action patterns control for microscopic car traffic operations (Michon, 1985). The justification for this discrepancy is that riding a bicycle is considered to be a combination of tasks executed based on rules to perform maneuvres (time horizon of seconds) and automatic actions for the control of the bicycle (pedaling and steering, being split-second control) (Gavriilidou et al., 2019; Rasmussen, 1983).

In order to model these operations, two-layers are distinguished by Gavriilidou et al. (2019), following the concept of a plan-action decision structure proposed by Choudhury et al. (2010) and applied to model pedestrian walking behavior by Fukuda et al. (2014). The input to the upper level is the chosen route from the origin to the destination. In the upper layer, cyclists choose intermediate destinations and build up their path within the chosen route while interacting with other traffic users and with the infrastructure. We call this the *operational mental* layer. Examples of path choices are shown in Fig. 4. For the execution of each of these path choices, bicycle control dynamics in the form of pedaling and steering are necessary. This is the lower layer which we name *operational physical* layer.

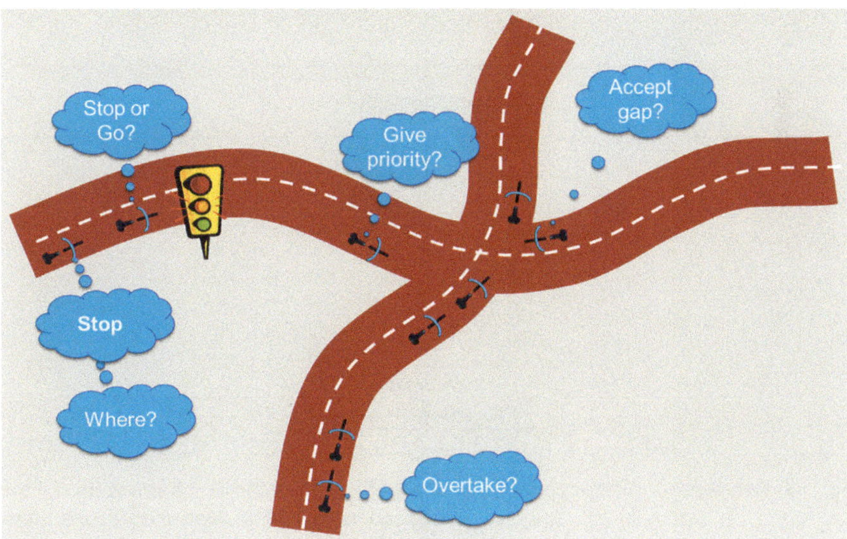

Fig. 4 Examples of path choices made by cyclists.

The complete framework is visualized in Fig. 5. Five types of path choices have been identified in the operational mental layer and each of them is captured by a separate model. The choices correspond to situations when (i) cyclists decide to overtake, but also when they are approaching an unsignalized intersection intending to cross or merge and need to decide (ii) whether to accept a gap in the conflicting traffic stream. Another choice at unsignalized intersections which is at the discretion of cyclists is to (iii) yield to oncoming traffic. Moreover, situations at a red traffic light are covered, where cyclists decide (iv) whether they stop and (v) where to position themselves in the queue.

Decisions (output) made in the mental layer are communicated as input either into another path choice within the mental layer or into the physical layer. The former is visualized by the two arrows within the mental layer pointing toward the queuing position. When the output of the mental layer choice for yielding is to give priority by coming to a complete stop, then a stopping (queuing) position decision needs to be made before proceeding with decisions in the physical layer. The same process holds when a decision is made to stop at a red light as opposed to a red-light-running decision.

The operational physical layer consists of the controls that each individual exerts in consecutive time steps once a path choice has been made. These controls are steering and pedaling (or braking) to determine the cycling direction and speed, respectively. This layer is described by a single dedicated model covering steering and pedaling (or braking) jointly.

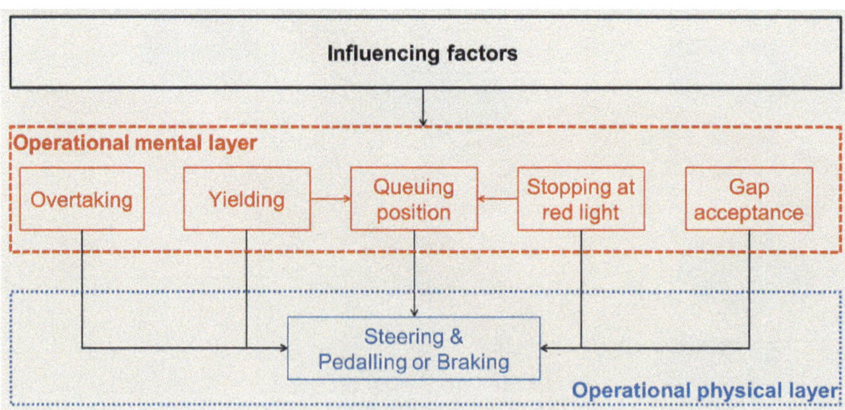

Fig. 5 Two-layer microscopic bicycle traffic operations framework. *From Gavriilidou, A., Daamen, W., Yuan, Y., Hoogendoorn, S., 2019. Modelling cyclist queue formation using a two-layer framework for operational cycling behaviour. Transport. Res. Part C Emerg. Technol. 105, 468–484.*

By applying these controls, the state of each individual cyclist (i.e., speed, position and headway) is affected. The new states of the cyclists that emerge from the physical layer are fed back into the mental layer to allow for path choice updates when necessary. This means that there is two-way communication between the two layers.

In the following sections, both models on the operational mental layer and models on the operational physical layer are introduced.

5.1.1 Mental layer models

The mathematical models used for the decisions in the mental layer are mostly discrete choice models. In the cases of gap acceptance and red-light running, the choice is binary, namely to do it or not (Jiang et al., 2013; Johnson et al., 2011; Pai and Jou, 2014; Richardson and Caulfield, 2015; Schleinitz, 2016; Wu et al., 2012).

The other decisions, however, have more possible states. This has been handled with two different modeling approaches in the literature, namely rule based models and discrete choice models. Overtaking can be predicted based on rules that check the speed difference, the lateral and longitudinal distance between two cyclists. The threshold values to determine which state is expected have been identified using clustering techniques (Mohammed et al., 2019). Yielding at an unsignalized intersection has been modeled with a discrete choice model whose choice set consisted of discretized time intervals for the cyclist to arrive at the intersection (Gavriilidou, 2021). The choice of a queuing position has also been modeled with a discrete choice model where the cycle path was discretized into a finite number of cells that cyclists can choose as their stopping position (Gavriilidou et al., 2019).

5.1.2 Physical layer models

More research effort has been put on modeling the bicycle control dynamics, as several models have been developed for the physical layer. Very simple models represent cyclists by their speeds and positions in continuous space (e.g., cycle paths approaching intersections). The position and speed for the next time step are determined using mathematical formulas and/or basic physical laws. Typically, the main aim of these models is not to describe cyclist behavior in all detail, but as part of, e.g., a traffic control model to represent flows at multimodal signalized intersections (Dabiri and Hegyi, 2018; Dabiri et al., 2019; Jiang et al., 2013). Although these models are fast, they are usually not very accurate.

Models that are discussed in further detail are the Cellular Automata models, the social force models, utility based models and game theory models.

Early microscopic cyclist models made use of modeling paradigms developed for cars, such as Cellular Automata models. Cellular Automata models use a cellular representation of space and cyclists move from cell to cell following a set of predefined rules and the corresponding cell transition probability. The cell size, rule set and characteristics of the cyclist have been adjusted compared to the car models to reflect the heterogeneity of cyclist behavior, their lower speeds and their smaller sizes (Gould and Karner, 2009; Mallikarjuna and Rao, 2009; Mohammed et al., 2021; Tang et al., 2018; Vasic and Ruskin, 2012; Yao et al., 2009). More complex, environment-dependent rules can be incorporated to represent thought processes (e.g., specific routing decision, incidents, evacuations). CA models seems to be the most used model for representing bicycle flow, but are also used to represent a mixed traffic flow environment, see further Section 6.2.

Social force models determine cyclist movement in continuous space by representing the intended direction and interactions with their environment as force vectors. Applied forces can be attractive for example toward the desired destination or repulsive for example from obstacles and other traffic users (Huang et al., 2017; Li et al., 2011; Liang et al., 2012). The magnitude of each of these forces depends on proximity as well as characteristics of the other traffic users, but also of the considered cyclist, infrastructure like curbs, or events like changing traffic lights. The forces are based on a geometrical shaped social force field surrounding all agents (elliptical shape for all user types (Huang et al., 2017) or discriminatively ellipses for cyclists and circles for pedestrians (Yuan et al., 2017, 2018). Forces are estimated whenever two influencing shapes overlap, that is, when the two traffic participants are deemed to be in each other's influencing zone. A resulting vector is determined for each time step and using Newton's second law of motion, $F = m \cdot a$, the acceleration of the cyclist is calculated.

Utility based models provide agents with a finite number of alternatives, reflected in a choice set that combines changes in speed and direction, e.g., in the form of a fan-shaped choice grid (Gavriilidou et al., 2019). Typically, discrete choice models are used to reflect this approach, where alternatives in a choice set are assumed to yield a utility and depending on the type of choice model, these utilities will be compared. Using data, models that have been developed in this category aim to find the most likely utility functions, consisting of attributes and weights, to mimic realistic cycling behavior.

Attributes are for example the occupation of the solution, proximity to destination, deviation from current path and velocity.

Game theory models apply the principle of least effort and make assumptions on the strategy that cyclists adopt when interacting with each other. The effort is represented by forces exerted on the cyclist, but also communication between cyclists, e.g., eye contact, can be added. The applied strategies can be cooperative, non-cooperative (or zero-acceleration) or even hostile (Hoogendoorn et al., 2021).

5.2 Macroscopic theory and models

The macroscopic modeling of traffic operations dates to the groundbreaking work of Bruce Greenshields, who back in 1934 discovered the *Fundamental Diagram* of (car) traffic. The diagram relates the *flow* q (number of vehicles passing a cross section per hour) to the *density* k (average number of cars per kilometer):

$$q = Q(k)$$

For bicycle flows, the fundamental diagram can also be established. Zhang et al. (2014) show results from a simple, single file bicycle-following experiment show that a relation between flow and density can be established empirically. Interestingly, the authors show that fundamental diagrams for cars, pedestrians and cyclists are closely related, and that key differences are a matter of scaling. Fig. 3 shows the relation found in their paper.

5.2.1 *Derivation of the fundamental diagram from microscopic principles*

Let us consider a single file bicycle flow. The leader of the file is cycling at a speed of v and all the other cyclists are following at the same speed. The gross distance between a cyclist and her predecessor is s. It is reasonable to assume that this distance is an increasing function of the speed (the higher the speed, the bigger the distance) since higher speeds require more space for safe breaking in case of a stop. We assume:

$$s = s(v) = s_0 + T \cdot v$$

Here, s_0 is the stopping distance (in m, when $v = 0$) and T is the reaction time (in s). This *bicycle following rule* can be derived under the assumption that a cyclist aims to maintain sufficient distance when her predecessor brakes with a fixed deceleration while she decelerates with the same deceleration T s later (Fig. 6).

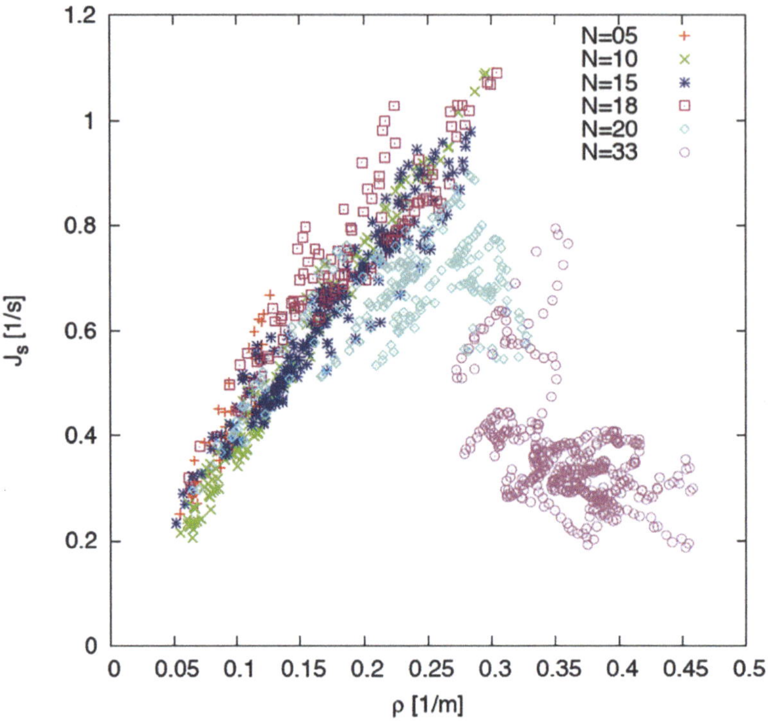

Fig. 6 Relation between density ρ and flow J_s. The data stems from a narrow circular path in which a certain number of cyclists N riding in a single file is moving without overtaking. *From Zhang, J., Mehner, W., Holl, S., Boltes, M., Andresen, E., Schadschneider, A., Seyfried, A., 2014. Universal flow-density relation of single-file bicycle, pedestrian and car motion. Phys. Lett. A 378 (44), 3274–3277.*

Looking at the file of cyclist, the density k in the file is equal to $k = 1/s$. This is easily shown by noticing that if the file (excluding the leader) consists of n cyclists, it has length $n \cdot s$. The density is equal to the number of cyclists n divided by the length $n \cdot s$, i.e., $1/s$. Now, since all cyclists in the file have the same speed v, the average speed $u = v$. Therefore:

$$\frac{1}{k} = s_0 + T \cdot u \leftrightarrow u = \frac{1}{T}\left(\frac{1}{k} - s_0\right)$$

This shows that we can express the density as a function of the average speed, and vice versa, the speed as a function of the density. This relation ($u = u(k)$) is known as the fundamental diagram. Since the speed is bounded by the maximum average speed u^0 of a bicycle flow, we get:

$$u = u(k) = \min\left(\frac{1}{T}\left(\frac{1}{k} - s_0\right), u^0\right)$$

This relation has interesting applications, not in the least since it allows us to determine the average speed of a bicycle flow to the density. This essentially results in a travel time function than can be used in a *network model* to determine the travel time TT on a link of length L, i.e.,:

$$TT(k) = L/u(k)$$

The relation can also be used to determine levels-of-service and relate these to, e.g., density levels.

Note that the analysis can be easily generalized to multi-file situations.

5.2.2 Continuity equation and the flow-density relation

The continuity equation describes the relation between flow, density, and speed:

$$q = k \cdot u$$

It describes the fact that the flow (or flow-rate) at a cross-section is determined by number of bicycles that are found (per meter) upstream of this cross-section multiplied by the speed these cyclists are moving. In combining this with the fundamental relation between speed and density derived above, we can determine a relation between the flow and the density:

$$q = q(k) = u(k) \cdot k = \min\left(\frac{1}{T}\left(\frac{1}{k} - s_0\right), u^0\right) \cdot k$$
$$= \min\left(\frac{1}{T}(1 - s_0 \cdot k), u^0 \cdot k\right)$$

This expression has some interesting features. First, we see that $q(0) = 0$. This means that when the density is equal to zero, there is no flow. Secondly, we see that $q(1/s_0) = 0$. This means that when the density $k = 1/s_0$, the speed is equal to zero and hence the flow is also equal to zero. We refer to this density as the *jam density*, i.e., $k_{jam} = 1/s_0$. This jam density might for example occur at a traffic light, when cyclists are waiting for green.

Finally, the function $q(k)$ reaches a maximum value at some density. This occurs at the density value $k = k_{crit} = \frac{1}{u^0 \cdot T + s_0}$. The flow $q(k_{crit}) = \frac{u^0}{u^0 \cdot T + s_0}$ is the *maximum flow* that we can expect, also referred to as the *capacity* C.

5.2.3 Queuing models

So far, we have looked at static macroscopic models that relate the macroscopic flow variables density, speed, and flow. These relations are very useful and are often an essential component of network simulation models that are used for strategic or planning purposes, or are used for so-called particle models (Daamen, 2004).

The dynamics of flows, e.g., the way queues build up and dissolve at a controlled intersection or at a bottleneck, is not properly captured when only considering the static properties of a flow. Here, we will consider two different models, namely queuing models and continuum flow models.

A queuing model is often used to describe flow operations at a *bottleneck* (e.g., a controlled intersection, a bridge, a roundabout). We assume that we know the (dynamic) *capacity profile* of the bottleneck. For instance, for a controlled intersection we know the capacity C of the road (the maximum flow that can occur when the traffic light is green) *and* we know that no flow passes the stop line when the light is red. This gives a capacity profile:

$$c(t) = \begin{cases} C & \text{if light is green} \\ 0 & \text{if light is red} \end{cases}$$

Next to the capacity profile, we need to know how many cyclists are arriving at the bottleneck. The demand profile $a(t)$ describes the number of cyclists per time unit (e.g., hour) that arrive at the bottleneck location.

Now, we have all the ingredients to determine the dynamics of the queue $r(t)$ at the bottleneck location, where $r(t)$ describes the number of cyclists in the queue at time instant t. Let us start with the outflow $d(t)$ from the queue:

$$d(t) = \begin{cases} c(t) & \text{if } r(t) > 0 \\ \min\{c(t), a(t)\} & \text{if } r(t) = 0 \end{cases}$$

This expression shows that when there is a queue ($r(t) > 0$), the queue dissipates according to the prevailing capacity at the bottleneck. When there is no queue ($r(t) = 0$), the outflow of the bottleneck is determined by the minimum of the prevailing demand $a(t)$ and capacity $c(t)$. This means that a queue starts when the demand $a(t)$ is larger than the capacity $c(t)$.

Let us define the (cumulative) arrival curve $A(t)$ as the *cumulative* number of cyclists that have arrived at the bottleneck, i.e.:

$$A(t) = \int_{t_0}^{t} a(s)ds$$

The (cumulative) departure curve $D(t)$ is defined by the *cumulative* number of cyclists departing from the bottleneck, i.e.:

$$D(t) = \int_{t_0}^{t} d(s)ds$$

Then, we can easily see that the number of vehicles in the queue is equal to:

$$r(t) = A(t) - D(t)$$

Queuing models are powerful tools to analyze properties of bottlenecks. They can be used to determine the delays that a cyclist will experience when arriving at a bottleneck, i.e.:

$$\text{delay}(i) = D^{-1}(i) - A^{-1}(i)$$

where $D^{-1}(i)$ and $A^{-1}(i)$ denote the inverse function of the departure and the arrival curves (i.e., the time when cyclist i respectively leaves or arrives at the bottleneck). This also shows that we can determine the collective delays of all cyclists by looking at the surface between the arrival and the departure curves, i.e.:

$$\text{collective delay } (t) = \int_{t_0}^{t} (A(s) - D(s))ds$$

Other measures that can be determined are the maximum queue length, the maximum delay, etc. It is left to the reader to determine how these measures can be computed. The measures of performance are very useful in analyzing the performance of an intersection controller, or other types of bottlenecks.

5.2.4 Continuum models and shockwave theory

Queuing models are useful tools for many types of applications. However, they fail to capture the spatial component of queueing. Continuum models, such as kinematic wave models or Lighthill-Witham Richards (LWR) models—named after the academics that first proposed using these models—are able to prescribe the spatial dynamics of queuing. The model assumes that the traffic flow variables flow, density and speed are continuous functions of time and space, e.g., $k = k(t, x)$. Moreover, they assume that for all time instants and locations, we know the fundamental diagram *and* that flow, speed, and density satisfy $q(t,x) = k(t,x) \cdot u(t,x) = Q(k(t,x))$. Next to this, we assume that the conservation of bicycle relation holds:

$$\frac{\partial k}{\partial t} + \frac{\partial q}{\partial x} = 0$$

This expression states that the density changes over time due to the change in the flow over space. The latter can be seen as the difference between inflow (density increases) and outflow (density decreases). We can also rewrite this equation as follows:

$$\frac{\partial k}{\partial t} + \frac{\partial q}{\partial x} = \frac{\partial k}{\partial t} + \frac{\partial Q(k)}{\partial x} = \frac{\partial k}{\partial t} + \frac{dQ}{dk} \cdot \frac{\partial k}{\partial x} = 0$$

Readers that are familiar with flow modeling will understand why this model is referred to as the kinematic wave model: disturbances in the density—i.e., changes in the density in space—described by $\partial k / \partial x$ move over time in the direction $c(k) = dQ(k)/dk$, that is with the so-called *kinematic wave speed*. Large disturbances, so-called *shocks*, move with (shockwave) speed:

$$\omega_{21} = \frac{Q(k_2) - Q(k_1)}{k_2 - k_1}$$

This expression is often used to determine the speed of the head and the tail of a queue, which both delineate shocks. For instance, when a queue that has built up in front of a controlled intersection (red phase) is released (green phase), bicycle traffic will move out of the queue with capacity flow, while the density is equal to the critical density. This means that for the conditions downstream of the queue we have $k_2 = k_{crit}$ and $Q(k_2) = C$. In the queue itself, there is no flow, and the density is equal to the jam density, i.e., $k_1 = k_{jam}$ and $Q(k_1) = 0$. This means that the shockwave speed at the head of the queue equals:

$$\omega_{21} = \frac{C}{k_{crit} - k_{jam}}$$

In the same way, we can determine the dynamics of the tail of the queue. For more details about kinematic wave and shockwave theory, we refer to Lighthill and Whitham (1955) or any other textbook on LWR theory.

6. Simulation models

There are few existing simulation packages (standalone simulation environment/software) that include high-fidelity and robust sub-models for all of the behavioral levels presented in Fig. 2/Section 2. Often, strategic or planning models used by city planners or transportation analysts have an emphasis on demand modeling, traffic assignment, and mode/route choice, but relatively coarse descriptions of cycling operations, see Section 6.1. On the other hand, microscopic simulation models are often limited to modeling traffic operations and route choice—the concerned models include both existing commercial packages and simulation tools reported in literature as discussed in Section 6.2.

6.1 Planning models

Traditionally, transportation planners focus on motorized traffic due to for example, the size of infrastructure investments and economic losses caused by traffic jams. Their models are often based on either the four-step model, for example the Swedish national model (Beser and Algers, 2002) or the activity-based approach, for example the Tel Aviv model (Shiftan and Ben-Akiva, 2011). One would expect incorporation of cycling choice behavior in the transportation planning models. Unfortunately, its integration happens rarely and slowly. Cycling is often missing, treated as a rest category, or combined with walking into slow/active modes, which results in incorrect estimates and it makes it impossible to derive the impact of potential policy measures. One of the exceptions is the Dutch National Model System (Landelijk Model System (LMS), Rijkswaterstaat, 2017), which does not only have the bike as access/egress mode, but also as an independent mode, and even distinguishes between bikes and ebikes. Regional models, such as Traffic Model Metropolitan Region of Amsterdam (Verkeersmodel Metropoolregio Amsterdam, VENOM, VENOM Organisation (2017)) and several regional Dutch Omnitrans models are working on a Bike module, with calibrated OD matrices and networks.

Until recently data and hence information and knowledge on cycling choice behavior has been scarce. In recent years, developments in large-scale data collection tools, such as for example Wi-Fi and GPS, together with technological advancements such as smartphones have made it possible to collect (on a larger scale) revealed preference data concerning cyclists. Hence, allowing research into cycling mode and route choice modeling to bridge the gap with motorized modes and providing input for the transport planning models.

For example, recent development in traffic planning software (e.g., PTV-Visum) has included a dedicated bicycle assignment method enabling route assignments which better reflect route choices made by cyclists. The underlying demand model is based on activity-based modeling idea, capturing the characteristics of multimodal transport (cars, public transport, cycling and walking) in the entire network. Similar software packages consider bicycle aspect in a multimodal environment include EMME, OmniTRANS, SATURN. This way the model can better replicate the behavior of cyclists and evaluate measures for cycling.

6.2 Microscopic simulation models

As discussed, most microscopic simulation models and simulation packages for bicycle traffic and travel mainly encapsulate bicycle operations and partial route choice. As for modeling route choice behavior, the underlying modeling paradigm is by and large based on utility-based approaches (discrete choice models). The idea is to provide a floor-field (map navigation) on top of the operational level to cover the route choice decision, they look at the value of the probability of transition from the current location to a specific neighboring location (destination), with respect to movement constraints and/or the relevant determinants. Typical factors in route selection would encompass network-related ones, such as cycling infrastructure (slopes, pavement surface conditions, bus stops, parking facilities, junctions), and/or context ones, including travel time, route length, their interactions with other road users, or even personal socio-demographic attributes. Not all the determinants as identified in Section 4.2 are included in the existing simulation models. For instance, MATSim is able to consider attributes of infrastructure (slopes, surface) next to travel time in the cyclist route choice decision. Simulation studies have validated this modeling idea (Ziemke et al., 2017). In Vissim, users can predefine static routing or apply iterative dynamic assignment module to create route choice regarding determinants like travel time. Also the route choice can be imported from its macroscopic counterpart–Visum.

As for describing bicycle operational level, in the existing car-centric simulation packages (e.g., Aimsun, Vissim, MATSim), cyclists are modeled as non-lane-based vehicles in a multi-modal context. The purpose is mainly to see the impact of cyclists over an area (e.g., an urban segment or an intersection), rather than representing realistic trajectories for individual cyclists or reproducing fully valid operational behaviors. Also in open-source packages (e.g., SUMO), no exclusive movement model for bicycles is implemented. Existing models need to be re-purposed: bicycles are seen as slow vehicles, or as fast pedestrians. Therefore, the default bicycle operational behavior is not calibrated or validated. From literature, different research groups have made effort to develop specific simulation applications based on the various modeling paradigms, ranging from simple kinematic models, to more sophisticated types, CA type, social-force based, utility-based and game theory models, as identified in Section 5.1, however, to the best of our knowledge, there is no ready-to-use bicycle simulation models covering a wide range of applications and scenarios.

7. Summary and conclusions

In this chapter, we discussed different aspects of (mathematical) modeling of bicycle traffic and cyclist's travel choices. In doing so, we looked at different types of decisions that cyclists make on different temporal and spatial levels. These decisions—or their collective results—can be modeled via different mathematical constructs.

Travel choices, e.g., where activities are performed, the mode that is chosen to travel, or the route a cyclist takes, are often modeled using *discrete choice models*. These models describe the chance that an individual chooses—or the share of a population that chooses—a particular alternative to perform an activity or to travel, assuming that the option is chosen that yields the highest subjective utility.

These discrete choice models also have been put forward to model operational decision making. But also other modeling approaches, e.g., game theory, are used to describe the behavior of individual cyclists. Flow operations are also modeled on a more aggregate level, i.e., *macroscopically*, when traffic flow variables density, average speed, and flow, or using simple queuing models.

We have also presented some of the available models that combine these different concepts in simulation packages.

References

Annema, J.A., 2013. Transport resistance factors: time, money and effort. In: Wee, G.P., Annema, J.A., Banister, D. (Eds.), The Transport System and Transport Policy: An Introduction. Edward Elgar Publishing, pp. 101–124.

Beser, M., Algers, S., 2002. SAMPERS—The new Swedish national travel demand forecasting tool. In: National Transport Models. Springer, Berlin, Heidelberg, pp. 101–118.

Björklund, G., Mortazavi, R., 2013. Influences of Infrastructure and Attitudes to Health on Value of Travel Time Savings in Bicycle Journeys. Centre for Transport Studies.

Böcker, L., Dijst, M., Prillwitz, J., 2013. Impact of everyday weather on individual daily travel behaviours in perspective: a literature review. Transp. Rev. 33 (1), 71–91.

Box, G.E.P., 1976. Science and statistics. J. Am. Stat. Assoc. 71 (356), 791–799. https://doi.org/10.1080/01621459.1976.10480949.

Brackstone, M., Montanino, M., Daamen, W., Buisson, C., Punzo, V., 2012. Use, calibration, and validation of traffic simulation models in practice: results of Web-based survey. In: TRB 2012-Transportation Research Board 91rd Annual Meeting, pp. 1–12.

Broach, J., Dill, J., Gliebe, J., 2012. Where do cyclists ride? A route choice model developed with revealed preference GPS data. Transport. Res. Part A Policy Pract. 46 (10), 1730–1740.

Choudhury, C.F., Ben-Akiva, M., Abou-Zeid, M., 2010. Dynamic latent plan models. J. Choice Model. 3 (2), 50–70.

Daamen, W., 2004. Modelling Passenger Flows in Public Transport Facilities. TRAIL Ph.D. thesis. ISBN: 9040725217.

Daamen, W., Buisson, C., Hoogendoorn, S.P. (Eds.), 2014. Traffic Simulation and Data: Validation Methods and Applications. CRC Press.

Dabiri, A., Hegyi, A., 2018. Personalised optimal speed advice to cyclists approaching an intersection with uncertain green time. In: 2018 European Control Conference (ECC). IEEE, pp. 1666–1671.

Dabiri, A., Hegyi, A., Goñi-Ros, B., 2019. Optimal speed advice for cyclists using a roadside sign at signalized intersections with uncertainty in traffic light timing. Transport. Res. Record 2673 (7), 239–247.

Fishburn, P.C., 1968. Utility theory. Management Sci. 14 (5), 335–378.

Fraser, S.D., Lock, K., 2011. Cycling for transport and public health: a systematic review of the effect of the environment on cycling. Eur. J. Pub. Health 21 (6), 738–743.

Fukuda, D., Seo, T., Yamada, K., Yaginuma, H., Matsuyama, N., 2014. An econometric-based model of pedestrian walking behavior implicitly considering strategic or tactical decisions. In: Pedestrian and Evacuation Dynamics 2012. Springer, pp. 615–624.

Furth, P.G., 2012. Bicycling infrastructure for mass cycling: a trans-Atlantic comparison. In: Pucher, J., Buehler, R. (Eds.), City Cycling. Massachusetts Institute of Technology Press, Cambridge, MA, pp. 105–140.

Gavriilidou, A., 2021. Cyclists in Motion: From Data Collection to Behavioural Models. Doctoral dissertation, Ph.D. thesis, Delft University of Technology.

Gavriilidou, A., Daamen, W., Yuan, Y., Hoogendoorn, S., 2019. Modelling cyclist queue formation using a two-layer framework for operational cycling behaviour. Transport. Res. Part C Emerg. Technol. 105, 468–484.

Geurs, K.T., van Wee, B., 2013. Accessibility: perspectives, measures and applications. In: van Wee, B., Annema, J.A., Banister, D. (Eds.), The Transport System and Transport Policy: An Introduction.

Gould, G., Karner, A., 2009. Modeling bicycle facility operation: cellular automaton approach. Transport. Res. Rec. 2140 (1), 157–164.

Handy, S., Van Wee, B., Kroesen, M., 2014. Promoting cycling for transport: research needs and challenges. Transport Rev. 34 (1), 4–24.

Hansen, K.B., Nielsen, T.A.S., 2014. Exploring characteristics and motives of long distance commuter cyclists. Transport Policy 35, 57–63.

Hoogendoorn, S.P., Bovy, P.H., 2001. Generic gas-kinetic traffic systems modeling with applications to vehicular traffic flow. Transport. Res. Part B Method. 35 (4), 317–336.

Heinen, E., Van Wee, B., Maat, K., 2010. Commuting by bicycle: an overview of the literature. Transport Rev. 30 (1), 59–96.

Hood, J., Sall, E., Charlton, B., 2011. A GPS-based bicycle route choice model for San Francisco, California. Transport. Lett. 3 (1), 63–75.
Hoogendoorn, S.P., Gavriilidou, A., Daamen, W., Duives, D., 2021. Game theoretical framework for bicycle operations: a multi-strategy framework. Transport. Res. Part C Emerg. Technol. 128, 103175.
Huang, L., Wu, J., You, F., Lv, Z., Song, H., 2017. Cyclist social force model at unsignalized intersections with heterogeneous traffic. IEEE Trans. Indus. Inform. 13 (2), 782–792.
Jiang, H., Wen, T., Jiang, P., Han, H., 2013. Research on cyclists microscopic behaviour models at signalized intersection. In: 16th International Conference Road Safety on Four Continents. Beijing, China (RS4C 2013). 15–17 May 2013.
Johnson, M., Newstead, S., Charlton, J., Oxley, J., 2011. Riding through red lights: the rate, characteristics and risk factors of non-compliant urban commuter cyclists. Acc. Anal. Prevent. 43 (1), 323–328.
Li, M., Shi, F., Chen, D., 2011. Analyze bicycle-car mixed flow by social force model for collision risk evaluation. In: 3rd International Conference on Road Safety and Simulation, pp. 1–22.
Liang, X., Baohua, M., Qi, X., 2012. Psychological-physical force model for bicycle dynamics. J. Transport. Syst. Eng. Inform. Technol. 12 (2), 91–97.
Lighthill, M.J., Whitham, G.B., 1955. On kinematic waves II: a theory of traffic flow on long crowded roads. Proc. R. Soc. 229 (1178), 317–345.
Mallikarjuna, C., Rao, K.R., 2009. Cellular automata model for heterogeneous traffic. J. Adv. Transport. 43 (3), 321–345.
Mcnally, M.G., Rindt, C.R., 2007. The activity-based approach. In: Handbook of Transport Modelling. vol. 1, pp. 55–73.
Menghini, G., Carrasco, N., Schüssler, N., Axhausen, K.W., 2010. Route choice of cyclists in Zurich. Transport. Res. Part A Policy Pract. 44 (9), 754–765.
Michon, J.A., 1985. A critical view of driver behavior models: what do we know, what should we do? In: Human Behavior and Traffic Safety. Springer, Boston, MA, pp. 485–524.
Mohammed, H., Bigazzi, A.Y., Sayed, T., 2019. Characterization of bicycle following and overtaking maneuvers on cycling paths. Transport. Res. Part C Emerg. Technol. 98, 139–151.
Mohammed, H., Sayed, T., Bigazzi, A., 2021. Microscopic modeling of cyclists on off-street paths: a stochastic imitation learning approach. Transportmetrica A: Transport Sci., 1–22.
Muñoz, B., Monzon, A., Daziano, R.A., 2016. The increasing role of latent variables in modelling bicycle mode choice. Transport Rev. 36 (6), 737–771.
Pai, C.W., Jou, R.C., 2014. Cyclists' red-light running behaviours: an examination of risk-taking, opportunistic, and law-obeying behaviours. Acc. Anal. Prevent. 62, 191–198.
Rasmussen, J., 1983. Skills, rules, and knowledge; signals, signs, and symbols, and other distinctions in human performance models. IEEE Trans. Syst. Man Cybernet. 13 (3), 257–266.
Richardson, M., Caulfield, B., 2015. Investigating traffic light violations by cyclists in Dublin city centre. Acc. Anal. Prevent. 84, 65–73.
Rijkswaterstaat, 2017. Het Landelijk Model Systeem. Wvl1217zb010. In Dutch.
Schleinitz, K., 2016. Cyclists' Road Safety—Do Bicycle Type, Age and Infrastructure Characteristics Matter? Ph.D. thesis, Technische Universität Chemnitz.
Schneider, F., 2021. Spatial Activity-Travel Patterns of Cyclists. Doctoral Dissertation, PhD Thesis, Delft University of Technology.
Schneider, F., Daamen, W., Hoogendoorn, S., 2021. Trip chaining of bicycle and car commuters: an empirical analysis of detours to secondary activities. Transportmetrica A: Transport Sci., 1–24.

Shiftan, Y., Ben-Akiva, M., 2011. A practical policy-sensitive, activity-based, travel-demand model. Ann. Region. Sci. 47 (3), 517–541.

Tang, T.Q., Rui, Y.X., Zhang, J., Shang, H.Y., 2018. A cellular automation model accounting for bicycle's group behavior. Phys. A Stat. Mech. Appl. 492, 1782–1797.

Ton, D., Duives, D.C., Cats, O., Hoogendoorn-Lanser, S., Hoogendoorn, S.P., 2019. Cycling or walking? Determinants of mode choice in the Netherlands. Transport. Res. Part A Policy Pract. 123, 7–23.

Ton, D., Cats, O., Duives, D., Hoogendoorn, S., 2017. How do people cycle in Amsterdam, Netherlands?: estimating cyclists' route choice determinants with gps data from an urban area. Transport. Res. Rec. 2662 (1), 75–82.

Ton, D., Duives, D., Cats, O., Hoogendoorn, S., 2018. Evaluating a data-driven approach for choice set identification using GPS bicycle route choice data from Amsterdam. Travel Behav. Soc. 13, 105–117.

Vasic, J., Ruskin, H.J., 2012. Cellular automata simulation of traffic including cars and bicycles. Phys. A Stat. Mech. Appl. 391 (8), 2720–2729.

VENOM Organisation, 2017. VENOM handbook Richtlijnen & afspraken. INT/2017/3882. In Dutch.

Vidal, et al., 2022. This book series.

Wang, Y., Chau, C.K., Ng, W.Y., Leung, T.M., 2016. A review on the effects of physical built environment attributes on enhancing walking and cycling activity levels within residential neighborhoods. Cities 50, 1–15.

Wu, C., Yao, L., Zhang, K., 2012. The red-light running behavior of electric bike riders and cyclists at urban intersections in china: an observational study. Acc. Anal. Prevent. 49, 186–192.

Yao, D., Zhang, Y., Li, L., Su, Y., Cheng, S., Xu, W., 2009. Behavior modeling and simulation for conflicts in vehicles-bicycles mixed flow. IEEE Intell. Transport. Syst. Mag. 1 (2), 25–30.

Yuan, Y., Goñi-Ros, B., van Oijen, T.P., Daamen, W., Hoogendoorn, S.P., 2017. Social force model describing pedestrian and cyclist behaviour in shared spaces. In: International Conference on Traffic and Granular Flow. Springer, Cham, pp. 477–486.

Yuan, Y., Goñi-Ros, B., van Oijen, T.P., Daamen, W., Seer, S., Hoogendoorn, S.P., 2018. Calibration and validation of a social force model describing walking and cycling behavior in shared spaces using empirical trajectory data. In: Proceedings of the 9th Conference on Pedestrian and Evacuation Dynamics. Lund, Sweden.

Zhang, J., Mehner, W., Holl, S., Boltes, M., Andresen, E., Schadschneider, A., Seyfried, A., 2014. Universal flow-density relation of single-file bicycle, pedestrian and car motion. Phys. Lett. A 378 (44), 3274–3277.

Ziemke, D., Metzler, S., Nagel, K., 2017. Modeling bicycle traffic in an agent-based transport simulation. Proc. Comp. Sci. 109, 923–928.

CHAPTER NINE

Cyclists' interactions with other road users from a safety perspective

Heather Kaths*
School of Architecture and Civil Engineering, University of Wuppertal, Wuppertal, Germany
*Corresponding author: e-mail address: kaths@uni-wuppertal.de

Contents

Abstract

This chapter provides an overview of the literature about selected interactions between cyclists, pedestrians, motorists, heavy-duty vehicles, busses, pedestrians in urban areas. Hydén's Safety Pyramid is used as a framework for organizing interactions as frequent, inconsequential encounters, potential, slight and serious conflicts or crashes with varying levels of severity. The interactions are organized in this chapter by where they occur and by the interacting road user. First, cyclists' interactions on road segments are investigated, focusing on cyclist-pedestrian interactions, interactions between cyclists and passing motorists, interactions at bus stops, and interactions between cyclists. Interactions that take place at intersections are then explored and the gap acceptance of cyclists and motorists and the problematic interactions between cyclists and heavy-duty vehicles are examined. Finally, a short overview of interactions in shared space is given. Most of the literature concerns dangerous interactions between cyclists and other road users or those at the top of Hydén's Safety Pyramid. Fewer studies were found that investigate normal encounters and the potential benefits of interacting.

Advances in Transport Policy and Planning, Volume 10
ISSN 2543-0009
https://doi.org/10.1016/bs.atpp.2022.04.008

The chapter concludes with a discussion about the mechanisms behind dangerous interactions in general and what can be done by urban and infrastructure planners, traffic and vehicle engineers, and developers of technologies to transform dangerous interactions into normal encounters.

Keywords: Cycling, Bicycle traffic, Cyclists, Urban traffic, Road user interactions, Traffic safety, Road safety

1. Introduction

How a cyclist interacts with other road users and his or her environment has an enormous impact on the cycling experience. Both the perceived and objective safety, or lack thereof, as well as the efficiency, comfort, and enjoyment of cycling are all impacted by the frequency and characteristics of cyclists' interactions with others. Infrastructure planning and design play a pivotal role in shaping interactions experienced by cyclists while the experience and outcome of each interaction is influenced by the type of interacting partner.

Christer Hydén (1987) proposed the well-known Safety Pyramid that describes the relationship between the frequency and severity of encounters, conflicts, or crashes between road users (see Fig. 1). The large bottom section of the pyramid represents normal interactions between road users, referred to as encounters. These types of events are very frequent and do not pose any danger to either of the interacting parties. Positioned above normal encounters are potential, slight, and serious conflicts, which in this order decrease in frequency while increasing in seriousness. At the top of the

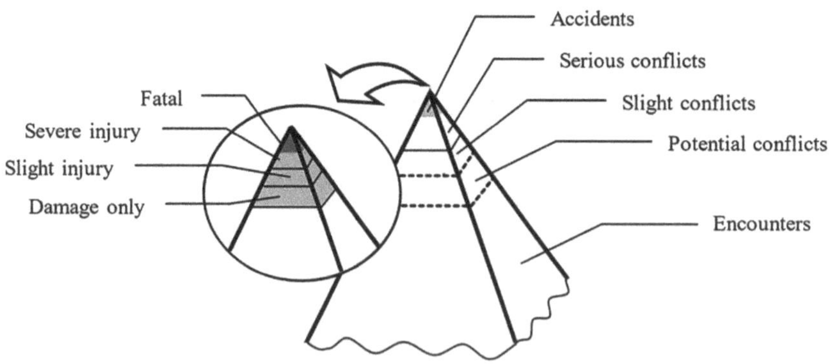

Fig. 1 Christer Hydén's Safety Pyramid. *From Laureshyn, A., Várhelyi, A., 2018. The Swedish Traffic Conflict Technique: Observer's Manual. LUND University.*

pyramid are crashes, which are relatively rare events in comparison to encounters or conflicts. This theory was extended upon by many (mainly Swedish) researchers to form the Traffic Conflict Technique, which can be used to infer the number of infrequent, severe events based on the observation of different types of more frequent conflicts (Laureshyn and Várhelyi, 2018).

One important implication of the Safety Pyramid theory is that the majority of interactions between road users are not dangerous. These encounters can even add value to a cyclist's journey. One of the positive aspects of cycling in comparison to traveling by private automobile is the opportunity for the cyclist to interact with his or her environment and communicate with other people while moving. During her interviews in the cycling metropolitan Copenhagen, Freudendal-Pedersen noted that many cyclists report "smelling, hearing, and feeling the city is different when you 'are not caged in a metal box'." (Freudendal-Pedersen, 2015, p. 37).

Nevertheless, cyclists undoubtedly bear a disproportionately large burden in terms of traffic injuries and fatalities at the top of the pyramid. In the European Union, for example, cyclists account for a total of 8% of road fatalities (European Road Safety Observatory, 2018), while at the same time constituting only 2% of all person kilometers (Steenberghen et al., 2017). If one looks at the causation of cyclist crashes in terms of road user behavior, it is clear that the cyclists themselves are not usually at fault. For example, in Germany, 75% and 79% of collisions between a bicycle and a private car or truck were primarily caused by the motor vehicle driver, respectively (German Federal Ministry of Transport, 2012).

Several methods are useful in studying dangerous interactions between road users. Crash data, either from police reports or from the reconstruction of collision scenes, and hospital records provide insight into cyclist crashes. It can be difficult to draw overarching conclusions from crash data because of the relatively low frequency of events and the corresponding long observation times necessary to collect adequate sample sizes. According to the Safety Pyramid theory, there is a relationship between the frequency of potential, slight and serious conflicts, and the occurrence of crashes. Based on this proposition, many researchers have focused on the investigation of conflicts and near misses to gain insight into safety-related problems. Critical incidents are tracked and mapped on a large-scale in projects such as SimRa (Karakaya et al., 2020) and BikeMaps (Nelson et al., 2015). A final method is to ask people through surveys or interviews about their experiences as cyclists interacting with other road users.

Depending on many factors, such as urban planning, road infrastructure design, traffic laws, culture, norms, and modal split, the dominating interactions of cyclists differ across cities and countries. In most places, the vast majority of interactions, and thus conflicts and crashes, experienced by cyclists are with motorists. In 2020, across Europe, 83% of cyclist fatalities resulting from a crash with another road user followed a collision with a motor vehicle (53% with a car, 7% with a bus, and 13% with a truck) (Adminaité-Fodor and Jost, 2020). Fatal crashes with other cyclists accounted for only 1% of cyclist deaths while crashes with pedestrians led to less than 1% of all cyclist deaths. However, near misses and non-fatal crashes with pedestrians account for between 1.2% and 6.4% of all incidents in the reviewed literature (O'Hern and Oxley, 2019; Poulos et al., 2015). These numbers vary drastically by country.

Not only traffic safety but also traffic flow and efficiency are regulated by road user interactions. This is especially true in urban areas where many people and modes of transport come together in a smaller area. Bicycle traffic, particularly in countries with a high modal split of cycling, can have an important impact on the overall traffic flow and efficiency. This effect is most pronounced at intersections, where streams of bicycle traffic interact with and influence the flow of other modes. For example, a flow of 600 bicycles/hour on one intersection approach can reduce the capacity of right-turning motor vehicle traffic on the same approach by approximately 50% and of left-turning vehicles on the opposite approach by nearly 65% (Grigoropoulos et al., 2022) in right-hand traffic. Not only the presence of bicycle traffic but also the behavior of each cyclist and the methods for interaction between different road users are hypothesized to impact overall efficiency.

A good deal of research power has gone into quantifying and mathematically modeling the interactions of cyclists with other cyclists, pedestrians, and motorists to create realistic microscopic traffic simulations. These tools are used to virtually design, test, and evaluate road infrastructure and traffic control measures. If the behavior models, and specifically the interaction models, that underpin microscopic traffic simulation do not reflect the actual behavior of all types of road users, the results of simulation studies will lack realism and accuracy (Twaddle et al., 2014). This body of research offers a pool of knowledge about cyclists' normal, non-critical encounters.

In this chapter, the interactions between cyclists and other road users are explored by focusing on different components of the urban road network. I begin with an analysis of interactions on road segments, followed by an examination of interactions at intersections, and conclude with a short review of interactions in shared spaces. An overview of the findings of peer-reviewed papers that explore cyclists' encounters, conflicts, and crashes with pedestrians, motorists, busses, and other cyclists is presented and a link between the interaction and the risk to cyclists is assessed. Selected reports that are deemed to be of high quality are included in the literature review. Research gaps are noted and topics for future research are identified.

2. Interactions on road segments

Road segments are stretches of roads between intersections on which road users generally move longitudinally in one of potentially two directions of travel. According to the European Road Safety Observatory, 64% of cyclist fatalities in Europe occur on road segments (European Commission, 2020a). For comparison, 81% of pedestrian fatalities (European Commission, 2020b) and 82% of car occupant fatalities (European Commission, 2021) occur on road segments in Europe.

Depending on the infrastructure design, cyclists face interactions with different road users. If bicycle traffic is guided on the roadway, either using marked bicycle lanes or mixed traffic roadways, cyclists will interact mainly with motorists, heavy-duty vehicles, busses, and other cyclists. Interactions with pedestrians and other cyclists dominate on physically separated bicycle infrastructure, shared paths, and sidewalks. In this section, literature on the interactions between cyclists and pedestrians, busses, motorists, and other cyclists are summarized. Particular attention is placed on interactions that are risky to cyclists or have a significant impact on traffic flow and efficiency.

2.1 Pedestrians

Interactions between cyclists and pedestrians occur when bicycle traffic is physically separated from motor vehicles and cyclists are relocated to paths shared with or adjacent to pedestrian traffic. Shared-use sidewalks and pathways are infrastructures that are intended for use by both cyclists and pedestrians without any separation between the two modes. Segregated facilities, on the other hand, allocate space to each road user group using surface markings or different building materials. The majority of the literature found in this review is focused on the occurrence of near misses or crashes between pedestrians and cyclists. Very little was found concerning the benefits of interaction and the value of personal encounters in the cycling experience.

Researchers in the German city of Berlin found that 75% of bicycle-pedestrian crashes took place between, rather than at, intersections (Schreiber, 2013). Similarly, a study in Finland indicated that most near misses and collisions between cyclists and pedestrians happen when the road users move in the same direction (Mesimäki and Luoma, 2021). The infrastructure characteristics, particularly the width and the separation between cyclists and pedestrians, have a large impact on the safety and comfort of both types of road users. Incidents are much more likely to occur on shared-use rather than separated facilities (Mesimäki and Luoma, 2021; Poulos et al., 2015). Poulos et al. (2015) found the crash rate for cyclists riding on pedestrian paths to be 26.4 crashes per 1000 h, which is considerably higher than for other road environments. For example, the crash rate was found to be 8.8 crashes per 1000 h on shared pedestrian and bicycle paths, 5.8 crashes per 1000 h on cycle lanes, and 4.7 crashes per 1000 h on roadways.

Hatfield and Prabhakharan (2016) looked at the behavior of pedestrians and cyclists on shared-use facilities and found that cyclists were more likely to follow the left-hand rule (in Australia) than pedestrians and typically gave way to pedestrians. However, passing on the wrong side, passing too close and too quickly, and not giving warning were all observed in the study. Mesimäki and Luoma (2021) found that both pedestrians and cyclists feel less safe on shared-use facilities and were less happy to ride or walk on them compared to paths segregating road users.

A major source of conflict between cyclists and pedestrians is their differing patterns of behavior. Cyclists typically use their bicycles to travel quickly along a specific route. Pedestrians, on the other hand, are not always motivated by reaching their destination as quickly as possible and tend to change their path, direction, and speed spontaneously. In addition, pedestrians are more likely to be distracted, for example by conversations, the use of mobile phones, or by listening to music (Hatfield and Prabhakharan, 2016). Likely because of these differences in behavior, cyclists can experience anger towards pedestrians. Marín Puchades et al. (2017) found that cyclists' anger towards pedestrians was associated with an increased likelihood for near misses with this type of road user. Furthermore, cyclists tend to blame pedestrians more for a conflict on shared-use infrastructure than they do for a conflict at an intersection or on a sidewalk, where the pedestrian is perceived as having the right-of-way (Paschalidis et al., 2016).

2.2 Busses

Busses create unique interaction constellations for cyclists because of their regular stops, which tend to be located on road segments. Researchers have noted an increased risk of injury to cyclists when a bus stop is present (Heydari et al., 2017; Osama and Sayed, 2017; Strauss et al., 2013). However, the number of incidents at bus stop zones is relatively low. For example, 1.1% of all personal injuries registered in Germany in 2018 happened at a bus stop (Berger et al., 2020).

Depending on the location and design of the bus stop and the type of cycling facility, cyclists encounter different types of interactions. A bus stop is a space designated for waiting, boarding, and alighting transit passengers and can be integrated into the sidewalk, a road median, or on a dedicated boarding island. The cycling infrastructure, on the other hand, can either be on-road or physically separated. There is a wide range of solutions for combining cycling and bus infrastructure. While it is not possible to delineate and discuss all the possibilities in this chapter, some of the most common solutions are summarized and points for (dangerous) interactions are discussed and depicted in Fig. 2:

a. *Physically separated cycling facility*: The cycling facility is located between the sidewalk and the waiting area of the bus stop or between the bus stop and the roadway at the edge of the sidewalk area. In either situation, cyclists and bus passengers must interact. (Afghari et al., 2014) found that cyclists tend to maintain their speed and do not perform evasive actions to avoid pedestrians at bus stops. Pedestrians on the other hand were found to reduce their speed and move out of the way of approaching cyclists. Greenshields et al. (2018) reported that the most common causes of serious conflicts between cyclists and pedestrians on this type of facility were caused by inattentiveness of the pedestrians, lack of space, crowding, visibility problems, and other features that restrained movement at the bus stop.

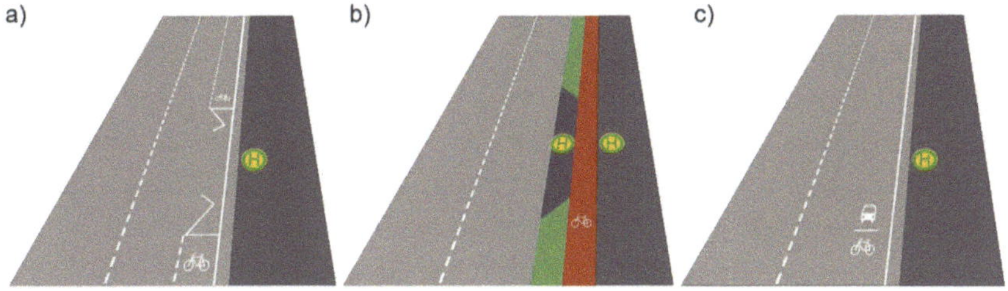

Fig. 2 Examples of solutions for combining cycling infrastructure with a bus stop.

b. *On-road cycling facility*: A break in on-road bicycle lanes allows for busses to access passengers waiting at a bus stop on the sidewalk. This results in a temporary interruption in the separation between bus and bicycle traffic. Cyclists riding behind the bus when it pulls over to the bus stop can either pass the bus by moving into the roadway or wait behind the bus. A problematic situation can arise when a bus driver pulls out of the bus stop and into the roadway while a cyclist is carrying out an overtaking maneuver. Kaparias et al. (2021) noted that cyclists ride significantly faster when there is a bus stop present. The authors suggested that this is due to the increased width of the road at bus stops. I propose, however, this might be due to the need to accelerate to merge into motor vehicle traffic to pass stopped busses.

c. *Shared bus-cycling facility*: In some places, busses and cyclists share a designated lane for only these two modes. De Ceunynck et al. (2017) found close interactions to be common on these types of lanes and observed many instances in which a bus passed with a lateral clearance of less than 1 m or followed a cyclist at a headway less than 2 s.

Because crashes with motor vehicles, trucks, and busses have more severe consequences in terms of injury and fatalities, it is likely that bus stops combined with on-road cycling facilities pose a greater risk to cyclists. Further research is needed to examine different bus stop/cycling infrastructure configurations and compare the number and severity of conflicts and crashes at each type.

2.3 Motorists

Motorists and cyclists must interact on road segments without marked cycling infrastructure (mixed traffic) and on segments with on-road infrastructures, such as painted bicycle lanes or other markings to indicate the presence of bicycle traffic. Mainly, these interactions are characterized by a faster-moving motorist approaching, following, and/or passing a slower-moving cyclist. Researchers have largely focused on the behavior of motorists, likely because they have a better overview and more control in the interaction. However, if a rear-end or sideswipe crash takes place, the cyclist is likely to bear the brunt of the impacts. Indeed, motorists passing cyclists with an insufficient lateral distance is a crucial safety problem on road segments (Johnson et al., 2010; Pai, 2011; Stone and Broughton, 2003). Even when passes with a low lateral distance do not result in a collision or critical interaction, the comfort and subjective safety of the cyclist is decreased (Beck et al., 2021), which can lead to reduced bicycle use in the long term (Parkin et al., 2007) and a decrease in the uptake of cycling (Aldred and Crosweller, 2015).

Many jurisdictions around the world have introduced minimum lateral clearance distances to reduce rear-end and sideswipe crashes between cyclists and passing motorists. For example, motorists are required to maintain a minimum passing distance of 1 m in Australia and 1.5 m in Germany. Several US American States stipulate a minimum passing distance of 3 ft. (~0.9 m) or 5 ft. (~1.5 m). Despite these measures, issues with insufficient lateral passing distance persist. Non-compliance rates found in the literature range between 2% and 16% (Debnath et al., 2018; Love et al., 2012; Oh et al., 2019). Although this range of compliance rates can likely be explained in part by the size of the required passing distance, not enough research is available to systematically compare this effect. Additional factors, such as characteristics of the roadway, the traffic culture, and the modal split likely affect passing distances as well. The availability of open sensor systems for detecting passing distances, such as 1M+ (Henao et al., 2021) will enable the widespread analysis of lateral passing distances.

The infrastructure design has been found to have an important impact on the lateral positioning of both motorists and cyclists during a passing maneuver. For example, close passes are observed more often on curved road segments as opposed to straight sections (Debnath et al., 2018). As would be expected, narrow traffic lanes lead to closer passing behavior (Debnath et al., 2018; Nolan et al., 2021). The presence of a marked bicycle lane has multiple positive effects. Firstly, the lateral position of the cyclist in relation to parked cars is increased (Duthie et al., 2011), which reduces the likelihood of a dooring incident and indicates a feeling of comfort. Secondly, the lateral distance between a cyclist and a passing motorist increases in the presence of a bicycle lane (Chuang et al., 2013; Love et al., 2012; Nolan et al., 2021; Oh et al., 2019). Finally, the subjective safety of cyclists using a bicycle lane is higher during passing events (Beck et al., 2021). The presence of protected bicycle lanes has been found to greatly increase the lateral passing distance in comparison to painted bicycle lanes (Nolan et al., 2021). Other markings that indicate the presence of bicycle traffic, such as "sharrows" (painted pictograms on the pavement indicating the presence of cyclists) have not been found to increase the lateral passing distance between motorists and cyclists or to encourage cyclists to ride in a safer position away from parked cars (Oh et al., 2019).

The characteristics of the motorist and cyclist play a role in the lateral passing distance and the perceived danger of an interaction. Passes carried out by trucks and other large vehicles are perceived as being particularly dangerous (Aldred, 2016; Aldred and Crosweller, 2015; Beck et al., 2021), push cyclists to the side of the road (De Ceunynck et al., 2017), and result in less lateral stability of the cyclist (Chuang et al., 2013). The lateral position of the cyclist is an important determinant of the lateral spacing granted by the motorist; for each foot of additional lateral space of the cyclist from the curb or parked vehicles, a motorist moves 0.5 feet further to the center of the road (Duthie et al., 2011). As a result, the lateral clearance distance between motorists and cyclists decreases when cyclists ride further into the vehicle lane. Researchers have found that motorists tend to grant wider lateral passing distances to female cyclists (or those who appear to be female) (Chuang et al., 2013; Walker, 2007).

There has been significantly less attention from researchers about the actions and reactions of cyclists in situations with a passing motorist. Duthie et al. (2011) estimated that cyclists deviate about 0.2 m from their intended path when being passed by a motor vehicle. Chuang et al. (2013) found that the steering angle, the speed, and the variation in speed of the cyclist affected the passing behavior of the motorist. In terms of safety-critical behavior, Johnson et al. (2010) found that cyclists rode in a safe/legal manner before a crash, near miss, or another type of incident on a road segment in 88.9% of the cases.

Although passing maneuvers are the most common and (therefore) problematic type of interaction on road segments, another problem on multiple lane roads is the tendency of motorists to make a sudden lane change maneuver and fail to notice or react to cyclists (Johnson et al., 2010).

2.4 Other cyclists

Road segments are characterized by a direction of travel and can be either one-way or bi-directional. As such, interactions between cyclists can be categorized as following, passing, or meeting events. A following event is a situation in which a faster-moving cyclist approaches a slower cyclist traveling in the same direction and adjusts his or her speed to follow the slower cyclist. During a passing event, the faster moving cyclist passes a slower cyclist by changing their velocity (speed and or direction). A meeting event is defined as a situation in which two cyclists traveling in opposite directions approach each other and adjust their velocity to maneuver around one another.

A passing event is characterized by the following three parameters:

- *Speed*: Khan and Raksuntorn (2001) found an average speed difference between passing and passed cyclists of 2.6 m/s, which was found to remain relatively constant throughout the maneuver. A minimum speed difference of 1.5 m/s was noted. If the difference dropped below this threshold, the passing cyclist was found to increase his or her speed. In contrast, Botma and Papendrecht (1991) found passing cyclists maintain a constant speed while carrying out a passing maneuver. Falkenberg et al. (2003) found that the passing cyclist usually does not have to reduce his or her speed in reaction to the cyclist who is to be passed.
- *Length/duration of passing event*: There is a weak indication that the length of the passing maneuver increases with the width of the infrastructure. Passing maneuver lengths of 57 m (11.0 s) and 24 m (4.5 s) were found for 2.4 m and 1.8 m wide separated bicycle paths (Botma and Papendrecht, 1991). Longer passing maneuvers with an average of 91.4 m were observed on a 3 m wide bicycle path (Khan and Raksuntorn, 2001).
- *Lateral spacing*: A German study found the average, minimum and maximum lateral spacing between cyclists to be 0.60 m, 0.20 m, and >1.00 m, respectively (Falkenberg et al., 2003). A US American study estimated larger values for the average, the minimum, and maximum lateral spacing of 1.78 m, 1.35 m, and 2.36 m, respectively (Khan and Raksuntorn, 2001). As well as the type and width of the facility, other conditions, such as whether it was in an urban or rural region, may influence lateral spacing.

Meeting events were examined in a controlled experiment in the Netherlands (Yuan et al., 2018). Findings show that both cyclists in an interaction deviate from their intended lateral position and that women deviate more from their desired path than men do. The observed cyclists began deviating from their intended paths when they were about 30 m apart and the maximum lateral deviation is between about 0.5 m and 0.8 m. Khan and Raksuntorn (2001) measured an average lateral spacing at the moment that two cyclists meet of 1.95 m on a 3 m wide separated bicycle path.

The number of passing and meeting events influences the Level of Service (LOS) for cyclists. Botma (1995) suggested using the number of hindrance events, which are passing, meeting or combined passing, and meeting events, as an indicator of the LOS for cyclists on separated facilities. Each hindrance event is presumed to force a cyclist to adjust their speed or path, which in turn decreases efficiency, comfort, and possibly safety. This method has been adopted in a modified form in both the American Highway Capacity Manual (National Research Council, 2000, 2010) and the German "*Handbuch für die Bemessung von Straßenverkehrsanlagen*" (Forschungsgesellschaft für Straßen- und Verkehrswesen, 2015). Although the number of passing and meeting events is widely used in determining LOS on bicycle facilities, it has been noted that they are relatively difficult to measure in the field (Gould and Karner, 2010).

Researchers have placed more attention on the flow of bicycle traffic in the last couple of years. Within the European research project *allegro* (unraveling slow mode traveling and traffic) at the TU Delft, experiments were carried out to study how cyclists interact with each other and the implications of these interactions on the flow of bicycle traffic. Hoogendoorn and Daamen (2016) introduced a model for bicycle traffic headway that takes into account the lateral flexibility of cyclists and classifies headways as constrained (a cyclist is following another cyclist and cannot or does not want to overtake) or unconstrained. They estimate that all cyclists move freely when headways greater than 4 s are present. Wierbos et al. (2019) examined the positioning of cyclists on facilities with varying widths and found support for the theory that cyclists divide available space into sub-lanes. Values for the capacity of cycling infrastructure of various widths are derived. Still, the mechanisms that underpin the behavior of cyclists in areas with large volumes of bicycle traffic and the variations due to type of infrastructure, country, culture, type of bicycle, and characteristics of the cyclists themselves require more attention.

3. Interactions at intersections

While it is possible to separate bicycle, motor vehicle, and pedestrian traffic on road segments, road users must come together and interact with one another at at-grade intersections. Throughout the European Union, 36% of cyclist fatalities occur at intersections, which is extremely high in comparison to other modes. Interestingly, in the European countries with high modal splits of bicycle traffic, cyclist fatalities are more likely to take place at intersections rather than on road segments (European Commission, 2020a). In this section, two topics are discussed, the gap acceptance of cyclists and other road users interacting with cyclists and critical interactions with heavy-duty vehicles. Please note that all turning directions mentioned in this chapter are based on right-hand traffic.

At signalized intersections, priority is granted to a large degree by the traffic signal. Conflicting streams, such as crossing and left-turning road users, are often served in the same signal phase and road users must yield to one another based on traffic laws. At non-signalized intersections, road users must determine and grant the right of way for each interaction (again based on traffic laws). Gaps are the distance in space or time between two road users following each other or to the nearest approaching road user in an opposing traffic stream. Gap acceptance describes the minimum gap size utilized by road users to cross an opposing stream and has an enormous effect on traffic flow and cyclist safety at intersections.

A critical safety issue for cyclists is interactions with heavy-duty vehicles. Although interactions with heavy-duty vehicles are important on road segments as well, this topic is included in this section because of the acute problem with interactions between cyclists riding straight across the intersection and heavy-duty vehicles turning right.

3.1 Gap acceptance

Gap acceptance plays an important role in the interaction of conflicting traffic streams at intersections. The most common examples of gap acceptance are left-turning vehicles or cyclists serviced in the same phase as vehicles or cyclists moving straight across the intersection in the opposite direction. Another example is road users turning left or right that must pass through a stream of pedestrians or cyclists crossing adjacently in the same phase. In many places, the turning vehicle or cyclist must wait for a large enough gap in the prioritized stream. Of course, there are different regulations for interactions in different countries.

The only factor found to affect the gap acceptance of cyclists is the type of stop they perform. Opiela et al. (1980) studied the gap acceptance of 260 cyclists as they crossed two lanes of one-way motor vehicle traffic. They found gap acceptance to be affected by the type of stop, with cyclists who came to a rolling stop accepting much shorter gaps compared to those who came to a complete stop. The observed gap acceptance data was found to follow a logarithmic distribution. The critical gap, which represents the intersection between the gap acceptance and gap rejection, was found to be 3.2 s. Hoogendoorn and Daamen (2016) estimated a so-called empty space distribution, which can be used to determine the number of gaps that can be used by crossing traffic.

Gap acceptance across the driving population regulates the overall traffic efficiency at intersections. Many researchers have investigated traffic volumes and the resulting delay at intersections. Allen et al. (1998) studied the relationship between the bicycle traffic volume on a given intersection approach and the percentage of the green phase in which the conflict area for left and right turning vehicles is blocked by cyclists. They concluded that there are a sufficient number of large gaps and therefore very little impact on traffic flow when the volume of bicycle traffic is less than 60 cyclists/hour. A linear equation was developed to predict the proportion of green time during which the conflict zone is occupied based on the volume of bicycle traffic. Extrapolation was used to predict that a full blockage of the conflict zone occurs at 2646 cyclists/hour green. Grigoropoulos et al. (2022) found in Germany that a flow of 600 cyclists/hour at an intersection approach reduces the capacity of right-turning motor vehicle traffic at the same approach by approximately 50% and of left-turning vehicles on the opposite approach by nearly 65%.

Gap acceptance plays a central role in the safety of cyclists at intersections. A major safety concern at signalized intersections involves vehicles turning right in the same signal phase as cyclists traveling straight across the intersection, which are often positioned to the right of the turning vehicle traffic. This leads to situations in which drivers do not see cyclists (look-but-failed-to-see-error) or accept gaps in bicycle traffic that are not large enough.

3.2 Heavy-duty vehicles

The most dangerous interactions for cyclists in urban areas are those with heavy-duty vehicles. In Europe, 13% of cyclist fatalities resulting from a crash with another road user followed an impact with a truck. Several countries with relatively high modal splits of cycling, including Denmark and Switzerland, have shares of cyclist fatalities from truck-cyclist crashes above 20% of all cyclist collision fatalities. Part of the problem is that when cyclist-heavy duty vehicle crashes occur, the consequences for the cyclist are likely to be more severe than for collisions with any other type of road user (Kim et al., 2007; Manson et al., 2013). In addition, as a result of megatrends such as urbanization and increased online shopping, the number of heavy-duty vehicles in urban areas is growing and researchers have noted a troubling lack in developments concerning city logistics (Dablanc, 2007). These factors together suggest that the bicycle-truck problem in urban areas will likely become worse in the future.

Pokorny and Pitera (2019) provide a summary of 43 studies relating to crashes and conflicts between cyclists and heavy-duty vehicles. They report that the most serious risk factor for cyclist-truck collisions is limited visibility; mainly the problematic blind spots beside, in front, to the sides, and behind the truck in which drivers are not able to see cyclists, pedestrians, and any other road users. Other problems with blind spots, such as lack of awareness about the problem, cyclists' incorrectly presuming that a truck driver can see them, improper adjustment of mirrors by truck drivers, leading to larger blind spots, and a lack of proper truck equipment are found to be risk factors for cyclist-heavy duty vehicle collisions.

Large trucks and rigid trucks, particularly those linked with construction activities, are particularly dangerous for cyclists due to their large blind spots, large turning radii, and limited maneuverability (Niewoehner and Berg, 2005). For this reason, and because large trucks are known to cause congestion in urban areas, many cities are implementing policies to replace large trucks with many smaller trucks (Taniguchi, 2014). However, trucks are not only dangerous for cyclists when they are driving but also when they are parked. The number of smaller-sized delivery vehicles carrying the packages and parcels ordered online is growing at a rapid rate and in many cases, there is insufficient temporary parking available for these trucks. Hence, many truck drivers park on sidewalks and bicycle lanes out of necessity and temporarily block these facilities for their intended users. Based on observations of cyclists' interactions in Munich, Germany, Silva et al. (2020) reported that cyclists often break traffic laws by moving into an adjacent vehicle lane to pass a delivery vehicle (even though these vehicles only block the lane for a short period). This behavior puts cyclists at risk for dangerous interactions with passing motorists (see the previous section about motorists).

4. Shared space

In the previous two sections, I investigated infrastructure designs with a large degree of separation between active and motorized modes of transport. This is a common approach to ensure high traveling speeds for motor vehicles while ensuring safe conditions for pedestrians and cyclists. The concept of shared space is different in that there is no physical segregation between the modes of transport and the speed of faster road users is reduced to ensure safe interactions for all. Because of the lack of physical separation, there is an increased need for interaction and cooperation. As a result, shared spaces are characterized by more conflicts, greater attentiveness of all road users, and smaller differences in traveling speed between modes (Kaparias et al., 2013). Researchers in Austria have found the variance in observed speeds per road user is smaller in shared space than on other types of infrastructure because road users do not need to start and stop as often (Schönauer et al., 2012). However, although injuries are rare, physical contact between road users is common in shared spaces and conflicts are a cause for concern of both pedestrians and cyclists (Gkekas et al., 2020).

The density of the shared space has a large impact on the behavior, interaction, and comfort of road users. As expected, cyclists' traveling speeds are lower (Alsaleh et al., 2020; Beitel et al., 2018; Essa et al., 2018) and the number of conflicts between cyclists and pedestrians is higher (Beitel et al., 2018) in shared spaces with high pedestrian densities. The higher density also leads to more close interactions, which lowers the perceived safety of pedestrians (Kiyota et al., 2000). Subjectively, cyclists and pedestrians see high density and inattentiveness as risk factors for conflicts and crashes (Gkekas et al., 2020). As discussed in previous sections, it appears that pedestrians are more likely to adjust their behavior and yield to a cyclist than the other way around in a shared space (Che et al., 2021).

No studies were found in the review that investigate the behavior and interactions in shared spaces with motorized vehicles.

5. Discussion

Interactions between cyclists and other road users are a normal part of moving through an environment on a bicycle and are not in themselves problematic. The opposite is true; the lack of a hard shell and a slower traveling speed allows cyclists the opportunity to experience and interact with the surrounding environment and with other people using the road. So where does the problem lie? A major issue is the failure to perceive and then predict the development of a potential problem.

Based on an in-depth analysis of cyclist-motorist crashes in Sweden, Räsänen and Summala (1998) reported two common mechanisms in collisions. First, road users fail to detect or see an interacting cyclist or motorist and a potentially critical situation. They found that in 37% of studied crashes, neither road user perceived the danger before the crash occurred. Similarly, an Australian review reported that in over 60% of collisions, a major contributing factor was that neither the cyclist nor the driver saw the other road user before the collision happened (Australian Transport Safety

Bureau, 2006). A common problem is that people tend to thoroughly check for other road users in areas where they are expected and neglect, or quickly scan, spaces where they are not. Many cyclist-motorist crashes happen at non-signalized intersections when a vehicle turning right crashes into a cyclist that approaches from their right-hand side (Gerstenberger, 2015; Herslund and Jørgensen, 2003; Räsänen and Summala, 1998; Summala et al., 1996). In this situation, the motorist expects interacting road users to approach from the left-hand side and therefore visually searches this area more thoroughly than the space on the right-hand side (Summala et al., 1996). Even if they do scan the right side, they are more prone to a "look-but-failed-to-see-error" because the cyclist does not fit into the driver's fixed search strategy (Herslund and Jørgensen, 2003).

How can urban infrastructure planners and traffic engineers address this issue? They must design and build infrastructure that is uniform, direct, and easy to understand for all road users. This will support the positioning of all persons in spaces where they are expected by other road users. It is also important to ensure high visibility for cyclists, motorists, and pedestrians to physically be able to see one another. Finally, technology may assist motorists in detecting other road users and upcoming interactions before they become critical. A key example of this is drivers' assistance systems that detect cyclists and pedestrians in the blind spots of large trucks and warn the truck driver.

The second common failure according to Räsänen and Summala (1998) is the incorrect prediction of the upcoming behavior of other road users. People express their intention and upcoming manoeuvers with one another using implicit and explicit communication strategies. Implicit communication strategies convey messages to other road users without using direct signals. Examples include changing speed or direction or looking in a certain direction. Explicit communication on the other hand involves direct signals such as hand waving, honking a horn, or ringing a bell on a bicycle. Successful communication forms the basis of all normal encounters and is essential in resolving conflicts (Abendroth et al., 2019).

What can be done to address the failure to predict the behavior of other road users? Again, clear and easily understandable infrastructure is the key. Rules and regulations that ensure predictable behavior and the enforcement of these rules may help create a predictable road environment. However, a much more effective measure may be a simple reduction in speed limits and the introduction of traffic calming measures. When traveling at slower speeds, road users have more time to correct misinterpretations of upcoming behaviors. And if a collision does happen, the consequences are less severe at low speeds in comparison to higher speeds. Again, technology may offer assistance in predicting the behavior of other road users. Developers of automated driving systems are very keen to create systems that can implicitly and explicitly communicate with human cyclists, pedestrians, and motorists, predict behaviors and react in ways that are understandable to others.

In situations in which a cyclist detects and perceives an upcoming risk, correctly predicts the behavior of the interacting partner, and communicates their intention, a final potential problem is the failure to properly adjust their operational behavior (e.g. speed and direction). This is particularly relevant for cyclists in comparison to users of other modes because riding a bicycle requires physical skill, balance, and strength in a dimension different from walking or sitting and driving a motor vehicle. If a cyclist loses operational control during an interaction, he or she is at risk of a fall, which can have serious consequences as well. This factor is particularly important for elderly cyclists and children.

What can be done to help cyclists adjust their speed and direction and react to critical situations without losing control of their bicycles? Once again technology may be able to assist. For example, researchers at the TU Delft are in the process of developing assistance systems that help cyclists stay upright when riding at slow speeds (TU Delft, 2019).

Bicycle traffic is becoming increasingly diverse. Pedelecs and other electrically supported bicycles, pod bicycles, cargo bicycles, e-scooters, and other forms of micromobility are growing in popularity. Each of these new forms of mobility is distinct in terms of driving dynamics and use. The interactions between users of these new modes and other road users may be similar to those of cyclists, but not identical. As these new modes become more commonplace, researchers will have the opportunity to examine interactions at all levels of the Safety Pyramid.

6. Conclusion

The topic explored in this chapter is very broad. I categorized cyclists' interactions according to the infrastructure (road segment, intersection, or shared space) and by the type of interaction (cyclist, motorist, heavy-duty vehicle, bus, or pedestrian). Interaction constellations that are known to lead to conflicts or crashes with potentially severe outcomes for cyclists, such as motorists overtaking cyclists on roadways, are the focus of the vast majority of the papers identified in this review. Fewer papers were found that examine normal interactions, or encounters according to the Safety Pyramid, and most of these were undertaken with the goal of modeling bicycle traffic for application in microscopic traffic simulations. Another aspect that has not been thoroughly covered in the literature is the subjective experience of interacting, particularly with consideration of the benefits interactions bring to the cycling experience.

References

Abendroth, B., Bengler, K., Beruscha, F., Bogner, E., Bruder, R., Deml, B., Imbsweiler, J., Joisten, P., Kiss, M., Lepczyk, D., 2019. Hands off, Human Factors off? Welche Rolle spielen Human Factors in der Fahrzeugautomation? R. Bruder & H. Winner, Darmstadt.

Adminaité-Fodor, D., Jost, G., 2020. How safe is walking and cycling in Europe? Europen Transport Safety Council.

Afghari, A.P., Ismail, K., Saunier, N., Sharma, A., Miranda-Moreno, L., 2014. Pedestrian-cyclist interactions at bus stops along segregated bike paths: a case study of Montreal. Proceedings of the 2014 Transportation Research Board Annual Meeting.

Aldred, R., 2016. Cycling near misses: their frequency, impact, and prevention. Transp. Res. Part A Policy Pract. 90, 69–83. https://doi.org/10.1016/j.tra.2016.04.016.

Aldred, R., Crosweller, S., 2015. Investigating the rates and impacts of near misses and related incidents among UK cyclists. J. Transp. Heal. 2, 379–393. https://doi.org/10.1016/j.jth.2015.05.006.

Allen, D., Hummer, J., Rouphail, N., Milazzo, J., 1998. Effect of bicycles on capacity of signalized intersections. Transp. Res. Rec. J. Transp. Res. Board 1646, 87–95. https://doi.org/10.3141/1646-11.

Alsaleh, R., Hussein, M., Sayed, T., 2020. Microscopic behavioural analysis of cyclist and pedestrian interactions in shared spaces. Can. J. Civ. Eng. 47, 50–62. https://doi.org/10.1139/cjce-2018-0777.

Australian Transport Safety Bureau, 2006. Deaths of Cyclists Due to Road Crashes. Australian Government.

Beck, B., Perkins, M., Olivier, J., Chong, D., Johnson, M., 2021. Subjective experiences of bicyclists being passed by motor vehicles: the relationship to motor vehicle passing distance. Accid. Anal. Prev. 155, 106102. https://doi.org/10.1016/j.aap.2021.106102.

Beitel, D., Stipancic, J., Manaugh, K., Miranda-Moreno, L., 2018. Assessing safety of shared space using cyclist-pedestrian interactions and automated video conflict analysis. Transp. Res. Part D Transp. Environ. 65, 710–724. https://doi.org/10.1016/j.trd.2018.10.001.

Berger, R., Medicus, M., Schmotz, M., Schüller, H., Plesker, M., 2020. Verkehrssicherheit an Haltestellen des ÖPNV. Forschungsbericht/unfallforsch. der Versicherer 63.

Botma, H., 1995. Method to determine level of service for bicycle paths and pedestrian-bicycle paths. Transp. Res. Rec. J. Transp. Res. Board, 38–44.

Botma, H., Papendrecht, H., 1991. Traffic operation of bicycle traffic. Transp. Res. Rec. J. Transp. Res. Board, 65–72.

Che, M., Wong, Y.D., Lum, K.M., Wang, X., 2021. Interaction behaviour of active mobility users in shared space. Transp. Res. Part A Policy Pract. 153, 52–65. https://doi.org/10.1016/j.tra.2021.08.017.

Chuang, K.-H., Hsu, C.-C., Lai, C.-H., Doong, J.-L., Jeng, M.-C., 2013. The use of a quasi-naturalistic riding method to investigate bicyclists' behaviors when motorists pass. Accid. Anal. Prev. 56, 32–41. https://doi.org/10.1016/j.aap.2013.03.029.

Dablanc, L., 2007. Goods transport in large European cities: difficult to organize, difficult to modernize. Transp. Res. Part A Policy Pract. 41, 280–285. https://doi.org/10.1016/j.tra.2006.05.005.

De Ceunynck, T., Dorleman, B., Daniels, S., Laureshyn, A., Brijs, T., Hermans, E., Wets, G., 2017. Sharing is (s)caring? Interactions between buses and bicyclists on bus lanes shared with bicyclists. Transp. Res. Part F Traffic Psychol. Behav. 46, 301–315. https://doi.org/10.1016/j.trf.2016.09.028.

Debnath, A.K., Haworth, N., Schramm, A., Heesch, K.C., Somoray, K., 2018. Factors influencing noncompliance with bicycle passing distance laws. Accid. Anal. Prev. 115, 137–142. https://doi.org/10.1016/j.aap.2018.03.016.

Delft, T.U., 2019. Smart Motor in Handlebars Prevents Bicycles From Falling Over (WWW Document). https://www.tudelft.nl/en/2019/tu-delft/smart-motor-in-handlebars-prevents-bicycles-from-falling-over.

Duthie, J., Brady, J.F., Mills, A.F., Machemehl, R.B., 2011. Effects of on-street bicycle facility configuration on bicyclist and motorist behavior. Transp. Res. Rec. J. Transp. Res. Board 2190, 37–44. https://doi.org/10.3141/2190-05.

Essa, M., Hussein, M., Sayed, T., 2018. Road users' behavior and safety analysis of pedestrian–bike shared space: case study of Robson Street in Vancouver. Can. J. Civ. Eng. 45, 1053–1064. https://doi.org/10.1139/cjce-2017-0683.

European Commission, 2020a. Facts and Figures Cyclists. Brussels.

European Commission, 2020b. Facts and Figures Pedestrians. Brussels.

European Commission, 2021. Facts and Figures Car Cccupants. Brussels.

European Road Safety, 2018. Observatory. Annual accident report 2018.

Falkenberg, G., Blase, A., Bonfranchi, T., Cosse, L., Draeger, W., Vortisch, P., Kautzsch, L., Stapf, H., Zimmermann, A., 2003. Bemessung von Radverkehrsanlagen unter verkehrstechnischen Gesichtspunkten. Berichte der Bundesanstalt fuer Strassenwesen. Unterr. Verkehrstechnik 103.

Forschungsgesellschaft für Straßen- und Verkehrswesen, 2015. Handbuch für die Bemessung von Straßenverkehrsanlagen (HBS).

Freudendal-Pedersen, M., 2015. Cyclists as part of the city's organism: structural stories on cycling in copenhagen. City Soc. 27, 30–50. https://doi.org/10.1111/ciso.12051.

German Federal Ministry of Transport, 2012. National Cycling Plan 2020. Berlin.

Gerstenberger, M., 2015. Accidents at Intersections: Basic Analysis of Causation and Approaches for Improvements. Doctoral Dissertation, Technical University of Munich.

Gkekas, F., Bigazzi, A., Gill, G., 2020. Perceived safety and experienced incidents between pedestrians and cyclists in a high-volume non-motorized shared space. Transp. Res. Interdiscip. Perspect. 4, 100094. https://doi.org/10.1016/j.trip.2020.100094.

Gould, G., Karner, A., 2010. Modeling bicycle facility operation. Transp. Res. Rec. J. Transp. Res. Board 2140, 157–164. https://doi.org/10.3141/2140-17.

Greenshields, S., Chowdhury, S., Jones, P., 2018. Bus Stop Bypasses: Analysis of pedestrian and cyclist behaviour via video. London.

Grigoropoulos, G., Leonhardt, A., Kaths, H., Junghans, M., Baier, M.M., Busch, F., 2022. Traffic flow at signalized intersections with large volumes of bicycle traffic. Transp. Res. Part A Policy Pract. 155, 464–483. https://doi.org/10.1016/j.tra.2021.11.021.

Hatfield, J., Prabhakharan, P., 2016. An investigation of behaviour and attitudes relevant to the user safety of pedestrian/cyclist shared paths. Transp. Res. Part F Traffic Psychol. Behav. 40, 35–47. https://doi.org/10.1016/j.trf.2016.04.005.

Henao, A., Apparicio, P., Maignan, D., 2021. One metre plus (1M +): a multifunctional open-source sensor for bicycles based on Raspberry Pi. Sensors 21. https://doi.org/10.3390/s21175812.

Herslund, M.-B., Jørgensen, N.O., 2003. Looked-but-failed-to-see-errors in traffic. Accid. Anal. Prev. 35, 885–891. https://doi.org/10.1016/S0001-4575(02)00095-7.

Heydari, S., Fu, L., Miranda-Moreno, L.F., Jopseph, L., 2017. Using a flexible multivariate latent class approach to model correlated outcomes: a joint analysis of pedestrian and cyclist injuries. Anal. Methods Accid. Res. 13, 16–27. https://doi.org/10.1016/j.amar.2016.12.002.

Hoogendoorn, S., Daamen, W., 2016. Bicycle headway modeling and its applications. Transp. Res. Rec. J. Transp. Res. Board 2587, 34–40. https://doi.org/10.3141/2587-05.

Hydén, C., 1987. The development of a method for traffic safety evaluation: the Swedish traffic conflict technique. Lund University, Sweden.

Johnson, M., Charlton, J., Oxley, J., Newstead, S., 2010. Naturalistic cycling study: identifying risk factors for on-road commuter cyclists. Adv. Automot. Med. Assoc. Adv. Automot. Med. Annu. Sci. Conf. 54, 275–283.

Kaparias, I., Bell, M.G.H., Dong, W., Sastrawinata, A., Singh, A., Wang, X., Mount, B., 2013. Analysis of pedestrian–vehicle traffic conflicts in street designs with elements of shared space. Transp. Res. Rec. J. Transp. Res. Board 2393, 21–30. https://doi.org/10.3141/2393-03.

Kaparias, I., Miah, S., Clegg, S., Gao, Y., Waterson, B., Milonidis, E., 2021. Measuring the effect of highway design features on cyclist behavior using an instrumented bicycle. In: 2021 7th International Conference on Models and Technologies for Intelligent Transportation Systems (MT-ITS), pp. 1–6, https://doi.org/10.1109/MT-ITS49943.2021.9529276.

Karakaya, A.-S., Hasenburg, J., Bermbach, D., 2020. SimRa: using crowdsourcing to identify near miss hotspots in bicycle traffic. Pervasive Mob. Comput. 67, 101197.

Khan, S., Raksuntorn, W., 2001. Characteristics of passing and meeting maneuvers on exclusive bicycle paths. Transp. Res. Rec. J. Transp. Res. Board 1776, 220–228. https://doi.org/10.3141/1776-28.

Kim, J.-K., Kim, S., Ulfarsson, G.F., Porrello, L.A., 2007. Bicyclist injury severities in bicycle–motor vehicle accidents. Accid. Anal. Prev. 39, 238–251. https://doi.org/10.1016/j.aap.2006.07.002.

Kiyota, M., Vandebona, U., Katafuchi, N., Inoue, S., 2000. Bicycle and pedestrian traffic conflicts on shared pavements. In: Fourteenth Velo-City International Conference Proceedings, Munich.

Laureshyn, A., Várhelyi, A., 2018. The Swedish Traffic Conflict Technique: Observer's Manual. LUND University.

Love, D.C., Breaud, A., Burns, S., Margulies, J., Romano, M., Lawrence, R., 2012. Is the three-foot bicycle passing law working in Baltimore, Maryland? Accid. Anal. Prev. 48, 451–456. https://doi.org/10.1016/j.aap.2012.03.002.

Manson, J., Cooper, S., West, A., Foster, E., Cole, E., Tai, N.R.M., 2013. Major trauma and urban cyclists: physiological status and injury profile. Emerg. Med. J. 30, 32–37. https://doi.org/10.1016/j.aap.2012.03.00210.1136/emermed-2011-200966.

Marín Puchades, V., Prati, G., Rondinella, G., De Angelis, M., Fassina, F., Fraboni, F., Pietrantoni, L., 2017. Cyclists' anger as determinant of near misses involving different road users. Front. Psychol. https://doi.org/10.3389/fpsyg.2017.02203.

Mesimäki, J., Luoma, J., 2021. Near accidents and collisions between pedestrians and cyclists. Eur. Transp. Res. Rev. 13, 38. https://doi.org/10.1186/s12544-021-00497-z.

National Research Council, 2000. Highway Capacity Manual 2000. Transportation Research Board, Washington, DC.

National Research Council, 2010. Highway Capacity Manual 2010. Transportation Research Board, Washington, DC.

Nelson, T.A., Denouden, T., Jestico, B., Laberee, K., Winters, M., 2015. BikeMaps.org: a global tool for collision and near miss mapping. Front. Public Heal. 3. https://doi.org/10.3389/fpubh.2015.00053.

Niewoehner, W.B., Berg, F.A., 2005. Endangerment of pedestrians and bicyclists at intersections by right turning trucks. In: Proceedings of the 19th International Technical Conference on the Enhanced Safety of Vehicles (ESV). Washington D.C.

Nolan, J., Sinclair, J., Savage, J., 2021. Are bicycle lanes effective? The relationship between passing distance and road characteristics. Accid. Anal. Prev. 159, 106184. https://doi.org/10.1016/j.aap.2021.106184.

O'Hern, S., Oxley, J., 2019. Pedestrian injuries due to collisions with cyclists Melbourne, Australia. Accid. Anal. Prev. 122, 295–300. https://doi.org/10.1016/j.aap.2018.10.018.

Oh, J.-S., Feizi, A., van Houten, R., Kwigizile, V., Mastali, M., 2019. Bicycle passing distance law: effectiveness and necessity. J. Transp. Heal. https://doi.org/10.1016/j.jth.2019.100758.

Opiela, K.S., Khasnabis, S., Datta, T.K., 1980. Determination of characteristics of bicycle traffic at urban intersections. Transp. Res. Rec. J. Transp. Res. Board 743, 30–38.

Osama, A., Sayed, T., 2017. Evaluating the impact of socioeconomics, land use, built environment, and road facility on cyclist safety. Transp. Res. Rec. J. Transp. Res. Board 2659, 33–42. https://doi.org/10.3141/2659-04.

Pai, C.-W., 2011. Overtaking, rear-end, and door crashes involving bicycles: an empirical investigation. Accid. Anal. Prev. 43, 1228–1235. https://doi.org/10.1016/j.aap.2011.01.004.

Parkin, J., Wardman, M., Page, M., 2007. Models of perceived cycling risk and route acceptability. Accid. Anal. Prev. 39, 364–371. https://doi.org/10.1016/j.aap.2006.08.007.

Paschalidis, E., Basbas, S., Politis, I., Prodromou, M., 2016. "Put the blame on…others!": The battle of cyclists against pedestrians and car drivers at the urban environment. A cyclists' perception study. Transp. Res. Part F Traffic Psychol. Behav. 41, 243–260. https://doi.org/10.1016/j.trf.2015.07.021.

Pokorny, P., Pitera, K., 2019. Truck-bicycle safety: an overview of methods of study, risk factors and research needs. Eur. Transp. Res. Rev. 11, 29. https://doi.org/10.1186/s12544-019-0371-7.

Poulos, R.G., Hatfield, J., Rissel, C., Flack, L.K., Murphy, S., Grzebieta, R., McIntosh, A.S., 2015. An exposure based study of crash and injury rates in a cohort of transport and recreational cyclists in New South Wales. Australia. Accid. Anal. Prev. 78, 29–38. https://doi.org/10.1016/j.aap.2015.02.009.

Räsänen, M., Summala, H., 1998. Attention and expectation problems in bicycle-car collisions: an in-depth study. Accid. Anal. Prev. 30, 657–666. https://doi.org/10.1016/S0001-4575(98)00007-4.

Schönauer, R., Stubenschrott, M., Huang, W., Rudloff, C., Fellendorf, M., 2012. Modeling concepts for mixed traffic: steps towards a microscopic simulation tool for shared space zones. Transp. Res. Board 91st Annu. Meet, 1–16.

Schreiber, M., 2013. Innerörtliche Unfälle mit Fußgängern und Radfahrern, Gesamtverband der Deutschen Versicherungswirtschaft e. V. Unfallforschung der Versicherer, Berlin.

Silva, C., Moeckel, R., Clifton, K., 2020. Proof of concept for a grounded theory approach to understanding interactions occurring on bicycle facilities. Transp. Res. Rec. J. Transp. Res. Board 2674, 94–104. https://doi.org/10.1177/0361198120943588.

Steenberghen, T., Tavares, T., Richardson, J., Himpe, W., Crabbé, A., 2017. Support Study on Data Collection and Analysis of Active Modes Use and Infrastructure in Europe. Final Report. Eur. Union, Luxemberg.

Stone, M., Broughton, J., 2003. Getting off your bike: cycling accidents in Great Britain in 1990–1999. Accid. Anal. Prev. 35, 549–556. https://doi.org/10.1016/S0001-4575(02)00032-5.

Strauss, J., Miranda-Moreno, L.F., Morency, P., 2013. Cyclist activity and injury risk analysis at signalized intersections: a Bayesian modelling approach. Accid. Anal. Prev. 59, 9–17. https://doi.org/10.1016/j.aap.2013.04.037.

Summala, H., Pasanen, E., Räsänen, M., Sievänen, J., 1996. Bicycle accidents and drivers' visual search at left and right turns. Accid. Anal. Prev. 28, 147–153. https://doi.org/10.1016/0001-4575(95)00041-0.

Taniguchi, E., 2014. Concepts of city logistics for sustainable and liveable cities. Proc. Soc. Behav. Sci. 151, 310–317. https://doi.org/10.1016/j.sbspro.2014.10.029.

Twaddle, H., Schendzielorz, T., Fakler, O., 2014. Bicycles in urban areas: review of existing methods for modeling behavior. Transp. Res. Rec. J. Transp. Res. Board 2434, 140–146. https://doi.org/10.3141/2434-17.

Walker, I., 2007. Drivers overtaking bicyclists: objective data on the effects of riding position, helmet use, vehicle type and apparent gender. Accid. Anal. Prev. 39, 417–425. https://doi.org/10.1016/j.aap.2006.08.010.

Wierbos, M.J., Knoop, V.L., Hänseler, F.S., Hoogendoorn, S.P., 2019. Capacity, capacity drop, and relation of capacity to the path width in bicycle traffic. Transp. Res. Rec. J. Transp. Res. Board 2673, 693–702. https://doi.org/10.1177/0361198119840347.

Yuan, Y., Goñi-Ros, B., Daamen, W., Hoogendoorn, S.P., 2018. Investigating cyclist interaction behavior through a controlled laboratory experiment. J. Transp. Land Use 11, 833–847. https://doi.org/10.5198/jtlu.2018.1155.

CHAPTER TEN

Cycling and socioeconomic (dis) advantage

Eugeni Vidal Tortosa[a,*], Eva Heinen[a,b,c], and Robin Lovelace[a]
[a]Institute for Transport Studies, University of Leeds, Leeds, United Kingdom
[b]Faculty of Architecture and Design, Research Centre on Zero Emission Neighbourhoods (ZEN) in Smart Cities, Norwegian University of Science and Technology (NTNU), Trondheim, Norway
[c]Department of Spatial Planning, TU Dortmund University, Dortmund, Germany
*Corresponding author: e-mail address: e.vidaltortosa@leeds.ac.uk

Contents

Abstract

The socioeconomically disadvantaged have much to gain from cycling uptake, as they are most likely to suffer transport disadvantage and be less physically active. This chapter reviews research on "cycling and socioeconomic disadvantage" from two different perspectives: (1) socioeconomic inequalities in cycling levels and (2) spatial inequalities in the provision of cycling facilities. We found evidence of variable relationships between socioeconomic disadvantage and cycling levels. In European "high-cycling" countries, all income groups seem to cycle with minor variations. In Western "low-cycling" countries such as the UK, Canada, and Australia, middle- and high-income groups tend to cycle more. By contrast, in the US, slightly higher levels of cycling among low-income groups or no significant differences were found. In South America, there is a consistent negative association between income and cycling. Education was found positively associated with cycling in Europe, North America, and Oceania, but negatively in South America. Most studies found that disadvantaged populations have lower access to cycling networks and particularly to docked-based Bike Share Schemes (BSS). Dockless BSS may, however, help to reduce geographical inequalities relative to BSS. These results lead to the conclusion that socioeconomic inequalities in cycling should receive greater consideration in

Advances in Transport Policy and Planning, Volume 10
ISSN 2543-0009
https://doi.org/10.1016/bs.atpp.2022.04.009

research into cycling uptake and in practice, at design, implementation, and monitoring stages of interventions to enable cycling uptake. Further work is needed in a range of areas relating to cycling and socioeconomic disadvantage, including research from both perspectives—socioeconomic inequalities in cycling levels and spatial inequalities in the provision of cycling facilities—in middle- and low-income countries, new methods to reliably assess spatial inequalities in the provision of cycling facilities, more insight into trends in inequalities, and in-depth analysis of the barriers to cycling among disadvantaged populations.

Keywords: Cycling, Cycling levels, Cycling infrastructure, Cycling networks, Bike share, Socioeconomic disadvantage, Transport equity, Health inequalities

1. Introduction

The socioeconomically disadvantaged are one of the groups that have much to gain from cycling uptake (Lee et al., 2012). First, because they tend to suffer greater transport disadvantage, due to factors including lack of access to private automobiles or public transport (Rachele et al., 2018). Cycling, as an affordable and convenient mode, can help these groups to access jobs, education, and other local services. Second, because the socioeconomically disadvantaged are less physically active and have a higher incidence of obesity and chronic diseases (Giles-Corti, 2002; Lindström et al., 2001). Regular cycling can contribute to increasing their levels of physical activity and improving their health and well-being (Oja et al., 2011).

There are some remarkable reviews in North America on equity in active modes and cycling planning (Doran et al., 2021; Lee et al., 2017). Also, Dill and McNeil (2021) provided a review of equity and vehicle sharing including bikeshare. However, no work, to our knowledge, has evaluated the international literature available on the extent to which socioeconomically disadvantaged groups cycle and have access to cycling facilities.

This chapter provides a review on the topic "cycling and socioeconomic disadvantage" from two different perspectives: (1) socioeconomic inequalities in cycling levels and (2) spatial inequalities in the provision of cycling facilities. Studies on socioeconomic inequalities in cycling levels analyze the relationships between cycling levels (cycling demand) and different socioeconomic factors such as income, education, and occupation. Research on spatial inequalities in the provision of cycling facilities assesses whether cycling infrastructure (cycling supply) is evenly distributed geographically. Spatial inequalities in the provision of cycling facilities may influence socioeconomic inequalities in cycling levels and vice versa.

In this chapter, the term cycling facilities is used to mean bicycle lanes and physical stations or service geography designations of Bike Share Schemes (BSS), including dock-based and dockless systems. Other types of cycling amenities such as bike racks for parking, shelters, service centers, and specialized traffic signs or signals are not considered.

We intended this review to have a global geographical scope. However, due to the scarcity of research in Asian or African countries, we decided to focus only on regions with substantial cycling inequalities research activity: Europe, North America, South America, and Oceania. Because of clear differences in approaches and findings between them, the results from the literature review are generally grouped by these continents.

2. Socioeconomic inequalities in cycling levels

This section reviews the literature on the relationships between cycling levels and the key socioeconomic factors income, education, and occupation. Although the relationship between these socioeconomic factors and race and ethnicity is intimately intertwined, we focus strictly on the former.

Table 1 outlines each of the studies reviewed in this section. It shows the continent and the country, area, or city where the study was conducted; the cycling measure, the trip purpose, the level of analysis, and the socioeconomic factor (income, education, occupation) analyzed; and the sign of association found.

2.1 Income

In Europe, the association between income and cycling levels seems to depend on how common cycling is in each country. In high-cycling European countries, such as the Netherlands, Germany, and Belgium, all socioeconomic groups seem to cycle with minor variations (Pucher and Buehler, 2008). In the Netherlands, the 2010/2011 Dutch National Travel Survey reported no substantial differences in total bicycle share by income groups (individuals from all socioeconomic levels made an average between 26% and 28% of their trips cycling), although low-income groups were found to cycle significantly more to work (Harms et al., 2014). Also in the Netherlands, Ton et al. (2018) found no significant association between income and cycling; however, Fishman et al. (2015) and Gao et al. (2017) found that higher-income groups cycle more. In Germany, a positive association was found between income and utility cycling (Finger et al., 2019).

Table 1 Studies on socioeconomic inequalities in cycling levels

Continent	Country, area, or city	Cycling measure[a]	Trip purpose[b]	Level of analysis[c]	Socioeconomic factor	Sign of association[d]	Reference
Europe	Netherlands (NL)	MET hours	All	Ind.	Income, Education, Occupation	+/+/−	Fishman et al. (2015)
Europe	Netherlands (NL)	Minutes/week	All	Ind.	Income, Education	+/+	Gao et al. (2017)
Europe	Netherlands (NL)	Bicycle share	All	Ind.	Income, Education	o/o	Harms et al. (2014)
Europe	Netherlands (NL)	Binary variable (yes/no)	All	Ind.	Income, Education, Occupation	o/+/o	Ton et al. (2018)
Europe	Flanders (BE)	% cyclists vs non-cyclists	Com.	Ind.	Education	+	de Geus et al. (2007)
Europe	Ghent (BE)	Bicycle share	All	Ind.	Income	−	Witlox and Tindemans (2004)
Europe	Germany (DE)	>600 MET min/week	Util.	Ind.	Income, Education, Occupation	−/+/+	Finger et al. (2019)
Europe	Antwerp (BE), Barcelona (ES), London (GB), Örebro (SE), Rome (IT), Vienna (AT), and Zurich (CH)	% cyclists vs non-cyclists	All	Ind.	Education, Occupation	+/+	Raser et al. (2018)
Europe	England (GB)	Categorical variable and % of cycling	Util./ Leis.	Ind.	Education	1+	Goodman and Aldred, 2018)

Europe	London (GB)	% cyclists, minutes, and km cycled/day	All	Ind.	Income	+	Green et al. (2010)
Europe	England and Wales (GB)	Bicycle share	Com.	Aggr.	Income, Occupation	+/+	Parkin et al. (2008)
Europe	England (GB)	Binary variable (yes/no), minutes/week	Util./ Leis.	ind.	Deprivation, Education, Occupation	l+/+/+	Vidal Tortosa et al. (2021a)
Europe	England (GB)	Binary variable (yes/no), trips, and miles/week	Util./ Leis.	ind.	Income, Education, Occupation	u+/l+/o	Vidal Tortosa et al. (2021b)
North America	8 Canadian cities (CA)	Bicycle share	Com.	Aggr.	Income	+	Fuller and Winters (2017)
North America	Canada (CA)	Binary variable (yes/no)	Util.	Ind.	Income, Education	+/+	Winters et al. (2007)
North America	Cities > 250,000 (US)	Bicycle share	Com.	Aggr.	Income	o	Dill and Carr (2003)
North America	6 small US cities (US)	Binary variable (yes/no)	Com.	Ind.	Income, Education	o/o	Handy and Xing (2011)
North America	United States (US)	Bicycle share	Com.	Ind.	Income, Education	−/+	Plaut (2005)
North America	United States (US)	Bicycle share	All	Ind.	Income	−	Pucher et al. (2011)
Oceania	Brisbane (AU)	Categorical variable (types of cycling)	Util./ Leis.	Ind.	Income, Education, Occupation	+/+/+	Heesch et al. (2015)

Continued

Table 1 Studies on socioeconomic inequalities in cycling levels—cont'd

Continent	Country, area, or city	Cycling measure[a]	Trip purpose[b]	Level of analysis[c]	Socioeconomic factor	Sign of association[d]	Reference
Oceania	Melbourne (AU)	Binary variable (yes/no)	All	Ind.	Income, Education, Occupation	+/+/+	Kavanagh (2005)
Oceania	Sydney Greater Metropolitan Area (AU)	Binary variable (yes/no)	All	Ind.	Income, Occupation	+/+	Merom et al. (2010)
Oceania	New Zealand (NZ)	Bicycle share	Com.	Aggr.	Income	o	Tin Tin et al. (2009)
South America	Brazil (BR)	Categorical variable (types of cycling)	Com./Leis.	Ind.	Income, Education	−/−	Bandeira et al. (2017)
South America	Santiago (CL)	Binary variable (yes/no)	Util.	Ind.	Income	m- f+	Aguilar-Farias et al. (2019)
South America	Santiago (CL)	Binary variable (yes/no)	All	Ind.	Income, Education	−/−	Ortúzar et al. (2000)
South America	Bogotá (CO)	Bicycle share	Com.	Ind.	Income	−	Guzman and Bocarejo (2017)

[a]MET = Metabolic Equivalents of Tasks.
[b]Util. = Utility, Leis. = Leisure, Com. = Commuting.
[c]Aggr. = Aggregate, Ind. = Individual.
[d]'+' = Positive, '−' = Negative, 'o' = No association, 'l+' = Positive for leisure, 'u+' = Positive for utility, 'm− f+' = Negative for males, positive for females.

By contrast, in Ghent (Belgium), the highest-income group was found to cycle less (Witlox and Tindemans, 2004). Higher cycling levels and safer and more inclusive cycling infrastructure in these countries might encourage everyone to cycle regardless of their socioeconomic status.

In low-cycling European countries, such as the UK, most studies found a positive association between income and cycling. For example, in England and Wales, higher-income populations were found to cycle more to work than lower-income populations (Parkin et al., 2008). In London, not only the highest-income group was found to cycle more often, but also longer and further (Green et al., 2010). Also in England, Vidal Tortosa et al. (2021a) found that people from deprived areas cycle significantly less for leisure but not for utility; however, Vidal Tortosa et al. (2021b) found that low-income groups tend to cycle less for utility cycling, but not for leisure. The use of different methods and databases (the Active Lives Adult Survey in the former study and the English National Survey in the latter) may explain the inconsistencies between these two studies conducted in England. Greater overall cycling among affluent groups in the UK has been attributed to several factors such as crime, safe storage, bicycle availability, image issues (Parkin et al., 2008) as well as cultural and identity reasons (Steinbach et al., 2011).

In North America, mixed results are reported. In Canada, income was found to have a positive association with commuting cycling (Fuller and Winters, 2017) and utility cycling (Winters et al., 2007). However, in the US, the 2009 National Household Travel Survey indicated a higher cycling share in the lowest-income quartile (Pucher et al., 2011). Also in the US, Plaut (2005) found income negatively associated with commuting cycling, although a study conducted in US cities >250.000 inhabitants (Dill and Carr, 2003) and another in 6 small US cities (Handy and Xing, 2011) did not find such association. Pucher et al. (2011) attributed higher levels of cycling among the lowest-income groups in the US to two factors. First, low-income groups are less likely to own a car, and cycling is an inexpensive mode of transportation. Second, low-income households in the US tend to be more concentrated in central cities, where trips are shorter and therefore more cyclable. In Oceania, most studies report that higher-income groups cycle more. Three studies with data from Brisbane, Melbourne, and Sydney (Australia) found a positive relationship between income and cycling (Heesch et al., 2015; Kavanagh, 2005; Merom et al., 2010); the only study conducted in New Zealand found no association (Tin Tin et al., 2009).

In South America, the existing literature agrees: cycling is used mainly by low-income groups. This is the conclusion of studies conducted in Brazil for commuting and leisure (Bandeira et al., 2017), in Bogotá (Colombia) for commuting (Guzman and Bocarejo, 2017), and in Santiago (Chile) for all types of cycling (Ortúzar et al., 2000). Interestingly, in Santiago (Chile), low socioeconomic status was found associated with a greater likelihood of utility cycling in men, but with a lower likelihood of utility cycling in women (Aguilar-Farias et al., 2019). Three factors could explain greater cycling levels by low-income groups in South America. First, the levels of socioeconomic inequalities and transport disadvantage in this continent is particularly high (Vecchio et al., 2020), and consequently, the number of individuals who have no other option but to cycle to work, education or other services ("captive" cyclists) is probably higher. Second, low-income groups in South America tend to live in peri-urban areas (Libertun de Duren, 2018), that is, probably too far to access the city center on foot, but perhaps not by bicycle. Third, the degree of stigmatization of cycling (seen as a means of transport for the poor) in these countries is particularly high (Ortúzar et al., 2000; Tucker and Manaugh, 2018).

2.2 Education

Most research conducted in European countries agrees that people with higher levels of education cycle more. In the Netherlands, three studies found a positive association between education and cycling (Fishman et al., 2015; Ton et al., 2018); however, another one reported no differences in bicycle share by education level (Harms et al., 2014). In Flanders (Belgium) and Germany, education was found positively associated with cycling to work and total cycling (de Geus et al., 2007; Finger et al., 2019). A study that compared socio-demographic differences between cyclists and non-cyclists using data from 7 European cities including Antwerp, Barcelona, London, Örebro, Rome, Vienna, and Zurich found that within the group of cyclists the share of participants with higher education was higher compared to non-cyclists (Raser et al., 2018).

In the UK, education is also associated with more cycling, although not all studies agree on the type of cycling in which this association occurs. In England, people with higher education levels were found more likely to cycle for leisure, but not for utility within most local authorities (Goodman and Aldred, 2018). Also in England, Vidal Tortosa et al. (2021b) found that those with any educational qualifications cycle more for leisure but not for utility; however, Vidal Tortosa et al. (2021a) found that people with higher educational levels cycle more for both leisure and utility. Again, the use of different methods and databases between these two studies may explain the differences in their results.

Also in North America and Oceania, most studies found that people with higher education levels cycle more. In Canada, Winters et al. (2007) found a positive relationship between education and utility cycling. In the US, Plaut (2005) reported that non-motorized commuters were better educated than car commuters. This association was not found, however, in 6 small US cities (Handy and Xing, 2011). In Australia, education was positively associated with both leisure and utility cycling in Brisbane (Heesch et al., 2015) and with overall cycling in Melbourne (Kavanagh, 2005).

In South America, by contrast, the two studies reviewed showed that people with lower education levels tend to cycle more. In Brazil, workers with lower education levels were found more likely to cycle to work and during leisure time than those with higher education (Bandeira et al., 2017). In Santiago (Chile), people with lower education levels were found more willing to cycle (Ortúzar et al., 2000). A greater limitation of transport options among disadvantaged groups and higher stigmatization of the bicycle as a means of transport in these countries might explain the different pattern.

2.3 Occupation

The relationship between occupation and cycling levels has received less scientific attention. In Europe, mixed results are reported. In the Netherlands, one study found that part-time workers, unemployed, and retired people have a greater likelihood of cycling than full-time workers (Fishman et al., 2015); however, another paper found no association between working hours and cycling (Ton et al., 2018). A study conducted in 7 European cities including Antwerp, Barcelona, London, Örebro, Rome, Vienna, and Zurich found that the proportion of employed individuals was higher among cyclists than non-cyclists (Raser et al., 2018).

In Germany, the higher the occupation status the higher the use of cycling for transport (Finger et al., 2019). In England and Wales, "higher professionals" were found positively associated with cycling to work, although the rest of the higher and middle socioeconomic classes were negatively associated (Parkin et al., 2008). Also in England, higher socioeconomic groups and part-time workers were found more likely to cycle for both utility and leisure cycling (Vidal Tortosa et al., 2021a, 2021b). In Australia, two studies, conducted in Brisbane and Sydney, found higher cycling levels among full-time workers (Heesch et al., 2015; Merom et al., 2010); and another study conducted in Melbourne found more cycling among professionals and blue-collar workers (Kavanagh, 2005).

Most of the associations found between cycling levels and income, education, and occupation were calculated adjusting for these and other socioeconomic and socio-demographic factors such as age and gender. This suggests that each of these factors (income, education, and occupation) may affect cycling levels independently of the other factors.

3. Spatial inequalities in the provision of cycling facilities

There is evidence that investment in cycling facilities results in increases in cycling levels (Buehler and Dill, 2016; Hosford et al., 2019; Lee et al., 2017). Therefore, and given that socioeconomic groups tend to live clustered in geographic areas, spatial inequalities in the distribution of cycling facilities could lead to socioeconomic inequalities in cycling levels.

This section reviews the literature on spatial inequalities in the distribution of cycling facilities distinguishing between research assessing access to cycling networks and access to Bike Share Schemes (BSS).

Table 2 outlines each of the studies reviewed in this section. It shows the continent and the country, area, or city where the study was conducted; the facility assessed (Cycling network/Dock-based BSS/Dockless BSS); and the result of the accessibility assessment regarding disadvantaged populations.

3.1 Cycling networks

In the European continent, a recent study reported that deprived areas[a] in England have a higher density of cycling infrastructure, both cycle lanes (on-road) and cycle tracks (off-road), and lower levels of traffic stress (Vidal Tortosa et al., 2021a).

In North America, most studies found important deficiencies among certain disadvantaged groups in accessing cycling networks. In Canada, one study conducted in 8 cities reported that low-income populations have

[a] *Small areas of England with a higher Index of Multiple Deprivation (IMD). The IMD is based on seven different domains of deprivation: Income Deprivation, Employment Deprivation, Education, Skills and Training Deprivation, Health Deprivation and Disability, Crime, Barriers to Housing and Services, and Living Environment Deprivation (DfCLG, 2015).*

Table 2 Studies on spatial inequalities in the provision of cycling facilities

Continent	Country, area, or city	Facility assessed	Accessibility assessment result (regarding disadvantaged populations)	Reference
Europe	England (GB)	Cycling network	Greater	Vidal Tortosa et al. (2021a)
North America	8 Canadian cities (CA)	Cycling network	Lower	Fuller and Winters (2017)
North America	Montreal, Longueuil and Laval (CA)	Cycling network	Lower (immigrants, children, and old people), Greater (low-income people)	Houde et al. (2018)
North America	Victoria, Kelowna, and Halifax (CA)	Cycling network	Greater (in 2 out of 3 cities)	Winters et al. (2018)
North America	Vancouver (CA)	Cycling network	Lower (children and Chinese people), Greater (University-educated adults)	Firth et al. (2021)
North America	22 large US cities (US)	Cycling network	Lower (low SES and minority residents)	Braun et al. (2019)
North America	Portland (US)	Cycling network	Greater (low-income people), Lower (black, youth, and old people)	Dill and Haggerty (2009)
North America	Baltimore (US)	Cycling network	Greater (black and low-income people), Lower (Hispanic people)	Kent and Karner (2019)
North America	Minnesota (US)	Cycling network	Lower	Wang and Lindsey (2017)
Oceania	Melbourne (AU)	Cycling network	Lower	Crawford et al. (2008)
Oceania	Melbourne (AU)	Cycling network	Evenly distributed (although more off-road infrastructure in affluent areas)	Pistoll and Goodman (2014)

Continued

Table 2 Studies on spatial inequalities in the provision of cycling facilities—cont'd

Continent	Country, area, or city	Facility assessed	Accessibility assessment result (regarding disadvantaged populations)	Reference
South America	Rio de Janeiro and Curitiba (BR)	Cycling network	Lower	Tucker and Manaugh (2018)
South America	Santiago (CL)	Cycling network	Lower	Mora et al. (2021)
South America	Bogotá (CO)	Cycling network	Lower	Teunissen et al. (2015)
Europe	Glasgow (GB)	Dock-based BSS	Lower	Clark and Curl (2016)
Europe	London (GB)	Dock-based BSS	Lower	Goodman and Cheshire (2014)
Europe	London (GB)	Dock-based BSS	Lower	Lovelace et al. (2020)
North America	Island of Montreal (CA)	Dock-based BSS	Greater	Fuller et al. (2013)
North America	5 Canadian cities (CA)	Dock-based BSS	Lower (in 4 out of 5 cities)	Hosford and Winters (2018)
North America	29 large cities (US)	Dock-based BSS	Lower	Barajas, 2018
North America	Phoenix (US)	Dock-based BSS	Lower	Conrow et al. (2018)
North America	7 large US cities (US)	Dock-based BSS	Generally lower (non-white, low-educated, low-income people)	Aultman-Hall and Ursaki (2015)
South America	5 Brazilian cities (BR)	Dock-based BSS	Lower	Duran et al. (2018)
South America	Manizales (CO)	Dock-based BSS	Lower	Cardona et al. (2017)

Table 2 Studies on spatial inequalities in the provision of cycling facilities—cont'd

Continent	Country, area, or city	Facility assessed	Accessibility assessment result (regarding disadvantaged populations)	Reference
North America	32 US cities (US)	Dock-less BSS and Dock-based BSS	Dock-based BSS lower. Dockless BSS more evenly distributed	Meng and Brown (2021)
North America	Seattle (US)	Dock-less BSS	Lower	Mooney et al. (2019)
North America	San Francisco (US)	Dock-less BSS and Dock-based BSS	Dock-based BSS lower; Dockless BSS greater for the disadvantaged	Qian et al. (2020)

less access to cycling lanes (Fuller and Winters, 2017); however, another study carried out in the medium-sized cities of Victoria and Kelowna (Winters et al., 2018) found the opposite result. In Montreal, Longueuil, and Laval, low-income individuals were found to have greater accessibility to the cycling networks, but recent immigrants, older populations, and children lower (Houde et al., 2018). In Vancouver, areas with more children and where more Chinese people live were found to have less access to protected bike lanes, and areas with more university-educated adults to have more infrastructure in general and local street bikeways in particular (Firth et al., 2021). This study also found that, in general, the disparities did not change over time. In the US, a study based on data from 22 large cities found that, overall, people with lower socioeconomic status (SES) and minority residents had lower access to bicycle lanes (Braun et al., 2019). Similarly, in Minnesota, the cycling infrastructure was found to benefit disproportionately wealthier populations (Wang and Lindsey, 2017). In Portland, minority communities, youth, and the elder had some limitation in accessing cycling lanes; however, low-income populations had greater accessibility (Dill and Haggerty, 2009). In Baltimore, black and low-income communities were found to have slightly better access by bicycle to specific services, but Hispanics worse (Kent and Karner, 2019).

In Australia, a study conducted in Melbourne showed a progressive positive association between density of cycling paths and areas of higher socioeconomic status (Crawford et al., 2008). However, another study with more recent data from Melbourne found that cycling infrastructure was generally equitably distributed, although the off-road infrastructure was slightly higher in more affluent areas (Pistoll and Goodman, 2014).

Findings from South American cities generally coincide: the poor areas tend to be under-served. In Rio de Janeiro and Curitiba (Brazil), the wealthiest areas were found to have more than twice the supply of cycling infrastructure than the poorest areas (Tucker and Manaugh, 2018). In Santiago (Chile), most bicycle lanes were found concentrated in central communes where middle- and upper-middle income groups live (Mora et al., 2021). In Bogotá (Colombia), the low-income areas were found less accessible to the *cicloruta* bicycle network and the *ciclovía* recreational program, even though most of their users come from low-income areas (Teunissen et al., 2015).

3.2 Bike share schemes

One of the main barriers to cycle among disadvantaged populations is not having access to a bicycle, either due to the cost of ownership or lack of secure storage space (McNeil, 2011). Bike Share Schemes (BSS) could provide a solution for these constraints.

There is extensive literature on equity in the distribution of dock-based BSS. In Europe, all the studies reviewed that assessed the distribution of BSS stations report that disadvantaged areas are on average under-served. In London, the provision of bike-sharing stations in non-deprived areas was found disproportionately higher than in deprived areas, although the system seems to have become more inclusive in recent years (Goodman and Cheshire, 2014; Lovelace et al., 2020). In Glasgow, people with higher qualifications and in employment were found to live, on average, closer to bike-sharing stations (Clark and Curl, 2016).

In North America, most studies suggest that BSS stations benefit affluent populations. In the Canadian cities of Vancouver, Toronto, Ottawa-Gatineau, and Montréal the disadvantaged had lower access to bike-sharing stations, but in Hamilton, greater access (Hosford and Winters, 2018). However, another study conducted in the Island of Montréal found that individuals with lower incomes live significantly closer to bike-sharing stations (Fuller et al., 2013). The use of different methods and datasets may explain the inconsistencies in the results of these two studies conducted in Montréal. A report conducted in 7 major US cities found that white people have higher access to BSS stations in Chicago, Boston, New York City,

Denver, and Seattle; people with higher education in Chicago, New York City, Denver, and Seattle; and people with higher income in Chicago, New York City, Washington DC, and Seattle (Aultman-Hall and Ursaki, 2015). Also in Phoenix, low-income populations were found under-represented in accessing BSS (Conrow et al., 2018). Barajas (2018) examined the distribution of bike-sharing stations in terms of job locations in 29 US cities. Their findings were that almost all of the dock-based BSS served significantly more higher-income and higher-skilled jobs. No papers looking at the spatial distribution of BSS stations in Oceania were found.

Finally, in South America, the two studies reviewed agree that wealthier areas have greater access to bike-sharing stations. In Porto Alegre, Recife, Rio de Janeiro, Salvador, and Sao Paulo (Brazil), the coverage of BSS stations favored wealthier and centrally located neighborhoods with a higher proportion of white population (Duran et al., 2018). In Manizales (Colombia), the upper-class groups had higher access than the middle and lower (Cardona et al., 2017).

Two factors might explain why disadvantaged areas are generally under-served in accessing BSS. First, promoters may consider that the demand for bike-sharing bicycles in disadvantaged areas is lower, although there is evidence that shows that the proportion of low-income cyclists is higher among bike-sharing users than among regular cycling (Buck et al., 2013). Second, since the crime level in disadvantaged areas is usually higher, promoters may fear more vandalism and bike theft in these areas.

Literature on equity in dockless BSS is scarcer. Qian et al. (2020) compared the dock-based and dockless BSS in San Francisco and found that dockless systems could provide greater availability of bikes for disadvantaged populations than for other communities. Interestingly, they also found that the existence of electric bikes helps mitigate the bikeshare usage gap between disadvantaged and non-disadvantaged communities. Meng and Brown (2021) examined 32 US cities with both dock-based and dockless BSS. They found that the distribution of docked systems was extremely unequal and that dockless systems greatly reduced geographical inequalities relative to docked. Mooney et al. (2019) explored equity of spatial access to dockless BSS in Seattle and reported inequalities similar to prior findings in studies of docked BSS.

A closely related issue to the spatial inequalities in the provision of cycling facilities is the relationship between the provision of cycling facilities and urban gentrification. Studies looking at this relationship provide a counterpoint to the perceived benefits of cycling in disadvantaged areas.

On the one hand, the provision of bicycle lanes and public bicycles in disadvantaged communities may create opportunities to mitigate transport disadvantage and reduce health inequalities. On the other, these cycling facilities (along with other "revitalization" measures) can raise housing prices, with the consequent potential for displacement of the poorest populations. This has been extensively studied in US cities such as New York (Stein, 2011), San Francisco (Stehlin, 2015, 2019), Portland (Flanagan et al., 2016), Chicago (Lubitow, 2016), Philadelphia (Stehlin, 2019), Detroit (Stehlin, 2019), Los Angeles and Minneapolis (Hoffmann and Lugo, 2014), and Memphis (Smiley et al., 2016).

4. Research gaps and priorities for further research

Several important research gaps in both of the areas reviewed in this chapter remain. More research in socioeconomic inequalities in cycling levels and in spatial inequalities in the provision of cycling facilities is needed in low- and middle-income countries. This is especially important in countries such as China or India, which together represent 37% of the entire world population and, where cycling has traditionally been one of the most important modes of transportation. Investigation of cycling inequalities in these countries is essential to help reduce their issues in transport disadvantage, which are generally higher than in Western countries.

Second, the existing methods to assess spatial inequalities in the provision of cycling facilities have significant limitations. Current studies examine how the proximity of cycling infrastructure (bicycle networks or BSS) varies by area or social group. However, most of these studies do not analyze the quality of the infrastructure or whether the infrastructure is adapted to the needs of different groups. Do bicycle lanes in disadvantaged areas lead to the destination or public stations used by their residents? Are the BSS in disadvantaged areas adapted to the times, prices, and types of payment methods more suitable for these groups? Moreover, most of these studies focus on the distribution of cycling facilities (cycling networks or BSS), but not on how cyclable areas are. There is evidence that cycling facilities are associated with higher cycling levels; however, the consideration of other spatial factors linked to cycling levels such as urban form, connectivity, hilliness, transport safety, aesthetics, and crime (Fraser and Lock, 2011; Wang et al., 2016) is often neglected.

Third, more insight into the direction that each of the areas reviewed in this chapter is taking is needed. Are these inequalities increasing or decreasing over time? Monitoring these trends would indicate to what extent current policies are being effective in reducing inequalities.

Finally, research on barriers to cycling among socioeconomically disadvantaged populations has focused primarily on access to cycling facilities. More research is needed on other environmental and non-environmental factors such as access and ownership of bicycles, safe bicycle storage at work and home, and cultural and social norms.

5. Conclusions

This chapter reviewed research on cycling and socioeconomic disadvantage from two different perspectives: socioeconomic inequalities in cycling levels and spatial inequalities in the provision of cycling facilities. We found evidence of variable relationships between socioeconomic disadvantage and cycling levels in the literature. Cycling is one of the only modes of transport that is more common among relatively rich people in some places, but more common among relatively poor people in others. In European countries with high levels of cycling, all income groups seem to cycle with minor variations. In Western low-cycling countries such as the UK, Canada, and Australia, middle- and high-income groups tend to cycle more. By contrast, in the US, studies report slightly higher levels of cycling among low-income groups or no significant differences. In South America, where most countries are low- or middle-income and cycling is rare, there is a consistent negative association between income and cycling. This might be explained by greater transportation disadvantages, the location of the poorer populations in peri-urban areas, and higher stigmatization of cycling in this continent. Education is consistently found to be positively associated with cycling in research undertaken in Europe, North America, and Oceania. This could be attributed to greater awareness of the environmental and health benefits of cycling of those with higher levels of education. In South America, however, the literature finds a negative association with education. The mixed results and the limited number of studies for occupation make it difficult to draw conclusions on this relationship.

Regarding spatial inequalities in the provision of cycling facilities, disadvantaged groups were found generally more under-served. One study, in England, found disadvantaged areas more accessible to cycling infrastructure, and another one, in Australia, no significant differences. However, in North America, where the majority of research into this topic has been undertaken, disadvantaged groups were mostly found under-served.

In South America, the lack of access of the disadvantaged is consistent. This is despite the fact that low-income groups seem to comprise the majority of cyclists in most North American and South American cities. In Europe, North America, and South America disadvantaged populations were also found to have lower access to bike-sharing stations. Most of the recent studies on Dockless BSS show, however, that these systems can help reduce the geographical inequalities found in docked systems.

These results lead to the conclusion that socioeconomic inequalities in cycling should receive greater consideration in research into cycling uptake and in practice, at design, implementation, and monitoring stages of interventions to enable cycling uptake.

Further work is needed in a range of areas relating to cycling and socioeconomic disadvantage, including research from both perspectives—inequalities in cycling levels and in the provision of cycling facilities—in middle- and low-income countries, new methods to reliably assess spatial inequalities in access to cycling facilities, more insight into trends in inequalities, and in-depth analysis of the barriers to cycling among disadvantaged populations.

Answers to these questions and greater consideration of socioeconomic inequalities in cycling when implementing cycling policies will be highly beneficial for those who suffer from inequalities in transport and health. Further research in these areas will also yield benefits for society as a whole, since it will contribute to the reduction of motorized transport and associated costs to people and environments worldwide.

References

Aguilar-Farias, N., Cortinez-O'Ryan, A., Chandia-Poblete, D., Heesch, K.C., 2019. Prevalence and correlates of transport cycling in Chile: results from 2014 to 2015 national surveys. J. Transp. Health 14, 100594. https://doi.org/10.1016/j.jth.2019.100594.

Aultman-Hall, L., Ursaki, J., 2015. Quantifying the Equity of Bikeshare Access in U.S. Cities. Transportation Research Center.

Bandeira, A.d.S., da Silva, K.S., Del Duca, G.F., Zilch, G.R., de Oliveira, E.S.A., de Barros, M.V.G., Nahas, M.V., 2017. Factors associated with bicycle use for commuting and for leisure among Brazilian workers. Sport Sci. Health 13, 63–68. https://doi.org/10.1007/s11332-017-0350-0.

Barajas, J.M., 2018. How equitable is bikesharing? Exploring population characteristics and access to employment. In: Proceedings of the 97th Annual Meeting of the Transportation Research Board.

Braun, L.M., Rodriguez, D.A., Gordon-Larsen, P., 2019. Social (in)equity in access to cycling infrastructure: cross-sectional associations between bike lanes and area-level sociodemographic characteristics in 22 large US cities. J. Transp. Geogr. 80, 102544. https://doi.org/10.1016/j.jtrangeo.2019.102544.

Buck, D., Buehler, R., Happ, P., Rawls, B., Chung, P., Borecki, N., 2013. Are bikeshare users different from regular cyclists?: a first look at short-term users, annual members, and area cyclists in the Washington, D.C., region. Transp. Res. Rec.: J. Transp. Res. Board 2387, 112–119. https://doi.org/10.3141/2387-13.

Buehler, R., Dill, J., 2016. Bikeway networks: a review of effects on cycling. Transp. Rev. 36, 9–27. https://doi.org/10.1080/01441647.2015.1069908.

Cardona, M., Zuluaga, J., Escobar, D., 2017. Análisis de la red de ciclo-rutas de Manizales (Colombia) a partir de criterios de accesibilidad territorial urbana y cobertura de estratos socioeconómicos. vol. 38, Revista Espacios, p. 11.

Clark, J., Curl, A., 2016. Bicycle and Car share schemes as inclusive modes of travel? A socio-spatial analysis in Glasgow, UK. Soc. Incl. 4, 83. https://doi.org/10.17645/si.v4i3.510.

Conrow, L., Murray, A.T., Fischer, H.A., 2018. An optimization approach for equitable bicycle share station siting. J. Transp. Geogr. 69, 163–170. https://doi.org/10.1016/j.jtrangeo.2018.04.023.

Crawford, D., Timperio, A., Giles-Corti, B., Ball, K., Hume, C., Roberts, R., Andrianopoulos, N., Salmon, J., 2008. Do features of public open spaces vary according to neighbourhood socio-economic status? Health Place 14, 889–893. https://doi.org/10.1016/j.healthplace.2007.11.002.

de Geus, B., De Bourdeaudhuij, I., Jannes, C., Meeusen, R., 2007. Psychosocial and environmental factors associated with cycling for transport among a working population. Health Educ. Res. 23, 697–708. https://doi.org/10.1093/her/cym055.

DfCLG, 2015. The English Indices of Deprivation 2015. Research report.

Dill, J., Carr, T., 2003. Bicycle commuting and facilities in major US cities: if you build them, commuters will use them. Transp. Res. Rec.: J. Transp. Res. Board 1828, 116–123. https://doi.org/10.3141/1828-14.

Dill, J., Haggerty, B., 2009. Equity Analysis of Portland's Draft Bicycle Master Plan—Findings. vol. 135, Urban Studies and Planning Faculty Publications and Presentations.

Dill, J., McNeil, N., 2021. Are shared vehicles shared by all? A review of equity and vehicle sharing. J. Plan. Lit. 36, 5–30. https://doi.org/10.1177/0885412220966732.

Doran, A., El-Geneidy, A., Manaugh, K., 2021. The pursuit of cycling equity: a review of Canadian transport plans. J. Transp. Geogr. 90, 102927. https://doi.org/10.1016/j.jtrangeo.2020.102927.

Duran, A.C., Anaya-Boig, E., Shake, J.D., Garcia, L.M.T., Rezende, L.F.M.d., Hérick de Sá, T., 2018. Bicycle-sharing system socio-spatial inequalities in Brazil. J. Transp. Health 8, 262–270. https://doi.org/10.1016/j.jth.2017.12.011.

Finger, J.D., Varnaccia, G., Gabrys, L., Hoebel, J., Kroll, L.E., Krug, S., Manz, K., Baumeister, S.E., Mensink, G.B.M., Lange, C., Leitzmann, M.F., 2019. Area-level and individual correlates of active transportation among adults in Germany: a population-based multilevel study. Sci. Rep. 9, 16361. https://doi.org/10.1038/s41598-019-52888-x.

Firth, C.L., Hosford, K., Winters, M., 2021. Who were these bike lanes built for? Social-spatial inequities in Vancouver's bikeways, 2001–2016. J. Transp. Geogr. 94, 103122. https://doi.org/10.1016/j.jtrangeo.2021.103122.

Fishman, E., Böcker, L., Helbich, M., 2015. Adult active transport in the Netherlands: an analysis of its contribution to physical activity requirements. PLoS One 10, e0121871. https://doi.org/10.1371/journal.pone.0121871.

Flanagan, E., Lachapelle, U., El-Geneidy, A., 2016. Riding tandem: does cycling infrastructure investment mirror gentrification and privilege in Portland, OR and Chicago, IL? Res. Transp. Econ. 60, 14–24. https://doi.org/10.1016/j.retrec.2016.07.027.

Fraser, S.D.S., Lock, K., 2011. Cycling for transport and public health: a systematic review of the effect of the environment on cycling. Eur. J. Public Health 21, 738–743. https://doi.org/10.1093/eurpub/ckq145.

Fuller, D., Winters, M., 2017. Income inequalities in bike score and bicycling to work in Canada. J. Transp. Health 7, 264–268. https://doi.org/10.1016/j.jth.2017.09.005.
Fuller, D., Gauvin, L., Kestens, Y., 2013. Individual- and area-level disparities in access to the road network, subway system and a public bicycle share program on the island of Montreal, Canada. Ann. Behav. Med. 45, 95–100. https://doi.org/10.1007/s12160-012-9433-y.
Gao, J., Helbich, M., Dijst, M., Kamphuis, C.B.M., 2017. Socioeconomic and demographic differences in walking and cycling in the Netherlands: how do these translate into differences in health benefits? J. Transp. Health 6, 358–365. https://doi.org/10.1016/j.jth.2017.06.001.
Giles-Corti, B., 2002. Socioeconomic status differences in recreational physical activity levels and real and perceived access to a supportive physical environment. Prev. Med. 35, 601–611. https://doi.org/10.1006/pmed.2002.1115.
Goodman, A., Aldred, R., 2018. Inequalities in utility and leisure cycling in England, and variation by local cycling prevalence. Transp. Res. Part F: Traffic Psychol. Behav. 56, 381–391. https://doi.org/10.1016/j.trf.2018.05.001.
Goodman, A., Cheshire, J., 2014. Inequalities in the London bicycle sharing system revisited: impacts of extending the scheme to poorer areas but then doubling prices. J. Transp. Geogr. 41, 272–279. https://doi.org/10.1016/j.jtrangeo.2014.04.004.
Green, J., Steinbach, R., Edwards, P., Datta, J., 2010. Cycling in London: A Study of Social and Cultural Factors in Transport Mode Choice. (Technical Report). LSHTM, London.
Guzman, L.A., Bocarejo, J.P., 2017. Urban form and spatial urban equity in Bogota, Colombia. Transp. Res. Procedia 25, 4491–4506. https://doi.org/10.1016/j.trpro.2017.05.345.
Handy, S.L., Xing, Y., 2011. Factors correlated with bicycle commuting: a study in six small US cities. Int. J. Sustain. Transp. 5, 91–110. https://doi.org/10.1080/15568310903514789.
Harms, L., Bertolini, L., te Brömmelstroet, M., 2014. Spatial and social variations in cycling patterns in a mature cycling country exploring differences and trends. J. Transp. Health 1, 232–242. https://doi.org/10.1016/j.jth.2014.09.012.
Heesch, K.C., Giles-Corti, B., Turrell, G., 2015. Cycling for transport and recreation: associations with the socio-economic, natural and built environment. Health Place 36, 152–161. https://doi.org/10.1016/j.healthplace.2015.10.004.
Hoffmann, M.L., Lugo, A., 2014. Who is 'world class'? Transp. Just. Bicycle Policy 4, 17.
Hosford, K., Winters, M., 2018. Who are public bike share programs serving? An evaluation of the equity of spatial access to bike share service areas in Canadian cities. Transp. Res. Rec. 2672 (36), 42–50.
Hosford, K., Winters, M., Gauvin, L., Camden, A., Dubé, A.-S., Friedman, S.M., Fuller, D., 2019. Evaluating the impact of implementing public bicycle share programs on cycling: the international bikeshare impacts on cycling and collisions study (IBICCS). Int. J. Behav. Nutr. Phys. Act. 16, 107. https://doi.org/10.1186/s12966-019-0871-9.
Houde, M., Apparicio, P., Séguin, A.-M., 2018. A ride for whom: has cycling network expansion reduced inequities in accessibility in Montreal, Canada? J. Transp. Geogr. 68, 9–21. https://doi.org/10.1016/j.jtrangeo.2018.02.005.
Kavanagh, A.M., 2005. Urban area disadvantage and physical activity: a multilevel study in Melbourne, Australia. J. Epidemiol. Community Health 59, 934–940. https://doi.org/10.1136/jech.2005.035931.
Kent, M., Karner, A., 2019. Prioritizing low-stress and equitable bicycle networks using neighborhood-based accessibility measures. Int. J. Sustain. Transp. 13, 100–110. https://doi.org/10.1080/15568318.2018.1443177.
Lee, R.E., Adamus-Leach, H.J., Cheung, K.C., Soltero, E.G., Lopez, Y., Saavedra, F., Noor, M., Mama, S.K., 2012. Researching those who have the most to gain: focused physical activity promotion in lower socioeconomic populations. Curr. Cardiovasc. Risk Rep. 6, 355–361. https://doi.org/10.1007/s12170-012-0243-3.

Lee, R.J., Sener, I.N., Jones, S.N., 2017. Understanding the role of equity in active transportation planning in the United States. Transp. Rev. 37, 211–226. https://doi.org/10.1080/01441647.2016.1239660.
Libertun de Duren, N.R., 2018. Why there? Developers' rationale for building social housing in the urban periphery in Latin America. Cities 72, 411–420. https://doi.org/10.1016/j.cities.2017.10.006.
Lindström, M., Hanson, B.S., Östergren, P.-O., 2001. Socioeconomic differences in leisure-time physical activity: the role of social participation and social capital in shaping health related behaviour. Soc. Sci. Med. 52, 441–451. https://doi.org/10.1016/S0277-9536(00)00153-2.
Lovelace, R., Beecham, R., Heinen, E., Vidal Tortosa, E., Yang, Y., Slade, C., Roberts, A., 2020. Is the London cycle hire scheme becoming more inclusive? An evaluation of the shifting spatial distribution of uptake based on 70 million trips. Transp. Res. Part A: Policy Pract. 140, 1–15. https://doi.org/10.1016/j.tra.2020.07.017.
Lubitow, A., 2016. Mediating the 'white lanes of gentrification' in Humboldt Park. Bicycl. Justice Urban Transform., 249–259.
McNeil, N., 2011. Bikeability and the 20-min neighborhood: how infrastructure and destinations influence bicycle accessibility. Transp. Res. Rec. 2247, 53–63. https://doi.org/10.3141/2247-07.
Meng, S., Brown, A., 2021. Docked vs. dockless equity: comparing three micromobility service geographies. J. Transp. Geogr. 96, 103185. https://doi.org/10.1016/j.jtrangeo.2021.103185.
Merom, D., van der Ploeg, H.P., Corpuz, G., Bauman, A.E., 2010. Public health perspectives on household travel surveys. Am. J. Prev. Med. 39, 113–121. https://doi.org/10.1016/j.amepre.2010.04.007.
Mooney, S.J., Hosford, K., Howe, B., Yan, A., Winters, M., Bassok, A., Hirsch, J.A., 2019. Freedom from the station: spatial equity in access to dockless bike share. J. Transp. Geogr. 74, 91–96. https://doi.org/10.1016/j.jtrangeo.2018.11.009.
Mora, R., Truffello, R., Oyarzún, G., 2021. Equity and accessibility of cycling infrastructure: an analysis of Santiago de Chile. J. Transp. Geogr. 91, 102964. https://doi.org/10.1016/j.jtrangeo.2021.102964.
Oja, P., Titze, S., Bauman, A., de Geus, B., Krenn, P., Reger-Nash, B., Kohlberger, T., 2011. Health benefits of cycling: a systematic review: cycling and health. Scand. J. Med. Sci. Sports 21, 496–509. https://doi.org/10.1111/j.1600-0838.2011.01299.x.
Ortúzar, J.d.D., Iacobelli, A., Valeze, C., 2000. Estimating demand for a cycle-way network. Transp. Res. Part A: Policy Pract. 34, 353–373. https://doi.org/10.1016/S0965-8564(99)00040-3.
Parkin, J., Wardman, M., Page, M., 2008. Estimation of the determinants of bicycle mode share for the journey to work using census data. Transportation 35, 93–109. https://doi.org/10.1007/s11116-007-9137-5.
Pistoll, C., Goodman, A., 2014. The link between socioeconomic position, access to cycling infrastructure and cycling participation rates: an ecological study in Melbourne, Australia. J. Transp. Health 1, 251–259. https://doi.org/10.1016/j.jth.2014.09.011.
Plaut, P.O., 2005. Non-motorized commuting in the US. Transp. Res. Part D: Transp. Environ. 10, 347–356. https://doi.org/10.1016/j.trd.2005.04.002.
Pucher, J., Buehler, R., 2008. Cycling for everyone: lessons from Europe. Transp. Res. Rec.: J. Transp. Res. Board 2074, 58–65. https://doi.org/10.3141/2074-08.
Pucher, J., Buehler, R., Seinen, M., 2011. Bicycling renaissance in North America? An update and re-appraisal of cycling trends and policies. Transp. Res. Part A: Policy Pract. 45, 451–475. https://doi.org/10.1016/j.tra.2011.03.001.
Qian, X., Jaller, M., Niemeier, D., 2020. Enhancing equitable service level: which can address better, dockless or dock-based bikeshare systems? J. Transp. Geogr. 86, 102784. https://doi.org/10.1016/j.jtrangeo.2020.102784.

Rachele, J.N., Sugiyama, T., Turrell, G., Healy, A.M., Sallis, J.F., 2018. Automobile dependence: a contributing factor to poorer health among lower-income households. J. Transp. Health 8, 123–128. https://doi.org/10.1016/j.jth.2017.11.149.

Raser, E., Gaupp-Berghausen, M., Dons, E., Anaya-Boig, E., Avila-Palencia, I., Brand, C., Castro, A., Clark, A., Eriksson, U., Götschi, T., Int Panis, L., Kahlmeier, S., Laeremans, M., Mueller, N., Nieuwenhuijsen, M., Orjuela, J.P., Rojas-Rueda, D., Standaert, A., Stigell, E., Gerike, R., 2018. European cyclists' travel behavior: differences and similarities between seven European (PASTA) cities. J. Transp. Health 9, 244–252. https://doi.org/10.1016/j.jth.2018.02.006.

Smiley, K.T., Rushing, W., Scott, M., 2016. Behind a bicycling boom: governance, cultural change and place character in Memphis, Tennessee. Urban Stud. 53, 193–209. https://doi.org/10.1177/0042098014556590.

Stehlin, J., 2015. Cycles of investment: bicycle infrastructure, gentrification, and the restructuring of the San Francisco Bay area. Environ. Plan A 47, 121–137. https://doi.org/10.1068/a130098p.

Stehlin, J.G., 2019. Cyclescapes of the Unequal City: Bicycle Infrastructure and Uneven Development. University of Minnesota Press.

Stein, S., 2011. Bike lanes and gentrification. Prog. Plann., 34–37.

Steinbach, R., Green, J., Datta, J., Edwards, P., 2011. Cycling and the city: a case study of how gendered, ethnic and class identities can shape healthy transport choices. Soc. Sci. Med. 72, 1123–1130. https://doi.org/10.1016/j.socscimed.2011.01.033.

Teunissen, T., Sarmiento, O., Zuidgeest, M., Brussel, M., 2015. Mapping equality in access: the case of bogotá's sustainable transportation initiatives. Int. J. Sustain. Transp. 9, 457–467. https://doi.org/10.1080/15568318.2013.808388.

Tin Tin, S., Woodward, A., Thornley, S., Ameratunga, S., 2009. Cycling and walking to work in New Zealand, 1991-2006: regional and individual differences, and pointers to effective interventions. Int. J. Behav. Nutr. Phys. Act. 6, 64. https://doi.org/10.1186/1479-5868-6-64.

Ton, D., Duives, D.C., Cats, O., Hoogendoorn-Lanser, S., Hoogendoorn, S.P., 2018. Cycling or walking? Determinants of mode choice in the Netherlands. Transp. Res. Part A: Policy Pract. https://doi.org/10.1016/j.tra.2018.08.023.

Tucker, B., Manaugh, K., 2018. Bicycle equity in Brazil: access to safe cycling routes across neighborhoods in Rio de Janeiro and Curitiba. Int. J. Sustain. Transp. 12, 29–38. https://doi.org/10.1080/15568318.2017.1324585.

Vecchio, G., Tiznado-Aitken, I., Hurtubia, R., 2020. Transport and equity in Latin America: a critical review of socially oriented accessibility assessments. Transp. Rev. 40, 354–381. https://doi.org/10.1080/01441647.2020.1711828.

Vidal Tortosa, E., Lovelace, R., Heinen, E., Mann, R.P., 2021a. Infrastructure is not enough: interactions between the environment, socioeconomic disadvantage, and cycling participation in England. JTLU 14, 693–714. https://doi.org/10.5198/jtlu.2021.1781.

Vidal Tortosa, E., Lovelace, R., Heinen, E., Mann, R.P., 2021b. Cycling behaviour and socioeconomic disadvantage: an investigation based on the English National Travel Survey. Transp. Res. Part A: Policy Pract. 152, 173–185. https://doi.org/10.1016/j.tra.2021.08.004.

Wang, J., Lindsey, G., 2017. Equity of bikeway distribution in Minneapolis, Minnesota. Transp. Res. Rec.: J. Transp. Res. Board 2605, 18–31. https://doi.org/10.3141/2605-02.

Wang, Y., Chau, C.K., Ng, W.Y., Leung, T.M., 2016. A review on the effects of physical built environment attributes on enhancing walking and cycling activity levels within residential neighborhoods. Cities 50, 1–15. https://doi.org/10.1016/j.cities.2015.08.004.

Winters, M., Friesen, M.C., Koehoorn, M., Teschke, K., 2007. Utilitarian bicycling. Am. J. Prev. Med. 32, 52–58. https://doi.org/10.1016/j.amepre.2006.08.027.
Winters, M., Fischer, J., Nelson, T., Fuller, D., Whitehurst, D.G.T., 2018. Equity in spatial access to bicycling infrastructure in mid-sized Canadian cities. Transp. Res. Rec.: J. Transp. Res. Board 2672, 24–32. https://doi.org/10.1177/0361198118791630.
Witlox, F., Tindemans, H., 2004. Evaluating bicycle-car transport mode competitiveness in an urban environment. An Activity-Based Approach. World Trans. Policy Pract. 10, 11.

CHAPTER ELEVEN

Cycling, climate change and air pollution

Christian Brand[a,c,*], Henk-Jan Dekker[b], and Frauke Behrendt[b]
[a]University of Oxford, Oxford, United Kingdom
[b]TU Eindhoven, Eindhoven, The Netherlands
[c]UK Energy Research Centre, Oxford, United Kingdom
*Corresponding author: e-mail address: christian.brand@ouce.ox.ac.uk

Contents

Abstract

Cycling is considered a healthy and sustainable form of getting from A to B. The net effects of the various forms of cycling and e-biking on mobility-related air pollutant emissions are complex. This chapter synthesizes research on the potential of cycling and e-biking to reduce (and contribute) to air pollutant emissions from mode shift away from motorized transport. Life cycle analysis of greenhouse gas emissions from production, use and end-of-life of active and motorized vehicles is used to compare the most common urban transport modes and determine whether cycling and e-biking reduce

Advances in Transport Policy and Planning, Volume 10
ISSN 2543-0009
https://doi.org/10.1016/bs.atpp.2022.04.010

overall emissions or not. By doing so the Chapter provides a summary of research on cycling as a low carbon and clean mobility option in context of the climate emergency and the air quality crisis in cities.

Keywords: Transport emissions, Mode shift, Active mobility, E-bikes, Climate change mitigation, Urban transport, Rural transport, Life cycle analysis

1. Introduction

"A cycle is silent, emits no fumes, takes up little road space and when it collides with another cyclist or pedestrian, injuries are usually slight. Many Cambridge car owners use cycles for local journeys."

Cambridge traffic plan, 1950

Yes, things have changed since the 1950s when the Cambridge traffic census showed that cycle traffic was sometimes three times greater than motor traffic. Today, cycling has largely been marginalized in favor of the "motor car." But cycling is still cleaner, quieter and more space-efficient than cars—whether the bicycles are electric or not. Personal cars are responsible for a large part of transport emissions. In the UK, for example, carbon dioxide (CO_2)[a] emissions from car travel are responsible for 61% of the sector's emissions (Philips et al., 2022), and despite increasing sales of hybrid, and electric vehicles, average tailpipe emissions of new cars are still increasing in large part due to increased sales of larger and heavier cars such as sports utility vehicles (SUVs). There is also a growing consensus that the technological switch to electric cars may not solve this sufficiently or fast enough to meet our climate goals (Brand, 2021). Replacing car trips by more sustainable modes is therefore one of the most effective ways to reduce transport emissions.

To put this into context, transport today accounts for 21% of global carbon emissions (IEA, 2021) and 29% of European carbon emissions (ICCT, 2021). It is now the largest emitting sector in many developed countries. While Europe and North America dominate historic transport emissions, much of the projected growth in emissions is in Asia. Even if current and committed policies were to succeed, transport's carbon emissions would still grow almost 20% by 2050 (OECD/ITF, 2021). Highly ambitious policies could cut these emissions by 70% (OECD/ITF, 2021)—but not to zero.

[a] Carbon dioxide accounts for roughly 99% of the direct transport carbon dioxide equivalent (CO_2-eq) emissions, based on a 100-year global warming potential.

Modal shifts away from carbon-intensive to low-carbon modes of travel hold considerable potential to mitigate carbon emissions from transport (Cuenot et al., 2012). One of the more promising ways to reduce transport CO_2 emissions is to promote and invest in "active travel" (i.e., walking, cycling, e-biking) while "demoting" motorized modes that rely on fossil energy sources (Bearman and Singleton, 2014; de Nazelle et al., 2010; ECF, 2011; Frank et al., 2010; Goodman et al., 2012; Keall et al., 2018; Neves and Brand, 2019; Quarmby et al., 2019; Sælensminde, 2004; Scheepers et al., 2014; Woodcock et al., 2018). Out of all the various forms of active travel, cycling and e-biking have arguably the biggest potentials to reduce emissions, particularly in urban areas. While "conventional" cycling has been around for more than two centuries, e-bikes are rising quickly in popularity, including shared schemes, and these electrical vehicles have the potential to replace short-to medium-distance trips, also in sub-urban and rural settings.

To better understand the emission-reduction impacts of cycling, it is important to assess the key determinants of (and changes in) travel pollutant emissions and include a detailed, comparative analysis of the distribution and composition of emissions by transport mode (e.g., bike, car, van, public transport, e-bike) and journey purpose across a wide range of contexts (e.g., intra-urban, inter-urban, rural). With the increasing popularity of electrified forms of cycling that have zero emissions at point of use, it is also important to assess the main *sources* of emissions (e.g., from vehicle use, energy supply or vehicle manufacturing). We focus here on emissions of greenhouse gases and the key local air pollutants relevant to public health, i.e., particulate matter and nitrogen oxides. Other impacts of substituting car travel for cycling such as less noise pollution, better use of space in cities, (de)congestion, increased crash risks, and more active lifestyles are of course also important but are outside the scope of the Chapter.

This Chapter first compares impacts of the key urban transport modes on a per passenger-km basis using a life cycle analysis (LCA) approach. For cycling, this includes conventional bikes and e-bikes in both private and shared settings for moving people and their goods –freight transport and last-mile logistics are not covered here. It then synthesizes the evidence on mode substitution as a key determinant of cycling's environmental impact. Given a set of emission factors (which can be determined with a LCA analysis) we can compare the environmental impact of different modes. This in turn allows us to calculate what degree of mode shift needs to occur to result in a certain net reduction of emissions. For example, if e-biking predominantly replaces walking trips, we can assume that the environmental impact of this shift will be negative (i.e., a relative increase in emissions and impact). Ideally, cycling and e-biking replace trips by private cars running by fossil fuels.

2. Travel emissions: how do "cycling" and "cyclists" compare?

2.1 Determinants and distribution of emissions

Travel emissions are determined by transport mode choice and usage, which in turn are influenced by journey purpose (e.g., commuting, visiting friends and family, shopping), individual and household characteristics (e.g., location, socio-economic status, car ownership, type of car, bike access, perceptions related to the safety, convenience and social status associated with active travel), land use and built environment factors (which impact journey lengths and trip rates), accessibility to public transport, jobs and services, and meteorological conditions (Adams, 2010; Alvanides, 2014; Anable and Brand, 2019; Bearman and Singleton, 2014; Brand and Boardman, 2008; Brand and Preston, 2010; Cameron et al., 2003; Carlsson-Kanyama and Linden, 1999; Götschi et al., 2017; Ko et al., 2011; Nicolas and David, 2009; Stead, 1999; Timmermans et al., 2003).

Mobility-related pollutant emissions are highly variable and distributed highly unequally across a wide range of contexts (Brand and Boardman, 2008; Büchs and Schnepf, 2013; Ko et al., 2011; Preston et al., 2013; Susilo and Stead, 2009). In many cases the prevalence of cycling is low, implying that measurement and detection of statistically significant effects of cycling on mobility-related carbon emissions are a major challenge (Brand et al., 2014). Some people travel a lot, especially by motorized means, while others do not travel at all on a given day (Brand et al., 2013). A major European study found that the top 10% of survey participants were responsible for 59% of carbon emissions from daily travel, and that those with better car access, higher incomes and poor bus accessibility producing higher emissions overall (Brand et al., 2021a). This is important for targeting mitigation efforts at the highest emitters while not increasing emissions of the lowest. The latter might however be desirable from a mobility justice perspective in that traveling more might allow these groups to access otherwise unavailable job opportunities or other services. If active modes are not chosen for this, overall emissions might increase somewhat, which would need to be offset by further reductions among the highest emitters.

2.2 Life cycle emissions of private and shared bikes

Life cycle assessment (LCA) is a way to study the environmental impact of (in this case) transport modes from cradle to grave. A typical LCA of transport mode emissions take into account the emissions generated by making the vehicle, using it, fuelling/charging it and any end-of-life treatment. In the production phase the materials from which the vehicle is made are considered, as well as the energy expended during production. The use phase can be the most complex, involving not just the direct emissions but also—in the case of shared operations—indirect emissions from service operations caused by the collection, charging, and redistribution of shared e-bikes, often done by internal combustion engines vehicles.

While cycling and e-biking cannot be considered a "zero-carbon emissions" mode of transport due to the amount of carbon produced from vehicle manufacturing and energy supply, life cycle emissions from cycling can be more than 30 times lower for each trip than driving a fossil fuel car, and about ten times lower than driving an electric one (Brand et al., 2021a). Table 1 gives an overview found in the literature of average rates of carbon emissions (in grams of carbon dioxide equivalent, CO_2-eq, per passenger-km, or pkm) for the main modes of urban transport. The main reasons for variation in the values for "conventional bicycle" are due to different accounting methods: for example, some studies include an infrastructure component or emissions from changes to dietary intake, both of which can be larger than the vehicle manufacturing component (OECD/ITF, 2020). Emissions from public transport depend mainly on the mode (bus, light rail, or metro) and different occupancy rates in the study areas. Urban rail typically

Table 1 Average life cycle GHG emissions for key transport modes, private ownership and use, excluding infrastructure component.

Avg. life cycle GHG emissions (in grams of CO_2-eq per pkm)	Conventional bicycle	*E*-bike	Urban public transport	Car
Cherry (2007)	5	22	48	306
Blondel et al. (2011)	21	22	101	271
Weiss et al. (2015)	5	25	110	240
OECD/ITF (2020)	7	24	67	149
Brand et al. (2021a)	5	15	65	190
de Bortoli (2021) (data for Paris)	11	18	7 (metro), 125 (diesel bus)	202

has lower average emission rates than buses, with OECD/ITF (2020) providing "global averages" of 66 gCO_2-eq per pkm for metro/urban train and 91 gCO_2-eq per pkm for bus. Note these can be substantially lower in public transport systems that run on low carbon electricity, such as Norway, Denmark and France. In Paris, for instance, life cycle emissions can be as low as 7 gCO_2-eq per pkm for metro and 9 gCO_2-eq per pkm for suburban rail (de Bortoli, 2021). The variation in car emission rates is as expected, as they vary by the fuel mix and age of the car fleet, car size and weight, occupancy rates (which vary by trip purpose) and trip speeds (slower speeds in urban areas mean higher per-km emissions).

Fig. 1 provides a "central estimate" of average GHG emissions broken down into the main LCA components. LCA GHG emissions depend on the materials used in vehicle manufacturing, the propulsion technologies and their energy vectors, ridership characteristics, the frequency with which infrastructure (e.g., roads, railways, bike lanes) is used, as well as operational practices. Using central estimates with regards to vehicle lifetimes, electricity generation mix, and vehicle occupancy rates, the data in Fig. 1 suggest that

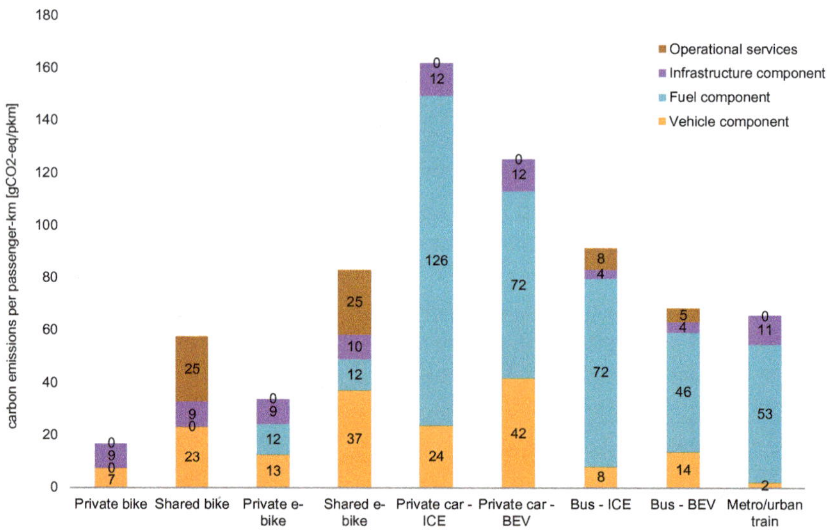

Fig. 1 Life cycle GHG emissions of urban transport modes by LCA component, in gCO_2-eq/pkm (central estimates). Notes: ICE = internal combustion engine vehicle; BEV = battery electric vehicle. *Adapted from OECD/ITF. 2020. Good to Go? Assessing the Environmental Performance of New Mobility, accessed at https://www.itf-oecd.org/good-go-assessing-environmental-performance-new-mobility. Paris: International Transport Forum, OECD Publishing. assessment tool, using central estimates with regards to vehicle lifetimes, electricity generation mix, and vehicle occupancy rates.*

private bikes and e-bikes that are regularly used have the lowest life-cycle GHG emissions per kilometer traveled. This is the result of low material requirements per vehicle, no external energy required for vehicle operation in the case of private bikes, energy efficient use of electricity for e-bikes and no energy needed for operational services. Crucially, the difference between the vehicle component for private and shared (e-)bikes is due to different vehicle lifetimes assumed in the comparative analysis. Interestingly, infrastructure-related GHG emissions are most relevant for individual vehicles requiring the use of significant amounts of lane km of roads, including parking (i.e., for private cars). We used a single, reputable source (OECD/ITF, 2020: see Annex A for methodological details and data sources) for comparing modes as the inherent uncertainties in LCA studies make a direct comparison across modes difficult. We discuss below how the emission performance for each LCA component can be improved.

2.3 Private or shared: which is lower carbon over the life cycle?

While the majority of bikeshare systems employ conventional bicycles, the number of e-bicycle sharing schemes (e-BSS) have been growing worldwide. Galatoulas et al. (2020) have provided an inventory showing that in 2018, 23% of the newly launched bike-sharing systems used (at least in parts) e-bikes; in 2019 that number was 32%. In the decade prior to 2018 the share of e-bike systems never exceeded 11%. Of all e-BSSs, 59% are European, 27% in the Americas, and 13% in Asia (outside these regions only Australia and Egypt have an e-BSS). However, many of the European systems are quite small in scale (mean fleet size of 166 vehicles), whereas systems introduced in North America or Asia are generally larger (mean fleet size 465). In terms of dockless vs. station based systems, it is hard to draw generalizations. For instance, many systems launched in North America in 2018 were dockless, but this dropped sharply in 2019, whereas in Europe, dockless systems seem to be on the rise. As of November 2019, the largest e-BSSs outside China were located in Madrid, Brussels, Amsterdam, and Milan.

However, life cycle assessments of these systems are rare. While a growing number of studies on shared e-scooters is appearing (see e.g., de Bortoli, 2021), bikeshare systems are rarely studied from this environmental perspective. OECD/ITF (2020) provided a range of estimates about the impact of both private and shared (e-)bikes. While privately-owned e-bikes have a slightly higher environmental impact than conventional bicycles, both have the lowest life-cycle energy requirements of all vehicles

(OECD/ITF, 2020). Elliot et al. (2018) estimated that e-bikes in New Zealand generated 20 gCO_2-eq/pkm. Similarly, OECD/ITF found that conventional bikes generated 7 g CO_2-eq/pkm and private e-bikes 24 gCO_2-eq/pkm (both excluding infrastructure component). But the literature is fairly clear that life cycle carbon emissions are higher for current shared systems: shared systems with conventional bicycles can emit 48 g CO_2-eq/pkm while a shared e-bike system produces 74 g CO_2-eq/pkm (OECD/ITF, 2020). This is not to say that shared systems can have lower emissions rates. Indeed, a well balanced, well used system can have lower per-pkm emissions than an underused one that requires lots of relocation of bikes. A range of actions can improve the environmental performance of shared services, including:

- Use low carbon materials in vehicle manufacturing (steel is better than aluminium);
- Design solutions that extend vehicle life, and;
- Improvements in operations due to lower servicing requirements per kilometer of service.

2.3.1 Vehicle production and end-of life treatment

Emissions from bike manufacture are a major part of vehicle life cycle emissions (de Bortoli, 2021). OECD/ITF (2020) put the share of production in total emissions at around 50% for private and shared e-bikes, with similar figures for *shared* conventional bikes. Central estimates (and % shares) reported in OECD/ITF (2020) were:

- 7 gCO_2-eq/pkm out of a total of 7 g for private bikes (100%);
- 13 gCO_2-eq/pkm out of a total of 24 g for private e-bikes (51%);
- 23 gCO_2-eq/pkm out of a total of 48 g for shared bikes (49%), and;
- 37 gCO_2-eq/pkm out of a total of 74 g for shared e-bikes (50%).

Elliot et al. (2018) found a higher share of production emissions at over 87% of total GHG emissions of e-bikes in New Zealand, which is largely due to the approximately 80% share of renewable electricity generation in New Zealand—much higher than the global average figure underpinning the OECD/ITF data. Note none of the above figures include the infrastructure component, which has been estimated at around 9–10 gCO_2-eq/pkm for both conventional and e-bikes (OECD/ITF, 2020).

In terms of end-of-life treatment, emissions have been shown to be relatively small. Elliot et al. (2018), for example, found that end-of-life contributes about 4% to total GHG emissions.

The economic lifetime and annual distance traveled of a vehicle are important considerations here: the longer a vehicle can be used the lower the per-pkm emissions associated with production and end of life treatment. For private bikes and e-bikes, OECD/ITF (2020) assumed mean lifetimes of 5.6 years (taking into account a 30% reduction in the typical lifetime of 8 years due to theft, accidents, and vandalism) and an annual distance traveled of 2400 km per vehicle. For shared bikes and e-bikes OECD/ITF assumed a vehicle lifetime of just 2.0 years (taking into account a 60% reduction in lifetime due to tampering, vandalism, loss and damage, etc.) with an annual distance traveled of 2900 km per vehicle.

2.3.2 Transportation and delivery to point of purchase

Vehicle transportation and delivery is generally a small component of total emissions. In the case of New Zealand, relatively close to production in China, Elliot et al. (2018) found it contributed only 1% to the total impact. OECD/ITF (2020) likewise found that the transport of shared e-bikes contributed around 3 gCO_2-eq/pkm out of 74 gCO_2-eq/pkm (4% of total emissions), with similar percentages for other types of bicycles. Vehicle transportation is therefore less actionable than other aspects of the vehicle life cycle (other than perhaps creating local production facilities in the US and Europe).

2.3.3 Emissions from energy/fuel supply to the vehicle

Neither cycling nor using e-bikes incurs direct emissions at point of use. But using e-bikes implies there are emissions associated with supplying the energy used in charging. The associated GHG and local air pollution emissions depend heavily on the electricity generation mix, with OECD/ITF (2020) providing a central estimate of 12 gCO_2-eq/pkm (assuming a global average generation mix that includes large shares of fossil fuel generation). Of course, very low carbon electricity as produced today in Norway, France or Costa Rica (to name but a few leaders here), or called for by future scenarios transitioning electricity production away from fossil to renewable sources, would reduce this to near zero. However, higher carbon electricity as in Poland or India would roughly double this value. Elliot et al. (2018) showed how New Zealand's relatively green energy production (80% renewables) can minimize charging impact. As a result, the use phase of e-bikes in the country contributes less than 10% to total impact, whereas for conventional fossil fuelled cars this is over 90%.

While shared e-bike systems are on the rise, they are very new phenomena and charging practices are not clear in the literature. To avoid emissions associated with collection for recharging, docked bikeshare systems that double as charging stations are a promising solution. The bike-share operator PBSC Urban Solutions has taken a stance against swappable batteries and prefers to use docks that start charging as soon as a user puts the bike into the dock (PBSC Urban Solutions, 2019). This system requires 4h for a full charge, but 30min of charging is enough for 12km of riding. Dockless bikeshare systems need other solutions and, like free-floating e-scooters, typically require operators to manually swap batteries, which can be highly polluting if conventional fossil fuel vehicles are used for this (OECD/ITF, 2020). Apart from emissions associated with collection for recharging, there might still be emissions from collection in order to redistribute the bikes to match the demand.

2.3.4 Emissions from energy/fuel supply to the user

Does cycling and e-biking lead to increased dietary intake and associated net carbon emissions? The evidence is inconclusive on whether day-to-day active travel (as opposed to performance/sport activity) significantly increases overall dietary intake when compared to motorized travel. When people burn more calories through exercise they don't typically consume as many extra calories in their diet (Elder and Roberts, 2007). Related to this, the effects of an increase in active travel on health outcomes such as BMI (essentially body weight) are inconclusive. One longitudinal study in the Netherlands reported no significant effects (Kroesen and De Vos, 2020) while another longitudinal study in European cities showed a significant, if small, effect of a decrease in BMI for those who traveled actively (Dons et al., 2018). A study using consumption data obtained from a consumer survey found that a 10% rise in active transport share was associated with a 1% *drop* in food-related emissions, which may be related to overall health awareness or concerns as well as impacts on well-being and mental health (Ivanova et al., 2018). Another recent study by Mizdrak et al. (2020) made the *explicit assumption* that increased energy expenditure is directly compensated with increased energy intake, while acknowledging that this is an unproven assumption. More speculative, a surplus intake of calories is common in Western societies, resulting in weight gain over the years. This would at least speak for there not being an immediate need to compensate for extra calorie expenditure—people who do daily moderate physical activity from cycling just get a little fitter and loose weight.

2.3.5 Operational impact of shared systems: rebalancing, collection and redistribution

Private (e-)bikes have no operational impact since they are used, stored and charged individually by private individuals. However, shared (e-)bike systems do have operational costs since they require rebalancing (and recharging in the case of e-bikes). Rebalancing is especially problematic in hilly cities where people tend to leave bicycles downhill, forcing daily redistribution by van—although this applies less so for e-bikes. Rebalancing is a major source of emissions associated with shared mobility systems. OECD/ITF (2020) estimates the number for operational services of bike-share systems at 25 gCO_2-eq/pkm. This is 51% of total emissions associated with shared bikes, and 34% for shared e-bikes. Service operation can therefore be a significant contributor to environmental impacts of bicycle-share systems. Changes in operational practices, in particular the minimisation of the ratio of servicing vehicle km to (e-)bike km (achievable with increases in the average number of e-bikes per service vehicle trip or the reduction of service trip distances, or both) can lead to net reductions in GHG emissions (OECD/ITF, 2020).

There are other strategies to encourage users to help with the rebalancing of bikes in shared bicycle systems. Zürich operator Bond (previously smide), for instance, indicates "bonus zones" where users receive free user minutes if they park their bikes there; this incentivises trips into under supplied areas. The same applies to parking the bikes at a charging station (Guidon et al., 2019). In the Polish Tricity area (Gdánsk, Gdynia, Sopot), a hybrid system was applied where users were allowed to park bikes outside public transit stops for an extra fee but received a bonus if they parked them at a docking station (Bieliński and Ważna, 2020).

2.4 Summary: cycling and e-biking are the lowest carbon emitters on a life cycle basis

There is a growing body of evidence that both e-bikes and conventional bicycles (when privately owned) have significantly lower life-cycle GHG emissions per passenger-km than most road-based urban transport vehicles; they are also comparable with efficient rail-based systems such as metro, light rail and urban rail that run on low carbon electricity such as in Paris (de Bortoli, 2021). Yet the verdict on the exact magnitude of how much better e-bikes are is still out, as this will depend on future optimization of technologies, system management, and the share of low carbon electricity in recharging. Given their typically higher average trip distance, and their ability to carry loads, e-bikes and e-cargo bikes have significant potential to replace more and/or different trips than conventional bikes, also in intra-urban and rural areas. Perhaps surprisingly, life cycle GHG emissions can be higher for current generation of shared systems, which can be comparable to efficient, diesel-based urban bus services. However, the potential for improvements is significant here.

3. Mode shift: what are potential and observed emission reductions from shifting to cycling?

3.1 Which trips and trip purposes are amenable to mode shift?

For most journey purposes cycling covers short to medium length trips. Most studies focus on these "short" (up to 5 km) to "medium" (up to 20 km) length trips, as they are amenable to at least a partial modal shift towards active travel (Beckx et al., 2013; Carse et al., 2013; de Nazelle et al., 2010; Goodman et al., 2014; Keall et al., 2018; Neves and Brand, 2019; Vagane, 2007). Travel diary data from thousands of survey participants across seven European cities reported *mean* trip lengths of 1.1 km for walking, 4.8 km for cycling and 9.4 km for e-biking (Castro et al., 2019), with relatively wide distributions that suggest that some people traveled a lot further than the mean values suggest. Typically, the majority of trips in this range is made by car or bus (Beckx et al., 2013; U.S. Department of Transportation, 2017; JRC, 2013; Keall et al., 2018; Neves and Brand, 2019).

E-bikes in particular have significant substitution potential, some call them a "game changer," as e-bikers have been found to take longer trips by e-bike and bicycle, compared to cyclists. E-bikes work better in hilly areas, allow for more luggage to be carried, and generally increase travel speed. As a result e-bikes have a larger potential for mode substitution away from cars (Castro et al., 2019; Fyhri and Beate Sundfør, 2020; Kroesen, 2017; Mason et al., 2015; McQueen et al., 2020).

So, what is the potential for reductions in carbon emissions due to mode substitution? In the UK, for instance, about 3 out of 5 car trips are under 8 km (5 miles), producing 21% of car CO_2 emissions (BEIS, 2019; DfT, 2018)—largely for commuting, shopping and personal business purposes. "Medium" length trips of between 8 km and 16 km produce a further 18% of car CO_2, with longer trips of between 16 km and 25 km adding a further 8% of car CO_2. If we assume that a trip duration of 1 h is a reasonable "threshold" (i.e., maximum) for regular trips by e-bikes, the corresponding max. Distance is about 25 km. So overall, trips up to 25 km in length could be substituted by cycling or e-biking. These represent about 40–50% of car CO_2, or about 30–40% of passenger transport CO_2 emissions. In contrast, the 40–50% of mileage and carbon emissions from all person transport that come from long distance travel (i.e., over 100 km) are "out of reach" for mode substitution to cycling (van Goeverden et al., 2016).

3.2 Potential effects: "what if" scenario and potential impacts studies

Much of the work on climate change emissions impacts of cycling has been based on analyses of the *potential* for emissions mitigation (Yang et al., 2018) or the generation of "what if" scenarios that explore the likely impacts of hypothetical increases in cycling (Goodman et al., 2019; Lovelace et al., 2011; Tainio et al., 2017; Woodcock et al., 2018). The potential effects depend largely on the study contexts, the ambitions of the underlying "what-if" assumptions, and geographic scales.

3.2.1 Global scale

Mason et al. (2015) developed a "high shift cycling scenario" and found that a 11% combined cycling/e-bike share of urban passenger travel distance worldwide by 2030 would cut CO_2 emissions from urban transport by about 7%, rising to a 14% combined cycling/e-bike share and a near 11% reduction by 2050. E-bikes played a critical role in the scenario. The study highlighted a range of issues that must be addressed for e-bikes to succeed as a mass transportation mode in many countries, including safety and (upfront) cost. Governments should encourage and subsidize low-powered, speed-limited e-bike usage while placing direct restrictions on high-polluting gasoline cars and motorbikes (Mason et al., 2015).

3.2.2 European scale

The European Cyclists' Federation (ECF) estimated that the carbon emissions benefits of an annual distance cycled of 146 billion kilometers for the EU28 (Steenberghen et al., 2017) amounts to about 16 million tons of CO_2 avoided each year (ECF, 2018). Using more conservative assumptions about mode substitution, trip generation and default emissions rates for motorized transport contained in the WHO's Health Economic Assessment Tool for walking and cycling (Götschi et al., 2020), this level of cycling amounts to about 12 million tons of CO_2 emissions avoided each year (source: own calculation using the online tool). To put these figures into context, total CO_2 emissions from cars in the EU were about 520 million tons in 2015 (T&E, 2018). Therefore, existing cycling activity makes a modest contribution to climate change mitigation in Europe.

3.2.3 National scale

A study in the UK (Stott, 2020) estimated that if cycling's popularity returned to 1940s levels (when the average Brit cycled six times further per year than today) and these trips replaced car journeys, that would create a net saving of 7.7 million tons of CO_2 per year in the UK alone. To put these figures into context, total carbon emissions from cars and taxis in the UK were 68 million tons in 2019 (DfT, 2021). Hence, the potential net savings from cycling at 1940s levels amount to about 11% of annual GHG emissions from cars.

It has also been estimated that e-bikes, if used to replace car travel, have the "physical capability" (simulated as how far people are capable of traveling, based on physical ability, travel patterns and infrastructure provision at fine spatial scale) to cut car CO_2 emissions in England by up to 50% (about 30 million tons of CO_2 per year) (Philips et al., 2022). The greatest opportunities were found to be in rural and sub-urban settings: city dwellers already have many low-carbon travel options, so the greatest impact would be on encouraging e-bike use outside urban areas (Philips et al., 2022). In Denmark, Germany, Switzerland and the Netherlands, they already know this (Hansen and Nielsen, 2014).

In Sweden, Winslott Hiselius and Svensson (2017) found that a 14–20% reduction of transport-related emissions can be achieved, or 272–394 kgCO_2 saved per e-bike per year. Fyhri et al. (2017) studied a case in Oslo, Norway, and found a reduction of 87–144 kg of CO_2 per year. Bucher et al. (2019) argue that a wide uptake of e-bikes for commuting in Switzerland could reduce emissions from diesel and gasoline by 10–20%.

All of the above studies stress that these potential shifts will require a mixture of push and pull measures: segregated cycling infrastructure can help, as can measures raising the cost or convenience of driving.

3.2.4 Regional and city scale

McQueen et al. (2020) found that in Portland, Oregon, a 15% e-bike mode share (by distance traveled) would reduce car trip mode share from 85% to 75%, leading to a 12% reduction in CO_2 emissions and averaging 225 kgCO_2 saved per e-bike per year.

3.2.5 Individual scale

Brand et al. (2021a) estimated that an average person in European cities who "shifted travel modes" from car to bike decreased life cycle CO_2 emissions by 3.2 kgCO_2/day—equivalent to the emissions from driving a car for 10 km, eating a serving of lamb or chocolate, or sending 800 emails. Scaling this up to twice a week, 50 weeks a year gives an estimate of 320 kgCO_2/year, or about a quarter of the average per capita car emissions in Europe of about 1 ton of CO_2/year (T&E, 2018).

Many studies to date have focused on commuting. Life cycle CO_2 emissions from social, shopping, personal business and recreational journeys have been shown to be more strongly associated to car use, and that shopping and personal business trips were found to be significantly shorter, therefore increasing the potential for mode shift to cycling (Brand et al., 2014, 2021a,b).

3.3 Observed effects: cross-sectional and longitudinal studies

Empirical evidence of observed mode shifts is rarer, methodologically challenging and often limited to smaller scale studies focusing on a single city or urban areas. For instance, a longitudinal panel study of 50 participants in the Cardiff, Wales area showed that, taking into account individual travel patterns and constraints, cycling can realistically substitute for between 41% and 69% of "short" car trips up to 5 km, saving between 5% and 10% of CO_2 emissions from car travel. This was on top of 5% of "avoided" emissions from cars due to existing walking and cycling.

In a recent study of daily travel behavior (i.e., all trips recorded on a given weekday) of more than 3500 participants across seven European cities, "cyclists" had 84% lower life cycle CO_2 emissions from all daily travel than "non-cyclists" (Brand et al., 2021a). The study also found that mobility-related life cycle CO_2 emissions were 14% *lower* for those participants who cycled one trip per day more, and 62% *lower* for those who used a car or van for one trip a day less (while keeping everything else constant).

A separate analysis using longitudinal panel data of nearly 2000 urban dwellers found that increases in cycling significantly lowered carbon footprints, even in urban European contexts with a high incidence of cycling (Brand et al., 2021b). The study found that an increase in cycling at follow-up *independently* lowered mobility-related lifecycle CO_2 emissions, thus suggesting that active travel substituted for motorized travel and did not constitute additional, induced travel. It estimated that those who switch one trip per day from car driving to cycling—and do this regularly for about 200 days a year—reduce their carbon footprint by about 0.5 t over a year, representing a substantial share of average per capita CO_2 emissions and equivalent of a one-way flight from London to New York. If just one in five urban residents permanently changed their travel behavior in this way, the study estimated that it would cut emissions from all car travel in Europe by about 8% (Brand et al., 2021b).

Bigazzi and Wong (2020) conducted a meta-analysis of 24 studies on e-bike mode substitution. They concluded that generalizations are hard to make since local substitution patterns vary significantly. Overall, however, the median mode substitution that could be gleaned from this literature is that 33% of e-bike trips replace public transit, 27% conventional bicycle, 24% cars and 10% walking (see also Fig. 2). Kroesen (2017) and Sun et al. (2020) found that in the high-cycling context of the Netherlands, many e-bike trips replaced trips by conventional bike rather than car trips. However, Ling et al. (2015) point out that these might for instance be senior citizens who were no longer comfortable cycling and would have switched to a car had they not chosen e-bikes. We therefore have to consider that one

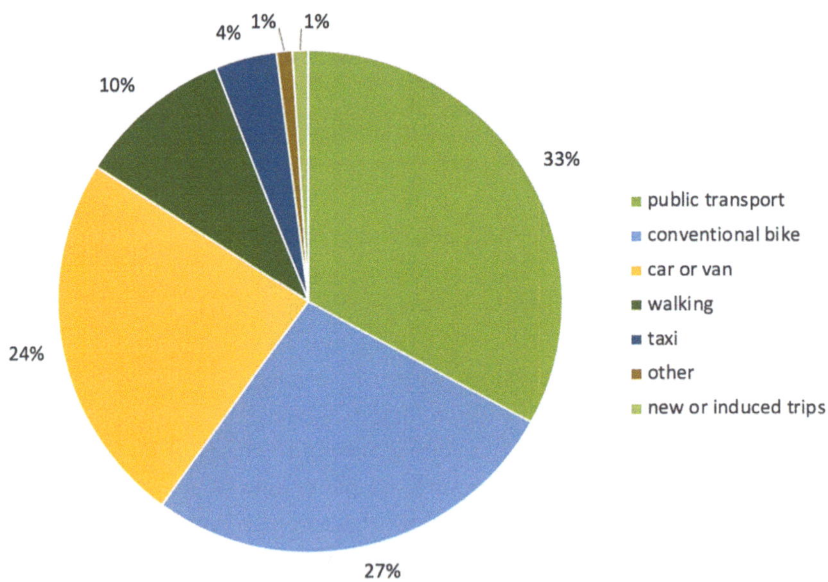

Fig. 2 Median mode substitution to e-biking based on meta-analysis of 24 studies. *Bigazzi, A., Wong, K. 2020. Electric bicycle mode substitution for driving, public transit, conventional cycling, and walking. Transp. Res. D Transp. Environ., 85, 102412.*

potential positive impact from the uptake of e-bikes is keeping existing cyclists on the bike longer. Senior citizens who might shift to more climate-impacting motorized modes can continue cycling longer when they employ e-bikes (Jones et al., 2016; Leger et al., 2019). It might also convince more women to take up cycling (Wild et al., 2021).

There are a few case studies from Sweden, which are worthwhile to consider since they are European but do not have the relatively high cycling levels of the Netherlands and Denmark. Winslott Hiselius and Svensson (2017) show that in Sweden e-bikes predominantly replace car trips. As expected, a larger share of conventional bicycle and public transit trips were replaced in urban areas than in rural contexts, but in both rural and urban contexts the net environmental impact of e-bike uptake is a reduction of CO_2 emissions.

One randomized controlled trial of 98 Swedish drivers investigated the effect of using e-bikes on modal choice, number of trips, distance traveled, and perceptions of e-bikes as a substitute for the car (Söderberg f.k.a. Andersson et al., 2021). The study found that those people who were given an e-bike increased cycling by 1 trip and 6.5 km per day and person, which led to a 25% increase in total cycling, with the increase due to a reduction in car use by 1 trip and 14 km per person and day; a decrease in car mileage of 37%. This overall reduction in car travel is higher than in studies conducted by Kroesen (2017) in the Netherlands (28%) or Cairns et al. (2017) in Brighton (20%). This can partly be explained by the fact that car levels in these cases were already lower to begin with than in the case in Skövde, Sweden. Interestingly, study participants reported that e-bikes reduce barriers linked to time, distance, and physical exertion, especially in hilly areas. The study further claimed that e-bike use was related to hedonic, rational, and altruistic gains by individuals. These factors can explain why e-bikes may have a larger appeal to car drivers than conventional cyclists.

3.4 What about mode shift from bike sharing systems?

The potential for BSS to reduce emissions is more complicated than for private ownership of e-bikes. The existing literature has a strong focus on the dominant conventional bike sharing systems and has yet to grapple with more recently introduced e-BSS. In car-dominant cities in the US or Australia, research suggests a reduction of car kilometers traveled as the result of the introduction of these systems. However, in a European context, cities tend to have higher levels of public transit and active transport. As Fishman et al. (2014) illustrated for London, car kilometers actually rose as a result of the introduction of bicycle share systems as few car trips were substituted while many new kilometers were added by the trucks driving around to rebalance bicycles. Luo et al. (2019) studied dockless vs. docked BSS in the US and concluded that dock-less BSS are problematic in this regard, as they may require at least 34% of car trips to be replaced by shared bike trips for a net positive impact, which is higher than most systems currently achieve. In contrast, docked systems may have more potential to decrease GHG emissions because they require fewer car trips to be substituted to have positive net emission effects (Luo et al., 2019).

The mode substitution effects of e-BSS have only recently been investigated. Specific mode substitution data for an e-bike sharing system exists for the Tricity area in Poland. Bieliński and Ważna (2020) found that shared e-bikes did not, in the majority of cases, substitute car trips, but rather acted as replacements for public transit trips or as first mile/last mile trips to public transit stops (replacing walking). Because the area is somewhat hilly, the municipal government chose e-bikes rather than conventional bicycles in the hopes of substituting car trips or encouraging e-bike use as feeder transport for public transit—successfully, as 39% of respondents to the questionnaire in this study used it in this way. All the same, as in other studies on bike-share systems or e-bikes, the e-Bike Sharing System was far more likely to replace public transit trips than car trips.

3.5 Local air pollution effects

So far we have largely focussed on the climate change mitigation effects of using conventional bikes or e-bikes and any mode shift from motorized mobility. Human health damages from local air pollution caused by road traffic are significant, in particular in urban areas where most people live and/or work (House of Commons, 2018). Urban transport is also one of the reasons why many urban areas are in breach of air pollution regulatory limits. Road transport is often the principal source of pollution, though domestic and background emissions also contribute to the problem (Hitchcock et al., 2014). Current regulatory breaches in many countries relate to nitrogen dioxide (NO_2), generated from emissions of nitrogen oxides (NO_X), and particulate matter, the latter both in its coarser PM_{10} form (particles with an average diameter of 10 μm or less) and the fine

$PM_{2.5}$ form (2.5 μm or less). NO_X is mainly a by-product of fuel combustion, while PM results from fuel combustion as well as road, brake and tyre wear (Grigoratos and Martini, 2014, 2015).

As with GHG emissions, neither conventional bikes nor e-bikes produce any tailpipe emissions of NO_X and PM. However, they produce very small amounts of PM from road, brake and tyre wear. Similar to life cycle emissons of the global air pollutant CO_2, their use is also responsible for air pollutant emissions from electricity generation, as well as vehicle manufacturing, maintenance and disposal. These occur generally at some distance from highly populated areas, hence health impacts are somewhat reduced by dispersion and dilution over distance and time (as compared to carbon emissions, which contribute to climate change independent from where they occur).

The literature on local air pollution effects is sparse when compared to climate emissions effects. Much of the evidence suggests that when compared to cars and vans, non-tailpipe air pollutant emissions for e-biking are several times lower per kilometer than for motorcycles and cars, have comparable emission rates to buses and higher emission rates than bicycles (Cherry et al., 2009). This is mainly because in-use emission rates are proportional to the vehicle weights—up to the power of four in case of road abrasion emissons. Comparing emissions of the main air pollutants and environmental health impacts (primary $PM_{2.5}$) from the use of conventional vehicles (CVs) and electric vehicles (EVs) in 34 major cities in China, Ji et al. (2012) found that e-bikes yield lower environmental health impacts per passenger-km than the three CVs investigated: gasoline cars (2 ×), diesel cars (10 ×), and diesel buses (5 ×).

In terms of health impacts of air pollution from mode shift to cycling, it is important to compare to the emissions rates of the substituted modes (i.e., car or bus). In terms of $PM_{2.5}$ and NO_X emissions, Brand and Hunt (2018) showed substantial differences between petrol, diesel and electric vehicles, particularly for NO_X where conventional diesel cars emit nearly six times more per km than conventional petrol cars. Battery electric vehicles (BEV) do not emit any NO_X when in use. $PM_{2.5}$ (and PM_{10}, not shown) emissions are more equally distributed, although there are clear differences as well, with non-diesel cars and vans emitting two thirds of the fleet average, and less than half of diesel cars and vans. BEV have zero exhaust emissions and contribute the lowest PM emissions of these vehicle types. As mentioned above, they do contribute a small but important share of non-exhaust emissions of particulate matter due to tyre, brake and road surface wear

(Grigoratos and Martini, 2014; Loeb, 2017; Ntziachristos and Boulter, 2016; Timmers and Achten, 2016; Williams et al., 2018).[b] BEV are estimated to emit 5–19% less PM_{10} from non-exhaust sources per km than internal combustion engine vehicles (ICEVs) across vehicle classes (OECD, 2020). However, BEV do not necessarily emit less $PM_{2.5}$ than ICEVs. Although lightweight BEVs emit an estimated 11–13% less $PM_{2.5}$ than ICEV equivalents, heavier weight BEVs emit an estimated 3–8% more $PM_{2.5}$ than ICEVs (OECD, 2020). In the absence of targeted policies to reduce non-exhaust emissions, consumer preferences for greater autonomy and larger vehicle size could therefore drive an increase in $PM_{2.5}$ emissions in future years with the uptake of heavier BEVs. This also means that in order to reduce air pollution policy should favor a shift away from BEVs to cycling.

4. Implications for policy and planning

4.1 Realizing the significant potential for mode shift

The evidence presented above shows that private bikes and e-bikes that are regularly used have the lowest life-cycle GHG emissions per pkm. It also shows that cycling and e-biking substitutes, at least in parts, for motorized travel, and that increases in cycling are not just additional, induced travel or due to route substitution (which can be the case for new infrastructure developments where new routes show significant uptake of cycling). This means that, even if not all car trips could be substituted by cycling and other forms of active travel, the potential for decreasing emissions is considerable and, as shown above, range between 5% (real world observation, cycling, conservative) and 50% (capability-based e-bike scenario).

Policy interventions that target mode shift and behavior change have been shown to achieve emissions reductions closer to the bottom than the top of that range (Grischkat et al., 2014; Semenescu et al., 2020), so policy ambition needs to rise sharply and involve a raft of bold "push" and "pull" measures that transform the mobility system and wean us off

[b] Non-exhaust emissions from road vehicles are in general terms enhanced by increased vehicle weight. Timmers and Achten (2016), for instance, acknowledge the benefits of regenerative brakes on electric vehicles and made a conservative estimate of zero brake-wear emissions for electric vehicles. Hence, their claim that electric vehicle particulate matter emissions are comparable to those of conventional vehicles was based upon the greater tyre and road surface wear, and resuspension associated with a greater vehicle weight.

motorized mobility and "car dependency" (OECD/ITF, 2021). Clearly, given the shorter distances covered by cyclists, land use and urban planning are critical—with car restraint and limiting or pricing car parking being important in addition to making cycling and other active travel options the better, more reliable and more convenient options for short (and medium) length journeys. Urban density and accessibility to jobs and services by active modes are important. This is exemplified by the growing number of city and local authorities that pursue urban planning around the concepts of the 15-min city (Moreno et al., 2021) or the 20-min neighborhood (Nieuwenhuijsen and Khreis, 2016; Tranter and Tolley, 2020).

4.2 Minimize the impacts of shared systems and make it easier to own and use a private vehicle

Private cycling and e-biking perform better in terms of life cycle emissions than shared vehicles, which is largely due to the much lower economic lifetime of vehicles in shared systems—one study showed the lifetime mileage of shared bikes to be 2.4 times lower than for private bikes (OECD/ITF, 2020). Incidentally this is also the case for shared and private e-scooters. Yet, the use of shared vehicles should be encouraged where space is at a premium, resources are limited and private ownership may be beyond the means of potential users, particularly in areas of "transport poverty" (Pabayo et al., 2012). Policymakers should therefore consider measures that minimize the impacts of shared systems by, for instance, decreasing the impact of servicing and operations (e.g., redistribution with zero emission vehicles) and increasing the longevity of the vehicle (and battery).

While subsidies for purchasing e-bikes are already in place in some EU countries and cities, this could be extended and/or marketed more, and could be more balanced in relation to measures that encourage uptake of electric cars. Apart from safe and convenient infrastructure, and safe traffic conditions, policy measures specific to e-bikes are:

1. secure storage facilities;
2. covered parking facilities as well as bike path winter maintenance;
3. including space for e-bike parking in building regulations;
4. converting existing car parking into bicycle parking facilities, and;
5. charging of e-bikes should be made as convenient as possible. This is particularly important for people's home and work locations, but also for all other trip destinations such as education, shopping or leisure.

4.3 Expand the scope to rural and sub-urban settings

People living in urban areas tend to have access to a range of low-carbon travel options and infrastructure. There is a risk that increased levels of cycling may decrease public transport ridership and walking more than car use. The above studies have shown, however, that cycling and e-biking in cities does indeed shift modes away from cars and reduce daily carbon emissions. Yet, a potentially greater impact would be on encouraging e-bike use outside urban areas. E-bikes offer an opportunity to substitute for fossil-fuel motorized mobility on "longer" journeys (defined here as in the 8–25 km range, based on mean speeds of 25 km/h and up to 1 h travel time) but this may need a range of policy and planning "carrots" (in particular, safe and high-quality infrastructure and financial support to reduce the up-front costs) and "sticks" (restraint/no access for motorized mobility, reduced traffic speed via road design, speed limits/enforcement) to mirror the success of countries such as the Netherlands, Switzerland and Germany, which have had some success in increasing rural e-biking, largely due to developing decent rural and intercity route systems.

5. Summary conclusion

Cycling and e-biking have been shown to have significant if limited carbon reduction benefits for short to medium length trips across a range of urban settings. The effects are more pronounced when cycling provision is coupled with car restraint policies. What is less clear (in terms of empirical evidence) is the role it can play in reducing carbon emissions from inter-urban and rural travel, and how soon the effects materialize. The relatively high emissions from the operation (rebalancing, recharging logistics) of current shared systems suggests we need to develop, implement and evaluate more balanced (e-)bike sharing systems and assess how they perform in environmental terms. Achieving high levels of mode shift away from cars is hugely contextual, so we need more robust evidence on the "why," "how" and "in what circumstances" mode shift has been achieved in real world settings. What is also less clear is the potential of multimodal substitution; for instance, what are the conditions and policies needed to shift a 50 km car trip to work to a multimodal trip involving a 10 km e-bike ride, a 35 km train journey and a 5 km shared ebike trip? There are also a number of mobility modes "between car and bike" that might be interesting to study—L-category or micro-mobility modes that are still marginal today but could play a role in meeting mobility needs of certain segments of the population (Héran and Bigo, 2020). An improved knowledge of the effects of active travel will provide a more robust evidence base to underpin climate change mitigation strategies and pathways at the local, national (CCC, 2020) and international (IEA, 2020) levels.

Nearly half of the fall in daily carbon emissions during global lockdowns in 2020 came from reductions in transport emissions (Le Quéré et al., 2020). The pandemic forced countries around the world to adapt to reduce the spread of the virus. Cycling and walking have been the "big winners" in many countries, including the US and Europe. This is despite cycle commuters being very likely to work from home. Cycling and e-biking has offered an alternative to public transport and driving (shared, taxi, etc.) that keeps social distancing intact. It has helped people to stay safe during the pandemic and it could help reduce emissions as confinement is eased, particularly as the high prices of used and new electric vehicles are likely to put many potential buyers off for now. Electric cars have a range of mobility justice issues (Henderson, 2020) and cannot reduce GHG emissions fast enough on their own (IEA, 2021, Brand et al., 2020). Even if all *new* cars were electric from now on, it would still take 15–20 years to replace the world's fossil fuel car fleet (Keith et al., 2019).

So, the race is on. Cycling and e-biking can contribute to tackling the climate emergency and urban air quality crisis *earlier* than electric cars while also providing affordable, more equitable, reliable, clean, healthy and congestion-busting transportation.

References

Adams, J., 2010. Prevalence and socio-demographic correlates of "active transport" in the UK: analysis of the UK time use survey 2005. Prev. Med. 50, 199–203.

Alvanides, S., 2014. Active transport: why and where do people (not) walk or cycle? J. Transp. Health 1, 211–213.

Anable, J., Brand, C., 2019. Energy, pollution and climate change. In: Docherty, I., Shaw, J. (Eds.), Transport Matters. Policy Press, Bristol.

Bearman, N., Singleton, A.D., 2014. Modelling the potential impact on CO2 emissions of an increased uptake of active travel for the home to school commute using individual level data. J. Transp. Health 1, 295–304.

Beckx, C., Broekx, S., Degraeuwe, B., Beusen, B., Int Panis, L., 2013. Limits to active transport substitution of short car trips. Transp. Res. D Transp. Environ. 22, 10–13.

BEIS, 2019. Greenhouse Gas Reporting: Conversion Factors 2019. Department for Business, Energy & Industrial Strategy, London. accessed at https://www.gov.uk/government/publications/greenhouse-gas-reporting-conversion-factors-2019. (on 12 Nov 2019).

Bieliński, T., Ważna, A., 2020. Electric scooter sharing and bike sharing user behaviour and characteristics. Sustainability 12, 9640.

Bigazzi, A., Wong, K., 2020. Electric bicycle mode substitution for driving, public transit, conventional cycling, and walking. Transp. Res. D Transp. Environ. 85, 102412.

Blondel, B., Mispelon, C., Ferguson, J., 2011. Cycle more Often 2 cool down the planet!: Quantifying CO2 savings of cycling. European Cyclists' Federation, Brussels. Retrieved from https://ecf.com/system/files/Cycle_More_Often_2_Cool_Down_the_Planet.pdf.

Brand, C., 2021. Cycling Is Ten Times more Important than Electric Cars for Reaching Net-Zero Cities. accessed at The Conversation UK. https://theconversation.com/cycling-is-ten-times-more-important-than-electric-cars-for-reaching-net-zero-cities-157163.

Brand, C., Boardman, B., 2008. Taming of the few - the unequal distribution of greenhouse gas emissions from personal travel in the UK. Energy Policy 36, 224–238.

Brand, C., Hunt, A., 2018. The Health Costs of Air Pollution from Cars and Vans, Report for Clean Air Day 2018. Available at Global Action Plan, London. https://www.cleanairday.org.uk/News/the-health-costs-of-air-pollution-from-cars-and-vans.

Brand, C., Preston, J.M., 2010. '60-20 emission'—the unequal distribution of greenhouse gas emissions from personal, non-business travel in the UK. Transp. Policy 17, 9–19.

Brand, C., Goodman, A., Rutter, H., Song, Y., Ogilvie, D., 2013. Associations of individual, household and environmental characteristics with carbon dioxide emissions from motorised passenger travel. Appl. Energy 104, 158–169.

Brand, C., Goodman, A., Ogilvie, D., 2014. Evaluating the impacts of new walking and cycling infrastructure on carbon dioxide emissions from motorized travel: A controlled longitudinal study. Appl. Energy 128, 284–295.

Brand, C., Anable, J., Ketsopoulou, I., Watson, J., 2020. Road to zero or road to nowhere? Disrupting transport and energy in a zero carbon world. Energy Policy 139, 111334.

Brand, C., Dons, E., Anaya-Boig, E., Avila-Palencia, I., Clark, A., de Nazelle, A., Gascon, M., Gaupp-Berghausen, M., Gerike, R., Götschi, T., Iacorossi, F., Kahlmeier, S., Laeremans, M., Nieuwenhuijsen, M.J., Pablo Orjuela, J., Racioppi, F., Raser, E., Rojas-Rueda, D., Standaert, A., Stigell, E., Sulikova, S., Wegener, S., Int Panis, L., 2021a. The climate change mitigation effects of daily active travel in cities. Transp. Res. D Transp. Environ. 93, 102764. https://doi.org/10.1016/j.trd.2021.102764.

Brand, C., Götschi, T., Dons, E., Gerike, R., Anaya-Boig, E., Avila-Palencia, I., de Nazelle, A., Gascon, M., Gaupp-Berghausen, M., Iacorossi, F., Kahlmeier, S., Int Panis, L., Racioppi, F., Rojas-Rueda, D., Standaert, A., Stigell, E., Sulikova, S., Wegener, S., Nieuwenhuijsen, M.J., 2021b. The climate change mitigation impacts of active travel: evidence from a longitudinal panel study in seven European cities. Glob. Environ. Chang. 67, 102224.

Bucher, D., Buffat, R., Froemelt, A., Raubal, M., 2019. Energy and greenhouse gas emission reduction potentials resulting from different commuter electric bicycle adoption scenarios in Switzerland. Renew. Sustain. Energy Rev. 114, 109298.

Büchs, M., Schnepf, S.V., 2013. Who emits most? Associations between socio-economic factors and UK households' home energy, transport, indirect and total CO2 emissions. Ecol. Econ. 90, 114–123.

Cairns, S., Behrendt, F., Raffo, D., Beaumont, C., Kiefer, C., 2017. Electrically-assisted bikes: potential impacts on travel behaviour. Transp. Res. A: Policy Pract. 103, 327–342.

Cameron, I., Kenworthy, J.R., Lyons, T.J., 2003. Understanding and predicting private motorised urban mobility. Transp. Res. D Transp. Environ. 8, 267–283.

Carlsson-Kanyama, A., Linden, A.-L., 1999. Travel patterns and environmental effects now and in the future:: implications of differences in energy consumption among socio-economic groups. Ecol. Econ. 30, 405–417.

Carse, A., Goodman, A., Mackett, R.L., Panter, J., Ogilvie, D., 2013. The factors influencing car use in a cycle-friendly city: the case of Cambridge. J. Transp. Geogr. 28, 67–74.

Castro, A., Gaupp-Berhausen, M., Dons, E., Standaert, A., Laeremans, M., Clark, A., Anaya, E., Cole-Hunter, T., Avila-Palencia, I., Rojas-Rueda, D., Nieuwenhuijsen, M., Gerike, R., Panis, L.I., de Nazelle, A., Brand, C., Raser, E., Kahlmeier, S., Götschi, T., 2019. Physical activity of electric bicycle users compared to conventional bicycle users and non-cyclists: insights based on health and transport data from an online survey in seven European cities. Transp. Res. Interdiscip. Perspect. 100017.

CCC, 2020. Reducing UK Emissions: 2020 Progress Report to Parliament. Climate Change Committee, London. accessed at https://www.theccc.org.uk/publication/reducing-uk-emissions-2020-progress-report-to-parliament/.

Cherry, C. (2007). Electric Bike Use in China and Their Impacts on the Environment, Safety, Mobility and Accessibility. UC Berkeley: Center for Future Urban Transport: A Volvo Center of Excellence. Retrieved from https://escholarship.org/uc/item/8bn7v9jm.

Cherry, C.R., Weinert, J.X., Xinmiao, Y., 2009. Comparative environmental impacts of electric bikes in China. Transp. Res. D: Transp. Environ. 14 (5), 281–290. https://doi.org/10.1016/j.trd.2008.11.003.

Cuenot, F., Fulton, L., Staub, J., 2012. The prospect for modal shifts in passenger transport worldwide and impacts on energy use and CO2. Energy Policy 41, 98–106.

de Bortoli, A., 2021. Environmental performance of shared micromobility and personal alternatives using integrated modal LCA. Transp. Res. D Transp. Environ. 93, 102743. https://doi.org/10.1016/j.trd.2021.102743.

de Nazelle, A., Morton, B.J., Jerrett, M., Crawford-Brown, D., 2010. Short trips: an opportunity for reducing mobile-source emissions? Transp. Res. D Transp. Environ. 15, 451–457.

DfT, 2018. Analyses from the National Travel Survey, Statistical Release 18 January 2018. Department for Transport, London. https://assets.publishing.service.gov.uk/government/uploads/system/uploads/attachment_data/file/674568/analysis-from-the-national-travel-survey.pdf.

DfT, 2021. Transport and Environment Statistics: 2021 Annual Report. Department for Transport, London. accessed at https://assets.publishing.service.gov.uk/government/uploads/system/uploads/attachment_data/file/984685/transport-and-environment-statistics-2021.pdf.

Dons, E., Rojas-Rueda, D., Anaya-Boig, E., Avila-Palencia, I., Brand, C., Cole-Hunter, T., de Nazelle, A., Eriksson, U., Gaupp-Berghausen, M., Gerike, R., Kahlmeier, S., Laeremans, M., Mueller, N., Nawrot, T., Nieuwenhuijsen, M.J., Orjuela, J.P., Racioppi, F., Raser, E., Standaert, A., Int Panis, L., Götschi, T., 2018. Transport mode choice and body mass index: cross-sectional and longitudinal evidence from a European-wide study. Environ. Int. 119, 109–116.

ECF, 2011. Cycle more Often 2 Cool down the Planet! - Quantifying CO2 Savings of Cycling. European Cyclists' Federation (ECF), Brussels.

ECF, 2018. The Benefits of Cycling: Unlocking their Potential for Europe. European Cyclists' Federation, Brussels. accessed at https://ecf.com/sites/ecf.com/files/TheBenefitsOfCycling2018.pdf.

Elder, S.J., Roberts, S.B., 2007. The effects of exercise on food intake and body fatness: a summary of published studies. Nutr. Rev. 65, 1–19.

Elliot, T., McLaren, S.J., Sims, R., 2018. Potential environmental impacts of electric bicycles replacing other transport modes in Wellington, New Zealand. Sustain. Prod. Consum. 16, 227–236.

Fishman, E., Washington, S., Haworth, N., 2014. Bike share's impact on car use: evidence from the United States, Great Britain, and Australia. Transp. Res. D Transp. Environ. 31, 13–20.

Frank, L.D., Greenwald, M.J., Winkelman, S., Chapman, J., Kavage, S., 2010. Carbonless footprints: promoting health and climate stabilization through active transportation. Prev. Med. 50 (Suppl 1), S99–105.

Fyhri, A., Beate Sundfør, H., 2020. Do people who buy e-bikes cycle more? Transp. Res. D Transp. Environ. 86, 102422.

Fyhri, A., Heinen, E., Fearnley, N., Sundfør, H.B., 2017. A push to cycling—exploring the e-bike's role in overcoming barriers to bicycle use with a survey and an intervention study. Int. J. Sustain. Transp. 11, 681–695.

Galatoulas, N.-F., Genikomsakis, K.N., Ioakimidis, C.S., 2020. Spatio-temporal trends of E-bike sharing system deployment: A review in Europe, North America and Asia. Sustainability 12, 4611.

Goodman, A., Brand, C., Ogilvie, D., 2012. Associations of health, physical activity and weight status with motorised travel and transport carbon dioxide emissions: a cross-sectional, observational study. Environ. Health 11, 52.

Goodman, A., Sahlqvist, S., Ogilvie, D., 2014. New walking and cycling routes and increased physical activity: one- and 2-year findings from the UK iConnect study. Am. J. Public Health, e1–e9.

Goodman, A., Rojas, I.F., Woodcock, J., Aldred, R., Berkoff, N., Morgan, M., Abbas, A., Lovelace, R., 2019. Scenarios of cycling to school in England, and associated health and carbon impacts: application of the 'propensity to cycle tool'. J. Transp. Health 12, 263–278.

Götschi, T., de Nazelle, A., Brand, C., Gerike, R., 2017. Towards a comprehensive conceptual framework of active travel behavior: a review and synthesis of published frameworks. Curr. Environ. Health Rep. 4, 286–295.

Götschi, T., Kahlmeier, S., Castro, A., Brand, C., Cavill, N., Kelly, P., Lieb, C., Rojas-Rueda, D., Woodcock, J., Racioppi, F., 2020. Integrated impact assessment of active travel: expanding the scope of the health economic assessment tool (HEAT) for walking and cycling. Int. J. Environ. Res. Public Health 17.

Grigoratos, T., Martini, G., 2014. Non-exhaust traffic related emissions. Brake and Tyre wear PM: literature review. In: JRC Science and Policy Reports. Joint Research Centre, European Commission, Ispra.

Grigoratos, T., Martini, G., 2015. Brake wear particle emissions: a review. Environ. Sci. Pollut. Res. Int. 22, 2491–2504.

Grischkat, S., Hunecke, M., Böhler, S., Haustein, S., 2014. Potential for the reduction of greenhouse gas emissions through the use of mobility services. Transp. Policy 35, 295–303.

Guidon, S., Becker, H., Dediu, H., Axhausen, K.W., 2019. Electric bicycle-sharing: A new competitor in the urban transportation market? An empirical analysis of transaction data. Transp. Res. Rec. 2673, 15–26.

Hansen, K.B., Nielsen, T.A.S., 2014. Exploring characteristics and motives of long distance commuter cyclists. Transp. Policy 35, 57–63.

Henderson, J., 2020. EVs are not the answer: A mobility justice critique of electric vehicle transitions. Ann. Am. Assoc. Geogr. 110, 1993–2010.

Héran, F., Bigo, A., 2020. Malus poids, émissions de CO_2 : intéressons-nous enfin aux véhicules intermédiaires! accessed at https://theconversation.com/malus-poids-emissions-de-co-interessons-nous-enfin-aux-vehicules-intermediaires-148650.

Hitchcock, G., Conlan, B., Kay, D., Brannigan, C., Newman, D., 2014. Air Quality and Road Transport: Impacts and Solutions. RAC Foundation, London.

House of Commons, 2018. Improving Air Quality. Environment, Food and Rural Affairs, Environmental Audit, Health and Social Care, and Transport Committees - House of Commons, London. last accessed at https://publications.parliament.uk/pa/cm201719/cmselect/cmenvfru/433/43305.htm. on 18/04/2018.

ICCT, 2021. Transport Could Burn up the EU's Entire Carbon Budget. International Council for Clean Transportation, London, New York, Berlin. accessed at https://theicct.org/blog/staff/eu-carbon-budget-apr2021.
IEA, 2020. World Energy Outlook 2020. International Energy Agency, Paris. accessed at https://www.iea.org/reports/world-energy-outlook-2020/achieving-net-zero-emissions-by-2050.
IEA, 2021. Net Zero by 2050. International Energy Agency, Paris. accessed at https://www.iea.org/reports/net-zero-by-2050.
Ivanova, D., Vita, G., Wood, R., Lausselet, C., Dumitru, A., Krause, K., Macsinga, I., Hertwich, E.G., 2018. Carbon mitigation in domains of high consumer lock-in. Glob. Environ. Chang. 52, 117–130.
Ji, S., Cherry, C.R., Bechle, M.J., Wu, Y., Marshall, J.D., 2012. Electric vehicles in China: emissions and health impacts. Environ. Sci. Technol. 46 (4), 2018–2024. https://doi.org/10.1021/es202347q.
Jones, T., Harms, L., Heinen, E., 2016. Motives, perceptions and experiences of electric bicycle owners and implications for health, wellbeing and mobility. J. Transp. Geogr. 53, 41–49.
JRC, 2013. Analysis of National Travel Statistics in Europe. Seville, European Commission, Joint Research Centre, ISBN: 978-92-79-32358-4.
Keall, M.D., Shaw, C., Chapman, R., Howden-Chapman, P., 2018. Reductions in carbon dioxide emissions from an intervention to promote cycling and walking: A case study from New Zealand. Transp. Res. D Transp. Environ. 65, 687–696.
Keith, D.R., Houston, S., Naumov, S., 2019. Vehicle fleet turnover and the future of fuel economy. Environ. Res. Lett. 14, 021001.
Ko, J., Park, D., Lim, H., Hwang, I.C., 2011. Who produces the most CO2 emissions for trips in the Seoul metropolis area? Transp. Res. D Transp. Environ. 16, 358–364.
Kroesen, M., 2017. To what extent do e-bikes substitute travel by other modes? Evidence from the Netherlands. Transp. Res. D Transp. Environ. 53, 377–387.
Kroesen, M., De Vos, J., 2020. Does active travel make people healthier, or are healthy people more inclined to travel actively? J. Transp. Health 16, 100844.
Le Quéré, C., Jackson, R.B., Jones, M.W., Smith, A.J.P., Abernethy, S., Andrew, R.M., De-Gol, A.J., Willis, D.R., Shan, Y., Canadell, J.G., Friedlingstein, P., Creutzig, F., Peters, G.P., 2020. Temporary reduction in daily global CO2 emissions during the COVID-19 forced confinement. Nat. Clim. Change.
Leger, S.J., Dean, J.L., Edge, S., Casello, J.M., 2019. "If I had a regular bicycle, I wouldn't be out riding anymore": perspectives on the potential of e-bikes to support active living and independent mobility among older adults in Waterloo, Canada. Transp. Res. A: Policy Pract. 123, 240–254.
Ling, Z., Cherry, C.R., Yang, H., Jones, L.R., 2015. From e-bike to car: A study on factors influencing motorization of e-bike users across China. Transp. Res. D Transp. Environ. 41, 50–63.
Loeb, J., 2017. Particle Pollution from Electric Cars Could Be Worse than from Diesel Ones. *E&T Magazine* [Online]. last accessed at https://eandt.theiet.org/content/articles/2017/03/particle-pollution-from-electric-cars-could-be-worse-than-from-diesel-ones/ on13/04/2018.
Lovelace, R., Beck, S.B.M., Watson, M., Wild, A., 2011. Assessing the energy implications of replacing car trips with bicycle trips in Sheffield, UK. Energy Policy 39, 2075–2087.
Luo, H., Kou, Z., Zhao, F., Cai, H., 2019. Comparative life cycle assessment of station-based and dock-less bike sharing systems. Resour. Conserv. Recycl. 146, 180–189.
Mason, J., Fulton, L., McDonald, Z., 2015. A Global High Shift Cycling Scenario: The Potential for Dramatically Increasing Bicycle and E-Bike Use in Cities around the World, with Estimated Energy, CO2, and Cost Impacts. Institute for

Transportation & Development Policy and the University of California, Davis, Davis, CA. accessed at https://itdpdotorg.wpengine.com/wp-content/uploads/2015/11/A-Global-High-Shift-Cycling-Scenario_Nov-2015.pdf. on 10/07/2020.
McQueen, M., MacArthur, J., Cherry, C., 2020. The E-bike potential: estimating regional e-bike impacts on greenhouse gas emissions. Transp. Res. D Transp. Environ. 87, 102482.
Mizdrak, A., Cobiac, L.J., Cleghorn, C.L., Woodward, A., Blakely, T., 2020. Fuelling walking and cycling: human powered locomotion is associated with non-negligible greenhouse gas emissions. Sci. Rep. 10, 9196.
Moreno, C., Allam, Z., Chabaud, D., Gall, C., Pratlong, F., 2021. Introducing the "15-Minute City": sustainability, resilience and place identity in future post-pandemic cities. Smart Cities, 4.
Neves, A., Brand, C., 2019. Assessing the potential for carbon emissions savings from replacing short car trips with walking and cycling using a mixed GPS-travel diary approach. Transp. Res. A: Policy Pract. 123, 130–146.
Nicolas, J.-P., David, D., 2009. Passenger transport and CO2 emissions: what does the French transport survey tell us? Atmos. Environ. 43, 1015–1020.
Nieuwenhuijsen, M.J., Khreis, H., 2016. Car free cities: pathway to healthy urban living. Environ. Int. 94, 251–262.
Ntziachristos, L., Boulter, P., 2016. EMEP/EEA Air Pollutant Emission Inventory Guidebook 2016: Technical Annex on 1.A.3.b.vi Road Transport: Automobile Tyre and Brake Wear and 1.A.3.b.vii Road Transport: Automobile Road Abrasion. European Environment Agency, Copenhagen.
OECD, 2020. Non-exhaust Particulate Emissions from Road Transport: An Ignored Environmental Policy Challenge. OECD Publishing, Paris. accessed at https://www.oecd.org/environment/non-exhaust-particulate-emissions-from-road-transport-4a4dc6ca-en.htm.
OECD/ITF, 2020. Good to Go? Assessing the Environmental Performance of New Mobility. International Transport Forum, OECD Publishing, Paris. accessed at https://www.itf-oecd.org/good-go-assessing-environmental-performance-new-mobility.
OECD/ITF, 2021. Reversing Car Dependency: Summary and Conclusions, ITF Roundtable Reports, No. 181. International Transport Forum, OECD Publishing, Paris. accessed at https://www.itf-oecd.org/sites/default/files/docs/reversing-car-dependency.pdf.
OECD/ITF (2021). ITF Transport Outlook 2021. Paris: International Transport Forum, OECD Publishing. Retrieved at https://www.itf-oecd.org/itf-transport-outlook-2021 on 20/03/2022.
Pabayo, R.A., Gauvin, L., Barnett, T.A., Morency, P., Nikiéma, B., Séguin, L., 2012. Understanding the determinants of active transportation to school among children: evidence of environmental injustice from the Quebec longitudinal study of child development. Health Place 18, 163–171.
PBSC Urban Solutions, 2019. What if "Old School" Is the Best School for Electric Bike-Share? Accessed at https://www.pbsc.com/blog/2019/11/what-if-old-school-is-the-bestschool-for-electric-bike-share. (2021).
Philips, I., Anable, J., Chatterton, T., 2022. E-bikes and their capability to reduce car CO2 emissions. Transp. Policy 116, 11–23.
Preston, I., White, V., Thumim, J., Bridgeman, T., Brand, C., 2013. Distribution of Carbon Emissions in the UK: Implications for Domestic Energy Policy. Joseph Rowntree Foundation, London.
Quarmby, S., Santos, G., Mathias, M., 2019. Air quality strategies and technologies: A rapid review of the international evidence. Sustainability 11.

Sælensminde, K., 2004. Cost–benefit analyses of walking and cycling track networks taking into account insecurity, health effects and external costs of motorized traffic. Transp. Res. A: Policy Pract. 38, 593–606.
Scheepers, C.E., Wendel-Vos, G.C.W., den Broeder, J.M., van Kempen, E.E.M.M., van Wesemael, P.J.V., Schuit, A.J., 2014. Shifting from car to active transport: A systematic review of the effectiveness of interventions. Transp. Res. A: Policy Pract. 70, 264–280.
Semenescu, A., Gavreliuc, A., Sârbescu, P., 2020. 30 years of soft interventions to reduce car use—A systematic review and meta-analysis. Transp. Res. D Transp. Environ. 85, 102397.
Söderberg f.k.a. Andersson, A., Adell, E., Winslott Hiselius, L., 2021. What is the substitution effect of e-bikes? A randomised controlled trial. Transp. Res. D Transp. Environ. 90, 102648.
Stead, D., 1999. Relationships between transport emissions and travel patterns in Britain. Transp. Policy 6, 247–258.
Steenberghen, T., Tavares, T., Richardson, J., Himpe, W., Crabbé, A., 2017. Support Study on Data Collection and Analysis of Active Modes Use and Infrastructure in Europe, COWI for the European Commission, Directorate-General for Mobility and Transport, Brussels. Accessed at https://core.ac.uk/download/pdf/154964697.pdf.
Stott, S., 2020. How green is cycling? Riding, walking, ebikes and driving ranked. Bikeradar. accessed at https://www.bikeradar.com/features/long-reads/cycling-environmental-impact/. www.ourmedia.co.uk.
Sun, Q., Feng, T., Kemperman, A., Spahn, A., 2020. Modal shift implications of e-bike use in the Netherlands: moving towards sustainability? Transp. Res. D Transp. Environ. 78, 102202.
Susilo, Y.O., Stead, D., 2009. Individual carbon dioxide emissions and potential for reduction in the Netherlands and the United Kingdom. Transp. Res. Rec. 2139, 142–152.
T&E, 2018. CO2 Emissions from Cars: The Facts. Transport & Environment, Brussels. accessed at https://www.transportenvironment.org/wp-content/uploads/2021/07/2018_04_CO2_emissions_cars_The_facts_report_final_0_0.pdf.
Tainio, M., Monsivais, P., Jones, N.R., Brand, C., Woodcock, J., 2017. Mortality, greenhouse gas emissions and consumer cost impacts of combined diet and physical activity scenarios: a health impact assessment study. BMJ Open 7.
Timmermans, H., van der Waerden, P., Alves, M., Polak, J., Ellis, S., Harvey, A.S., Kurose, S., Zandee, R., 2003. Spatial context and the complexity of daily travel patterns: an international comparison. J. Transp. Geogr. 11, 37–46.
Timmers, V.R.J.H., Achten, P.A.J., 2016. Non-exhaust PM emissions from electric vehicles. Atmos. Environ. 134, 10–17.
Tranter, P., Tolley, R., 2020. Chapter 11 - conclusion: re-imagining the city for a healthier future. In: Tranter, P., Tolley, R. (Eds.), Slow Cities. Elsevier.
U.S. Department of Transportation, 2017. National Household Travel Survey: Vehicle Trips. U.S. Department of Transportation, Federal Highway Administration, Washington, DC. accessed at https://nhts.ornl.gov/vehicle-trips. on 20/03/2020.
Vagane, L., 2007. Short car trips in Norway: is there a potential for modal shift? In: Proceedings of the European Transport Conference (ETC) 2007 held 17–19 October 2007. Leiden, The Netherlands.
van Goeverden, K., van Arem, B., van Nes, R., 2016. Volume and GHG emissions of long-distance travelling by Western Europeans. Transp. Res. D Transp. Environ. 45, 28–47.
Weiss, M., Dekker, P., Moro, A., Scholz, H., Patel, M.K., 2015. On the electrification of road transportation? A review of the environmental, economic, and social performance of electric two-wheelers. Transp. Res. Part Transp. Environ. 41, 348–366. https://doi.org/10.1016/j.trd.2015.09.007.

Wild, K., Woodward, A., Shaw, C., 2021. Gender and the E-bike: exploring the role of electric bikes in increasing Women's access to cycling and physical activity. Active Travel Stud. 1.

Williams, M.L., Lott, M.C., Kitwiroon, N., Dajnak, D., Walton, H., Holland, M., Pye, S., Fecht, D., Toledano, M.B., Beevers, S.D., 2018. The lancet countdown on health benefits from the UK climate change act: a modelling study for Great Britain. Lancet Planet. Health 2, e202–e213.

Winslott Hiselius, L., Svensson, Å., 2017. E-bike use in Sweden—CO2 effects due to modal change and municipal promotion strategies. J. Clean. Prod. 141, 818–824.

Woodcock, J., Abbas, A., Ullrich, A., Tainio, M., Lovelace, R., Sá, T.H., Westgate, K., Goodman, A., 2018. Development of the impacts of cycling tool (ICT): A modelling study and web tool for evaluating health and environmental impacts of cycling uptake. PLoS Med. 15, e1002622.

Yang, Y., Wang, C., Liu, W., 2018. Urban daily travel carbon emissions accounting and mitigation potential analysis using surveyed individual data. J. Clean. Prod. 192, 821–834.

CHAPTER TWELVE

Cycling during and after the COVID-19 pandemic

Angela Francke*
Cycling and Sustainable Mobility, Universität Kassel, Kassel, Germany
*Corresponding author: e-mail address: angela.francke@uni-kassel.de

Contents

Abstract

Since the outbreak of the COVID-19 pandemic at the beginning of 2020, there have been significant changes in mobility worldwide. This chapter gives a short overview of general mobility behavior changes and a detailed summary of changes in relation to cycling and bicycle-related reactions of municipalities in urban planning to address and cater to those changes.

Overall, there was a decrease in general mobility due to travel restrictions, school closures, or people working from home. Additionally, similar changes in the transport modes used could be observed in many different countries, with the significantly decreased number of trips with public transport while at the same time private car usage increased. This chapter focuses on cycling trips, which have increased since they offer a socially distanced way of traveling, especially compared to non-individual travel modes. These changes in mobility subsequently influenced accident numbers and emissions. Many cities worldwide reacted to the different circumstances and adopted new, often temporary, infrastructure measures that encouraged people to cycle and walk more. Measures taken include tactical urbanism, pop-up bike lanes and

Advances in Transport Policy and Planning, Volume 10
ISSN 2543-0009
https://doi.org/10.1016/bs.atpp.2022.04.011

expansion of the bicycle network, the closures of streets and intersections for cars, the adjustment of speed limits, and the encouragement to use bike-sharing.

The chapter also reflects on the potential of the pandemic and the urban planning interventions put in place as a catalyst for sustainable mobility behavior. The pandemic has opened the way for further mobility transition toward both active travel modes and environmental friendliness in general. Many changes that were observed will persist and may change the way we move and fulfill our mobility needs in the long-term, as the increase of mobile working or the shift toward virtual meetings continue. In the end, the changed circumstances due to the pandemic worked as a catalyst for implementing such measures, and the cities should further make use of this opportunity.

Keywords: Cycling, Sustainable mobility behavior, Mobility transition, Tactical urbanism, Pop-up bike lanes, Transport mode choice

1. Introduction

With the beginning of the COVID-19 outbreak and the restrictions put in place to prevent an uncontrolled spread of the virus, the circumstances for daily activities changed. In this time, people were suddenly asked to deal with an unprecedented societal transition in the form of travel restrictions, school closures, loss of employment, and new, often imperfect, digital solutions for product delivery and working from home. These new conditions resulted in changed mobility patterns. In general, COVID-19 hotspots shifted from one region to another, resulting in different restrictions. As a result, mobility behavior developed very differently in the course of the COVID-19 pandemic.

The reduction of overall mobility was reported in many cities and countries, with numbers reaching pre-pandemic times once the restrictions were removed. In most areas, the mobility behavior pattern showed these ups and downs, and it is difficult to compare the number and phases of lockdowns, restrictions in place and reduced and the measures put in place on a global level. While the effects could be observed worldwide, the focus of the following chapters will be to summarize the findings and give examples from mainly Europe, the Americas, and some Asian studies.

A remarkable shift in the modal split distribution was observed. Cycling was seen as a reliable and resilient option in pandemic times as it enabled social distancing and a low risk of contagiousness. Additionally, it combined further advantages like being outside, staying physically active, and strengthening the immune system. Knie et al. (2021) state that 11% of those surveyed specified that they had "*acquired a first, further or better bicycle due to corona*"

(p. 22). There are detailed studies on the effect of the pandemic on cycling traffic all over the globe which used different data sources, like app data, counters or surveys (e.g., Anke et al., 2021; Hong et al., 2020). Buehler and Pucher (2021) give a first compact review of those cycling studies.

The increase in cycling is also reflected in the higher demand for bicycles and its sales figures. According to the NPD Group, sales of bicycles between April 2020 and April 2021 were up by 57% in the United States (Sorenson, 2021). In France, the total number of bikes sold increased by 1.7% to 2.68 million in 2020, and e-bike sales increased even by 31% (Beckendorff, 2021). In the United Kingdom, a report sales in the cycling market grew by up to 60% at the start of the pandemic, and e-bikes sales more than doubled (Bicycle Association (2020). Data from the first half of 2021 show that sales increased (+52%) compared to pre-pandemic levels (Bicycle Association, 2021). The report also suggests that the demand for bikes could not be fully satisfied because of a lack of bike availability. In Germany, bike sales (including e-bikes) increased by 17%. E-bikes sales alone increased even more (44%). Total revenue from bike sales was 6.44 billion euros, an increase of 61% (Zweirad-Industrie-Verband (ZIV), 2021).

Besides the behavioral side as a response to the corona pandemic, the municipalities also put up interventions that were meant to support a shift to cycling-based movements in cities. Those urban planning measures were often temporarily and quickly installed, like the famous pop-up bike lanes, street closures, or tactical urbanism interventions. In sum, the focus of this article is to show and discuss which measures were taken and which mobility and especially cycling behavior were observed on a general level in the prominent global lockdown waves. This article additionally aims to study the opportunity the COVID-19 pandemic has on the increase of cycling and potential long-term effects. The question to discuss is what changes will be permanent and which changed circumstances lead to a long-term change of mobility pattern.

2. General mobility and cycling trends during the COVID-19 pandemic

The pandemic had a substantial impact on individual routines and mobility behavior. There have been several studies of COVID-19 impacts on mobility which mostly report similar results with trips by motorized transport as well as active mobility options increasing and public transport trips decreasing (e.g., Abdullah et al., 2020; Ahangari et al., 2020;

Anke et al., 2021; Knie et al., 2021; Nobis et al., 2021). In Table 1, the trends are summarized in general and for cycling as well as specific for urban and non-urban areas.

2.1 Mobility behavior

Mobility data in the United Kingdom shows a mobility reduction by approx. 65% during the first lockdown period. During the summer of 2020, overall mobility increased, but not to pre-pandemic levels, and then decreased again in November 2020 due to rising cases and new restrictions (Enders et al., 2020). In Germany, the Covid-19 Mobility Project (2021) shows that daily mobility decreased by up to 35–40% during lockdown periods in spring and winter 2020, but mobility numbers quickly went back to their normal levels with fewer restrictions. In Switzerland, Molloy et al. (2020) found a 50–60% reduction in the average traveled kilometers per day. A study with respondents coming from South and South-East Asian countries stated that the majority of the respondents (57%) did not go to work or school and the primary purpose of trips shifted significantly from work or study trips to shopping trips and travel distances were reduced (Abdullah et al., 2020). There was a significant shift in mode choice from public transport to private transport (cars, motorbikes) and non-motorized modes. About 87% of Indonesian respondents stated that they reduced their traveling (very) significantly and the lower frequency of travel correlates with a decrease in participation in out-of-home-activities (Irawan et al., 2021).

Teixeira and Lopes (2020) show that the ridership drop in New York City due to the pandemic was considerably smaller for bike-sharing (drop by 71%) than for subway ridership (90%). Additionally, the authors found evidence that a modal shift from public transport to bike-sharing occurred and therefore consider the bike-sharing system is a more resilient option than the subway system. Similarly, Heydari et al. (2021) view the bike-sharing system in London as a resilient part of the urban transportation system as shared bicycle usage did not decrease significantly. However, the authors show that usage times increased during lockdown periods, indicating changes in people's mobility behavior and the usage of bike-sharing systems as a substitution for public transport.

The subjective well-being has also changed differently for the different transport modes throughout the pandemic. For example, in April 2020 in Germany, 9% of respondents said they would feel more comfortable or

Table 1 Overview of trends in mobility behavior in reaction to the corona pandemic.

	Mobility trends during the COVID-19 pandemic	**Details of the cycling trends**
Key trends in general	Shift in the modal split distribution All transport modes decreased absolutely, except cycling Primary purpose of trips shifted from work or study trips to shopping/leisure trips Household income influences direction of mobility behavior change Changes most prominent for age 65 and under Emissions decreased, especially during hard lockdown times	Preference of individual transport modes, like cycling, because of possible social distancing Number of accidents decreased during lockdown periods, especially the amount of fatally injured cyclists
Key trends in urban areas	Increase in walking Increase in cycling Increase in private car use Decrease in public transport use	Average daily kilometers cycled increased Times of cycling trips and trip purposes changed (more leisure, more midday) Length of cycling trips changed (longer trips for leisure purpose) Cycling increased in more transit-oriented cities while it decreased in more bicycle-oriented university cities
Key trends in non-urban areas	Decrease in public transport use but to a lesser extent than in urban areas Change in car use	More bicycle activities in rural areas for recreational purpose

From Aloi, A., Alonso, B., Benavente, J., Cordera, R., Echániz, E., González, F., Ladisa, C., Lezama-Romanelli, R., López-Parra, Á., Mazzei, V., Perrucci, L., Prieto-Quintana, D., Rodríguez, A., Sañudo, R., 2020. Effects of the COVID-19 lockdown on urban mobility: empirical evidence from the City of Santander (Spain). Sustainability 2020, 12, 3870. https://doi.org/10.3390/su12093870; Follmer, R., Schelewsky, M., 2020. Mobilitätsreport 02, Ergebnisse aus Beobachtungen per repräsentativer Befragung und ergänzendem Mobilitätstracking bis Ende Juni. Ausgabe 31.07.2020, Bonn, Berlin, mit Förderung des BMBF.; Möllers, A., Specht, S., Wessel, J., 2021. The Impact of the Covid-19 Pandemic and Government Interventions on Active Mobility (Working Paper No. 34). University of Münster, Germany, Institute for Transport Economics.; Molloy, J., Schatzmann, T., Schoeman, B., Tchervenkov, C., Hintermann, B., Axhausen, K.W., 2020. Observed impacts of the Covid-19 first wave on travel behavior in Switzerland based on a large GPS panel. Transport Policy. Volume 104, 2021, 43–51. https://doi.org/10.1016/j.tranpol.2021.01.009; Anke, J., Francke, A., Schaefer, LM., Petzold, T., 2021. Impact of SARS-CoV-2 on the mobility behavior in Germany. Eur. Transp. Res. Rev. 13, 10. https://doi.org/10.1186/s12544-021-00469-3; Maier, O., 2021. Perspective of Cycling Industry - Cycling in Times of COVID.

much more comfortable if they used or would use a bicycle compared to pre-pandemic times; in summer and autumn 2020, this figure was 11%, in spring 2021, it was 13%. In autumn 2021, 15% of respondents said they would feel more comfortable or much more comfortable if they used or would use a bicycle than before the spread of the coronavirus (Nobis et al., 2021). Hong et al. (2020) applied app data to different types of cycling infrastructure. While the increase in non-commuting-cycling was the highest on safe cycling infrastructure (shared off-road infrastructure, park routes) after the implementation of the lockdown, the increase was also significant on roads with no specific cycling infrastructure, implying that people were encouraged to use these roads more because of lower traffic volumes and therefore, increased safety. The authors also reported higher increases on cycling routes with attractions (i.e., rivers, parks) and good connections to essential destinations (e.g., supermarkets).

Although most studies focused on urban mobility, the initial situation concerning transport modes is different in rural areas, with car use having a much higher share of the modal split. On the other hand, all other modes have a lower share of the modal mix in rural areas than in urbanized areas. During the pandemic, the use of public transport decreased. The most noteworthy change was car usage in rural areas, with 78% of responses stating a change. About 45% state that they use the car less (versus 20% of the urban drivers), and 33% use it more (versus 23% of urban drivers) (Anke et al., 2021).

The mobility reduction was most prominent for people under the age of 65 during the beginning of the pandemic and went back to or even above their pre-pandemic levels as the pandemic continued, and new routines were established (Knie et al., 2021). In contrast, overall mobility for older people has continued to decrease. In addition, people of the older age group were more sensitive to the risks of the virus and the risk of infection on public transport (Park and Cho, 2021).

According to Parker et al. (2021), people with lower incomes did not decrease their public transport travel as much. Under normal conditions, the mobility footprint increases with income: On average, the higher the income, the higher the mobility indicators, such as time spent on the road and distance traveled. At the beginning of the pandemic in 2020, there was a brief reversal of this relationship, with people from higher income levels having lower mobility indicators due to the possibility of working remotely (Follmer, 2020). The already lower modal split share of motorized private transport in low compared to high-income households had decreased even further from 45% to 40% from May 2017 to May 2020 but was almost returning to pre-pandemic levels in May 2021 in Germany (Knie et al., 2021). At the same time, the share of motorized private transport in the modal split of people with high household income has risen steadily from 54% in May 2017 to 58% in May 2020 to 61% in May 2021. The share of cycling in the modal split has hardly changed for low, medium, or high household income alike, suggesting that cycling use is not significantly dependent on socio-economic indicators in Germany. Schaefer et al. (2021) found that in the choice of changing transport modes, eco-consciousness played an essential role in using the bicycle instead of the car.

2.2 Trip purpose

As gyms were closed and curfews implemented, cycling was suitable for some people to keep physically active. In Germany, the reduction in mobility was most significant for work and educational purposes and smaller for recreational and leisure purposes (Knie et al., 2021). Meanwhile, the number of trips for shopping and errands was roughly the same in May 2020 compared to pre-pandemic times. Hong et al. (2020) used crowdsourced cycling data from the activity app Strava which correlated with automatic bicycle counters, to analyze changes in cycling activity in Glasgow, Scotland, UK. With the pandemic beginning in March 2020, commuting trips decreased significantly. However, the number of non-commuting trips started to increase, indicating that people used cycling more as a form of exercise.

People did not necessarily perceive the removal of their daily trips as enrichment. In a study from the Netherlands, 69% of the respondents stated they miss at least some facets of commuting, where the main aspects include the activity of commuting itself (53%), the ability to spend some time alone (25%), and feeling independent (24%). These specifications have varied greatly depending on the transport mode. For example, 55% of car commuters did not miss their commute, while 91% of bicycle and e-bike commuters missed at least one aspect of their commute. The study also shows that the longer the commute, the less it was missed (Rubin et al., 2020).

2.3 Accident numbers and emissions

The changes in mobility during the COVID-19 pandemic had different impacts on road traffic collisions and road deaths in different countries. While there was a reduction of both indicators in 32 out of 36 countries in April 2020 compared to April 2019, there was an increase in the other four countries (Yasin et al., 2021). Wegman and Katrakazas (2021) also found a reduction of traffic fatalities in 23 out of 24 countries in 2020 compared to a baseline of the previous years (2017–2019), the only exception being Switzerland. There are differences in reduction rates with almost no reduction in Finland, a reduction between 15% and 25% in Mexico, New Zealand, Great Britain, Japan, Greece, Slovenia, Belgium, Sweden, and France, and a reduction of more than 35% in Argentina and Iceland. In Great Britain, a reduction of 68% in April 2020 compared to the 3-year average for 2017 to 2019 was observed (Department for Transport, 2021). In contrast, there was an increase in road deaths by 50% in Slovakia and by 9% in Denmark in April 2020 compared to April 2019 (European Transport Safety Council, 2020). One explanation for the increase could be that the reduction in traffic has created emptier roads where risky driving, such as speeding, is much more likely to occur and lead to more severe injuries in collisions.

However, the change in road fatalities was not the same for all transport modes. Wegman and Katrakazas (2021) show a decrease for all transport modes in the countries studied, with the largest decrease for public transport-related fatalities (68%) and the smallest for cyclists (6%), which may be related to a decrease in public transport trips made. The Department for Transport (2021) even saw a rise in pedal cyclist fatalities by 41% in Great Britain, while serious injuries fell by 1% and slight injuries fell by 10% in 2020 compared to the 3-year average for 2017–2019. In this case, the increase in pedal cyclist fatalities is in line with the increase in pedal cyclist traffic. The numbers have continued to move in very different directions in different countries in 2021. While the National Center for Statistics and Analysis (2021) estimates an increase of 18.4% in motor vehicle traffic fatalities in the United States for the first half of 2021, a new high since 2006, provisional data shows a 7% drop in road deaths in 2021 compared to 2020 in Ireland, a record low since recording began in 1959 (Road Safety Authority, 2022).

The number of accidents has decreased during lockdown periods, especially the amount of fatally injured cyclists during hard lockdown times. In Germany in March 2020, the number of total severe accidents was down to 68% compared to the average number of 2017–2019, the number of fatal cyclist accidents at 67%, and the number of accidents with personal injury at 87%. Those decreases primarily occurred during the start of the lockdown and went up to almost the same amount afterward. The numbers of fatally injured bicyclists are shown in Fig. 1. As many people switched from public transportation to individual modes of transport, less experienced or novice

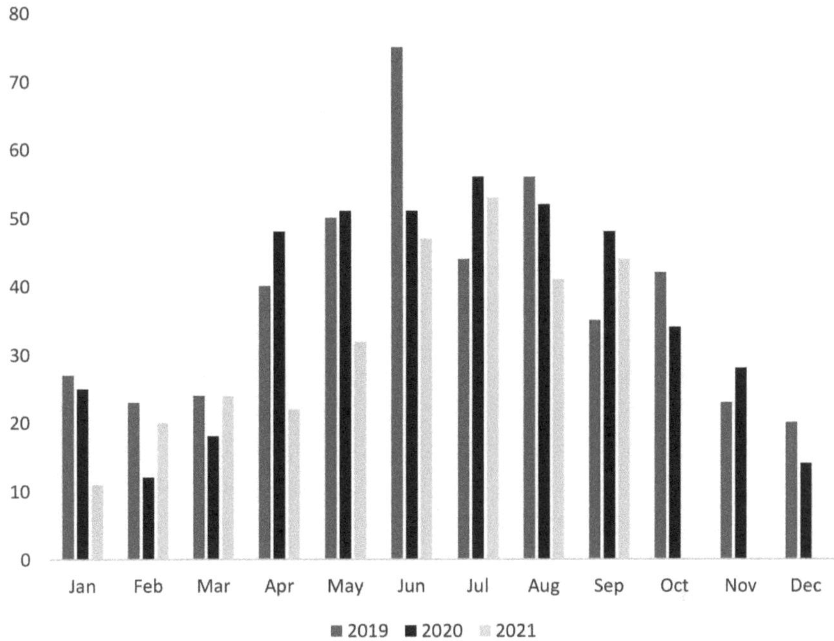

Fig. 1 Number of fatal injured bicyclists accidents in Germany, 2019–2021. *Source: own analysis with data from DESTATIS, 2022. Fachserie. 8, Verkehr. 7, Verkehrsunfälle. Monatlich, https:/www.statistischebibliothek.de/mir/receive/DESerie_mods_00000096 (accessed on 20 December 2021).*

car and bicycle riders were on the road. Further, the spring season was enjoyable and additionally stimulated the use of active mobility modes.

The change in traffic volume has not only triggered a change in the number of accidents but also in traffic-related emissions. The global CO_2 emissions decreased by about 17% in April 2020 compared with the average 2019 levels, about half of this being due to changes in surface transport (Le Quéré et al., 2020). The global daily fossil CO_2 emissions only from surface transport decreased by up to 7.5 $MtCO_2$ d ˆ-1 in April 2020 concerning annual mean daily emissions from this sector in 2019. As Jackson et al. (2021) expected, the global fossil CO_2 emissions returned to 2019 levels in 2021.

3. Measures to promote cycling during COVID-19

The COVID-19 pandemic has significantly affected mobility behavior. Various studies have shown the effect of the different phases of lockdown conditions on overall mobility, transport modes, trip lengths, and the relation between trip purposes. Certain factors such as gender, age, eco-consciousness, household income, or the risk of infection influenced the behavior's direction. In many places, the municipalities responded to the new circumstances: Temporary and permanent measures in infrastructure have been implemented. Examples of these and how they, in turn, have affected mobility behavior are presented in this part of the article.

Many cities worldwide have adopted new, often temporary, infrastructure measures to deal with the changed circumstances of the pandemic. Active travel modes, i.e., walking and cycling, emerged as they offer a socially distanced way of traveling, especially when compared to public transport. Additionally, some municipalities have seen the pandemic as an opportunity to start a transformation to become healthier and more environmentally friendly cities (Nikitas et al., 2021). Cycling, in particular, is seen as a low-cost, sustainable mode of transportation with a low risk of COVID-19 transmission (Kraus and Koch, 2021). It is a central pillar of the transition toward a more sustainable mobility system and helps to reach the UN climate goals. However, these activities needed more support, including a safe space, especially in the dense urban areas. Therefore, to encourage people to cycle more and ensure that doing so is safe, both in terms of risk of infection and protection from road safety risks (Adriazola-Steil et al., 2021), changes in the cycling infrastructure were necessary. There are various measures taken which include: (a) tactical urbanism, like road painting; (b) pop-up bike lanes and the extension of the bicycle network and the number of bicycle parking racks in general, (c) traffic calming with the closures of streets and intersections for cars and the implementation of speed limits or (d) the encouragement to use or facilitate the use of bike-sharing, which are described in detail below.

In general, the measures implemented to respond to the COVID-19 pandemic helped reduce congestion and improve traffic safety. Various actors have launched datasets to catalog these measures. For example, the European Cyclists' Federation (European Cyclist' Federation (ECF), 2020) launched the COVID-19 Cycling Measures Tracker, which lists cities across Europe with their planned and implemented measures. Of 2600 km announced, just 1500 km have been implemented, and 1.7 billion € have been allocated for cycling promotion as of February 2022. 77% of the listed measures are cycle lanes/tracks, 18% are traffic calming/reduction measures, 4% are car-free sections, and 1% are wider sidewalks. The city of Rome is leading the board of announced measures with 150 km of cycling measures announced and 15.7 km implemented, while London is leading the board of implemented measures with 75% (77 km) of cycling measures implemented.

Granada has implemented 100% of the announced 60 km of traffic calming/reduction. In relation to its population, the country of Luxembourg has announced and implemented the most kilometers with 89 km. Combs and Pardo (2021) also started a publicly available global dataset that lists over a thousand pandemic-related mobility measures. The most common measure is curb space reallocation with 27%, while the most frequently mentioned one is the expansion of street space for walking/cycling with 43%. NUMO, the New Urban Mobility alliance, et al. (n.d.) also manage a dataset where over 500 mobility responses to COVID-19 from 245 cities are listed (as of February 2022). The 572 initiatives listed use different approaches like communication, financial support, or changes to public space.

Furthermore, also at the country level, actions were taken. Within the EU, many countries also adopted the approach of promoting cycling in their COVID-19 recovery plans, aiming for a more sustainable recovery. According to the analysis of the European Cyclist' Federation (ECF) (2020), within these plans, around 1.7 billion € are reserved for cycling infrastructure, safety, tourism, and promotion (European Cyclist' Federation (ECF), 2021a).

3.1 Tactical urbanism

Many cities used actions of tactical urbanism to react to the urgency of the pandemic. In contrast to long-term, strategic urban planning, tactical urbanism is seen as a quick, low-cost approach to tackle problems in the urban environment to improve life quality and sustainability. Tactical urbanism involves the participation of local communities and neighborhoods and is mainly limited to small-scale, temporary actions. However, it is also used to initiate long-term changes or experiment with new ideas before larger investments are made (Lydon and Garcia, 2015). Tactical urbanism is mainly seen as a bottom-up approach (Graziano, 2021); however, Lydon and Garcia (2015) argue that local governments can also adopt it in a more top-down way to react to new demands quickly. This was primarily the case during the pandemic. Citizens should be encouraged to participate in the planning process by directly testing the interventions and giving feedback. Many cities tried to find solutions for the public space as a reaction to the pandemic. These temporary changes caused by the pandemic can also test future changes toward more sustainable cities in an urban lab. Marti and Espindola (2020) describe how tactical urbanism can be used in this sense: "*The actions of tactical urbanism implemented these weeks (rapid, low cost, reversible interventions like ground painting or using mobile urban furniture) constitute an interesting laboratory to explore and test permanent changes in the transformation of our streets in order to build more peaceful cities: cleaner and less polluted, human-centered and easily inclusive, slower and enabling new urban experiences.*" (p. 22). Because of the low cost of the measures, it is possible to implement them very quickly and change and adapt them continuously to the needs of a situation. Some of the following measures explained or parts of them can be categorized into tactical urbanism.

3.2 Pop-up bike lanes

One solution that has been widely adopted is the so-called pop-up bike lane. Pop-up bike lanes are created by the reallocation of road space from car traffic to bike traffic, transforming former car lanes, which are not as busy as a result of reduced mobility during the pandemic, into new, temporary cycleways (Lovelace et al., 2020). These bike lanes are marked by paint and cones or bollards, which create a physical separation from motor traffic, as shown in Fig. 2. The separation with standard equipment and paint from road construction sites were the most popular forms at the early stages of the pandemic. However, design guidelines for pop-up bike lanes were quickly developed

Fig. 2 A pop-up bike lane in Berlin Friederichshain-Kreuzberg. *Source: Peter Boytman Creative Commons CC0 1.0.*

that recommend a width of around 3 m to ensure safe passing while respecting social distancing measures (Adriazola-Steil et al., 2021; Mobycon, 2020).

This movement was a global one, and new pop-up bike infrastructure has also been implemented in many cities in North America, South America, and Australia, briefly described below. In Europe, approximately 2000 km of pop-up bike lanes have been announced (European Cyclist' Federation (ECF), 2021b). A leading example, which made headlines worldwide, is Bogota, Colombia. Among one of the first metropolises, they instantly added 84 km of temporary bike lanes to its already existing cycling network of 550 km (World Health Organization (WHO), 2020). This measure had the effect of doubling the number of cyclists while also increasing the interest of citizens in cycling in general.

Further major examples can be found in Brussels, Belgium, where about 25 km of cycle lanes were added; Berlin, Germany, with about 24 km of new lanes; or London, UK, with about 25 km of pop-up bike lanes. Paris, France, implemented around 80 km of cycling infrastructure, primarily as pop-up bike lanes. Most notably, Rue de Rivoli, a major thoroughfare in the city center, has been completely closed to private car traffic, and a wide cycle lane has been created. Paris also implemented several accompanying measures and accelerated its already existing plan to become cycling-friendly by 2024. In Vienna, Austria, temporary bike lanes of only 2.5 km were implemented, which were generally well used, but they were discontinued, despite the findings of great potential for adding even more bike lanes in Vienna (Frey et al., 2020). Barcelona, Spain, added 21 km of temporary bike lanes with plans to make these changes permanent (Medina et al., 2020). They also announced plans to create about 33 km of bike lanes until 2023, using the pop-up infrastructure to start a long-term transformation into more cycling-friendly (de Barcelona, 2021).

As a good example of how cycling is promoted in a smaller municipality, the COVID-19 transport recovery plan of Leicester City Council (2020) is described. Leicester, UK, based their plan on three essential principles: first, the need for more safe travel options in terms of the health of residents; second, the general need for sustainable mobility due to the climate crisis; and third, social equity. As a result, they announced in their plan in May 2020 the production of one mile of pop-up cycle track every week for 10 weeks alongside several other measures, including free maintenance through local bike shops and rental bicycles for employees. They also launched a new bike-sharing scheme in spring 2021 to provide additional safe and sustainable mobility options with reduced fees and even e-bikes for rent.

Overall, pop-up bike lanes have been a success story getting more people to cycle. Kraus and Koch (2021) calculate an average increase in cycling of about 42% triggered by pop-up bike lane programs compared to control cities. The increased numbers of cyclists also come from new cyclists who were not able or who did not dare to cycle before. With a reduced car traffic volume and a separation from the motorized traffic, the new cyclists were confident enough to both try to cycle and also to cycle longer routes. A survey from Berlin states several major advantages of the new pop-up bike lanes: greater distance from motorized traffic and pedestrians, more space for keeping distance and for overtaking, and more direct routes. These result in safer, faster, and more comfortable journeys (Götting and Becker, 2020).

In Berlin, Germany, the city government initiated the implementation of pop-up bike lanes in cooperation with the local council administration (Bezirksamt Friedrichshain-Kreuzberg, 2020). As a result, most people supported the project, with 94% of respondents stating their support (Götting and Becker, 2020). However, the project was also the focus of discussions about the legality of pop-up infrastructure (Berlin.de, 2021); in October 2020, a court decided that the implementation of pop-up bike lanes was legal and justified under the circumstances of the pandemic (Oberverwaltungs¬gericht Berlin-Brandenburg, 2020). Therefore, at the end of 2021, it was announced that the great majority of pop-up bike lanes in the district of Friedrichshain-Kreuzberg would be converted into permanent cycling infrastructure (Bezirksamt Friedrichshain-Kreuzberg, 2021). The local government states increased equity and safety for vulnerable road users as the main factors for the conversion of the infrastructure.

The installation of pop-up bike lanes also brought further long-term changes, as an investigation report about a pop-up bike lane in Berlin shows (Deutsche Umwelthilfe e.V, 2021). The bike lanes at Kantstraße and Neue Kantstraße were quantitatively observed from the first lockdown in April 2020 in Germany. Before the installation, the traffic volume on Kantstraße averaged 20,982 motor vehicles per day. From April 2020, i.e., after the installation of the pop-up cycle track, until the end of October 2021, there were only 16,387 motor vehicles per day. The number of motor vehicles has therefore reduced by 22%. On the other hand, the number of cycling movements has increased by 232% in the same period, from 1542 to 5125 cycling movements per day. With the reduced number of motor vehicles, the NO_2 pollution at Kantstraße has decreased from 33 $\mu g/m^3$ in 2019 to 26 $\mu g/m^3$ in 2020. The change exceeds the average reduction as an effect of the COVID-19 pandemic of about 2 $\mu g/m^3$. This pop-up cycle track will be converted into a regular cycle track (Latz, 2021).

Apart from the pop-up bike lanes, the public network was also extended for cycling and walking. Buehler and Pucher (2021) compiled a survey on the overall expansion of the bicycle network and found that in 32 of 42 European and 102 of 200 North-American cities, new bike lanes were built. For example, in London, the network expanded by 100 km, in Paris by 80 km, in New York City by 102 km, and in Montreal by 88 km.

3.3 Open streets

Another measure implemented by many cities was so-called open streets or slow streets (Lydon, 2021). A primary example of tactical urbanism is that these streets have been opened for use by cyclists and pedestrians and are partially closed for cars. If cars are allowed, pedestrians and cyclists have priority, and there are often traffic calming measures as well as speed limits in place to ensure that people can move safely and socially distanced in the road space. For example, in Brussels, a "slow street"-zone was created, spanning the entire city center, with priority for pedestrians and cyclists and a speed limit of 20 km/h (International Transport Forum (ITF), 2020). In addition, a citywide speed limit of 30 km/h was implemented, except for a few major roads. In Vienna, 25 temporary "encounter zones" were created, which allowed pedestrians to use the road space (Frey et al., 2020). However, due to the lack of additional structural design measures, pedestrians' usage of these zones was generally low, and the program was discontinued.

In the city of Oakland, USA, an extensive "slow streets" program was initiated by the Oakland Department of Transportation at the beginning of the pandemic in April 202 and designated around 119 km of its street network as potential slow streets with priority for cyclists and pedestrians, and only local motorized traffic allowed (City of Oakland, 2020). Using a tactical urbanism approach, the program was rolled out by using temporary measures like barricades, cones, and signs and relying on community feedback to choose new locations and improve implementation (OakDOT, 2020). An interim findings report showed that vehicle traffic dropped significantly on slow streets, no fatal or severe crashes involving cyclists or pedestrians occurred, and 77% of participants of an online survey stated that they support the program (OakDOT, 2020). Additionally, a new program called "Essential places" was launched to improve traffic safety in critical locations based on community feedback. In order to evaluate the program, the city used an online survey, which was available in multiple languages, to reach as many people as possible, as well weekly meetings with community organizations and local transportation advocate organizations (OakDOT, 2020).

In October 2020, the city began to replace temporary infrastructure elements that required high maintenance, such as cones and barricades, with more durable materials in specific locations (City of Oakland, 2022). It is also planned to implement permanent "slow streets" following long-term plans to convert existing neighborhood bike routes (OakDOT, 2022).

A similar program was implemented in Seattle, USA: approximately 40 km of neighborhood streets were converted to so-called Stay Healthy Streets. They were implemented to give people safe space for walking, cycling, or other activities while being closed through traffic (Seattle Department of Transportation, 2021). The program was focused on areas where a higher percentage of people of color, people with disabilities, and children live to increase equity of access to safe mobility and public space (Firth et al., 2021). The city has also used an online survey to assess whether these efforts have been successful and if the changes should be made permanent (Seattle Department of Transportation, 2021). This is, as mentioned, an essential part of those measures as they allow reaching a more diverse user group and receiving feedback from those users. This is the precondition for assessing and implementing measures that suit the needs of all groups of users.

3.4 Changes in bike sharing systems

With the increased demand for cycling during the pandemic, bike-sharing systems have played an essential role in meeting this need as they increase the accessibility of cycling. While in some cities, e.g., in Santander, Spain, the bike-sharing systems were suspended because of concerns of increased COVID-19 transmission risks (Aloi et al., 2020), most cities expanded their systems or implemented special offers to give people, who needed to travel, a safe option to do so. According to Teixeira et al. (2021), using bike-sharing to avoid public transport and maintain social distance were more relevant motivations for users. In contrast to the city of Leicester introducing a new bike-sharing scheme, other cities and bike-sharing operators implemented different measures. In Glasgow and Edinburgh, the UK, the first 30 min of every ride were made available free of charge (POLIS, 2020). Additionally, free memberships for the bike-sharing system were offered to healthcare workers (Wilson, 2020). In Berlin, 30-min rides on its system Nextbike were offered free. In Boston and Chicago, the USA, Lyft has introduced free and reduced-fare programs for essential workers and discounts for other users (Miketa and Sun, 2020). In New York City, a program that provided free trips to the city's "critical workforce" was implemented (Teixeira and Lopes, 2020). Some systems also implemented additional health measures, such as more frequent cleaning of the bike fleet and station facilities, to decrease the risk of COVID-19 transmission (Jobe and Griffin, 2021). However, it is also essential to highlight the need to communicate better these efforts to increase the perceived safety of the systems and attract more users.

4. Potential long-term changes in mobility behavior

Some impact of the pandemic changes may turn into long-term behavior. Of particular importance here is the extent to which the pandemic situation offers opportunities for promoting sustainable mobility. The pandemic and its measures can be understood as a disruptive event (Anke et al., 2021). Because of the perceived disruption, a so-called window of opportunity opened to change behavior as the set outside conditions had changed. The behavior had to adapt to that, and new mobility routines could develop.

Many people started to increase the use of their individual motorized transport. This has adverse side effects on the environment. Particularly problematic in this context is the permanence of these changed mobility patterns. The potential change in mobility behavior toward a more environmentally friendly one needs supporting factors to make maintaining it as easy as possible. The pandemic showed that many people changed from public transport to an individual transportation form. Since many people who used public transport before the pandemic have changed their mobility behavior so that it now no longer plays a role, awareness of it as a mobility option must again be fostered. This problem can be avoided or mitigated by implementing further investments and efforts to attract environmentally-friendly mobility options and the redesigning of places and infrastructure to encourage active mobility. This was their first, or greatest extent of, active mobility experience for many people. Fuller et al. (2021) show that improved cycling skills and confidence due to the national lockdown are relevant for continuous cycling after lockdown relaxations. Slightly more than 50% of respondents who were new to cycling or started again during the pandemic stated that they would rate improving their skills and confidence as an extremely or fundamental reason for continuing cycling after loosening the lockdown restrictions compared to 27% of those who had continuously cycled. Increased confidence was cited as extremely or very important by a similar number of respondents: 59% of those new to or restarted cycling and 25% of those who had cycled before and during the pandemic. For women, in particular, improved confidence and cycling skills were very or extremely important (42–49%) compared to male respondents (28–29%).

In general, the usage of digital services has become more popular. As routes were cut where possible during the COVID-19 pandemic and parts of the retail sector were forced to close temporarily, online retailing increased in importance. Instead of face-to-face meetings, the majority of people also reported that they, during and immediately after the first lockdown, preferred to hold online meetings (50%) or to make phone calls (83%) instead of face-to-face meetings with family and friends (Follmer and Schelewsky, 2020). An important influencing factor is also the increased work in the home office, which results in the reduction of numerous commutes and, at the same time, changes in leisure and errand routes. Before the COVID-19 pandemic, approximately 10–15% of the workforce in Germany worked at least partially from home (Follmer, 2020). In spring 2020—during the first lockdown—25% to 35% of the employees worked from home (Nobis et al., 2020), and around 40% were estimated at the EU level (European Union, 2020). In high-income groups, the opportunity to work from home is more frequent than average, and the numbers were even higher. The changes in transport modes already described—the avoidance of public transport and the switch to private cars—were particularly evident for high-income individuals and became more pronounced as the pandemic progressed. The fact that there will probably not be a (complete) return to "normal times" concerning the home office is shown by the continuation of this form of work in the course of the pandemic.

Although the home office was nothing new, the COVID-19 pandemic presented many companies and employees with new challenges. Each person's living situation is different, and the conditions for working from home vary in different factors like place of work, ergonomics, and care responsibilities (Bilge et al., 2020; Bockstahler et al., 2020). About 44% of people with care responsibilities without support work outside of typical working hours, 38% of people with care responsibilities with support work late into the night and on weekends (Bockstahler et al., 2020). This also impacts the daily traffic pattern, with bike traffic shifting more to midday and afternoon. Female respondents scored significantly higher on remote working stressors than male and diverse respondents (Bilge et al., 2020; Demmelhuber et al., 2020). Despite the possible risks of remote working, many people see advantages; almost half of the respondents would like to work from home as often after the pandemic as during it (Hans Böckler Stiftung, 2020). The study also shows that the more the respondents earn, the greater their desire to work from home is.

The increase in working remotely and virtual substitutes of real traffic will persist beyond the pandemic, even if in a reduced volume. An essential prerequisite for this is the promotion of digitalization, especially to further encourage digital alternatives that stimulate environmentally friendly mobility behavior and provide mixed land use to facilitate working from home. On the other hand, more digitalization will likely increase the distance to facilities, and the drop in requirement to be at work every day will reduce commuting travel. Both may increase distances and thus the ability to cycle for transport. The changed environmental conditions and thus the changed mobility behavior will also have long-term effects on traffic planning. Long-term, this might also lead to a relocation of homes which has further effects on the transport system. So far, these effects, especially the increased use of digital services, have not yet been sufficiently considered in the simulations and models. There is also a social dimension as not everyone can work from home and no safe public transport means no option to travel and therefore, possibly no income. The major challenge here is to increase the attractiveness of sustainable transport for all user groups and include this in the planner's perspective. It takes a tremendous effort to change mobility behavior again after one has become accustomed to a different mode of transport. The beginning of the lockdowns was clearly defined, acting as a robust signal for many that there was a genuine need to adjust their behavior, including mobility behavior substantially. However, the end of the pandemic still seems a bit amorphous and so lacks the decisive impulse that was present at the start. Another behavioral change would be more difficult in this situation, requiring additional education and communication measures.

To prevent contagion and enable physical activity, space in public areas is necessary, even in dense urban areas. It is necessary to reallocate space for cyclists and create areas for recreation and pedestrians. Specific measures proved to be very successful in promoting active mobility and reducing air pollution, like CO_2 and NO_2. These gains should not be squandered by a lack of further funding or research.

5. Summary and outlook on mobility after COVID-19

The different stages of the pandemic revealed how changeable mobility and cities are. Different studies have illustrated how pandemic-induced changes in mobility led to significant reductions in traffic accidents leading to personal injury or fatality and reduced congestion and CO_2 emissions. The new hygiene and social distances requirements and the changes in mobility, including increased need and willingness for both walking and cycling, had governments and municipalities all over the world respond with numerous temporary and permanent infrastructure measures. Many of these pandemic measures have brought to light the possibility of major changes being accomplished in a concise time frame when the political will (and the urgency) is there.

A significant number of cities have demonstrated that temporary traffic experiments, such as pop-up bike lanes or open streets, can be used to try out new structures and public space layouts. The cities used the opportunity to implement measures and evaluate these measures, which can be made permanent if successful and well-received. One's own - preferably positive - experience helps with the acceptance of measures. With users' feedback, the COVID-19 measures can be improved continuously and increase acceptance from all user groups. The pandemic has shown what is possible and how willing people are to change their mode of transport. The mere reduction of cars on the road at the beginning of the first lockdown in 2020 has been enough to alter the safety perception of some people sufficiently enough for them to see cycling as a viable option. The implementation of new bicycle infrastructure also supported this.

Cycling can be one of the environmentally-friendly alternatives to motorized private transport for individual transportation. Bicycles are an ideal mode of transportation to enable a resilient mobility system in a city. Some cities have shown creativity in encouraging citizens to be actively mobile, with free bicycle maintenance and repair measures. People who have switched to active mobility because of the pandemic need to be supported to stay there (e.g., via incentives from the employer or health insurance). It has been common for measures promoting active mobility to focus on urban areas usually. However, it is necessary to pay attention to rural areas as well, since the dependence on cars is still much higher there. Infrastructure and alternative, attractive solutions must first be implemented in these areas.

Even with cities' implementation of active mobility policies and infrastructure and the increased interest in cycling as a viable mobility option, there can be additional challenges. For example, sales of bicycles had already been rising before the pandemic, but the surge in demand caused them to increase at an even higher rate. The more considerable demand understandably led to supply bottlenecks, resulting in some would-be cyclists being unable to access bicycles. The further expansion of bike-sharing systems can be a solution here. Further, it is attractive for municipalities to encourage first-time cyclists to continue to use the bicycle post-pandemic.

The changed traffic situation forced by the COVID-19 pandemic opened a window of opportunity for behavioral change, i.e., the quiet streets or the opportunities for active mobility is a shared long-term memory in the collective mind. In this sense, the benefits and opportunities for changing mobility and its role as a catalyst in the mobility revolution have been a positive side effect of the pandemic that has affected humanity for the past years. This changed mobility system and this shared experience gave a glimpse of what the transport revolution can look like and what is possible—that is an opportunity. All the tactical urbanism measures showed that the greatest challenges of the transport transition are not technical and, in many aspects, do not require innovations. The political will to change is sufficient in most cases to implement lasting, substantial change in a concise time frame. Sustainable, safe mobility and a better quality of life can be created with relatively simple means; people just need to be enabled to gain new experiences in order to break with habitual behavior. So far, the pandemic period has provided many examples of getting started. What is done during such a situation to cope with the pandemic can prepare us better when a similar situation happens again in the future. The best practices and innovations have been and continue to be developed; cities and governments just need to start the transition.

References

Abdullah, M., Dias, C., Muley, D., Shahin, M., 2020. Exploring the impacts of COVID-19 on travel behavior and mode preferences. Transp. Res. Interdiscip. Perspect. 8, 100255. https://doi.org/10.1016/j.trip.2020.100255.

Adriazola-Steil, C., Pérez-Barbosa, D., Batista, B., Luke, N., Li, W., Sharpin, A., 2021. Safe Bicycle Lane Design Principles: Responding to Cycling Needs in Cities during COVID and beyond. World Resources Institute. http://doi.org/10.46830/wrigb.20.00063.

Ahangari, S., Chavis, C., Jeihani, M., 2020. Public Transit Ridership Analysis during the COVID-19 Pandemic. https://doi.org/10.1101/2020.10.25.20219105.

Ajuntament de Barcelona., 2021. Cyclable Network Set to Grow with an Additional 32.6 Kilometres of Bike Lanes. https://www.barcelona.cat/infobarcelona/en/tema/mobility-and-transport/cyclable-network-set-to-grow-with-an-additional-32-6-kilometres-of-bike-lanes-2_1108633.html. (accessed on 03 January 2022).

Aloi, A., Alonso, B., Benavente, J., Cordera, R., Echániz, E., González, F., Ladisa, C., Lezama-Romanelli, R., López-Parra, Á., Mazzei, V., Perrucci, L., Prieto-Quintana, D., Rodríguez, A., Sañudo, R., 2020. Effects of the COVID-19 lockdown on urban mobility: empirical evidence from the City of Santander (Spain). Sustainability 2020 (12), 3870. https://doi.org/10.3390/su12093870.

Anke, J., Francke, A., Schaefer, L.M., Petzold, T., 2021. Impact of SARS-CoV-2 on the mobility behavior in Germany. Eur. Transp. Res. Rev. 13, 10. https://doi.org/10.1186/s12544-021-00469-3.

Beckendorff, J., 2021. Frankreich 2020: E-Bikes lassen Fahrradbranche jubeln. RadMarkt - Das Branchenmaganzin. https://radmarkt.de/nachrichten/frankreich-2020-e-bikes-lassen-brasnche-jubeln.

Berlin.de, 2021. Rechtsstreit um Berliner Pop-up-Radwege in Berlin beendet. https://www.berlin.de/tourismus/infos/verkehr/nachrichten/6450506-4357821-rechtsstreit-um-berliner-popupradwege-in.html.

Bicycle Association, 2020. Official Industry Stats Reveal Record Extent of Covid Cycling Sales Growth. Press release December 4, 2020. https://www.bicycleassociation.org.uk/news-press/official-industry-stats-reveal-record-extent-of-covid-cycling-sales-growth/.

Bicycle Association, 2021. BA MDS Reports Continued Surge: Sales Up 52%. Press release August 2, 2021. https://www.bicycleassociation.org.uk/news-press/mds-reports-continued-surge-bikes-up-56/.

Bilge, P., Alkan, A., Ağanoğlu, R., 2020. Managing work-life balance during the COVID-19 crisis. (https://www.dpg-physik.de/vereinigungen/fachuebergreifend/ak/akc).

Bockstahler, M., Jurecic, M., Rief, S., 2020. Working from Home Experience. An Empirical Study from the User Perspective during the Corona Pandemic. (http://publica.fraunhofer.de/dokumente/N-605596.html).

Buehler, R., Pucher, J., 2021. COVID-19 impacts on cycling, 2019–2020. Trans. Rev. 41 (4), 393–400. https://doi.org/10.1080/01441647.2021.1914900.

City of Oakland, 2020. City of Oakland Announces "Oakland Slow Streets" Program Starting Saturday to Enable Safer Walking, Cycling. https://www.oaklandca.gov/news/2020/city-of-oakland-announces-oakland-slow-streets-program-starting-saturday-to-enable-safer-walking-cycling (accessed on 03 January 2022).

City of Oakland, 2022. Oakland Slow Streets - Essential Places. (https://www.oaklandca.gov/projects/oakland-slow-streets).

Combs, T., Pardo, C., 2021. Shifting streets COVID-19 mobility data: findings from a global dataset and a research agenda for transport planning and policy. Transp. Res. Interdiscip. Perspect. 9. https://doi.org/10.1016/j.trip.2021.100322.

Covid-19 Mobility Project, 2021. Covid-19 Mobility Project. https://www.covid-19-mobility.org/de/ (accessed on 16 December 2021).

Demmelhuber, K., Englmaier, F., Leiss, F., Möhrle, S., Peichl, A., Schröter, T., 2020. Working from Home before and After the Coronavirus: Effects and Gender Issues. ifo Schnelldienst digital 1 (No. 14), 01–04. https://www.ifo.de/en/publikationen/2020/article-journal/working-home-and-after-coronavirus-effects-and-gender-issues.

Department for Transport, 2021. National statistics. The impact of lockdown on reported road casualties Great Britain, final results: 2020. https://www.gov.uk/government/statistics/reported-road-casualties-great-britain-annual-report-2020/the-impact-of-lockdown-on-reported-road-casualties-great-britain-final-results-2020.

Deutsche Umwelthilfe e.V., 2021. Untersuchungsergebnisse: Verkehrliche Auswirkung Pop-up Radweg Kantstraße. https://www.duh.de/presse/pressemitteilungen/pressemitteilung/sensationserfolg-pop-up-radweg-kantstrasse-in-berlin-untersuchung-der-deutschen-umwelthilfe-belegt-v/ (accessed on 20 December 2021).

Enders, A., Pickthall, A., Nicoletti, L., Cullinan, C., 2020. COVID-19 and Mobility. https://www.endersanalysis.com/reports/covid-19-and-mobility (accessed on 20 December 2021).

European Cyclist' Federation (ECF), 2020. COVID-19 Cycling Measures Tracker. https://ecf.com/dashboard.

European Cyclist' Federation (ECF), 2021a. Final analysis: Cycling becomes mainstream in EU member states' COVID-19 recovery plans. https://ecf.com/news-and-events/news/final-analysis-cycling-becomes-mainstream-eu-member-states-covid-19-recovery (accessed on 22 December 2021).

European Cyclist' Federation (ECF), 2021b. COVID-19 Cycling Measures Tracker. (https://ecf.com/dashboard (accessed on 20 December 2021).

European Transport Safety Council, 2020. The impact of COVID-19 lockdowns on road deaths in April 2020 (PIN briefing). (https://etsc.eu/pin-briefing-the-impact-of-covid-19-lockdowns-on-road-deaths-in-april-2020/).
European Union, 2020. Telework in the EU before and after the COVID-19: where we were, where we head to. https://ec.europa.eu/jrc/sites/default/files/jrc120945_policy_brief_-_covid_and_telework_final.pdf (accessed on 6 January 2022).
Firth, C., Baquero, B., Berney, R., Hoerster, K., Mooney, S., Winters, M., 2021. Not quite a block party: COVID-19 street reallocation programs in Seattle, WA and Vancouver, BC. SSM - Popul. Health. 14, 100769.
Follmer, R., 2020. Mobilitätsreport 01, Ergebnisse aus Beobachtungen per repräsentativer Befragung und ergänzendem Mobilitätstracking bis Ende Mai. Ausgabe 29.050.2020, Bonn, Berlin, mit Förderung des BMBF.
Follmer, R., Schelewsky, M., 2020. Mobilitätsreport 02, Ergebnisse aus Beobachtungen per repräsentativer Befragung und ergänzendem Mobilitätstracking bis Ende Juni. Ausgabe 31.07.2020, Bonn, Berlin, mit Förderung des BMBF.
Frey, H., Laa, B., Leth, U., Kratochwil, F., Scober, P., 2020. Mobilität in Wien unter COVID19 - Begleituntersuchung Temporäre Begegnungszonen und Pop-Up Radinfrastruktur. Technische Universität Wien.
Bezirksamt Friedrichshain-Kreuzberg, 2020. Temporäre Einrichtung und Erweiterung von Radverkehrsanlagen während der Pandemie-Krise. Pressemitteilung Nr.53. (https://www.berlin.de/ba-friedrichshain-kreuzberg/aktuelles/pressemitteilungen/2020/pressemitteilung.911780.php).
Bezirksamt Friedrichshain-Kreuzberg, 2021. Konsequente Verstetigung der Pop-Up-Radwege. Pressemitteilung Nr. 238. https://www.berlin.de/ba-friedrichshain-kreuzberg/aktuelles/pressemitteilungen/2021/pressemitteilung.1158571.php.
Fuller, G., McGuinness, K., Waitt, G., Buchanan, I., Lea, T., 2021. The reactivated bike: self-reported cycling activity during the 2020 COVID-19 pandemic in Australia. Transp. Res. Interdiscip. Perspect. 10, 100377. https://doi.org/10.1016/j.trip.2021.100377.
Götting, K., Becker, S., 2020. Reaktionen auf die Pop-Up-Radwege in Berlin. Ergebnisse einer explorativen Umfrage zur temporären Radinfrastruktur im Kontext der Covid-19 Pandemie. IASS Study. https://doi.org/10.2312/iass.2020.019.
Graziano, T., 2021. Smart technologies, Back-To-The-Village rhetoric, and tactical urbanism: post-COVID planning scenarios in Italy. Int. J. E-Plan. Res. 10 (2), 80–93. https://doi.org/10.4018/IJEPR.20210401.oa7.
Hans Böckler Stiftung, 2020. HOMEOFFICE: BESSER KLAR GEREGELT. Arbeitswelt. 15. https://www.boeckler.de/de/boeckler-impuls-homeoffice-besser-klar-geregelt-27643.htm.
Heydari, S., Konstantinoudis, G., Behsoodi, A.W., 2021. Effect of the COVID-19 pandemic on bike-sharing demand and hire time: evidence from Santander Cycles in London. PLoS ONE 16 (12). https://doi.org/10.1371/journal.pone.0260969.
Hong, J., McArthur, D., Raturi, V., 2020. Did safe cycling infrastructure still matter during a COVID-19 lockdown? Sustainability 12, 8672. https://doi.org/10.3390/su12208672.
International Transport Forum (ITF), 2020. Re-spacing our cities for resilience. In: COVID-19 Transport Brief: Analysis, Facts and Figures for Transport's Response to the Coronavirus.
Irawan, M., Belgiawan, P., Joewono, T., Bastarianto, F., Rizki, M., Ilahi, A., 2021. Exploring activity-travel behavior changes during the beginning of COVID-19 pandemic in Indonesia. Transportation. https://doi.org/10.1007/s11116-021-10185-5.
Jackson, R.B., Friedlingstein, P., Le Quere, C., Abernethy, S., Andrew, R.M., Canadell, J.G., Ciais, P., Davis, S.J., Deng, Z., Liu, Z., Peters, G.P., 2021. Global fossil carbon emissions rebound near pre-COVID-19 levels. Environ. Res. Lett. 17.

Jobe, J., Griffin, G.P., 2021. Bike share responses to COVID-19. Transp. Res. Interdiscip. Perspect. 10. https://doi.org/10.1016/j.trip.2021.100353.

Knie, A., Zehl, F., Schelewsky, M., 2021. Mobilitätsreport 05, Ergebnisse aus Beobachtungen per repräsentativer Befragung und ergänzendem Mobilitätstracking bis Ende Juli. Ausgabe 16.08.2021, Bonn, Berlin, mit Förderung des BMBF.

Kraus, S., Koch, N., 2021. Provisional COVID-19 infrastructure induces large, rapid increases in cycling. PNAS 13, 2021. https://doi.org/10.1073/pnas.2024399118.

Latz, C., 2021. Pop-Up-Radweg an Kantstraße soll dauerhaft umgesetzt werden. https://www.tagesspiegel.de/berlin/finanzierung-zugesagt-pop-up-radweg-an-kantstrasse-soll-dauerhaft-umgesetzt-werden/27647790.html (accessed on 29 December 2021).

Le Quéré, C., Jackson, R.B., Jones, M.W., 2020. Temporary reduction in daily global CO2 emissions during the COVID-19 forced confinement. Nat. Clim. Chang. **10**, 647–653. https://doi.org/10.1038/s41558-020-0797-x.

Leicester City Council, 2020. Leicester Covid-19 Transport Recovery Plan. (https://news.leicester.gov.uk/news-articles/2020/may/city-s-covid-19-transport-recovery-plan-published/ (accessed on 29 December 2021).

Lovelace, R., Talbot, J., Morgan, M., Lucas-Smith, M., 2020. Methods to prioritise pop-up active transport infrastructure. Transp. Findings (https://doi.org/*10.32866*/*001c*.*13421*).

Lydon, M., 2021. COVID19 Livable Streets Response Strategies [Dataset]. https://docs.google.com/spreadsheets/d/1tjam1v0NLUWkYedIa4dVOL49pyWIP IyGwRB0DOnm3Ls/edit#gid=0 (accessed on 20 December 2021).

Lydon, M., Garcia, A., 2015. Tactical Urbanism: Short-Term Action for Long-Term Change. The Streets Plans Collaborative, Inc., Island Press, Washington, DC.

Marti, M., Espindola, L., 2020. Opportunity in the time of COVID-19. J. Public Space 5 (3), 23–30. https://doi.org/10.32891/jps.v5i3.1373.

Medina, M.A., Alvarez, C., Clemente, Y., Zarfa, M., 2020. Bike Lanes: How Cities across the World Are Responding to the Pandemic. El Pais (https://english.elpais.com/society/2020-11-06/bike-lanes-how-cities-across-the-world-areresponding-to-the-pandemic.html (accessed on 03 January 2022).

Miketa, D., Sun, P., 2020. As mobility patterns change, cities shift gears. Plan. Theory (https://www.planning.org/planning/2020/jun/intersections-transportation/ (accessed on 29 December 2021).

Mobycon, 2020. Making safe space for cycling in 10 days: A guide to temporary bike lanes, from Friedrichshain-Kreuzberg, Berlin. (https://mobycon.com/updates/a-guide-to-temporary-bike-lanes-from-berlin/ (accessed on 20 December 2021).

Molloy, J., Schatzmann, T., Schoeman, B., Tchervenkov, C., Hintermann, B., Axhausen, K.W., 2020. Observed impacts of the Covid-19 first wave on travel behavior in Switzerland based on a large GPS panel. Transp. Policy 104 (2021), 43–51. https://doi.org/10.1016/j.tranpol.2021.01.009.

National Center for Statistics and Analysis, 2021. Early estimate of motor vehicle traffic fatalities for the first half (January–June) of 2021 (Crash•Stats Brief Statistical Summary. Report No. DOT HS 813 199). National High-way Traffic Safety Administration. https://www.transportation.gov/briefing-room/usdot-releases-new-data-showing-road-fatalities-spiked-first-half-2021.

Nikitas, A., Tsigdinos, S., Karolemeas, C., Kourmpa, E., Bakogiannis, E., 2021. Cycling in the era of COVID-19: lessons learnt and best practice policy recommendations for a more bike-centric future. Sustainability 2021 (13), 4620. https://doi.org/10.3390/su13094620.

Nobis, C., C. Eisenmann, V. Kolarova, Nägele, S., 2020. DLR-Befragung: Wie verändert Corona unsere Mobilität? Verkehrsmittelnutzung, Einkaufs-, Arbeits- und Reiseverhalten.

Nobis, C., Eisenmann, C., Kolarova, V., Nägele, S., Winkler, C., Lenz, B., 2021. Effects of COVID on Mobility Behaviour. (https://verkehrsforschung.dlr.de/en/projects/corotrans-effects-corona-pandemic-logistics-mobility-and-transportation-system/effects).

NUMO, the New Urban Mobility alliance; Polis; TNO; the Transportation Sustainability Research Center, University of California, Berkeley; Transformative Urban Mobility Initiative; the Urbanism Next Center at the University of Oregon; and the World Economic Forum's Global New Mobility Coalition (n.d.) COVID Mobility Works. https://www.covidmobilityworks.org/.

OakDOT, 2020. Oakland Slow Streets Interim Findings Report. City of Oakland Department of Transportation. https://www.oaklandca.gov/documents/oakland-slow-streets-interim-findings-report-september-2020-1 (accessed on 03 January 2022).

OakDOT, 2022. Slow Streets - Essential Places Presentation, January 2022. Oakland Department of Transportation, Safe Streets Division.

Oberverwaltungs¬gericht Berlin-Brandenburg, 2020. Pop-up-Radwege dürfen vorerst bleiben 32/20. Beschluss vom 6. Oktober 2020 OVG 1 S 116/20. https://www.berlin.de/gerichte/oberverwaltungsgericht/presse/pressemitteilungen/2020/pressemitteilung.1000806.php.

Park, B., Cho, J., 2021. Older Adults' avoidance of public transportation after the outbreak of COVID-19: Korean Subway evidence. Dent. Health 2021 (9), 448. https://doi.org/10.3390/healthcare9040448.

Parker, M., Li, M., Bouzaghrane, M., Obeid, H., Hayes, D., Frick, K., Rodríguez, D., Sengupta, R., Walker, J., Chatman, D., 2021. Public transit use in the United States in the era of COVID-19: transit riders' travel behavior in the COVID-19 impact and recovery period. Transp. Policy 111, 53–62. https://doi.org/10.1016/j.tranpol.2021.07.005.

POLIS, 2020. COVID-19: Keeping Things Moving—Glasgow and Edinburgh Launch Temporary Free Bike-Share. https://www.polisnetwork.eu/article/glasgow-and-edinburgh-launch-temporary-free-bike-share/?id=122791 (accessed on 30 December 2021).

Road Safety Authority, 2022. Provisional Review of Fatal Collisions. January to 31 December 2021. https://www.rsa.ie/news-events/news/details/2022/01/01/2021-records-lowest-number-of-road-fatalities-since-recording-began-in-1959.

Rubin, O., Nikolaeva, A., Nello-Deakin, S., te Brömmelstroet, M., 2020. What Can we Learn from the COVID-19 Pandemic about how People Experience Working from Home and Commuting? Centre for Urban Studies, University of Amsterdam.

Schaefer, K., Tuitjer, L., Levin-Keitel, M., 2021. Transport disrupted – substituting public transport by bike or car under covid 19. Transp. Res. A: Policy Pract. 153, 202–217. https://doi.org/10.1016/j.tra.2021.09.002.

Seattle Department of Transportation, 2021. Stay Healthy Streets. https://www.seattle.gov/transportation/projects-and-programs/programs/stay-healthy-streets (accessed on 04 January 2022).

Sorenson, D., 2021. The Cycling Market Pedals Ahead in 2021. NPD Group (https://www.npd.com/news/blog/2021/the-cycling-market-pedals-ahead-in-2021/).

Teixeira, J.F., Lopes, M., 2020. The link between bike sharing and subway use during the COVID-19 pandemic: the case-study of New York's Citi bike. Transp. Res. Interdiscip. Perspect. 6. https://doi.org/10.1016/j.trip.2020.100166.

Teixeira, J.F., Silva, C., Moura E Sá, F., 2021. The motivations for using bike sharing during the COVID-19 pandemic: insights from Lisbon. Transp. Res. F: Traffic Psychol. Behav. 82. https://doi.org/10.1016/j.trf.2021.09.016.

Wegman, F., Katrakazas, C., 2021. Did the COVID-19 pandemic influence traffic fatalities in 2020? A presentation of first findings. IATSS Res. 45. https://doi.org/10.1016/j.iatssr.2021.11.005.

Wilson, C., 2020. NHS staff in Glasgow offered free bike memberships. Glasgow Times (https://www.glasgowtimes.co.uk/news/18341164.nhs-staff-glasgow-offered-free-bike-memberships/ (accessed on 04 January 2022).

World Health Organization (WHO), 2020. Ciclovías Temporales. Bogotá, Colombia (https://www.who.int/news-room/feature-stories/detail/ciclov%C3%ADas-temporales-bogot%C3%A1-colombia (accessed on 20 December 2021).

Yasin, Y.J., Grivna, M., Abu-Zidan, F.M., 2021. Global impact of COVID-19 pandemic on road traffic collisions. World J. Emerg. Surg. 16, 51. https://doi.org/10.1186/s13017-021-00395-8.

Zweirad-Industrie-Verband (ZIV), 2021. Zahlen – Daten – Fakten zum deutschen Fahrrad- und E-Bike Markt 2020, Pressemitteilung. https://www.ziv-zweirad.de/marktdaten/detail/article/marktdaten-2020/.

Further reading

DESTATIS, 2022. Fachserie. 8, Verkehr. 7, Verkehrsunfälle. Monatlich, https://www.statistischebibliothek.de/mir/receive/DESerie_mods_00000096 (accessed on 20 December 2021).

Maier, O., 2021. Perspective of Cycling Industry - Cycling in Times of COVID.

Möllers, A., Specht, S., Wessel, J., 2021. The Impact of the Covid-19 Pandemic and Government Interventions on Active Mobility. Working Paper No. 34, University of Münster, Germany, Institute for Transport Economics.